Islam and Politics

Contemporary Issues in the Middle East

Islam and Politics

FOURTH EDITION

• • •

John L. Esposito

SYRACUSE UNIVERSITY PRESS

First Edition 1984

Fourth Edition 1998
08 09 10 11 12   10 9 8 7 6 5 4

The paper used in this publication meets the minimum requirements of American National Standards for Information Sciences—Permanence of Paper for printed Library Materials, ANSI Z39.48-1984. ⊚

Library of Congress Cataloging-in-Publication Data
Esposito, John L.
    Islam and politics / John L. Esposito. — 4th ed.
      p.   cm. (Contemporary issues in the Middle East)
    Includes bibliographical references (p.   ) and index.
    ISBN 0-8156-2774-2 (pbk. : alk. paper)
    1. Islam and politics—Middle East.   2. Islam and politics—
Africa, North.   3. Middle East—Politics and government.
4. Africa, North—Politics and government.   5. Political science—
Middle East—History.   6. Political science—Africa, North—
History.   I. Title.   II. Series.
BP63.A4M533   1998
320.917'671—DC21   97-51941

Manufactured in the United States of America

For Malcolm H. Kerr
(1931–84)

and Jean Esposito

John L. Esposito is founding Director of the Center for Muslim-Christian Understanding: History and International Affairs at Georgetown University and Professor of Religion and International Affairs and Professor of Islamic Studies. Esposito has served as President of the Middle East Studies Association of North America and of the American Council for the Study of Islamic Societies. He is Editor-in-Chief of *The Oxford Encyclopedia of the Modern Islamic World*. Among his publications are: *The Islamic Threat: Myth or Reality?*; *Islam: The Straight Path*; *Islam and Democracy* (with J. Voll); *Islam, Gender, and Social Change* (with Y. Haddad); *Political Islam: Revolution, Radicalism, or Reform?*; *The Iranian Revolution: Its Global Impact*; *Voices of Resurgent Islam*; *Islam in Asia: Religion Politics, and Society*; *Islam and Development*; and *Women in Muslim Family Law* (Syracuse University Press, 1982).

Contents

Foreword

*O*n February 1979, the Islamic storm broke with full fury. It had long been brewing; now its vortex was Iran. There, the Ayatollah Khomeini, after years of exile, returned to the tumultuous acclaim of a million or more Shia Muslim followers. With his return, the Iranian Islamic Republic was born and the rule of the *Faqih* (or jurisconsult), an innovation even in Islamic political theory, was inaugurated. In short order, the Iranian polity, which had undergone forced modernization under the shah, was theoretically restructured into what some have scoffingly dubbed a *"mullacracy."* American and Soviet interests alike were challenged by a politicoreligious phenomenon that both superpowers, each for different reasons, had cavalierly dismissed as incompatible with the wave of the future. Not only Iran but the greater Middle East felt the resultant shock waves, while national leaders in the states of the area found it prudent to propitiate increasingly assertive Islamic constituents.

The past five years have continued to witness the rippling effects of what has generically come to be termed "Islamic resurgence." In the West, confusion over the meaning of this phenomenon has been compounded by ethnocentricity, prejudice, and, interestingly enough, the limitations of our modern political science technical lexicon to describe with accuracy and nuance, the dynamics of what was taking place in another cultural setting. Developments tended to be construed in Western rather than Islamic terms, often with resultant conceptual skewing.

By the end of 1979, lay elements of the conglomerate political entourage that had triumphantly returned with Khomeini had been outmaneuvered by assertive *mullahs,* who were patently more agile in manipulating the levers of Iranian popular feeling. The American embassy in Teheran had been overrun by Islamic "students," and some fifty American diplomats taken hostage in an action for which precedent would be hard to find. Washington, viewed as the most prominent purveyor of westernization, had been excoriated by the grim-visaged leader of Iran as the "great satan." The Soviet Union, which had hoped to benefit from United States discomfiture in Iran, was to its chagrin castigated by Khomeini as a close second in the hierarchy of international peddlers of evil.

In November of that same year, the *Masjid al-Haram* in Mecca, the most sacred shrine of Islam, was seized by religious fundamentalists in an action reminiscent of the tenth-century Carmathian despoliation of that city. Only with difficulty could Saudi Arabian military forces oust the insurgents, who decried the Saudi government's policies as un-Islamic and excessively pro-Western— meaning, in the convoluted semantics of resurgent Islam, American-dominated. In quick succession, American embassies in Islamabad and Tripoli, almost three thousand miles apart, were attacked by Muslim mobs inflamed by Khomeini charges of United States collusion in the attack on the Mecca shrine. Whether these attacks were also consciously instigated by government authorities to legitimate the role of leaders, as in Libya, or represented spontaneous demonstrations of public frustration, as in Pakistan, was essentially irrelevant.

The model of Islam's success, in wresting control of Iran, encouraged Muslims elsewhere to reassert themselves in militant fashion. In doing so, they placed at the apex of their Islamic sense of outrage the perceived pervasive American presence. Two years later, in September 1981, President Muhammad Anwar al-Sadat of Egypt, whose close friendship with the United States outweighed in fundamentalist eyes his devotion to his Islamic faith and who had signed a peace treaty with "despised" Israel, was assassinated by uniformed Muslim fanatics.

Primary responsibility for the growing Muslim challenges to Western influence has often been attributed to the Iranian Islamic Republic's "revolution for export" concept. In fact, the link is considerably more complex than such a monocausal explanation suggests. For centuries Muslims everywhere have been afflicted by a deep sense of inferiority. Their once great power and civilization had over the centuries withered into relative impotence. Western political and economic intrusions into the domain of Islam had steadily eroded traditional spiritual and family values, raising the specter of ultimate cultural evanescence. True, there also existed a widespread belief that the *ulama,* the religious guardians of Islam, had over the centuries defaulted on their leadership role in the Islamic community, were often corrupt and shared blame for the low estate into which Islamic society had fallen. This, too, would have to be redressed, but the more immediate problem was Western neo-imperialism, real or imagined.

Few Muslims do not covet a better quality of life for themselves and their children. But could this not be achieved, many asked with increasing resonance, through means other than blind emulation of Western norms? That question has been fundamental to Muslim attempts at reform throughout the past two centuries. Some prominent thinkers among them have insisted that Islam, conceived as it was in the seventh century, lacks the adaptive capacity to meet the requirements of a modern age; others indignantly reject any such contention and assert in equally forceful fashion that Islam can modernize in its own way without compromising its spiritual values. For now the latter school seems in the ascendency as leaders of Muslim states everywhere give increased status to the *Shariah* (Islamic law) as a prime source of national legislation and, as a corollary, ban perceived symbols of Western depravity, such as alcohol.

Superficially, there appears to be a similarity of behavior in those states where smoldering Islamic discontent has erupted into open rebellion or demonstrations or threatens to do so. In fact closer scrutiny indicates that, below any surface mutuality of objectives, significant differences among Muslims persist. These are rooted in Islamic sectarianism, which even their newly regained pride cannot entirely assuage. Thus, for example, the Salafiyya insurgents who seized the Grand Mosque of Mecca, almost concurrently with the seizure of American diplomatic hostages in Iran, included in their litany of criticisms of the Saudi Arabian government alleged coddling of the kingdom's Shia minority. Paradoxically, the charge came at almost the same time that the Iranian Islamic Republic's Arab language broadcasts flayed Riyadh for allegedly discriminating against that same Shia minority. If further instance is needed, the Shia component of

Lebanese society, now a plurality over other confessional and sectarian components in that benighted country, openly disdains the views of long-time Lebanese Sunni politicians. The Islamic *ummah,* or community, though the fastest-growing religious grouping in the world today, largely through effective, worldwide missionary activities, is in perpetual ferment not only against perceived invidious Western influences but also because of such deep-seated organic schisms within it.

Global reactions to Islamic resurgence have been erratic and uncertain, and nowhere more so than in the United States. Occurrences in Iran and elsewhere in the Middle East, in the name of Islam, run counter to at least three ingrained American political beliefs:

First, the division between politics and religion, sacrosanct in our national ethos and one upon which most Americans have been politically weaned, has palpably been challenged. Americans tend to find it difficult to conceive of any amalgamation of politics and religion in twentieth-century political societies, even in the developing world.

Second, secular nationalism, that European import to the Middle East, which Americans sometimes decry as jingoistic and conducive to conflict but which they comprehend and even exercise in their own ways, was the appropriate stage through which developing nations must pass on the road to nationhood. Surely, then, whatever change might have taken place in the form of government in Iran, indigenous nationalism must still play a preeminent role in that country, even if now garbed in Islamic trappings. I recall vividly a meeting of State Department "experts" on the Middle East, convened shortly after the Khomeini takeover, at which several senior specialists, knowledgeable of Iran, categorically insisted that nationalism remained the dominant political force in that country and that the prevailing religious fervor was but a passing fancy! They may still prove to be right, but—as the protracted Iraq-Iran War has shown—Shiism and residual Iranian nationalism seem to be interacting to develop a dialectic of their own.

Third, American modernization buffs, both in government and academia, had for years argued that religion, and especially Islam, was a barrier to socioeconomic progress. In recognition of this, they had persuaded themselves that most modernizing Muslim governments and peoples saw Islam as a vestigial, nonregulatory force, applicable at most to personal status matters. Many reputable scholars, including some from the Middle East, who should have known better, derided Islam as irrelevant to nation building and chose to ignore it in modeling development plans for Middle East states. Now, unexpectedly, their blithe dismissal of religion as an element to be reckoned with had been thrown into a cocked hat. Had they been recklessly pushing the cause of modernization, based on Western models, to a point where they imperiled political stability in Islamic countries by decanting economic and political counsel that disregarded Muslim sensibilities? The Iranian case seemed to suggest that they had. By underrating the sociopolitical force of Islam and overrating the views of secularists and Islamic modernists, they had thrust themselves, unwittingly perhaps but partisanly, into the omnipresent modernist versus revivalist controversy that has long sundered Islamic society.

With such flawed preconceptions characterizing the initial American analysis of the Islamic resurgence phenomenon, small wonder that its significance and durability should have been misunderstood. While many academics and government officials had for a number of years predicted the downfall of the shah, few—very few, indeed—had predicted a clerical takeover of that country. Paradoxically, even as many Americans thought they perceived a monolithic quality in resurgent Islam, wherever it was reasserting itself, they also now slowly became aware of significant doctrinal differences between Sunni and Shia Islam. In fact, in the wake of the Khomeini takeover and as part of the reexamination of the Islamic phenomenon, a torrent of academic studies of Shia Islam and the Islamic factor in the Middle East burst forth upon us. Some were valuable contributions to our knowledge of the subject; many were sensationally vapid and simply written to capitalize on the latest fad. The media, with a few notable exceptions, was generally superficial in its reportage on Islamic resurgence and added to public confusion.

Former President Jimmy Carter, in his efforts to obtain the release of the American diplomatic hostages in Iran, had the good sense to seek counsel not only from government specialists but also from leading academic experts on Islam. From them he learned that a considerable corpus of *Shariah* exists dealing with the treatment of diplomats and that this corpus is more extensive in Shia than in Sunni Islam. This prompted the thought that if an approach could be made to Khomeini by one or more widely known Muslim religious savants, pointing out the illegality of his actions in terms of the *Shariah*, it might induce the Iranian leader to release them. Regrettably, no Muslim religious leader with the stature to be received by Khomeini or the courage to undertake so delicate a mission in what would patently have been in behalf of the United States could be found. Hence, the idea was never put to the test, although abortive approaches were made through various lesser lights on the religious plane. Had such an approach materialized, it might well have failed, but it suggested the need for a new religiopolitical level of dialogue to augment conventional diplomatic exchanges.

Some have hypothesized that Islamic resurgence has historically been a cyclical occurrence. Periods of high Islamic activism have regularly been followed by periods in which Islam appeared to be a spent political force. There is some historical evidence to support this, but we still have a great deal to learn about the staying power of Islamic resurgence. We would be well advised to recognize more than we have in the past that Islam, whether militantly assertive or seemingly passive, is omnipresent and represents a force with which we will have to come to terms. To do so requires understanding of its motivating factors.

It is precisely in this context that Professor John L. Esposito's volume *Islam and Politics* is so welcome an addition to the literature on the subject. A distinguished scholar who has specialized in examining the interaction between religion and politics in the Middle East, he is eminently qualified to write on this complex subject. His latest volume lays out, lucidly and concisely, the origins and evolution of Islam, beginning in the seventh century and its rapid diffusion from Morocco to China. He describes the subsequent modernist-revivalist controversies which have for years divided Muslim thinkers and caused sharp rifts among them in Egypt, Turkey, North Africa, Iran, Libya, the Indian subcontinent, and elsewhere. His vignettes on past and present Islamic leaders in these countries illumine their philosophies, purposes, and also their divergencies. Against this background, he assesses the role of Islam in the contemporary Middle East and sets forth the issues that Muslim leaders must face in today's world at home, in the broader Islamic community, and in an increasingly interdependent world from which they, too, cannot escape.

Notwithstanding the spate of recent literature on Islam, a comprehensive work placing it in clearer historical and contemporary perspective has still been needed. The task is difficult because of the breadth and complexity of the subject and its extensive geographic as well as intellectual scope. Professor Esposito's new volume admirably fills this gap. Scholarly, yet readable, it should prove invaluable to government practitioners, academics, and students alike.

Boston, Massachusetts
Summer 1984

HERMANN FREDERICK EILTS
Distinguished University Professor
of International Relations
Director, Center for International Relations
Boston University

Preface

*T*he Muslim world since publication of the third edition of *Islam and Politics* has seen many changes. However, Islam has continued to play a significant role in Muslim politics from North Africa to Asia. Diverse Islamic states and republics may be found in countries such as Iran, Sudan, Afghanistan, Pakistan, and Saudi Arabia. Islamic movements and institutions proliferate and are major political and social actors throughout the Muslim world. New voices have been raised warning of the threat of political Islam or "Islamic fundamentalism" or of an impending clash between the Muslim world and the West.

Because of the impact of religion on countries and movements, this revision updates major country case studies such as Iran, Egypt, Pakistan, and Sudan and additionally expands its coverage to North Africa, in particular Algeria and Tunisia. It also extends its coverage of Muslim militias and organizations to include Hamas, the Islamic Resistance Movement, in Palestine/Israel, and the Taliban, who have consolidated their rule over much of Afghanistan.

In recent years, the issue of democratization has become a more prominent theme in Muslim politics. Islamic activists or Islamists have become more visible as social and political actors in mainstream society, creating a network of social institutions (schools, hospitals, clinics, youth centers, banks, and publishing houses), participating in electoral politics, and assuming leadership positions in professional associations. In particular, Islamic candidates and parties have emerged as the leading opposition, and have served in cabinet level positions and in the parliaments of many countries. In Algeria, they were seemingly poised to come to power through parliamentary elections before the military intervened. In Turkey, Dr. Ecmettin Erbakan, leader of the Welfare (Refah) Party served as prime minister until military pressure led to his resignation. The performance and successes of Islamic organizations in electoral politics as well as the broader-based demands in many Muslim countries for greater political participation have led some to question whether Islam is compatible with democracy. Democratization in Muslim politics has challenged the intentions and credentials of many regimes and Islamists, as well as of western foreign policymakers. Thus, this issue and related questions of pluralism and the status and rights of women and minorities have been expanded.

Relations between the Muslim world and the West have never been more important in the post Cold War period. With 1.2 billion Muslims, Islam is the second largest of the world's religions. Muslims are not only a majority in more than 55 Muslim countries but also the second or third largest religious communities in Europe and America which makes Islam among the fastest growing of the world's religions. These realities have led some to speak of Islam as a political, cultural/civilization, and demographic threat to the West and top global stability. Thus, the fourth edition of *Islam and Politics* addresses the issue of the dangers of the Islamic threat or the clash of civilizations.

Finally, while I can not hope to thank all those colleagues and friends to whom I am indebted, I can thank a few especially important individuals whose support has enabled me to continue to research and write while directing the Center for Muslim-Christian Understanding at Georgetown University: my colleagues John Voll, Yvonne Haddad, and Amira Sonbol; Patricia Gordon, who manages the Center, and Ethel Stewart, our secretary; and Natana DeLong-Bas, the best of research assistants. As in everything I write and do, Jean Esposito has provided the space, inspiration, and support that make it all worthwhile.

Washington, D.C.   JLE
September 1997

Preface to the First Edition

*E*vents emanating from the Middle East during the early 1970s brought the West into an abrupt confrontation with the Arab world: 1973 witnessed both an Arab-Israeli war and in its wake an Arab oil boycott. The magnitude and gravity of this threat to the well-being of Western industrial states was felt not only at government and corporate levels but also at gas pumps and in homes. Rationing, skyrocketing fuel costs, economy cars, and energy conservation in the home and workplace became new realities, vividly driving home the economic and geopolitical significance of the Middle East. Yet Saudi Arabia and Iran, let alone Kuwait, Abu Dhabi, and Oman, remained remarkably unknown and obscure to most Westerners.

During the latter half of the 1970s, a series of events once more propelled the Islamic world into Western consciousness as the mass media chronicled political upheavals in Iran, Egypt, Saudi Arabia, Syria, Pakistan, and Afghanistan under such banners as "militant Islam" or "Islamic resurgence." Despite the diversity in geography and local politics, religion emerged as a common denominator in Muslim politics.

If the average citizen knew little about the Middle East, ignorance of the greater Islamic world, which extends from North Africa to Southeast Asia, was even more widespread. Moreover, most area specialists and readers seemed especially mystified by the visible Islamic character of contemporary events. The battle cry of revolutionaries or freedom fighters from Egypt to the Moro Islands of the Philippines was *Allahu Akbar!* (God is Most Great). Islamic ideology, symbols, language, and actors became employed both by opposition movements and incumbent governments to legitimate their activities. These events were especially puzzling because, although Muslims constitute one-seventh of the world's population, are a majority in some forty-three countries, and a significant minority in others, there was little popular awareness in the West of the most basic tenets of Islam and only minimal appreciation of the role of Islam in politics, law, and society.

Ignorance of Islamic politics has been further compounded by the problem of interpretation. What is one to make of competing and, at times, contradictory appeals to Islam? While Anwar al-Sadat invoked Islam and used the title "president of the believers," much of his opposition, including his assassins, belonged to Islamic movements that denounced him in the name of Islam. Many in the West who supported the Islamic "freedom fighters" of Afghanistan in their resistance to Soviet aggression viewed other Islamic revolutionaries such as those in Iran as Islamic "Marxists or fanatics."

The policies of self-styled Islamic governments have raised many questions about the nature of Islamic government, the role of the clergy in politics, and the place of Islamic law. In postrevolutionary Iran, the apparent early unity of Islamic forces soon disintegrated as the clergy-dominated Islamic Republican Party wrested power from Islamic moderates like Mehdi Bazargan and Abol Hasan Bani-Sadr. In Pakistan, although the commitment of the martial law regime of Gen. Zia ul-Haq to establish a more Islamic system of government was initially welcomed by many Pakistanis, the process of Islamization—which has come to include the banning of political parties, the postponement of elections, and media censorship in the name of Islam—has angered many religious as well as secular factions.

The diversity of actors and events in contemporary Islamic politics has raised numerous questions, among them, "Whose Islam?" In other words, who is to interpret the role of Islam and its place in state and society—rulers such as Sadat, Khomeini, or Qaddafi, religious leaders, or Islamic organizations? And secondly, "What Islam?" How does one distinguish between genuine Islamic practice and the calculated manipulation or misguided use of religion in politics to achieve questionable political goals?

Answering these and other questions raised by contemporary Muslim politics requires an appreciation of the relationship of religion to politics in Islam: both Islam's ideal and actual historical practice. Only then can one gain a proper perspective regarding the roots and appeal of Islamic revivalism as well as the problems and issues which accompany contemporary Islamic politics.

This volume will attempt to provide the historical background and the context in which to understand Islamic politics today, describe the roles of Islam in modern Muslim politics, and analyze the major obstacles and issues which attend the establishment of Islamically oriented states and societies.

Chapter 1, "Religion, Politics, and Society," reviews the relationship of Islam to politics as reflected in early Islamic history. It is in Islam's past that Muslims find the sources of their faith and the basis for contemporary formulations of an Islamic ideology for state and society.

Chapter 2, "Revival and Reform," analyzes the formative period of modern Islamic revival and reform. The reaction of premodern revivalist movements to the breakdown of medieval Muslim empires and the sociomoral decline of the Islamic community and the responses of Islamic modernist movements to European imperialism and modernization are reviewed, for both provide modern Muslim politics with an ideological legacy and an example of reformist activism.

Chapter 3, "Nationalism," investigates the role of Islam in anticolonial, independence movements and its place in the development of nationalist ideologies in North Africa, the Arab East, Iran, and the Indian subcontinent.

Chapter 4, "The Modern State," explores the diverse paths followed by newly independent Muslim states in nation building. Five case studies (Turkey, Saudi Arabia, Pakistan, Egypt, and Iran) are used to exemplify the spectrum of modern Muslim political developments, which range from secular to self-styled Islamic states. This is followed by an analysis of two Islamic organizations, the Muslim Brotherhood and the Jamaat-i-Islami, which have had and are continuing to have major influences on contemporary Islamic political activists and movements.

Chapter 5, "Contemporary Politics," discusses the sources and manifestations of the contemporary Islamic resurgence through an examination of the use of Islam by both incumbent governments and opposition movements in Libya, Pakistan, Iran, and Egypt.

Chapter 6, "Issues and Prospects," analyzes the underlying forces, questions, and issues that attend contemporary attempts to establish modern Islamic states and societies.

The geographic expanse of Islam, with its diversity of languages and political experiences, presents a complexity sometimes over-looked when Islam is simply reduced to its revelation and law. Analysis of contemporary events requires a grasp not only of the present political situation but also of the Islamic ideological framework and history (both real and ideal), which serve as a source of identity, inspiration, guidance, and legitimation for many Muslims today. I have deliberately restricted myself to the Middle East, selecting what I hope are a spectrum of positions. I had been tempted to cast my net more broadly to include the experiences of Southeast Asia and the Soviet Union. However, they are sufficiently different so that to do them justice would have required a volume twice this size.

There are many people from whom I have learned in the classroom, from their writings, and through conversation. In particular I am indebted to Muslim friends and colleagues whose friendship, guidance, and example have been extended as freely as their hospitality. In addition I am particularly grateful to Yvonne Haddad, John O. Voll, James P. Piscatori, and Laraine Carter for reading and commenting on the manuscript.

The preparation of any manuscript is a tedious process not only for the author but for his secretary. While I have the satisfaction of a finished product, Mary Cerasuolo must settle for my gratitude for a superb job—typing, proofreading, xeroxing. She suffered many of the stages of rewriting and pressures of a production schedule with a patient professionalism that characterizes all of her work. Lisa Ropple and Jennifer Carey cheerfully assisted in a variety of tasks. Finally, and most importantly, my wife Jean, as always, has been there.

Worcester, Massachusetts
Spring 1984

Islam and Politics

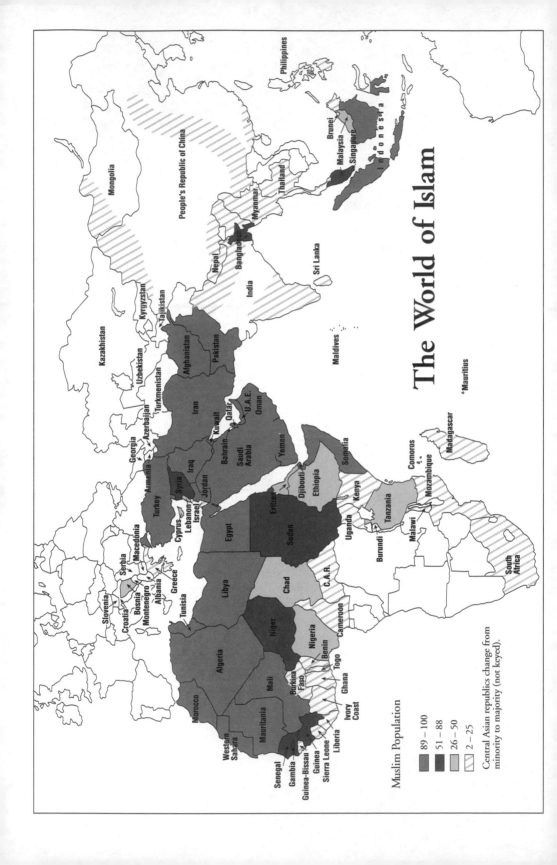

The World of Islam

Muslim Population

- 89 – 100
- 51 – 88
- 26 – 50
- 2 – 25

Central Asian republics change from minority to majority (not keyed).

... *1* ...

Religion, Politics, and Society

Normative Ideal and Historical Reality

*D*uring the seventh century, there arose in Central Arabia (modern-day Saudi Arabia) a movement that was to sweep across the world and become the second largest of the world's religions—Islam, a religion that today has some nine hundred million adherents. Islam was not simply a spiritual community. Rather, it also became a state, an empire. Islam developed as a religiopolitical movement in which religion was integral to state and society. Muslim belief that Islam embraces faith and politics is rooted in its divinely revealed book, the Quran, and the example *(Sunnah)* of its founder/prophet, Muhammad, and thus has been reflected in Islamic doctrine, history, and politics.

Allahu Akbar! (God is Most Great)—this declaration precedes the muezzin's call to prayer five times daily; it is the traditional Islamic battle cry. *Allahu Akbar!* summarizes the centrality of God and the wedding of personal religious conviction and political life in Islam. The source and foundation of all life is Allah (God)—the one and All Powerful, Creator and Sustainer, Master of the Universe, the Merciful and Compassionate, but also the Just Judge who will reward and punish all His creatures on the Last Day. The confession of faith testifies: "There is no God but God and Muhammad is His Prophet." Any understanding of Islamic belief and practice must begin with

God, who governs and intervenes in history, and with His Prophet Muhammad.

Muslims believe that throughout history, God sent messenger-prophets to warn and guide humankind: Adam, Noah, Abraham, Moses, and Jesus (Quran 3:40–43, 2:209, 7:155–58). "We believe in God, and the revelation given to us, and to Abraham, Ismail, Isaac, Jacob, and the tribes, and that which Moses and Jesus received and [all] the Prophets were given. We make no distinction between any of them. And to God we submit ourselves" (Quran 2:136).

Muslims believe, however, that God's revelations, as set down in the Jewish Torah and the Christian Gospels, were tampered with or distorted. In His mercy, God sent Muhammad as the final Messenger, "the last seal of the prophets" (Quran 33:40), and gave him the Quran, the revelation of God's will in its final and complete form. "It is He who sent down to you the Book with the truth, confirming what went before it; and He sent down the Torah and the Injil [Gospel] before that as a guidance to the people" (Quran 3:3). In the Quran, the transcendent God reveals his divine will for all creation. The Book and the Prophet provide the fundamental sources for the Straight Path (*Shariah*, or Islamic law) of Muslim life. The Prophet Muhammad is not only the messenger who received and proclaimed God's revelation, but also the "noble paradigm," the model or exemplar of Muslim life (Quran 33:21). Man's vocation, then, is to surrender (islam), to submit to, and thus to realize or carry out God's will. God has given all of creation as a trust to mankind (Quran 33:72, 31:20–29). Man, as bearer of this trust, is God's representative or vicegerent (Quran 2:30, 6:165) whose divinely mandated vocation is to be God's instrument in establishing and spreading an Islamic order, God's rule on earth.

The Islamic imperative is both personal and societal, individual and corporate. The Muslim community (*ummah*) is to be the principal vehicle for the realization of God's will. The Quran, the example of the Prophet, and the early Muslim community give eloquent and vivid testimony to this fact. "You are the best community ever brought forth for mankind, enjoining what is good and forbidding evil" (Quran 3:110).

Tribal solidarity in pre-Islamic Arabian society had represented the basic social bond. However, Islam replaced this with a community whose membership was based upon a common faith rather than male blood ties; religious rather than tribal affiliation became the basis of

Islamic society. All members of the *ummah* were to be equal before God. The duties and obligations of Muslim life, as well as their rewards or punishments, fall upon men and women alike. "Whoever does a righteous deed, whether man or woman, and has Faith, we will give him [her] a good life; and we shall reward them according to the best of their actions" (16:97). "The believers, men and women, are guardians of one another; they enjoin good and forbid evil, perform the prayer, give alms, and obey God and His Prophet" (9:71).

The divine mandate of the Quran took on form and substance in Medina under the guidance and direction of God's messenger the Prophet Muhammad.

Muhammad and the Muslim Community

Born in 570 but orphaned at a young age, Muhammad belonged to the Hashemite clan, a respected but poor branch of the Quraysh tribe which governed the city of Mecca in Central Arabia. Mecca was the center of commercial trade and religious pilgrimage. It contained a major religious shrine with its sanctuary, Kaba, a cube-shaped structure that housed idols of the various tribal gods and goddesses of the region. Most importantly, the shrine was the object of an annual pilgrimage and, therefore, a major source of Meccan prestige and revenue.

At twenty-five, Muhammad married his first wife, Khadijah, a wealthy widow and caravan owner, who was fifteen years his senior. Combining industriousness with a reputation for trustworthiness, he became a successful, respected member of Meccan society. However, his life changed dramatically in 610 when, at the age of forty and on the "Night of Power and Excellence" (Quran 97), he received the first in a series of divine revelations which were to extend over a period of twenty-two years and which were preserved in the Quran. In the tradition of biblical prophets, Muhammad was a warner as well as the bearer of good tidings (Quran 33:44–45).

He denounced the ungodliness of his society and announced God's prescriptions for its ills. Meccan political and religious elites reacted strongly to this claimant to prophetic authority. His message was an indictment of much that they represented. It condemned polytheism and professed an uncompromising monotheism; denounced their unbridled materialism and avarice and proclaimed a sweeping program of social reform, affecting business contracts and practices, the conduct of war, and the guidelines for family relations. The prophetic call for a community of believers, the divine appointment of Muhammad as its leader, and the claim that all human activity was accountable not to a tribe's customary laws or to blind vengeance but to an overriding divine law challenged the very foundation of Arabian society. It struck at the heart of the power and authority of Meccan political and religious elites.

Not surprisingly, Muhammad and his early converts were subjected to ridicule and rejection in Mecca. Thus, when a delegation from Yathrib invited Muhammad in 622 to emigrate (*hijra*) to their city, he accepted. The city had been torn by long-standing intertribal feuds, and Muhammad came as an arbiter or chief judge. He consolidated his political power and established a state informed by his prophetic message. Yathrib was renamed Medina (*madinat al-nabi,* City of the Prophet). The importance of the *ummah* in Islam and the significance of its establishment as a state were underscored by the fact that 622 (the beginning of the Islamic community/state at Medina) and not 610 (the year of God's first revelation to Muhammad) was reckoned as the first year of the Islamic calendar.

In the new community, Muhammad was the political as well as the religious leader. He was prophet, head of state, commander of the army, chief judge, and lawgiver. His authority and its acceptance were based upon his prophetic calling and Quranic mandate: "obey God and the Prophet" (3:32). "Those who swear allegiance/ convenant to you [Muhammad], convenant with God" (48:10). "Whoever obeys the Prophet, obeys God" (4:80). "It is not fitting for any believer, man or woman, to do as he pleases, when the matter has been decided by God and His Prophet" (33:36). Moreover, the Prophet was the model upon which Muslims were to pattern their lives: "You have a good model in God's Prophet" (33:21). Throughout the years, Muhammad's exemplary character and conduct, his continued reception of divine revelations, and his effectiveness and success reinforced his position of leadership.

Under Muhammad's guidance, Islam in Medina crystalized as both a faith and a sociopolitical system. From 622 to 632, through military action and astute diplomatic initiatives, the Muslim community expanded and established its hegemony over Central Arabia. Mecca was subdued and the tribes of Arabia were united into a single polity, an Arab commonwealth with a common ideology, centralized authority, and law. However, this unity should not be overestimated. The old tribal system of loyalties and values was not simply replaced but rather reformed and modified, Islamized. For the first time, an effective means had been found to unite and inspire Arabia's tribes so that a state emerged that could challenge the neighboring established empires of Byzantium and Persia and change the political and social life of the Middle East.

The Caliphate Period

The death of Muhammad in 632 plunged the community into two successive political crises involving political authority: the issue of succession and the problem of political fragmentation or civil war.

The caliphate period (632–1258) which followed unfolded in three phases: the Rightly Guided Caliphs (632–61), the Umayyad dynasty (661–750), and the Abbasid caliphate (750–1258). The caliphate period is particularly important both because it is the locus for the formation and development of Islamic ideology and institutions and because it is the reference point for Muslim self-understanding. The rule of the first four caliphs of Islam is significant not only for what they actually did but also for the period in which they lived, a time to which both conservative and modernist Islamic activists return for guidance in their attempts to delineate the Islamic character of modern states.

The Rightly Guided Caliphs

The caliphate period began in 632 when, as the majority of Muslims believe, Muhammad died without designating his replacement or establishing a system for the selection of his successor. After a brief, tense period of indecision, the leading companions of the Prophet (and thus leaders of the community) selected one of their own—Abu Bakr (the father of Muhammad's youngest wife, Aishah) as their leader. He had been a very close friend and adviser of the Prophet. One of the earliest converts to Islam, Abu Bakr was a man respected for his piety and political sagacity. Muhammad had appointed him to lead the Friday communal prayer during his absence. Abu Bakr became the first caliph of Islam, taking the title successor or caliph of the Prophet of God. As caliph he was the political and military leader of the community. Although not a prophet, he did enjoy a certain religious prestige as head of the community. This was symbolized by the caliph's leading the Friday congregational prayer and the mention of his name in the prayer.

Having resolved the question of political leadership and succession, Abu Bakr and the Muslim community turned to the consolidation of Arabia. Muhammad's death had precipitated a series of Arab tribal rebellions. For many tribal chiefs, their political pact with Medina ceased with Muhammad's death. Tribalism, the long-standing source of political and social identity, challenged the life and unity of the new Islamic state. In a series of battles that later Muslim historians would call the *riddah* (apostasy or renunciation of Islam) wars, Abu Bakr moved swiftly. Relying on Khalid ibn al-Walid, a brilliant general whom Muhammad had dubbed "The Sword of Allah," he crushed the tribal revolt, consolidated Muslim rule over the entire Arabian Peninsula, and thus preserved the unity and solidarity of the Islamic community/state.

The first four caliphs were all companions of the Prophet: Abu Bakr (632–34), Umar (634–44), Uthman (644–56), and Ali (656–61). While the crisis of political succession after Muhammad's death had been averted through the hasty selection of Abu Bakr, the Caliph Umar sought to avoid a similar problem. On his deathbed, Umar appointed an "election committee" to select his successor. After due consultation, Uthman ibn Affan, from the Umayyad, a leading Meccan family, was elected and the traditional sign of allegiance (the clasp of hand which symbolized the sealing of a pact or contract) was given. A pattern was established of selecting the caliph from the Quraysh, the Prophet's tribe, through a process characterized by consultation and an oath of allegiance.

It was not long, however, before tribal factionalism and the threat of rebellion resurfaced in the community. Uthman's family had been among Muhammad's strongest foes before they converted to Islam. Many of the Medinan elite—companions of the Prophet who were early Meccan emigrants and early Medinese converts—resented Uthman's accession to power and the increased prominence and wealth of his family members. Accusations that the caliph was weak and guilty of nepotism fueled political intrigue. In 656 Uthman was murdered by a group of Muslim mutineers from Egypt. Uthman's assassination was the first in a series of Muslim rebellions and religious fratricides which were to plague Islam's political development. The caliph's assassination by fellow Muslims was to be shortly followed by another Islamic problem of equal seriousness—Muslim civil war.

Ali, a cousin and son-in-law of the Prophet, succeeded Uthman as the fourth caliph. Muhammad had been raised with Ali in the household of Ali's father Abi Talib. Ali was devoted to Muhammad, and many of his followers believe that he was the first convert. He married the Prophet's only surviving child, Fatima, his daughter by Khadijah. They had two children: Hasan and Husayn. Many of Ali's supporters, believing that political succession belonged to the Prophet's family, had viewed Ali as the legitimate successor of Muhammad. They had been frustrated by the election of the first three caliphs, whom they viewed as interlopers. However, their satisfaction and vindication were short-lived, for throughout Ali's brief rule, his political authority was challenged by two opposition movements; the first a coalition led by the Prophet's wife Aishah and the second by the army of Muawiyah, the governor of Syria and a cousin of the Caliph Uthman. Ali's failure to find and prosecute Uthman's assassins became the pretext for both revolts. In the first, Ali crushed a rebellious army led by a triumvirate including the Prophet's young wife Aishah, whom Ali had once accused of infidelity. The "Battle of the Camel" (656), so named because fighting took place around the camel upon which Aishah was mounted, marked the first time a caliph had led his army against another Muslim army.

Of more long-range significance was Muawiyah's challenge to Ali's caliphate. Governor of Syria with a strong, standing army, Muawiyah had called for vengeance for his cousin Uthman's murder and had refused to accept Ali's appointment of another general to replace Muawiyah as governor of Syria. In 657 at Siffin (Syria), Ali led an army against his rebellious governor. When it looked as though Ali's forces would win the day, Muawiyah's men, raising Qurans on the tips of their spears, called for peaceful arbitration according to the Quran, crying out "Let God decide."[1]

The arbitration that then took place proved inconclusive militarily but had two important political results. A group of Ali's supporters, the Kharijites (seceders), who were disgusted with Ali's vacillation, broke with him. For the Kharijites, Muawiyah had committed a grave sin by challenging Ali's authority. Anyone who did so was no longer a Muslim and therefore became the lawful object of *jihad* (holy war), given a Muslim's absolute duty to do good and prevent evil.

In acquiescing to arbitration and not crushing Muawiyah, Ali had failed to perform his Islamic duty to subdue the rebels. The Kharijites were the first sect in Islam to express an uncompromising, egalitarian sociopolitical policy; namely, that leadership of the Islamic community belonged to the most observant of Muslims. Ali himself was no longer worthy of leadership because he had failed to prove himself a true believer. The Alids (followers of Ali), on the other hand, felt thwarted by Muawiyah's ruse. The rebel Muawiyah had not been subdued. Moreover, after Muawiyah left Siffin, he continued to govern Syria, extending his rule to Egypt. In 661, with Ali's assassination by a Kharijite, Muawiyah laid successful claim to the caliphate and established his capital in Damascus. The "golden age" of Muhammad and the Rightly Guided Caliphs of Medina came to an end.

In the caliphate period, the pattern for the organization and administration of the Islamic state had been initiated. The model for governance had followed, in large part, the example and practice of Muhammad. The caliph exercised direct political, military, judicial, and fiscal control of the Muslim community. He was selected through a process of consultation, nomination, and election. Administratively, conquered territories were divided into provinces. In general, the Arabs did not occupy conquered cities but established their own military garrison towns such as Basra and Kufa in Iraq and Fustat (Cairo) in Egypt. From these towns, conquered territories were governed and future expeditions were launched. They were administered by a governor, usually the military commander, and centered on its mosque, which served as the religious and public center of the towns.[2] An agent of the caliph, a revenue officer, oversaw the collection of taxes and other administrative activities. Revenue for the state came from the captured lands and taxes. The Islamic system of taxation took several forms: the tithe or wealth tax (*zakat*) and the tithe on land (*ushr*) paid by Muslims; the poll tax (*jizya*) and tribute (*kharaj*), later a general land tax paid by non-Muslims. All revenue was owned, collected, and administered by the state. The distribution of revenue was managed by the registry at Medina through a system of payments and pensions.

The internal civil and religious administration of conquered territories remained in the hands of local officials. Muslim society was divided into four major social classes. The elites of society were the Arab Muslims, with special status given to the companions of the Prophet because of their early support and role in establishing the *ummah*. Next came the non-Arab converts (*mawali*) to Islam. Although theoretically all Muslims were equal before God, practice varied in fact. The *dhimmi*, non-Muslim "People of the Book," were Jews and Christians who possessed a revealed scripture. In exchange for payment of the poll tax, these "protected" peoples were permitted to worship and be governed by their own religious laws and leaders and entitled to protection from outside aggression by the Muslim army. Finally, there were the slaves. Slavery had long existed among the Arabs. Although the Quran commanded the just and humane treatment of slaves (4:40, 16:73) and regarded their emancipation as a meritorious act, the system of slavery was adopted in modified form. Only captives in battle could be taken as slaves. Neither Muslims nor Jews and Christians could be enslaved in early Islam.

In the eyes of believers, the age of Muhammad and the Righteous Caliphs is the normative, exemplary period of Muslim life for a variety of reasons. It is viewed as the time when God sent down His final and complete revelation for humankind and His last prophet, Muhammad. Second, the Islamic community/state was created, bonded by a common religious identity and purpose. Third, the sources of Islamic law, the Quran, and the inspired leadership of Muhammad, which provided the basic guidance for the community, originated at this time. Fourth, the importance of Muhammad's exemplary behavior (*Sunnah*) and the early practice of the community was reflected in the creation and proliferation of *hadith* (traditions) literature. These narrative stories reflect the extent to which the Prophet, his family, and companions served as models for Muslim life. Fifth, it is this period of the early companions, or *salaf* (ancestors, or elders), that serves as the reference point for all Islamic revival and reform, whether traditionalist or modernist. Finally, the time of the Prophet and the early righteous caliphs was not only one of divine guidance but also one of validation. During this period, Muslims believe that the revealed message and Prophetic claims were realized and divinely validated in the full light of history by the success and power which resulted from the near miraculous victories and geographic expansion of Islam.

The Umayyad Dynasty

Muawiyah (661–80) assumed the caliphate and ushered in the
Umayyad era (661–750): imperial, dynastic, dominated by an Arab
military aristocracy. His move of Islam's capital from Medina to Damascus symbolized the new imperial age with its permanent shift from
the Arabian heartland of Medina (religious and political center) to an
established, cosmopolitan city. From this center, the Umayyads continued the expansion of Islamic rule and developed a strong centralized government, an Arab Empire. Within the amazingly brief period
of a hundred years, the early Islamic state had become an empire
whose boundaries extended from Spain across North Africa and the
Middle East to the borders of China. It was an empire greater than
Rome at its zenith.

Islam provided a unity of purpose and central authority enabling
Arabian tribes to achieve new levels of political organization and motivation. During the hundred-year period following the death of
Muhammad in 632, Muslim armies, driven by religious zeal and attracted by opportunities for plunder and booty, overran the Byzantine
and Sasanid (Persian) empires, which were already weakened by con-
stant warfare and internal strife. Success in this struggle (*jihad*) to
spread God's rule brought religious as well as political and economic
rewards. To die in battle was not to fail but, rather, to be counted
among the martyrs and thus be able to enter paradise immediately.
The conquests "were truly an *Islamic* movement. For it was Islam—
the set of religious beliefs preached by Muhammad, with its social
and political ramifications—that ultimately sparked the whole integration process and hence was the ultimate cause of the conquests'
success."[3]

Given common misconceptions regarding *jihad*, some clarification
is necessary. If Westerners are too quick to see Islam as a religion of
holy war, modern Muslim apologists have tended to present *jihad* in
early Islam as simply defensive in nature. In its most general sense
and application in Muslim life, *jihad* refers to the vocation of Muslims
to strive or struggle to realize God's will, to lead a virtuous life. This
includes the Muslims' universal mission and obligation to spread
God's will and rule. As Muslim armies advanced out of Arabia and
penetrated new areas, the peoples that they encountered were offered
three choices: conversion, that is, to become a member of the Muslim

community with its rights and duties; acceptance of Muslim rule as "protected" people; and, if neither of these options were accepted, then battle or the sword. The expansion of Islam resulted not only from the conquest of those who resisted Muslim rule but also from those who accepted the first two peaceful options. Indeed, in later centuries, the effective spread of Islam would be due to the peaceful activities of Muslim traders and Sufi (mystic) missionaries who won converts by their example and preaching. The Muslim obligation to spread God's righteous rule or governance of the *Shariah*, Islamic law, came to be formulated during Abbasid times (752–1258) in a division of the world into Islamic territory (*dar al-Islam*, land of Islam) and non-Islamic (*dar al-harb*, land of warfare).

The divisiveness of the first civil war between the caliph Ali and his general, Muawiyah, that led to the secession of the Kharijites and alienation of Ali's supporters complicated Umayyad attempts to establish effective governance. During the reign of Muawiyah's son and successor, Yazid, a second round of civil wars broke out. One of these, the revolt of Ali's son, Husayn, would shape and form the world view of Shii Islam and solidify the major division of Islam into Shii and Sunni. The repercussions of this initially minor rebellion would be magnified and felt in later Islamic history and its political potential realized in contemporary Iran in the twentieth century.

When the Umayyad Caliph Yazid came to power in 680, Husayn, who was living in Medina, refused to recognize his legitimacy and was persuaded to lead a rebellion in Kufa. However, Husayn did not receive the expected popular support, and at Karbala Husayn and his small army were surrounded and vanquished by an Umayyad army. The slaughter and "martyrdom" of the Alid forces gave rise to a movement of political protest centered on the martyred family of the Prophet, Ali and Husayn. The memory of Karbala provided the religiopolitical paradigm for Shii Islam. For Shii the injustice that had denied Ali, the cousin and son-in-law of the Prophet, his rightful succession to Muhammad had occurred again. They saw the forces of evil and injustice once more thwart the rightful rule of the Prophet's family. This outlook provided Shii Islam with its major theme—the battle of the forces of good (Shii) against those of evil (anti-Shii); its goal—the establishment of righteous rule and social justice; its model for political action—protest and martyrdom in God's way; and its model of political leadership—the *Imam*.

A fundamental political and legal difference between Sunni and Shii Muslims is the Sunni doctrine of the caliphate versus the Shii imamate. In Sunni Islam, the caliph is the selected/elected successor of the Prophet. He succeeded to political and military leadership of the community but had only limited religious status. For the Shii, in contrast, leadership is vested in the *Imam* (leader) who must be a direct descendant of the Prophet Muhammad and Ali, the first *Imam*. Moreover, he is the divinely inspired religiopolitical leader and serves both as the community's political leader and the final authoritative interpreter of God's will, Islamic law.

As a result of its political experiences, Shii Islam also differed from Sunni Islam in its perception of the meaning of history. For Sunni historians, success and power were the signs of a faithful community and validation of Muslim belief and claims. For the Shii, history was the theater for the struggle of a righteous remnant in protest and opposition against the forces of evil (Satan) to realize its messianic hope and promise—the establishment of the righteous rule of the *Imam*. Yet the reign and just social order of the *Imam* was to remain a frustrated hope and expectation for centuries as the Islamic community developed under the guidance and rule of Sunni caliphs.

It was the Umayyads, and later the early Abbasids, who introduced and developed many of the distinctive institutions of centralized government associated with the Islamic caliphate. The basis of Umayyad unity and stability was the establishment of an Arab monarchy and reliance upon an Arab warrior aristocracy. Contrary to the practice of Muhammad and the early caliphs, legitimate succession was made hereditary and was restricted to the Umayyad house. This innovation was the pretext for later Islamic historians to condemn Umayyad rule as kingship and, therefore, un-Islamic. However, a form of hereditary succession continued throughout the caliphal period even under the professedly more Islamic Abbasid caliphate.

Umayyad society, despite its Islamic character, was based upon the creation and perpetuation of an Arab aristocracy, which constituted a hereditary social caste.[4] The Arabs were the heart of the Umayyad's powerful military machine, which was the source of its power and security, and were the chief recipients of the fabulous wealth that poured into the empire as the Umayyads completed the conquest of the Sasanid and Byzantine empires. Arab Muslims en-

joyed special tax privileges. They were exempted from the more substantial taxes levied on the non-Arab Muslims and non-Muslims and
were only required to pay the wealth tax and the tithe on land. This
preferential system was to contribute to non-Arab Muslim discontent
and the movement to overthrow Umayyad rule.

Greater unity and control were fostered through the development
of a more centralized administration and the adoption of the administrative machinery (institutions and bureaucracy) and personnel of the
more developed Byzantine and Sasanid empires. The caliph continued to function as the head of state, personally engaged in its supervision, and was assisted by a bureaucracy composed of departments
or ministries that oversaw the collection and management of taxes,
lands, rents, payment of officials and the military, public works projects.[5] The progressive centralization and militarization of the state
resulted in an increasingly autocratic and absolutist government supported and protected by an Arab aristocracy.

As with the Umayyad government, law was an important area of
increasing centralization, Arabization, and Islamization; it was the
process through which the Umayyads borrowed from existing foreign
institutions and practices as well as adapted or added to such practices. We can see this particularly in the creation of two judicial institutions: the market inspector and the judge/*Shariah* courts. The
Byzantine system of government had included a market inspector.
The Umayyads adapted this practice by expanding the office to include not only market inspection but also the Islamic duty of assuring
that the religious/moral precepts of Islam were observed.[6] The market inspector, therefore, was also supervisor of public morals. His
duties included checking for defective weights and measures, fraudu-
lent business practices, and public observance of the fast during
Ramadan.

The judge, or *qadi*, was one of the administrative officials introduced by the Umayyads. Originally, he was a representative, or legal
secretary, of the provincial governor, a member of his administration,
charged with overseeing the implementation of government decrees
and settling disputes. Often these tasks were carried out by government officials along with their other duties. This was the first step in
the government's gaining greater control over the more ad hoc system of arbitration that had characterized Arab legal practice. By the

end of the Umayyad period (661–750), the office had become a separate and distinct government position, that of a judge responsible for
the enforcement of the *Shariah*. The cornerstone of the Islamic judicial
system—the *Shariah* Court—was laid.

Despite these developments, for many pious Muslims, Umayyad
rule, with its wealth and luxury, its imperial practices, and its privi-
leged Arab elites, seemed at odds with the Islamic message preached
by the Prophet and practiced by the early community at Medina. It
was not Islamic commitment and ideals but Arab power and wealth
that had unified Umayyad rule. The Umayyad's Islamic critics argued
that Islam was to permeate every area of life and thus should be
reflected in political, social, and legal life. Could this be said of the
example of many caliphs and the intrigues at the caliphal court? Were
the status and authority of the new elites due to their commitment to
Islam and the example of their personal lives, as had been true of the
Prophet, or to privilege and riches? For these devout Muslims, the
confused and contradictory character of Umayyad rule was epitomized by the condition of Islamic legal practice. The vastness of the
empire with its varying life-styles and customary laws, as well as the
judge's ability to settle disputes on the basis of his own personal dis-
cretion or judgment, had resulted in a great diversity in Islamic legal
practice.

Many asked: "Can God's will for humankind be discerned
through so subjective a process; can His law for the Muslims of Mecca
be so different from that for Medina, Kufa, or Damascus?" These
critics argued that if all Muslims were bound to submit to God's law
and realize His will in their personal and public lives, then the Islamic
way of life ought to be defined clearly and with more uniformity. The
result was the birth of the Islamic legal system as groups of pious
Muslims attempted to delineate in a comprehensive, detailed fashion
the Islamic pattern for Muslim life.[7] In Medina, Kufa, and other Muslim centers, groups of like-minded Muslims began reviewing Umayyad legal practice and found it to be a testimony to the Umayyad's
failure to implement Islam. They began to study the Quran and traditions of the Prophet in an attempt to understand and apply Islamic
principles and values to Muslim life. Their goal was to discern and
delineate the *Shariah*, God's revealed law which was to guide and
govern Muslim life. This process, begun during the late Umayyad
period, was to flourish under the Abbasids.

The elements of a growing Islamic opposition to Umayyad rule were as diverse as their motives: non-Arab Muslims who were second class citizens vis-à-vis Arab Muslims and denounced this as contrary to Islamic egalitarianism; Kharijites who continued to revolt in Mosul and Kufa; Shii or supporters of the family of Ali's claim to leadership of the Muslim community; Arab Muslims, such as those of Mecca, Medina, and Iraq, who were not among the established, favored Arab families; and finally pious Muslims, Arab and non-Arab alike, who viewed the "new cosmopolitan life" of luxury and social privilege as a departure from pristine Islam. For this last group, in particular, the renewal of Muslim society meant a return to the early normative period, to the example of Muhammad and the Rightly Guided Caliphs, and a restoration of the "Medinan ideal."

All opposition factions shared a common discontent with Umayyad rule and a tendency to couch their critique and their response in Islamic terms: "From being a society of Arabs who happened to be bound together by Islam, it must become a society of Muslims who happened to use the Arabic tongue and respect parts of the Arabic heritage."[8] The result was a broad-based, diverse anti-Umayyad sentiment which grew increasingly strong during the last decades of Umayyad rule (ca. 720–50). The opposition's justification and legitimation were cast in ideological terms: condemnation of Umayyad policies and practices as un-Islamic innovations; the call for a return to the Quran and the practices of the Prophet and the early community. Their agenda called for implementation of political, social, and legal reforms in the name of Islam, reforms that would establish a system of Islamic governance and social justice.

From 730 onwards, a series of Kharijite, Shii, and tribal revolts occurred. By 747 one insurrection in particular had survived—that of Abu Muslim, a freed slave of the Abbasid leader Ibrahim, who was a descendant of the Prophet's uncle al-Abbas. With strong Shii assistance, Islamic opposition groups gave their support. In 750 the Umayyads fell and Abu-l-Abbas, the brother of Ibrahim, was proclaimed caliph. Islam's capital moved from Syria to Iraq, from the long-established city of Damascus to the newly created Baghdad, the City of Peace. This royal citadel was to serve as the political, economic, and cultural center of the Islamic Empire. Under Abbasid rule (750–1258), the empire would be the seat not only of political power but also of great cultural activity and the flowering of Islamic civilization.

The Abbasid Caliphate

The Abbasids came to power under the banner of Islam: "The ideology of a restoration of primitive Islam, with variants reflecting different trends, had conquered the masses and, with the support of a majority of the learned men, became part of the program of all, or nearly all, the leaders of parties. It triumphed when the Abbasids adopted it as their slogan."[9]

Their revolution was justified by condemning Umayyad rule as impious and un-Islamic and by promising a more Islamic sociopolitical order. While Abbasid caliphs were fully as autocratic as their predecessors and were not hesitant to use ruthless force to crush their opposition, they took care to align their government and policies with Islam. They became patrons of the Islamic religious establishment, supported the development of Islamic disciplines, built mosques, and established schools.

The Abbasids adopted and refined Umayyad practice by borrowing heavily from the Persian tradition with its divinely ordained system of government. The caliph's claim to rule by divine mandate was symbolized by the altering of his title from "successor," or "deputy," of God's Prophet to "Deputy of God" and the appropriating of the Persian-inspired title "Shadow of God on Earth." The ruler's exalted status was further reinforced by his magnificent palace, retinue of court attendants, and the introduction of court etiquette appropriate for a monarch or emperor. For the religiously minded, the court at Baghdad was a far cry from the Medinan ideal.

From a community of believers, all equal before God and submissive to His divine will, headed by its elected, pious leader, Islam had now become an empire ruled by a caliph who inherited an office now cast in a royal mold. Although Muslims were only to submit to the one, true God alone, court etiquette required subjects to bow before the caliph, kissing the ground, a symbol of the caliph's absolute power and autocratic rule. Nothing could be farther from the Quranic ideal in which all power and homage belonged to God alone and all Muslims, as God's representatives on earth, were to constitute an egalitarian community.

The caliph enjoyed absolute power. If not in Islamic belief, in practice his word was law. He retained his position as the commander of the believers. He was the leader of the Friday, community prayer and of the community's armies in warfare and was to insure rule according to the Islamic law. Thus, the caliph possessed both religious prestige and political power and the duty to enforce Islamic law, defend the Islamic state, and guarantee internal security and peace.

Governmentally, there was a shift from the Arab, especially Syrian, dominated administration and military to a more broad-based, egalitarian system in which the non-Arab Muslims, especially the Persians, played a major role. The Abbasids relied on a strong military and an intricate, hierarchic bureaucracy through which they attempted to directly oversee and supervise every province of their empire. The central administration in Baghdad, building on previous Umayyad and Persian traditions, was highly structured. The government was organized into a system of ministries: treasury, army, intelligence, and so forth, headed by the chief minister, the vizier, who served as head of the caliphal cabinet, which supervised the large army of administrators and their staffs. In effect the caliphs increasingly delegated the conduct of government to the vizier and his ministers.

The empire was divided into provinces. Each province was administered by a governor and a superintendent of revenue, an agent of the caliph responsible for the collection and management of revenue (land and taxes) as well as other administrative tasks. The Islamic tax system became more equitable because Arab and non-Arab Muslims alike paid the same taxes, just as they enjoyed the same socioeconomic status and opportunities. Under Abbasid rule, Muslim society approximated more closely the early Islamic division of the *ummah:* Muslim and non-Muslim.

The development of the *Shariah* constitutes the Abbasid period's most significant contribution to Islam. Because part of the indictment against the Umayyads had been their failure to implement an effective Islamic legal system, the Abbasids gave substantial support to legal development. The work of the early law schools, which had only begun during the late Umayyad period (ca. 720), flowered under caliphal patronage of religious scholars (*ulama*, learned men). Islam has no clergy or priesthood. However, by the eighth century, the *ulama* had become a professional class of religious leaders. Their prestige and authority were based upon a reputation for knowledge of Islamic learning: Quran, prophetic traditions, law. As jurists, theologians, and educators, they became the interpreters and guardians of Islamic law and tradition.

A second motivation for legal development was the desire of many religious scholars to set forth clearly an Islamic ideal and mandate, which all too often was not to be found during the rule of less pious caliphs. In this way, the path to be followed, the Islamic charter for state and society, could be preserved independent of a caliph's moral character or political power. If the religious scholars could not control their caliph, they could attempt to get their way indirectly by delineating and preserving their interpretation of Islam in its law.

Although Muslims were enjoined to submit, that is, to realize God's will, no systematic delineation of Islamic law existed until the eighth century. The Quran is not a law book. Rather, the Quran sets forth general legal and ethical principles that are to guide and govern Muslim life. For the early Muslims, law consisted of Quranic prescriptions, Prophetic traditions, and decisions by the early caliphs and judges. These superceded and supplemented but did not replace Arab customary practice, or law. Under the Umayyads, as seen above, law continued to develop in the legal opinions of *qadis* (*Shariah* Court judges). Critical of Umayyad practice, the early schools of law had reviewed the Umayyad legal system in light of the Quran. However, the bulk of Islamic law developed as a self-conscious, systematic attempt by Muslim jurists to understand and apply revealed Islamic principles and values to the many exigencies of Muslim life. Thus was born Islamic jurisprudence or the science of law which by the end of the ninth century produced a detailed, systematic body of law that provided the established blueprint for Islamic state and society throughout subsequent centuries.

According to classical Islamic jurisprudence there are four sources or roots of law: (1) the Quran; (2) the *Sunnah* (example or model behavior) of the Prophet as preserved in the traditions; (3) analogical reasoning *(qiyas)*, that is, where a revealed prescription is lacking, a new regulation may be deduced by reasoning from a similar or analogous situation in scripture or the Prophetic traditions; and (4) the consensus, or agreement *(ijma)*, of the Islamic community on a point of law. The authority of consensus is based upon the Prophetic dictum: "My community will never agree upon an error." In practice the consensus was usually that of the religious scholars in a particular generation and not that of the entire community.

In fact the actual development of Islamic law was far more complex and creative than this idealized version preserved by Islamic jurisprudence. The classical statement of the sources of law overlooked the important roles played by the personal interpretation, or judgment (*ijtihad*), of early judges and jurists. Even more important was the bulk of customary practices which, if judged not contrary to Islam, were adopted and incorporated in the law books.

During the first two centuries of Abbasid rule (750–950), schools of law (groups of scholar-jurists) could be found in major centers of the empire. It was here, not in the courts, that Islamic law developed. Thus Islamic law was not the product of judicial decisions and review. There is no recognized case law system of legally binding precedents. Rather, given the Muslim's divinely revealed vocation to submit to and realize God's will, groups of jurists or legal scholars, not judges, sought to discover and delineate God's will for mankind in light of the Quran and example of Muhammad. As a result, Islamic law is as much a system of ethics as it is law, for it is concerned with what the Muslim "ought" or "ought not" to do. To violate the law is not only to risk legal sanctions on earth but divine judgment in the hereafter because law in Islam is viewed as God-ordained, not man-made. This is why all acts or duties were ethically categorized as: (1) obligatory, (2) recommended, (3) indifferent or permissible, (4) reprehensible, (5) forbidden or prohibited.

While there is a general unity in Islamic law, differences in approach and geographic location (and thus customary practice) among the law schools resulted in a legal diversity amidst this unity. Although there had been many schools of law, four major Sunni schools (Hanafi, Shafii, Maliki, and Hanbali) and one Shii school (Jafari) endured the test of time. The differences among law schools affect such questions as grounds for divorce, inheritance rights, and taxation. And, of course, a major difference between Sunni and Shii concerns leadership (caliphate vs. imamate) of the Muslim community. The content of Islamic law was seen as comprehensive because it set forth the divinely revealed blueprint for Muslim society. The law encompassed such areas as prayer and fasting as well as international and family laws. Muslim jurists divided all law into two general categories: duties to God (worship including prayer, tithing, pilgrimage, fasting); and duties to one's fellow man (social transactions which encompass public as well as personal life: civil, penal, commercial, and family laws).

By the tenth century, Islamic law, in the opinion of the *ulama*, was finalized and institutionalized. The consensus of legal scholars was that Islam's way of life had been adequately delineated. The task of

future generations was to follow God's path as set forth in the authoritative legal manuals. Individual, independent reasoning or personal
judgment was no longer deemed necessary or permissible—the door
of *ijtihad* (personal interpretation) was henceforth closed. Jurists were
not to write law books but commentaries. While individual religious
scholars like Taqi al-Din Ahmad Ibn Taymiyyah (1263–1328) and Jalal
al-Din al-Suyuti (1445–1505) demurred, the majority position resulted
in the traditional belief prohibiting substantive legal development by
jurists: "The power of absolute *ijtihad* was completely abolished; a
'relative' *ijtihad* was allowed. This meant either that one was allowed
to reinterpret law within one's own school of law or, and this was the
highest point of legislation, one could carry on an eclectic and comparative study of law of different schools and thus find some scope
for limited expansion in details."[10] The task of the judge and his Islamic law court was the "application," not "interpretation," of law.
Judges were organized under the direction of a central authority or
chief judge, appointed by the caliph. Assisting the courts were legal
specialists *(muftis)*, whose task was the interpretation of law as set
forth in the legal manuals of the schools. They communicated their
findings in legal opinions *(fatwas)* that both the judge and litigants
could use. In general the judiciary was dependent upon the caliph.
Judges were appointed, paid, and dismissed by the government. In
addition the caliph or his provincial governor retained the right to
review all decisions rendered by the courts.

  While in theory the *Shariah* was the only recognized law and judicial system of the Islamic Empire, in practice a parallel system of caliphal law and courts developed for a variety of reasons. First of all,
the idealism of the *Shariah* was often deemed impractical. For example, in criminal law, where two adult Muslim witnesses are lacking,
the rules of evidence require the court to accept an oath sworn in
God's name. Moreover, *Shariah* rules of procedure exclude circumstantial evidence and the cross-examination of witnesses. Second, and
perhaps of greater influence, was the caliph's desire to personally regulate and govern society. However, there was a problem. Although, in
practice, the caliph might exercise absolute power, in theory God was
the only lawmaker. To resolve this seeming contradiction, through a
series of legal fictions, a parallel system of caliphal jurisdiction was
introduced: the *Mazalim* (complaint) court system. Initially, the court
of *Mazalim* enabled the caliph to hear complaints against senior gov-

ernment officials (whose status or power may have inhibited the judge) or even against the judges themselves. In time the *Mazalim* became a system of courts whose scope and function were defined by the sovereign. An Islamic rationale for this dual legal system was established to justify such legal practices. In Islam the primary task of the caliph is to maintain a society governed by the Islamic law. However, in order to assure the proper implementation and administration of *Shariah* rule, the government was permitted to issue regulations or ordinances as long as these regulations were not contrary to the *Shariah*. Thus, in the name of Islam and the upholding of the *Shariah*, the right of the sovereign to issue ordinances, not laws, was justified. This method continued down through Islamic history and can be seen today in countries such as Saudi Arabia that have employed this rationale in introducing "regulations" such as the Mining Code (1963) and the Civil Service Law (1971), which supplement the *Shariah*.

Thus the Islamic Empire had two complementary jurisdictions: the *Shariah* Courts, which increasingly were restricted to matters of personal law, such as family law (marriage, divorce, and inheritance) and religious endowments, and the *Mazalim* courts, which dealt with public law such as criminal, land, taxation, and commercial regulations. Given the centrality of law as a model for the ideal Islamic society and its function as the basis for Islamic government, the place of Islamic law remains a major issue in Islamic politics.

The Abbasid period is remembered by Muslims not simply for its power and wealth or its completion of the process of state organization and law but especially for the development of Islamic culture and civilization. The Abbasids were committed patrons of culture and the arts. In addition to law, religious disciplines, such as Quran interpretation, tradition criticism, history, and biography, were developed. The process of Arabization, which had begun during the late Umayyad period, was completed by the end of the ninth century. Arabic language and tradition had interacted with, modified, and eventually dominated the peoples and cultures of the conquered territories. Arabic displaced Syriac, Aramaic, Coptic, and Greek, becoming the language of common discourse, government, and literature throughout much of the empire. Translation bureaus were established. Manuscripts were obtained from the far reaches of the empire and translated from their original languages (Greek, Syriac, Latin, Sanskrit, Persian) into Arabic at state-supported translation bureaus. Thus the best of literature and the sciences was made available. The period of translation and assimilation was followed by one of Muslim intellectual and artistic creativity in which significant contributions were made in many fields: literature and philosophy; art and architecture; science, medicine, and mathematics.[11] As Islam had challenged the world politically, it now did so culturally. This brilliant period, which Muslims came to view as the Golden Age of Islamic civilization, with its urban cultural centers in Cordova, Baghdad, Cairo, Nishapur, and Palermo, eclipsed Christian Europe, mired in the Dark Ages. As with the conquests and expansion of Islam, Muslims then (and now) regarded this phenomenal period as a sign of God's blessings and validation of Islam's message and the Muslim community's mission.

The Golden Age of Islamic civilization paralleled the progressive political fragmentation of imperial Islam. Abbasid political unity deteriorated dramatically after 950. Despite a strong central government, controlling a vast empire extending from the Atlantic to Central Asia with so many competing groups proved impossible. From 861 to 945, religious (in particular Kharijite and Shiite) and regional differences and competing political aspirations precipitated a series of revolts and secessionist movements. In Morocco and Tunisia, local rulers, while continuing to give nominal allegiance and to pay tribute to the caliph, exercised de facto rule over their territories, establishing their own local hereditary dynasties. Egypt saw the rise of the Shii Fatimid dynasty (909–1171). In Iran, Syria, and Iraq itself, local governors, who were often army commanders, increasingly asserted their independence as heads of semiautonomous states. By 945 the disintegration of a universal caliphate was evident as the Buyids, a family that ruled several such independent states in western Iran, invaded Baghdad and seized power. The Buyids assumed the title commander in chief, or commander of the commanders. Although Shiite, they did not change the Sunni orientation of the empire and left the caliph as nominal head of a fictionally unified empire. The Abbasids continued to reign but not to rule. From that time on, with an Abbasid on the throne as a symbol of legitimate government and Muslim unity, real power passed to a series of Persian (Buyid) and then Turkic (Seljuq) military dynasties or sultanates. The sultan ("power," ruler), as chief of the commanders, governed a politically fragmented empire. Finally, in 1258 the Mongols, under Hulagu, swept across Central Asia, conquered Persia, and descended upon Baghdad. They captured the capital and killed the Caliph al-Mutasim, who left no heir. The Islamic caliphate was terminated; the first stage of Islamic political history had come to an end.

While politically the Mongol conquest of the Abbasid caliphate may seem to be nothing more than the establishment of one more usurper dynasty, its Islamic significance was far more profound. Whatever the merits of the Persian-Turkic sultans that had seized power and governed from 945 to 1258, they were *Muslim*. The *ummah* continued to exist as a religiopolitical community/state with the caliph as its symbolic head and governed by Islamic law. Thus the ideological prerequisites for Muslim life remained intact; Muslims continued to live in an Islamic state, following the straight path (the *Shariah*) of Muslim life. Whatever the changing fortunes of Islamic history, for Muslim historical consciousness, the message and mission of the Islamic community had been validated from its Medinan beginnings in 622 by a long period of remarkable expansion, power, and wealth. Success and power were viewed as signs of God's pleasure and His reward for a faithful community. Muslim usurpers might come and go, but Islamic presence and rule had remained. But the conquest by Mongol invaders who were unbelievers meant the destruction of the land of Islam. It was a challenge to Muslim life, faith, and identity. In this sense, the Mongol threat was as traumatic and Islamically significant as that of European imperialism in the eighteenth century. Whatever the response, a successful resolution would entail the incorporation of Islam ideologically and politically once again in Muslim life.

Throughout the first six centuries of Islamic political history, despite the character of individual rulers and competing claims of various factions, religion provided the basic identity and ideological framework for political and social life. The world was divided into Islamic and non-Islamic territory. All Muslims were to strive to extend Islamic rule (the Pax Islamica), wherever possible. Thus merchants, traders, and soldiers were the early missionaries of Islam. Islam was part and parcel of the state's institutions: caliphate, judiciary, taxation, education, and social welfare systems. It affected the definition of citizenship and social classes and was symbolized in the new coinage system introduced by the Umayyads to replace that of the Byzantines. Coins were struck using Quranic phrases or images of Muhammad's lance or a *mihrab* (the prayer niche indicating the direction of Mecca). Islamic identity and ideology were so basic to politics that anticaliphal opposition movements—such as Muawiyah's challenge to Ali, Kharijite and Shiite revolts, social discontent, and the Abbasid revolution—also appealed to Islam to legitimate their actions. The political and social institutions, especially Islamic law, which represented an ideological synthesis of the Islamic way of life, would continue to constitute the essentials of Islamic government for future generations.

Medieval Muslim Empires: The Sultanate Period

The fall of Baghdad in 1258 did not sound the death knell of Islamic rule. Islam proved resilient. The postcaliphal period was both a dynamic and expansionist period of Islamic history. The political unity of the caliphate gave way to a burgeoning number of Muslim sultanates that governed an area that eventually extended from North Africa to Southeast Asia as Islam progressively penetrated East, West, and Central Africa; Central and Southeast Asia; and Eastern Europe. The continued expansion of Islam was accompanied by Muslim rule and large-scale conversions inspired both by the message of Islam as presented by Muslim preachers, especially the Sufi orders, and by conversions owing to the socioeconomic advantages of full membership, or citizenship, in the *ummah*. Despite the political fragmentation of the caliphate or lack of a universal central authority, an underlying unity of faith and culture continued to exist during the sultanate period. Muslim citizens of a particular state also maintained an awareness of a broader affiliation and identity with the more universal community. For Islamic faith and culture went hand in hand: "Whichever way Muslim faith and rule came, once it had endured any length of time there tended to follow the whole Islamic civilization as found in the area from which Islamization had come."[12]

By the sixteenth century, three major Muslim empires had emerged in the midst of the many sultanates: the Sunni Ottoman in West Asia and Eastern Europe, the Shii Safavid in Persia, and the Sunni Mughal in the Indian subcontinent. Harnessing gunpowder technology, these "gunpowder empires," whose central governments were supported by a blend of religious ideology and military strength, dominated the heartlands of the Islamic world: North Africa, the Middle East, and South Asia. Reminiscent of Abbasid times, great sultans like the Ottoman Sulayman the Magnificent (1520–1605), Shah Abbas (1588–1629) in Persia, and the Mughal emperor Akbar (1556–1605) in India were patrons of learning and the arts. The Islamic character of the state was reflected by the Ottoman conquerors who, after conquering the capital of the eastern Roman world and renaming Constantinople Istanbul, "crowned the hills with monumental mosques."[13] Their political and military achievements were accompanied by a dazzling cultural florescence. With the dynamic expansion of Islam during the sultanate period and the emergence of three Muslim empires, history continued to witness the vitality, success, and divine guidance of Allah's commonwealth. Baghdad's successors were now Istanbul, Isfahan, and Delhi.

While there were significant differences between the three great medieval Muslim empires, they each carried over the basic features of Islamic state and society. Islam provided legitimation, political ideology, and law; it informed the principal institutions of government. The head of state, the sultan, although a temporal ruler, derived his authority as emperor from God and was the defender/protector of Islam. He was an absolute monarch, ruling his empire as head of its military through a strong central government. While sovereign, the sultan often delegated the civil administration of his government to his grand vizier, his chief minister or steward, who oversaw an elaborate network of ministries.

The *Shariah* played a major role in all three empires. *Shariah*, as the official law of the empire, was the source of Islamic legitimation and identity and defined the norms of life. The ruler, however, also maintained his *Mazalim* courts and, in the name of *Shariah* governance, promulgated ordinances that in effect constituted much of the state's public law. The *Shariah* Courts continued to be generally restricted to matters of personal status: marriage, divorce, inheritance, and religious endowment.

The *ulama* often were a significant presence among the army of officials who served as government advisers and administrators. As in earlier Islamic history, they were the guardians of law and tradition and thus dominated the judicial, educational, and social service systems. They were indeed a religious establishment. Although the emperor retained absolute authority, the religious scholars through tacit alliance (Ottoman and Mughal) or independence (Safavid) wielded a great deal of influence. Their power and prestige can be appreciated if we recall the extent to which their activities impacted upon their societies. Legally, they were the judges and legal advisers (*muftis*) of the state, responsible for the administration and application of law. In addition to the office of chief judge, the religious institution was further centralized and administered from the capital by a chief religious functionary (head of religious affairs) known in the Ottoman Empire as a chief *mufti*, or *Shaykh al-Islam*, and in the Safavid and Mughal empires as the *Sadr al-sudir*.

The *ulama* also controlled the educational system, serving as its administrators and scholar-teachers. Royal patronage of learning resulted in a marvelous system of schools and universities, which provided the education required for all who aspired to public as well as religious office. This system of education reinforced both the prestige of the religious scholars and the Islamic identity and character of the state. Finally, they exercised considerable influence and power through their control over a broad range of social services. The income for such activities was generated from royal land grants, religious endowments and tithing. These funds were applied to the construction and maintenance of a variety of public services. mosques, hospitals, schools, lodges for travelers, and roads and bridges.

In conclusion, despite differences between the caliphate and sultanate periods and among the medieval Muslim empire sultanates themselves, there was a continuity grounded in their Islamic legacy and tradition. Islam constituted the basic ideological framework of meaning for political and social life. Moreover, whether the state was headed by a pious or impious caliph/sultan, or a usurper dynasty, none directly challenged the *Shariah* governance of the state. Thus, for the believer, there was a continuum of Muslim power and success which, despite the vicissitudes and contradictions of Muslim life, validated and reinforced the sense of a divinely mandated and guided community with a purpose and mission.

Islamic Political Thought

The integral relationship of religion to politics in Islam and its emphasis on the Muslim vocation to realize God's rule were reflected in the tendency to view political and social revolts (the apostasy wars, the social rights of non-Arab converts, the political secession of the

Shiites and Kharijites) as not simply political but religious issues. The rebellion of Arabian tribes after Muhammad's death was not just treason but apostasy. The systematic expression of the Islamic ideal had been preserved in Islamic law. Nevertheless, as we have seen, the historical reality was often at odds with the normative ideal. The early extraordinary expansion and development of Islam as a state necessitated immediate decisions by caliphs and generals rather than reflective planning by scholars and policy makers. The political and social infrastructure of the Umayyad and Abbasid empires did not grow out of the systematic interpretations and applications of Islamic ideology but rather from the ad hoc policies of successive regimes, which drew heavily from Byzantine and then Sasanid practice.

Given the comprehensive claim of the Islamic vision and the diverse nature of Islamic governments, the sharp discrepancy between revealed ideal and political reality posed a challenge to Muslims' consciences, in particular to those of the *ulama*, who saw themselves as the guardians of Islam. The Kharijites had been among the first to address the question: "What is the proper response to a conflict between the ideal and the real in Muslim political life?" Belief that a grave sinner was no longer a Muslim and was, in fact, the legitimate object of *jihad* had motivated their secessionist movement and been used to justify subsequent rebellions against caliphal authority. For others Umayyad authority and rule were based not upon the Medinan example of selection of a caliph through consultation but upon force and dynastic succession. Such a policy was un-Islamic and therefore a justification for the Abbasid revolution. Consequently, Islamic theories on the nature of the caliphate developed not as deductions or speculations on the nature of Islamic government but rather as justifications for a political reality often at odds with normative Islam. Sunni apologists responded to Shii and Kharijite objections to the actions of early Sunni caliphs (e.g., Ali's arbitration with Muawiyah or Yazid's rout of Husayn).

Other scholars addressed the disparity between Umayyad and Abbasid dynastic rule and the early normative practice of the Rightly Guided Caliphs. They responded to questions such as: (1) What constitutes an Islamic government? (2) To what extent is an Islamic government dependent upon the virtuous character of the caliph or the manner of his selection? (3) How should a Muslim respond to seemingly un-Islamic rulers or governments? Whatever the belief concern-

ing the unity of religion and politics, the historical experience of the
community often contradicted the Islamic ideal. The issues raised by
this discrepancy between faith and practice gave rise to the development of Islamic political thought.

Classical Sunni Islamic political theory took shape during Abbasid rule. Heavily indebted to and thus influenced by royal patronage, Muslim jurists and theologians had a twofold purpose: to
maintain the divine origin and purpose of the Islamic community and
to legitimate the claims and the rule of Abbasid caliphs.[14] During succeeding centuries, a wide variety of positions resulted, but no single
theory was universally adopted. For some the true caliphate was restricted to the first four Rightly Guided Caliphs. Others, like the great
historian Ibn Khaldun (d. 1406), pragmatically accepted the possible
compatibility of caliphate and kingdom: "Government and kingship
are a caliphate of God amongst men, for the execution of his ordinance amongst them."[15] The jurist, al-Mawardi (d. 1058), in his treatise
Al-Ahkam al-Sultaniyah (The Ordinances of Government), which became a classic exposition on Islamic government, presented a theoretical, idealized view of the caliphate. Many other jurist-theologians,
like Abu Hamid al-Ghazali (d. 1111) and al-Baqillani (d. 1013), followed suit. These scholars were not drafting government regulations
or guidelines but rather delineating a moral ideal. By the end of the
Abbasid period, the essentials of Islamic political theory were formed
with a number of common themes. God is the absolute sovereign and
ruler of the universe and the ultimate authority of the state. Through
a covenant, authority is delegated to mankind as God's instrument in
the world. The institution of the caliphate is based upon revelation,
the Quranic designation to serve as God's vicegerent, and not simply
upon reason. The caliph is elected or nominated by a group of influential community leaders "the people who loose and bind." He may
also be designated by his predecessor (the incumbent caliph). Election
or designation of a caliph is followed by community acceptance or
public acclamation. The moral idealism of caliphal political theory
was especially evident in the qualifications for office: justice; knowledge to interpret and apply the law; virtuous character; courage to
wage war; good physical health; and, finally, descent from the Quraysh—the Prophet's tribe. As the Commander of the Faithful, he
leads the community in war. The caliph's primary task is to uphold

and enforce the *Shariah*. He is the guardian or protector of Islam, Defender of the Faith.

The disintegration of the Abbasid caliphate during the tenth century raised an additional question for Islamic political thought: If the caliph in Baghdad was reduced to a nominal head of state, often restricted to his palace by the ruling army commander, were Muslims bound to revolt against a now un-Islamic usurper government? Al-Ghazali and Ibn Khaldun provided justifications for the acceptance of harsh political realities, maintaining that order was better than political chaos. Necessity or public interest legitimated acceptance of such sultan usurpers. As long as the sultan acknowledged the caliph as the spiritual and temporal head of the community, continued to mention the caliph's name at the Friday community prayer, and pledged to uphold *Shariah* rule, Islamic government continued to exist. Through such a legal accommodation, the symbol of Muslim unity and identity was preserved.

Despite the diversity of Islamic political thought, a common denominator emerged: the minimal requirement for an Islamic government was not the character of the head of state but rule according to the *Shariah*. Acknowledgment by the ruler that the *Shariah* was the state's official law preserved both the unity of the community and its Islamic framework or character. Islamic law, not the religious commitment or moral character of the ruler or government, was the criterion for the legitimacy of an Islamic state.

Conclusion

A review of the role of religion in politics and society in early Islam reveals a rich and complex history. Islam proved to be a faith in which religion was harnessed to political power. The Islamic community was both spiritual and temporal, church and state. Religious faith and ideology provided the ideological and motivational glue that united Arabian tribes and inspired and gave direction to the early period of expansion and conquest. Religion provided the world view, the framework of meaning for both individual and corporate life. Whether under the Rightly Guided Caliphs or Umayyad and Abbasid rulers, the ideological foundation of the community/state was Islam. The legitimacy and authority of the ruler, the officially acknowledged law of the state, and its judicial, educational, and social institutions were rooted in Islam. Though the historical and political realities of caliphal life were often at odds with its Islamic ideals, the primary principle of political identity and social cohesion nevertheless continued to be public and popular commitment to the *Shariah*. The Islamic ideal remained intact and authoritative, though often circumvented. For the believer, the Islamic character of Muslim history and political life was not belied by the disparities of history. Later generations of Muslims inherited the romantic, idealized understanding of the nature of Islamic political history and law that had been developed by the early *ulama* and had been transmitted and perpetuated in their writings, educational institutions, and religious instruction. This ideal, though it obscured many of the realities of Islamic history, provided the Islamic paradigm that inspired subsequent generations, from premodern revivalist movements to contemporary Islamic political activists, who would seek to emulate and realize an Islamic religiopolitical vision.

... *2* ...

Revival and Reform

Modern Islamic reform is often depicted simply as a reaction and response to Western imperialism—political and cultural domination by European colonial powers. However, the roots of modern reform lie in both Islamic and Western sources. Understanding twentieth-century Islamic politics requires an understanding of the character and legacy of both premodern Islamic revivalism, which addressed the internal weakness of Muslim society, and Islamic modernism, which responded to the challenge of Western colonialism. Premodern revivalism was primarily a response from within Islam to the internal sociomoral decline of the community. In many cases, it led to the creation of Islamic states such as Saudi Arabia, the Sudan, and Libya. Islamic revivalist movements like the Wahhabi in Arabia, Mahdi in the Sudan, and Sanusi in Libya were forerunners of both twentieth-century Islamic modernism and contemporary Islamic revivalism. As such they reveal much of the pattern of modern Islamic movements in their world view, ideology, language, and methods.

Islamic modernism broadened and built on the premodern revivalist legacy. By the mid-nineteenth century, concern for the internal weakness of the Islamic community was compounded by the threat of subjugation to the Christian West. European colonial domination of much of the Muslim world constituted for many Muslims the end result of a long period of decline. The political and religiocultural threat of Western imperialism brought forth a variety of Muslim responses ranging from conservative religious militant rejectionism to wholesale Western-oriented adaptationism, from *jihad* movements to modernist reform movements. As we shall see, Islamic modernism represented an Islamically rooted response to unite and strengthen a demoralized community. Its method was a reinterpretation of Islam that not only drew on Islamic tradition but also attempted to assimilate the best of modern science, thought, and institutions.

Premodern Islamic Revivalism

Islamic history has offered many examples of Muslim responses to the glaring disparity between God's revealed will for humankind and the historical development of the Islamic community. Among these were the early Kharijite and Shiite rebellions, the development of Islamic mysticism (Sufism) and law in the face of alleged "unIslamic" Umayyad practice, the "Islamic rationale" for the Abbasid revolution, and the reformist activities of great individual religious figures like the theologian al-Ghazali (d. 1111) and the jurist Ibn Taymiyyah (d. 1328). All had claimed to be responding to the sociomoral corruption of Muslim society; all had called for a return to the fundamentals of Islam to restore and revivify an errant community. Herein lie the historical roots for the long tradition of Islamic revival, a process of renewal and reform that have inspired both premodern and modern Muslim reform movements.

Throughout the eighteenth and nineteenth centuries, a wave of Islamic religiopolitical movements occurred from the Sudan to Sumatra. In the core areas of the Islamic world, the imperial sultanates (Ottoman, Safavid, and Mughal) had peaked in the sixteenth century; by the eighteenth century, their power and prosperity were fading into a period of decline. Among the common indices of imperial decline were internal political disintegration (the decline of central authority and the rise of semiautonomous regional and provincial governments), military losses, social dislocation and disruption, and a worsening economy, affected by European competition in trade and manufacturing. Political and economic decline were accompanied by a growing concern about spiritual and moral decay in eighteenth-century Islamic societies, which reflected a similar pattern of revival and reform, despite the distinctive differences caused by local conditions.

Within Sunni Islam, there developed an awareness that the continued vitality of the Islamic community would require renewal and reform from time to time. This belief in the need for a recurrent pro-

cess of revitalization was crystalized in the development of a revivalist tradition and a belief in a "renewer" or reviver of Islam. In addition experience of the disparity between public life and the Islamic
ideal contributed to the popular expectation of a messianic figure, the
Mahdi.

The renewer of Islam is sent at the beginning of each century to
restore true Islamic practice and thus regenerate a community which
tends, over time, to wander from the straight path. Belief in these
renewers is based upon a tradition of the Prophet: "God will send to
this *ummah* at the beginning of each century those who will renew its
faith."[1]

The Mahdi, "the guided one," in Sunni Islam is a popular rather
than doctrinal belief in an eschatological individual who will come in
the future to deliver the community from oppression by the forces of
evil and to restore true Islam and with it a reign of justice on earth.
This popular Sunni belief, never formally included in Sunni theology,
should be distinguished from the Shiite theological doctrine of the
Mahdi, which refers to the awaited return of the Hidden Imam. The
Shiite Mahdi is the divinely inspired religiopolitical leader of Shii Islam, the successor of Muhammad and Ali. He will come to inaugu-
rate a new age of peace and justice in the world. He is an absolute,
infallible guide and interpreter of revelation who rules by divine
right.

Among the principal ingredients of Islamic revivalism were a
sense that something had gone wrong in Islam and a diagnosis that
decline in Muslim fortunes was caused by a departure from the
straight path of Islam. Revivalists maintained that Islam had become
corrupted through its historical accretions from foreign (i.e., un-
Islamic) influences. Nowhere was this debilitating eclecticism believed
to be more clearly evident than in Sufism's absorption of popular
religious practices.

Sufism was an ascetic, mystical movement that had developed
during the early centuries of Islam. It had swept across the Islamic
world in the twelfth and thirteenth centuries, serving as an enor-
mously effective missionary movement. Islamic reformers maintained
that in becoming a mass movement, Sufi syncretism and eclecticism
had resulted in the assimilation of many innovations: ecstatic trances,
saint/tomb worship, and a passivity and fatalism that resulted from
the mystics' denigration of worldly affairs. The cure followed from

the diagnosis. Muslims must "return to Islam," that is, the correct practice of Islam with its emphasis upon active realization or implementation of God's will in this world. This purification was the prerequisite for a strong, powerful society as well as a requirement for eternal life. Muslims must reclaim the original Islam revealed in the Quran and the example of the Prophet and embodied in the life and practice of the early Medinan community.

Islamic revivalist movements sought to transform not only the religious but also the political and social life of the community. Their goal was nothing less than a moral reconstruction of Muslim society to restore its Islamic center. To accomplish this, they reasserted the right of individual reinterpretation. As discussed earlier, the majority of religious scholars had determined that individual interpretation of Islamic law was no longer necessary; instead Muslims were to follow the path of Islam as set forth in the regulations of the law manuals. Eighteenth- and nineteenth-century Islamic revivalists rejected this blind following of Muslim legal or theological teachings, believing that medieval law had been infiltrated by un-Islamic, historical accretions. They asserted their right to go back directly to the only immutable authority, the revealed sources of Islam, in order to rediscover and restore true Islam. In contrast to later Islamic modernism, premodern revivalism simply sought to restore and implement an existing ideal, not to reformulate or reconstruct new Islamic responses to modern change.

The Islamic rationale for change views the nature of Islam and the basis of religious renewal as both an individual and a communal affair. This reasoning provided a religiopolitical ideology that inspired premodernist Islamic movements and has continued to offer a paradigm for many contemporary Islamic movements today. Islamic ideological slogans and beliefs were harnessed to provide a legitimacy and a framework of meaning by which Islamic actors and movements mobilized popular support. We can see this approach to Islamic reform in several of the more prominent revivalist movements in Arabia, India, and Africa.

Arabia: Muhammad ibn Abd al-Wahhab

Muhammad ibn Abd al-Wahhab (1703–92) was the son of a learned jurist and theologian. He was educated at Mecca and Medina in Hanafi and Shafii law. He studied with teachers of the Hanbali school, the strictest of the Sunni law schools, and took Ibn Taymiyyah as his exemplar. Disillusioned by the moral laxity and spiritual malaise of his times, Muhammad ibn Abd al-Wahhab set out to reform his society, to return it to the practice of the Prophet. He denounced the ills of his society and called upon the people to abandon many popular religious beliefs and practices that he compared to pre-Islamic Arabian practice, the period of ignorance. The historical additions that overlay pure Islam constituted idolatry. In particular, he attacked the superstition and idolatrous practices of Sufism, denouncing them as "innovations," unwarranted deviations from true Islam. He called for a literal interpretation of the Quran and *Sunnah*. Muslims must return to the pure Islam of the first generation of Muslims, the righteous ancestors.

Muhammad ibn Abd al-Wahhab joined forces with a local tribal chief, Muhammad ibn Saud (d. 1765) of Dariyah, and from this alliance the so-called Wahhabi movement was born. Religious zeal and military might merged in a religiopolitical movement that waged holy war with a zeal reminiscent of the early Kharijites, viewing all Muslims who resisted as unbelievers. The tribes of Arabia were subdued and united in the name of Islamic egalitarianism. The Wahhabi forces' self-designation as Muwahiddun ("Unitarians," i.e., those who believe in and practice monotheism) was reminiscent of early Islamic radical monotheism and its iconoclasm. As Muhammad in Mecca had cleansed the Kaba of the tribal gods, so Abd al-Wahhab rejected all popular religious practices that smacked of idolatry—saint worship, pilgrimage to sacred tombs, devotional rituals: "to worship anyone or anything whether it be a king, prophet, Sufi saint, sacred tomb or tree is to create idols" (*Majmu'at al-rasa'il* 4:5). Because many of these practices were attributed to Sufi cultural accommodation, Sufism was suppressed; its shrines, tombs, and sacred objects were destroyed. In imitation of the Prophet's cleansing of the Kaba, Wahhabi iconoclastic zeal led to the destruction of sacred tombs in Mecca and Medina, including that of Muhammad and his early companions, as idolatrous shrines. Wahhabi forces destroyed Karbala, a major Shiite pilgrimage site in Iraq, which housed the tomb of Husayn. These latter actions have never been forgotten by Shii Muslims and have contributed to their negative attitude toward the Wahhabi of Saudi Arabia.

Abd al-Wahhab respected tradition but rejected an uncritical following of past authority. All postprophetic tradition, including the time-honored formulations of Islamic law, were subject to selective

criticism since the law itself had taken on un-Islamic customary practices. The starting point was to return again to a purified Islam. However, his interpretation was not that of twentieth-century Islamic
modernism which sought to reinterpret Islam in order to formulate
solutions for new situations. His was a literalist interpretation: the
revealed sources offered the immutable pattern of life, which must be
reclaimed and implemented in order to purify Islam, regenerate Muslim society, and restore its past glory.

India: Shah Wali Allah

In India the decline of Mughal power had spurred a number of
revivalist movements. Among the most influential was that of Shah
Wali Allah of Delhi (1702–62) and his disciples. Wali Allah rejected
the moral corruption of Indian society, indicted popular Sufism's indiscriminate syncretism, and called for a purification of Islam. Yet,
unlike Muhammad ibn Abd al-Wahhab, Wali Allah's surgery was less
radical. Rather than reject the present to restore the past, he sought to
modify present Muslim belief and practice in light of early Islamic
practice. Thus he set out to reform or purify Sufism rather than to
suppress it. Similarly, he advocated use of interpretation to reform
medieval Islam. Wali Allah believed that the rectification of Islamic
belief and practice would lead to a revitalization of Muslim society
and the restoration of Mughal power. Under the leadership of his son,
Shah Abdul Aziz (1746–1824), and then Sayyid Ahmad Barelewi
(1786–1831), the sociopolitical implications of Wali Allah's teachings
were developed and applied.

For Sayyid Ahmad, effective response to both the interior decay
of the community and the external thrust of the Sikhs, and later the
British, required *jihad*. Loss of political power meant that India was
no longer an Islamic territory but an "abode of war" (non-Islamic
territory). He and his followers, holy warriors, combined preaching
and military power in a *jihad* movement whose goal was the establishment of a purified Islamic state based upon social justice and
equality. Sayyid Ahmad saw the Muslims' loss of political power as
being caused by their failure to follow the law. He emphasized the
centrality of monotheism and denounced those polytheistic practices
(Sufi, Shii, and popular customs borrowed from Hinduism) that were
contrary to it.[2] With a band of followers, he made the pilgrimage to

Mecca in 1823. At Hudabiyya, the place where Muhammad's companions had made a pact to fight the Meccans, Sayyid Ahmad administered an oath of *jihad* to his followers.[3]

Sayyid Ahmad Barelewi was revered by his followers as a renewer of Islam. There was a belief that in each century God sends a leader who would strengthen Islam. The commitment of the holy warriors was reflected in their three thousand-mile trip in 1826 to the Northwest Frontier Province (Pakistan). This area was viewed as a proper area for *jihad* and the creation of a new Islamic state because its predominantly Muslim population was ruled by an oppressive non-Muslim Sikh regime. The holy warriors defeated the Sikhs at Balakot and established a religiopolitical state. Like the early caliphs, Sayyid Ahmad was proclaimed commander of the believers. In 1831 Sayyid Ahmad was killed in battle; his scattered movement continued until 1860.[4]

Africa: *Jihad* Movements

The general sense of Muslim decline and the desire for Islamic renewal were nowhere more evident than in nineteenth-century Africa. A series of *jihad* movements led to the establishment of Islamic states, including those led by Uthman dan Fodio (1754–1817) in Northern Nigeria, the Grand Sanusi in Libya (1787–1859), and the Mahdi of the Sudan (1848–85). A distinctive characteristic of most African revivalist movements was their leadership: reformist, militant, and politically oriented Sufi orders. Libya and the Sudan provide striking examples of *jihad* revivalist movements led by Sufis.

In Africa, as in most of the Muslim world, the Sufi orders had been the greatest missionaries of Islam. Sufism's openness and flexibility regarding indigenous African beliefs and practices subjected African Sufism to sharp criticism for opening the door to idolatrous superstition and an attitude of passive withdrawal which resulted from an otherworldly orientation. Reformers sought to realign Sufism with the more orthodox path, that is, to bring the inner path of Sufism into harmony with the more exterior path of Islamic law. This approach was more like that of Shah Wali Allah than that of Muhammad ibn Abd al-Wahhab. Sufi reformers did not eradicate but rather redefined Sufism, emphasizing a spirituality that stressed a this-worldly, activist Islam. The sociopolitical dimension of Islam was reintroduced as African Islamic movements, led by Sufi brotherhoods, fought to establish Islamic states. Prayer and political action were joined together in the earthly pursuit of God's will.

Among the major early African reformers was the Moroccan Ahmad ibn Idris (d. 1837), a jurist as well as a Sufi, who established his order, the Tariqa Muhammadiyya (Path of Muhammad), in Arabia. As with Muslim reformers throughout the Islamic world, he denounced tribal and regional particularism in the name of Islamic unity and solidarity as well as the moral and social abuses of a debilitated society. He called for Sufi reform through a return to the Quran and teachings of Muhammad. The finality of medieval Islamic teachings was rejected and the need for interpretation affirmed.

It was the disciples of Shaykh Ahmad ibn Idris who were to successfully transform his teachings into religiopolitical organizations. Among his more illustrious disciples was Muhammad Ali ibn al-Sanusi (1787–1859), founder of the Sanusiyyah Sufi order, a movement which would lead to the establishment of modern-day Libya.

Born in Algeria, the Grand Sanusi, as he was later known, studied in Cairo and Mecca, earning a reputation as a scholar of law and *hadith*. Al-Sanusi preached a purification of Sufism through a return to the Quran and *Sunnah*. He rejected much of Islamic law that had been based upon the reasoning and consensus of the *ulama*. For this and his claim to practice *ijtihad*, he earned the *ulama's* enmity. After the death of his teacher, Shaykh Ahmad ibn Idris, al-Sanusi moved to modern-day Libya, where he established the Sanusiyyah religious brotherhood. This order was both a reformist and missionary movement whose members penetrated areas of Central and West Africa establishing a network of settlements based upon the Sanusi ideology.

The Sanusi were militant activists who united tribal factions in the name of Islamic solidarity and brotherhood. Their Sufi devotional lodges served as religious, educational, and social centers, places for prayer and religious instruction as well as social welfare and military training. They were committed not only to establishing their own Islamic state and society but also to spreading Islam through extensive missionary activity in West and Central Africa. Although not seeking political conflicts, the Libyan descendants of al-Sanusi resisted European colonial expansionism: first French, and later Italian occupation and rule. Sayyid Muhammad Ali ibn Idris, grandson of the Grand

Sanusi, led the Sanusi resistance to Italian colonial rule (1911–51) and, at independence in 1951, became King Idris I of Libya.

In contrast to the Grand Sanusi of Libya, who had steadfastly resisted attempts to declare him caliph or Mahdi, the *jihad* movement of the Sudanese Mahdiyya order was led by Muhammad Ahmad (1848–85), who did proclaim himself Mahdi in 1881—the divinely selected and inspired guide for renewal, sent to restore God's rule and justice. Like Muhammad ibn Abd al-Wahhab, the Mahdi united his followers against fellow Muslims, in this case the Turks—Ottoman Egyptian rulers, whom he, too, declared infidels who "disobeyed the command of His messenger and his prophets . . . ruled in a manner not in accord with what God has sent, . . . altered the *Shariah* of our master, Muhammad, the messenger of God, and . . . blasphemed against the faith of God."[5] The corruption of Sudanese Islamic society was based upon the adoption of foreign (Turko-Egyptian and local non-Islamic) influences and practices: prostitution, gambling, tobacco, alcohol, music.

The Sudanese Mahdi shared with leaders of other Islamic revivalist movements the belief that they were reenacting the paradigmatic drama of early Islam—establishing as the Prophet had done in the seventh century the rule of God on earth. Moreover, the "Mahdi and his Ansar [followers] had seen the taking of Khartoum as but one in a series of conquests throughout the Muslim world."[6]

The Sudanese Mahdi, like Sayyid Ahmad Barelewi in India, Uthman dan Fodio in Nigeria, and Muhammad Ali ibn al-Sanusi in Libya, became the religiopolitical leader of an Islamic movement that sought to establish a theocratic state, which would re-create the ideal, early Islamic community/state. In common with other reformers, the Mahdi called for a purification of Islamic belief and practice, which had been corrupted by alien, un-Islamic customs and beliefs. Sufism was not rejected but reformed. However, unlike other revivalists, his view of normative Islamic practice did not rest upon asserting his right to exercise *ijtihad* but his claim as Mahdi to divine inspiration and guidance. As with the early Islamic victories of Muhammad, Mahdist victories were interpreted as divine validation of his mission. In 1885 the Mahdist movement successfully conquered the Sudan's Egyptian occupiers. A theocratic state, governed by Mahdist religious ideology, was created. The Mahdi had supreme power as God's delegate, with the *Shariah* as its only law. The Mahdist state ruled for fourteen years until it was finally defeated in 1899 by Anglo-Egyptian forces under Lord Herbert Kitchener.

Summary

Premodernist revival movements of the eighteenth and nineteenth centuries contributed to the pattern of Islamic politics and provided a legacy for twentieth-century Islam. Unlike Islamic modernism, these movements were motivated primarily in response to internal decay rather than external, colonial threat. As had been true from the early Islamic centuries, political disunity and sociomoral decline were viewed as owing to digression from the straight path because success and power were God's rewards for a faithful community. If Muslims had wandered, then they must renounce their society with its foreign (i.e., alien or non-Islamic) practices, reform Sufism, and return to Islam as lived during the early normative period of Muhammad and the Rightly Guided Caliphs. This purification process of renewal and reform was underscored by the growth of popular religious beliefs regarding the coming of renewers and of the Mahdi, the "rightly guided one."

Despite their individual differences and characteristics, premodern revivalist movements provided a common legacy to modern Islam in both their ideology and their methodology. First, they brought into sharp focus the weakened and disorganized condition of the community. Second, they provided the diagnosis and cure: departure from true Islamic belief/practice and thus the need for a return to Islam. Third, they reasserted a belief that Islamic monotheism meant the unity and totality of God's will for both the individual Muslim and the Islamic community. Religion is integral to all areas of life—political, social, and moral. Fourth, Islamic reform required the rejection of a blind acceptance of tradition, that is, a recognition that the medieval synthesis of Muslim life, contained in the corpus of Islamic law, included un-Islamic historical accretions. Fifth, they maintained that the restoration of true Islam necessitated personal interpretation that was based on the sole authoritative foundations of Islam—the Quran and prophetic practice as found in the early community. Sixth, these movements reemphasized the belief that the sociomoral revival of Islamic society required political action, an activism epitomized by *jihad*, the exertion to realize God's will through moral self-discipline, and, when necessary, military combat or warfare.

Islam and the West

At the beginning of the eighteenth century, many areas of the Islamic world had felt the impact of the economic and military challenge of an emerging modernizing West. A major shift of power was taking place as declining Muslim fortunes reversed the relationship of the Islamic world to the West—from that of an expanding offensive movement to a defensive posture. The dominant role Islam had played in world history was fast disappearing, while Christian Europe "was experiencing a prolonged period of outstanding creativity which was to prove historically decisive for all the world."[7] As Marshall Hodgson observed: "The most central Muslim areas were rapidly becoming a backwater."[8]

By the late nineteenth and early twentieth centuries, European imperial penetration of the Islamic world extended from Morocco to Indonesia. Military and economic presence often culminated in foreign political domination or rule: the French in North, West, and Equatorial Africa, and the Levant (now Lebanon and Syria); the British in Palestine, Transjordan, Iraq, the Arabian Gulf, and the Indian subcontinent; the Dutch in Southeast Asia. Where Muslims retained self-rule, as in the Ottoman Empire and Iran, they, too, were forced into a defensive posture against Western political and economic expansionism. British, French, and Russian ambitions chipped away at the territory and political stability of both empires.

Muslim responses to Christian Europe's power and dominance ranged from rejection to adaptation, from Islamic withdrawal to acculturation and reform. For many, colonial rule transformed the Islamically governed territory into a land of war, that is, non-Muslim territory. Although Christians had always been regarded as believers, "People of the Book," European colonizers were now denounced as unbelievers, enemies of Islam. Some Muslim leaders adopted the tradition-honored responses to foreign intrusions: holy war or emigration to a Muslim territory. In nineteenth-century India, Shah Abdul Aziz, the son of Wali Allah, issued a legal opinion or ruling on a point of Islamic law, declaring British India a land of war in which holy war or emigration were appropriate responses.[9] While some Muslims emigrated to Muslim territories,[10] a greater number joined *jihad* movements. Yet the majority of traditionalists advocated a policy of cultural isolation: withdrawal and non-cooperation. They equated any form of political cooperation with the West or adaptation of its culture as betrayal and surrender.

A third major Muslim response to the West emerged during the nineteenth century. It was led by reform-minded Muslims who sought to respond to, rather than simply to react against, the challenge of Western imperialism. Muslim reform was both secular and Islamic. The initial impetus for reform came from the West; Muslim governments during the nineteenth century sought to strengthen themselves by looking to Europe to modernize their military and bureaucracy. Modernization soon came to include the gradual westernizing of politics, law, and education. Two major examples of secular reform occurred in the Central Ottoman Empire and Egypt. By the late nineteenth and early twentieth centuries, Islamic modernist movements also developed, seeking to bridge the gap between tradition and modernity by offering an Islamic rationale for modern political, legal, and social change.

Modernization in the Central Ottoman Empire

Modernization in the Muslim world began in the nineteenth century. Because the source of European power was its modern armies, Muslim rulers like the Ottoman Sultan Mahmud II (1808–39) and his vassal in Egypt, Muhammad (Mehmet) Ali (1805–49), tried to emulate the West. They created military training schools staffed by Europeans. Delegations were sent to Europe to study languages, sciences, and politics. Translation bureaus and printing presses were established to make technical information more accessible. Military modernization was accompanied by government attempts to modernize their central administration, law, education, and economy. Rather than turning, as traditionalists did, to their Islamic past and to the *ulama* for advice, this new generation of reformers looked to Europe, to the West.[11] Like the Umayyad and Abbasid rulers, they were open to a selective, pragmatic process of assimilation, appropriating "foreign" ideas, methods, and techniques to develop a modern army and administration. However, early nineteenth-century modernization efforts were not extended to all areas of society in general. Westernizing modernization had its primary impact on the military-bureaucratic institutions of the state. Change was adopted by the state and implemented by a small political elite. These reforms were initiated, formulated, and imposed from above by ruling elites. They were responding to the external threat of European expansionism and not to internal, societal pressures for social change.

During the latter half of the nineteenth century, modernization progressively expanded into other spheres of life. Early attempts to strengthen military defense were followed by a more widespread modernization program in the Ottoman Empire under the Sultans Abdulmejid (1839–61) and Abdul Hamid II (1876–1909) and in Egypt under Khedive (Viceroy) Ismail. The piecemeal modernization initiated in the Central Ottoman Empire under Mahmud II was developed and systematized by his son, Abdulmejid, through an ambitious series of reforms known collectively as the Tanzimat (reorganizations). Islamic institutions were challenged by the establishment of state-supported, modern, European-inspired counterparts: new secular schools to train not only the military but a new bureaucratic corps; land reforms; new legal codes and courts to regulate civil, commercial, and penal affairs. Traditional institutions of the Islamic state succumbed to a gradual process of secularization: the separation of religion from the institutions and functions of the state. Opposition to the Tanzimat reforms came from conservative religious elements who viewed such innovations as unwarranted deviations *(bida)* from religion that undermined the traditional Islamic basis of the Ottoman Empire and would lead to the westernization and secularization of society. Even modern-oriented political leaders like Ahmed Vefik seriously questioned the grafting of these new imported concepts and institutions, fearing that: "An attempt to introduce, wholesale, European institutions into Turkey, and to engraft European civilization upon the ancient traditional Turkish political system, before it was prepared for so great an innovation, could not possibly prove successful and must inevitably so weaken the Ottoman Empire that it would lose the little strength and independence that it still possessed."[12]

Under Abdul Hamid II's Grand Vizier Midhat Pasha, the Tanzimat reforms were extended to introduce Western political institutions. The promulgation of the First Ottoman Constitution in 1876

was based upon French and Belgian models and included a constitutional monarchy with a two-chamber parliament. However, it quickly
became apparent that Abdul Hamid's commitment to modernization
was more military and technological than political. He refused to surrender the sultan's absolute power and, in fact, despotically set about
crushing liberal reforms and eliminating reformers through persecution and exile. To mask his true intentions Abdul Hamid appealed to
religion; he resurrected the title of caliph and tried to set a pan-Islamic movement in motion. He sought to rally Muslim support within
and without the Ottoman Empire by appealing to Muslim unity
against Christian nationalist movements that had sprung up among
his Christian Balkan subjects in southeast Europe. Nevertheless, political dissent among Muslim as well as non-Muslim Ottoman subjects
culminated in the revolution of 1908, led by the Committee of Union
and Progress (CUP). Some of the revolutionaries advocated a liberal
political ideology, Ottomanism, based upon a multinational concept
of the state. However, the CUP, reacting in part to the wave of Balkan
revolts, espoused an empire united by a policy of pan-Turanism, or
Turkification, which sought to force all Ottoman subjects, Christians
as well as Arab Muslims, to become Turks.

Both Balkan Christian ethnic groups (Armenian, Greek, Roman-
ian, Bulgarian) and Arabs (Muslim and Christian) reacted by pressing
for greater decentralization and autonomy as nationalist sentiments
grew. Among Arab Christians, the nationalist movement was spurred
by a literary revival in centers like Beirut, Damascus, and Aleppo,
which emphasized Arabic language, literature, and history rather
than religion as the sources of Arab national pride and identity. Societies such as the Arab Society of Arts and Sciences (1847) and the
Syrian Scientific Society (1857) fostered Arab consciousness and
group feeling. In 1875 Christian Arabs organized an Arab nationalist
secret society in Beirut. Although they sought support from among
the Arab Muslim majority, most Arab Muslims remained wary of
Arab Christians because of their close ties with Western Christian
missionaries who were viewed as an arm of European imperialism.
As we shall see, the British occupation of Egypt in 1882 would unite a
nascent Islamic modernist movement with nationalism. Islamic modernism would serve as a catalyst in the development of Egyptian and
Arab nationalism.[13]

Modernization in Egypt

In Egypt the Khedive Ismail (1863–79) had initially sought the cooperation of the *ulama* in modernizing Egyptian society. However, when the religious scholars proved intransigent, he adopted the policy of his predecessor, Muhammad Ali, of establishing new, Western secular institutions parallel to their traditional Islamic counterparts. Modern national secular schools were set up alongside the traditional religious system. Islamic law and courts were restricted to family law (marriage, divorce, inheritance) as the state adopted new legal codes based on French prototypes, which were applied by civil courts. The new skills required in a modern society bred new social groups, such as engineers, lawyers, doctors, and journalists, which were the products of the modern schools and "now challenged the political, intellectual, and social leadership the *ulama* had always enjoyed and forced them ever farther away from the center of the political arena."[14] The process of modernization was also accompanied by the emergence of nationalist sentiments that developed in opposition first to French and then to British dominance of Ismail's successor, the Khedive Tawfiq. The result was an anticolonial revolt in 1881 led by Urabi Pasha, Egypt's minister of war. This act provided the pretext for British military occupation of Egypt in 1882 and their de facto if not de jure rule of Egypt.

As a result of nineteenth-century government reform, the traditional Islamic basis of Muslim states was altered by a progressive secularization of society in which the ideology, law, and institutions of state were no longer Islamically legitimated but were indebted to imported models from the West. The net result was a growing bifurcation of Muslim society, epitomized in its educational as well as its legal system. The coexistence of traditional religious and modern secular schools, each with its own constituencies, trained two classes with divergent outlooks or world views: a westernized elite minority and a more traditional, Islamically oriented majority. The process of modernization also contributed to the erosion of the traditional bases for the power and prestige of the religious establishment as new classes of professionals assumed positions in education, law, and government, positions which had previously been the province of the *ulama*.

Islamic Modernism: Afghani and Abduh

The modern Muslim response to modernization was twofold. The progressive secularization by governments was accompanied in the late nineteenth century by the emergence of Islamic modernist movements in the Arab world and the Indian subcontinent. Secular reformers had tended to restrict Islam to the personal, moral sphere of life and turned to the West to rejuvenate the sociopolitical areas of life. But, during the latter half of the nineteenth century, there emerged a generation of Islamic reformers who sought to unite and strengthen Muslim communities through a reform of Islamic belief and society. Recognizing the scientific and political power of the modern West, they eschewed the rejectionist tendency of religious conservatives as well as the secularist policies of Western-oriented elites. For Islamic reformers, modernity posed no serious threat to an Islam that was correctly understood and interpreted. They maintained that the original message of Islam that had provided the ideal pattern for traditional Muslim society remained eternally valid.

Unlike conservative Muslims, however, Islamic modernists asserted the need to revive the Muslim community through a process of a reinterpretation or reformulation of their Islamic heritage in light of the contemporary world. Though they shared with premodern Islamic revivalist movements a call for renewal and reform through *ijtihad,* Islamic modernists did not simply seek to restore the past (i.e., early Islamic practice). Rather they advocated a reinterpretation and reformulation of their Islamic heritage to respond to the political, cultural, and scientific challenge of the West and modern life. They attempted to show the compatibility (and thus acceptability) of Islam with modern ideas and institutions, whether they be reason, science and technology, or democracy, constitutionalism, and representative government.

Jamal al-Din al-Afghani (1838-97) was a major catalyst for Islamic reform and change and the Father of Muslim nationalism.[15] As he roamed across the Muslim world from India to Egypt, Afghani called upon Muslims to unite in order to regenerate their community and culture. He appealed to their faith and pride. He reminded them of Islam's divinely revealed mandate and mission and stressed its past Islamic historical and cultural accomplishments: the conquests and expansion of Islam, the establishment of the Islamic Empire, and the flourishing of Islamic civilization.

Although Afghani did not advocate the rejectionist position of many conservative religious leaders, his call for a return to Islam, for Muslim unity and political autonomy made him acceptable to them. Afghani's espousal of modern science, his assertion that Islam was a religion of change and progress, his call for Muslim unity, solidarity, and political action in the face of European imperialism proved an attractive alternative for many of the younger generation. Afghani came at a critical juncture in Muslim history. He identified and brought into sharp focus the major concerns and issues facing the Islamic world, the causes of its weakness, and the major challenge to its very survival. He warned that the inner weakness of the Muslim community, coupled with the external political and cultural threat of European imperialism, seriously threatened the Islamic community. His genius was to serve as the catalyst that fired the imaginations and moved the wills of a generation of Muslims.

Born and educated in Iran and then British India, where he first encountered modern education and sciences, Afghani traveled throughout much of the Muslim world as well as London and Paris. He has been described as the "agent provocateur par excellence."[16] He was more a political activist than a philosopher or theorist. In many ways, he embodied his belief that: (1) Islam was a comprehensive, cohesive way of life, encompassing politics and society as well as worship; (2) the true Muslim carried out God's will in history. Whether in Persia, India, Afghanistan, Istanbul, or Egypt, his preaching was accompanied by an active involvement in local politics. While he taught Islamic philosophy, theology, and jurisprudence to those who gathered around him, he also implanted his political message: "the danger of European intervention, the need for national unity to resist it, the need for a broader unity of the Islamic peoples, the need for a constitution to limit the ruler's power."[17]

Afghani was distrusted by Muslim as well as British rulers. Invited to serve as an adviser to Iran by Shah Nasir al-Din, he was deported in 1891 for initiating the political agitation that led to the Tobacco Revolt. In 1892 he traveled to Istanbul at the request of Sultan Abdul Hamid. However, after Shah Nasir al-Din of Iran was assassinated in 1896 by a follower of Afghani, Sultan Abdul Hamid restricted his movement and activities.

Attributing the weakness of Muslim society to its stagnation and tendency to blindly follow and cling to past authority, Afghani emphasized Islam's dynamic, creative, and progressive character. Islam was no simple imitation of the past or complacent passivity but rather the religion of reason and action. True Islam encompassed worship of God as well as active realization or implementation of His will in state and society. Afghani stressed that Islam was more than just a religion in the Western sense of the term. It was a religion and civilization. Moreover, Islam was an ideology, supplying the raison d'être for Muslims both as individuals and as a sociopolitical community. The future strength and survival of the community was dependent upon the reassertion of Islamic identity and the reestablishment of Islamic solidarity. Afghani believed that Muslim revitalization of a subjugated community could be achieved not by ignoring or rejecting the West but by direct, active engagement and confrontation.[18] Muslims could claim and reappropriate the sources of Western strength (reason, science, and technology) because, he asserted, those sources had also been part of their Islamic heritage as witnessed by the past contributions of Islamic civilization in philosophy, medicine, science, and mathematics. Thus he exhorted Muslims to look to their own glorious Islamic past as the source for their inspiration, identity, and unity.

For Afghani Muslim renewal and reform had but one ultimate political purpose, liberation from the yoke of colonial rule. While acknowledging the importance of language and regional ties, Afghani maintained that Islam provided the common, most fundamental bond and basis for Muslim solidarity. Afghani's legacy continued in the Salafiyya (from *salaf,* ancestors) movement of his disciples Shaykh Muhammad Abduh (1849–1905) and Rashid Rida (1865–1935). Afghani did not choose between Islamic solidarity and the more local nationalist aspirations. He supported both Muslim nationalism and pan-Islamism. The reassertion of Muslim identity and solidarity were prerequisites for the restoration of political and cultural independence, and unity and solidarity were essential at both national and transnational levels.

Muhammad Abduh received a traditional religious education. When Afghani came to Cairo in 1871, Abduh became his most enthusiastic disciple. After qualifying as a religious scholar, Abduh joined the faculty at Cairo's al-Azhar University, renowned as the principal center of Islamic learning and orthodoxy. He also taught at Cairo's Dar al-Ulum, a new college that provided modern education for al-Azhar students who wished to qualify for government positions. During the 1870s, Abduh published newspaper articles reflecting Afghani's theories of political and social reform. Abduh became involved with Afghani in a nationalist opposition movement that culminated in Urabi Pasha's unsuccessful nationalist revolt in 1882 against British and French influence in Egypt. Britain occupied Egypt, and Abduh was sent into exile. He joined Afghani in Paris, where they organized a secret society and published *al-Urwa al-wuthqa* (The Indissoluble Link), a newspaper that embodied Afghani's message of resistance to European expansionism through Muslim solidarity and the revival of a dormant Islam through reinterpretation and reform.

However, after Abduh's return to Cairo from exile in 1888, he accepted the existing political framework and channeled his energies into religious, educational, and social reform rather than politics and agitation against political rule. Abduh was convinced that the transformation of Muslim society required both a reinterpretation of Islam and its implementation among the Egyptian people through national educational reform. Muslims must shed the dead weight of scholasticism and selectively appropriate what was best in Western civilization. His knowledge of the West resulted from his reading of modern European authors and travel in Europe. In 1898 Abduh and his disciple, Rashid Rida, published the first issue of the journal *al-Manar* (The Lighthouse) (1898–1935), which propagated Islamic reform. He worked to implement his ideas. In 1899 Abduh became *mufti* of Egypt, head of the nation's *Shariah* law court system. He pioneered court reform, and his legal opinions as *mufti* of Egypt had the character of authoritative rulings. Abduh reinterpreted Islamic law in light of modern conditions. His rulings ranged from the lawfulness of Muslims wearing European clothing to the permissibility of bank interest. Through his writing, teaching, preaching, and legal opinions, Abduh championed the cause of reform in Islamic law, theology, and education. His influence both in his own time and on successive generations of Muslims earned him the title Father of Islamic Modernism.

Rejecting the blind following of tradition, Abduh called for a new interpretation of Islam that would demonstrate its relevance to contemporary thought and life in the modern world. Abduh maintained that there was no inherent conflict between religion and reason or modern science. Change in Islamic practice was both possible and necessary. The renewal of Islam and Muslim society should be based not simply on Western secular modernization. Abduh sought to provide the rationale for the selective integration of Islam with modern ideas and institutions. Thus the needs of modern Muslim society could be accomplished through Islamic legal and social change.

Abduh argued that the Islamic basis for change was the division of Islamic law into two spheres: duties to God and social duties to other persons. He maintained that the former, which included beliefs and practices such as prayer, fasting, and pilgrimage, are immutable duties to God. However, the latter, which included social regulations such as criminal, civil, and family laws, are open to and subject to change. For example, Abduh advocated educational and legal reforms affecting the status of Muslim women. Recognizing the discrepancy between Quranic reforms, which had greatly improved women's status, and their social status in the nineteenth century, Abduh had criticized the waywardness of Muslim society: "To be sure, the Muslims have been at fault in the education and training of women, and of acquainting them with their rights; and we acknowledge that we have failed to follow the guidance of our religion, so that we have become an argument against it."[19]

Abduh was especially critical of polygamy and its deleterious effect on family life. The Quranic argument that Abduh developed regarding polygamy was adopted by most modern reformers and used by Muslim states to justify reforms in Muslim family law curtailing polygamy. According to Abduh, polygamy had been permitted in the Prophet's time as a concession to prevailing social conditions. The true intent of the Quran (4:3 and 4:129) was monogamy because it said that more than one wife was permissible only when equal justice and impartiality were guaranteed.[20] Because this is a practical impossibility, he concluded that the Quranic ideal must be monogamy.

Abduh's associate, Qasim Amin (1863–1908), developed the social dimension of the modernist movement by focusing on the plight of Muslim women as a cause for the deterioration of the family and society. For Amin the emancipation of women was integral to national development. He argued that true, uncorrupted Islam recognized the equality of both sexes. He criticized as un-Islamic customs such as the veiling and social seclusion of women, arranged marriages, the wife's lack of power to divorce, and the husband's unlimited rights of divorce. He believed that all these perpetuated the bondage of women. Following Abduh, Amin reemphasized the original Quranic intent that divorce be viewed as reprehensible although permissible when necessitated by failure of the marriage and of attempts at arbitration. As a step toward providing some relief, he recommended that women have equal rights of divorce with men.[21]

Reactions to Amin's feminist books, *Tahrir al-Marah* (The Emancipation of Women) and *al-Marah al-Jadidah* (The New Woman), and his ideas were swift and harshly critical. Conservative religious as well as some nationalist leaders dismissed Amin's stand as a desire to ape the West, which would undermine the family and weaken Egyptian society. However, his writings became a source of inspiration to many feminists. Madame Huda Sha'arawi, a leader of the feminist movement in Egypt a generation later, hailed him as "the hero of the feminist awakening and its founder."[22]

During the nineteenth and twentieth centuries, modernization was introduced into the Arab world in the military, bureaucracies, politics, law, economics, and education. The traditional Islamic ideological basis of state and society was progressively altered under the impact of Western secular nationalism. Muslims found themselves between two norms: the traditionalist belief that religion ought to determine the nature of political organization and that Islamic law provided the necessary standard and guidance for society, and the secular modernist Muslim preference for Western political concepts and institutions. With Afghani an Islamic movement arose that sought to take a middle position between the rejectionist tendency of many religious leaders and the unquestioned accommodationist proclivities of westernizing, secular Muslim elites.

Islamic modernism emphasized the political and cultural ascendency of Islam's past; the dynamic spirit and character of Islam and the acceptability of political, legal, and social modernization. Its purpose was twofold: to reawaken the Islamic community and restore its strength through Islamic reform, a modern reformulation of Islam; and to overthrow European imperialism in the Muslim world and regain autonomy and independence. Islamic modernism dispersed in many directions. It influenced a variety of Muslim leaders from Islamic to secular nationalist reformers and contributed to the development and acceptance of Egyptian and Arab nationalism alongside traditional pan-Islamism. What Fazlur Rahman had observed regarding pan-Islamism and nationalism in Afghani is true of the Islamic modernist legacy in general: "Actual influence has been in both directions of pan-Islamism and nationalism, sometimes in conflict with one another. Although the pan-Islamic idealism has not been successful in concrete terms, it continues to inspire various activist groups in different lands and lives so patently, if amorphously, in the aspirations of the people."[23]

Although it did not produce a unified movement, the reformist/ activist spirit of Islamic modernism provided a renewed awareness and sense of pride in Islamic history and identity, an Islamic rationale for modern reforms and an anticolonialist, ideologized Islam that reasserted Islam's relatedness to politics and society. It inspired Islamic reformist and national independence movements in other Muslim areas, such as North Africa, and contributed to the ideological basis of Islamic activism today.

Islamic Modernism in the Indian Subcontinent

For Muslims of the Indian subcontinent, 1857 was a turning point in their political history. From the sixteenth century, India had become a primary object of British, French, and Portuguese trade companies. By the nineteenth century, British military, economic, and political dominance in India was a reality. The Mughal emperor remained on the throne in Delhi more a figurehead than ruler of a Muslim India. The Indian Mutiny of 1857 (what some Indian historians prefer to call the first war for independence) provided the occasion for the declaration of formal British *raj* (rule) in India. Although both Muslims and Hindus had participated in the uprising, Muslims received the bulk of the blame and retribution. The Mughal emperor was dethroned. The centuries-long Indian Muslim Empire came to an end as the British government asserted direct rule over the subcontinent. Earlier Muslim debates about whether the colonial-dominated Mughal Empire was a *dar al-harb* were no longer necessary. The *dar al-Islam* had clearly ceased to exist as a non-Muslim government seized power; colonial control of a Muslim Empire gave way to the establishment of an Imperial Empire in India.

Just as in the eighteenth and early nineteenth centuries, India had produced Islamic revivalists like Shah Wali Allah and Sayyid Ahmad Barelewi, the post–1857 period generated Islamic movements in the

Indian subcontinent. As the Middle East had had Afghani and Abduh, Indian Islam produced, among others, Sayyid Ahmad Khan (1817–98) and his Aligarh movement. Ahmad Khan had come from an established Delhi family and worked for the East India Company. Although he knew many of those who had participated in the mutiny, he had withheld his support and remained loyal to the British. Initially overwhelmed by the chaos and destruction of the war of 1857, he considered emigrating from India. However, he soon committed himself to the regeneration of a devastated Muslim community. Unlike Afghani, Ahmad Khan was convinced that Islamic revolts and pan-Islamism were useless. He confined his attention to the Indian Muslim community and espoused a "real-politik loyalism."[24] Indian Muslims should accept the reality of foreign rule and within its limitations/boundaries restore and revivify their identity and community.

Like his Middle East counterparts, Ahmad Khan was convinced that the decline in Muslim fortunes was a sign that Islam was not being correctly understood and practiced; Islam was in need of reform. In the tradition of earlier Islamic revivalists like Wali Allah, he too rejected the unquestioned acceptance of medieval formulations of Islam and claimed the right to a fresh reinterpretation of Islam. In this way, Muslims might see that Islam was not only enduringly relevant to modern society but also not in conflict with Western science and technology. For Ahmad Khan modern science and education were critical for the renewal of Indian Islam. He believed it was imperative to demonstrate that there was no inherent conflict between religion, reason, and science: "If people do not shun blind adherence, if they do not seek the Light which can be found in the Quran and the independent *Hadith,* and do not adjust religion and science to the science of today, Islam will be extinct in India."[25]

In 1864 Ahmad Khan founded the Scientific Society, which translated important Western texts into Urdu. In 1874 he established the Muhammadan Anglo-Oriental College at Aligarh (renamed Aligarh Muslim University in 1920) and modeled it on Cambridge University, which he had visited. Its purpose was to educate Muslim leaders in both Western disciplines and their Islamic heritage. Much like Abduh, Sayyid Ahmad Khan devoted the major portion of his energies to a theological reinterpretation of Islam. This was motivated both by the internal needs of the Muslim community and by a desire to respond to the attacks of Christian missionaries and the distortions of oriental-ist scholars. He published a journal, *Tahdhib al-akhlaq*, which provided his modernist Islamic perspective on a broad range of topics. In addition he wrote a commentary on the Quran and a biography of Muhammad, *Essays on the Life of Mohammed*, in 1870.

Ahmad Khan saw the problem of Indian Islam quite clearly: "Today we need, as in former days, a modern theology by which we either render futile the tenets of modern sciences or [show them to be] doubtful, or bring them into harmony with the doctrines of Islam."[26] He was equally sure of his goal to "justify without any wavering what I acknowledge to be the original religion of Islam which God and the Messenger have disclosed, not that religion which the *ulama* and preachers have fashioned. I shall prove this religion to be true and this will be the difference between us and the followers of other religions."[27] Whereas Abduh maintained that there was no necessary contradiction between true religion and science, Khan, more strictly influenced by nineteenth-century European rationalism and natural philosophy, maintained that Islam was the religion of reason and nature. There could be no contradiction between the Word of God (Quran) and the Work of God (Nature). Because Islam was in harmony with the laws of nature, it must be compatible with modern scientific thought. Employing a rationalist interpretation of Islam, he felt free to interpret texts symbolically rather than literally in dealing with such questions as evolution, the existence of angels, and miracles.

Ahmad Khan, like Muhammad Abduh, also distinguished between Quranic injunctions concerned with religion in the strict sense and those relating to social matters. The former were immutable, the latter subject to change. This distinction enabled Sir Sayyid and followers like Mumtaz Ali and Chiragh Ali to view medieval formulations of Islamic legal and social practice as transient and to advocate widespread social and legal change.

Mumtaz Ali championed the social aspect of Ahmad Khan's reformism in India. Ali's special concern for women's rights led to the publishing of the journal *Tahdhib al-niswan*, through which he asserted the need for equality of women with men in marriage and social customs. Like his Egyptian counterpart, Qasim Amin, he stressed the right of equal educational opportunities for women, arguing it would make for better marriages between intellectually equal companions. Ali refuted the antifeminist exegesis of many classical Muslim scholars, maintaining that their interpretations did not reflect the meaning of the Quranic text but the customs and mores of the exegetes' own times. In language strikingly similar to the Egyptian Qasim Amin, Mumtaz Ali maintained that the inferior position of Muslim women was caused by their lack of education and subjection to marriage laws and customs that needed fundamental reform. He criticized child marriages and arranged marriages, asserting that marriage must be based on love and free choice. Ali also followed Ahmad Khan's Quranic interpretation (Quran 4:3, 129) regarding polygamy as a tolerated institution that must in contemporary society give way to the Quranic ideal—monogamy.

While Mumtaz Ali provided the modernist critique for social reform, Chiragh Ali, a close protege of Ahmad Khan, spoke more directly to the need for legal reform to implement needed social changes. For Chiragh Ali, Islam is distinct from any particular social system. Nevertheless, the law books of the four Sunni schools reflect the social system of Muslim society during the period of their formation. Failure to recognize this had led Muslims in the past to identify their social system and its institutions with the Quran and thus to regard them as ideal. Because society has changed, Chiragh Ali argued, Muslim law must also be updated to meet new social needs. The legal manuals of the law schools are not immutable sources to be blindly imitated. Ali argued that reform in Muslim family law was both desirable and Islamically possible. In many ways, such change would continue the process of reform begun in early Islam. If Muslim family law were viewed in the proper historical context, vis-à-vis pre-Islamic practices, Ali believed that Quranic reforms regarding the position of women in marriage, divorce, and inheritance would be judged truly fundamental and forward-looking: "Islam . . . changed the attitude towards women to one of respect, kindness and courtesy. The Muslim Law of inheritance, giving a woman exclusive right to her own property, compares favourably with the British law. Man's superiority is recognized by the Quran only in matters relating to his natural physical attributes."[28]

These Quranic intents and commands (the spirit and letter of its laws), however, were diverted through the ages by jurists who, in areas such as polygamy and divorce, developed laws that reflected customary practices often at odds with the Quran. Thus, Ali believed, an overhauling of traditional Islamic law to eliminate anachronistic customary practices alien to the Quran was essential to the modernization of the Muslim community.

Ahmad Khan's Aligarh movement, with its positive orientation toward modernization, served as a catalyst for the development of modernism in the Indian Muslim community. When Indian nationalism emerged during the late nineteenth century, he urged Muslims not to participate in the nationalist movement. He believed that even in a secular Indian nation, the Hindu majority would rule and thus threaten the continued existence and strength of the Muslim community. At first many Muslims did not follow his example. However, by the 1930s, Ahmad Khan's modernist legacy informed the Muslim nationalism of Muhammad Iqbal and Muhammad Ali Jinnah, leaders in the call for a separate Muslim state—Pakistan.

Conclusion

Islamic modernists were trailblazers, for they did not simply seek to return to the straight path of Islam but to chart its future direction. They were pioneers who planted the seeds for the acceptance of change, a struggle that has continued. While their secular counterparts simply looked to the West, Islamic reformers attempted to establish a continuity between their Islamic heritage and modern change. On the one hand, they based their principal arguments on revelation and Islamic history and identified themselves with their premodernist Islamic revivalist predecessors. On the other, they borrowed freely from Western thought and institutions. Still, as with secular political elites, Islamic modernists were a minority. They sought to inspire and motivate a more conservative religious majority. The reformers' rejection of the status quo (the unquestioned acceptance of traditional religious authority) and their assertion of a right to reinterpret and refashion Islam to meet the needs of the contemporary world often alienated the religious establishment.

As noted, modernist interpretation was not that of premodern revivalist leaders who had wished simply to reclaim and implement the teachings of the Quran and *Sunnah* of the Prophet. Rather than a restoration of early Islamic practices, modernists advocated an adaptation of Islam to the changing conditions of modern society. This process would result not simply in the reaffirmation of the past but in new laws and attitudes toward religious, legal, educational, and social reforms. Traditionalists criticized such changes as unwarranted innovations, an accommodation that permitted un-Islamic, Western Christian practices to infiltrate Islam. Reforms were condemned as *bida* (deviation from Islamic tradition), a term akin to heresy. Reformers' criticism that the *ulama* were out of touch with the modern world and in need of reform deepened the resistance to Islamic modernism of many, though not all, of the religious establishment. What then can we say specifically regarding the accomplishments and contribution of Islamic modernism?

First, Islamic modernism implanted an outlook, or attitude, toward both the past and the future. Pride in an Islamic past and the achievements of Islamic civilization provided Muslims with a renewed sense of identity and purpose. This countered the sense of weakness and religiocultural backwardness fostered by the reality of subjugation to the West and by the preaching of many Christian missionaries. At the same time, emphasis on the dynamic, progressive, and rational character of Islam enabled new generations of Muslims to embrace modern civilization more confidently.

Second, belief in the absolute relevance of Islam, its compatibility and adaptability to modernity, inspired reformers throughout much of the Islamic world.

Third, reformers' espousal of an assimilative and creative process for reinterpretation fostered a transformation in the meaning of traditional beliefs and institutions to accommodate and legitimate modern political and social change. As a result, future generations of Muslims, whether modernist or traditionalist oriented, have come to speak of Islamic democracy, to view traditional concepts of community consensus and consultation as conducive to parliamentary forms of representative government, and to accept forms of Muslim nationalism and Islamic socialism. Moreover, the use of *ijtihad* to formulate fresh responses to modern conditions came to be practiced quite readily by the religious establishment itself. In the name of Islam, nationalist ideologies such as the Arab nationalism/socialism of Egypt's Gamal Abd al-Nasser, Libya's Muammar Qaddafi, and Algeria's Islamic socialism were initially legitimated by *ulama*. Governments obtained *fatwas* to justify new policies regarding land reform, nationalism of banks and critical industries, and birth control.

Fourth, the anticolonial thrust of both Afghani and, later, Rashid Rida and his Salafiyya thought, with their emphasis on Islam as a self-sufficient alternative to the West, assured their continued influence among Islamic activists from Egypt's Muslim Brotherhood to contemporary Islamic revivalist organizations.

However, the Islamic modernist legacy is a mixed one. Neither Muhammad Abduh nor Ahmad Khan produced a systematic, comprehensive theology or reformist program. As we shall see, their disciples later traveled in many directions. The examples of both Muslim family law reform and the development of modern nationalism exemplify the diffuse and, at times, inconsistent nature of the modernist legacy. The spirit of Islamic modernism was a major factor in the development of early women's emancipation movements among upper- and middle-class Muslim women and the subsequent reform of Muslim family law that provided the major theater for modernist activity.

Although Islamic law had been displaced by European-based civil and criminal codes, Muslim family law had remained intact. During the post-World War I period, governments in Muslim countries enacted modern Muslim family law legislation that had a twofold purpose: to improve the status of women and to strengthen the rights of nuclear family members vis-à-vis more distant members of the extended family, favored by traditional law. Reforms occurred in three major areas: marriage, divorce, and inheritance. For example legislation was enacted to eliminate child marriages; restrict polygamy; curtail a man's unfettered, unilateral right to divorce his wife; and to increase a woman's grounds for divorcing her husband.

The Islamic modernist legacy was employed in drafting and justifying reform legislation. Governments cited reformist concepts, such as the right to *ijtihad* and the public interest, to justify legal changes for the betterment of Muslim society. The main argument for restricting polygamy was specifically based upon Muhammad Abduh's and Ahmad Khan's modernist reinterpretation of the Quran. Nevertheless, legal reforms were resisted because of the ad hoc use of modernist teachings and the drafting of modern legislation by modern political elites instead of by the traditional religious authorities. Traditionalists often viewed such reforms as an Islamic façade employed by westernized, secular elites to justify their desire to further ape the West. The state's unwillingness to directly challenge the continued strength of traditional Islam could be seen in the fact that, except for Tunisia, failure to observe modern family law reforms in most Muslim countries renders the act illegal but not invalid. Should a man, for example, ignore reform legislation in contracting a polygamous marriage, he is subject to prosecution for violating state law, but his marriage is not invalidated.

A second example of the failure to develop a united Islamic modernist movement and to provide a systematic reformist program is the differing paths followed by the disciples of early modernists. As will be seen, the Afghani-Abduh legacy took a more conservative turn in Rashid Rida's Salafiyya movement. At the same time, its influence contributed to the development of Egyptian and Arab nationalism. Under other Abduh followers, like Lutfi al-Sayyid, Ali Abd al-Raziq, and Taha Hussein, it resulted in a secular Egyptian nationalism.

Islamic revivalist and modernist movements provided a variety of Muslim approaches to the regeneration of a debilitated and subjugated community. This reformist legacy was often linked to the development of nationalism in the Arab East, Arab West (North Africa), and the Indian subcontinent.

... *3* ...

Nationalism

A s we have seen, a major crisis in Islamic history and in Muslim identity had been precipitated by the advent of European colonialism. By the end of the nineteenth century, the Islamic world had in large part succumbed to Western Christendom—economically, militarily, and, finally, politically. The disintegration of the traditional Islamic political order and the struggle against European colonialist intervention and rule provided both an identity crisis and a political purpose for Muslims in the twentieth century. The ground had been prepared by Muslim reformers like Jamal al-Din al-Afghani, with his call to resist imperialism, seek political liberation, and undertake an intellectual reawakening rooted in a return to Islam.

Two major political trends, often interrelated, predominated: anticolonial independence movements and the emergence of modern nationalism. Islam played an important role in each. First, in independence movements in North Africa and the Indian subcontinent, Islam served as a unifying rallying cry, providing an identity and allegiance, ideology and symbols, leadership and mosque-based communications centers. Second, the development of modern Muslim nationalism was indebted to Islamic modernist as well as secular nationalist leaders. Given the transnational religious ideology of Islam, the shift in loyalty from the pan-Islamic community to the more limited modern nation-state required a process of ideological redefinition and legitimation. Islam was integral to the development of nationalist ideologies: Egyptian, Arab, and Iranian nationalism as well as Tunisian, Algerian, Moroccan, and Pakistani nationalism.

The Arab East:
From Islamic Reform to Arab Nationalism

The Arab Christian Literary Movement and the Young Ottoman Turkification program had stirred early nationalist sentiments in the Ottoman Empire. However, Arab and Egyptian nationalism in the Middle East did not really develop until after World War I, the result of three major influences: (1) the breakup of the Ottoman Empire after World War I and the emergence of modern states that no longer shared a common (Islamic) religiously rooted ideology and religiously legitimated sociopolitical order, (2) the intensified struggle for independence from the political and religiocultural dominance of European imperialism, and (3) the ideological influence of the Salafiyya movement of Afghani's disciples, Muhammad Abduh and Rashid Rida.

In retribution for Ottoman support of Germany during World War I, the European Allies in the Treaty of Sèvres of August 1920 dismembered the Ottoman Empire, placing a major portion of the empire under a mandate (Great Power) system of government. The Arab provinces were placed under France and Britain. France took control of Syria and Lebanon; Britain governed Iraq, Palestine, and Transjordan. In Egypt British control had been tightened in response to Ottoman entrance into World War I on Germany's side; Britain declared Egypt a protectorate and deposed the Khedive, Abbas Hilmi II.

By the end of World War I, a strong independence movement led by Saad Zaghlul (1857–1927), a former disciple of Afghani, friend of Abduh, and leader of the "Egypt for Egyptians" movement, forced the British to end the protectorate in 1922. Egypt, granted a limited conditional form of independence, refused to accept anything but complete independence. Not until 1956 was the British occupation of Egypt finally terminated. In Egypt, as in the mandate areas, resentment toward continued European political, military, and economic hegemony fueled nationalist fervor and provided a common goal for opposition movements otherwise divided by class, region, tribe, or degree of religious (vs. secular) commitment.

Three ideological orientations emerged during this period: the Salafiyya reformism of Rashid Rida, Egyptian nationalism, and Arab nationalism. All were influenced by the Islamic reformist spirit of Afghani and Abduh that continued through the Salafiyya movement, a reform based upon a return to the practice of Muhammad and the early Muslim community. As the twentieth century unfolded, Abduh's disciples and friends took a number of directions ranging from the increasingly conservative position of Rashid Rida to the more acculturationist, secular nationalism of Saad Zaghlul, Lutfi al-Sayyid, Taha Hussein, and others. Thus the legacy of Islamic modernism/ though diffuse, informed nationalist leaders and ideology from Salafiyya reformism to Egyptian and Arab nationalism.

The Salafiyya Movement of Rashid Rida

Rashid Rida (1865–1935) has been called the "mouthpiece of Abduh."[1] While this describes his reverence for Muhammad Abduh and their close relationship, Rida developed his own distinctive position and legacy during the thirty-year period after Abduh's death (1905). With Rida Islamic reformism took a more fundamentalist turn. Born in Tripoli (then Syria and now Lebanon), after an early education at a local Quranic school, he studied at the Ottoman government school and at Shaykh Husayn al-Jisri's school in Tripoli, where he was exposed to modern learning as well as the Islamic classics. Here Rida met Muhammad Abduh and first became acquainted with Afghani and Abduh's newspaper, *al-Urwa al-wuthqa*. Rida's strong attraction to Afghani and Abduh and the extent to which their reformist ideas seemed to penetrate his very being are revealed in the following recollection:

> I found several copies of the journal among my father's papers, and every number was like an electric current striking me, giving my soul a shock, or setting it in a blaze, and carrying me from one state to another. . . . My own experience, and that of others, and history, has taught me that no other Arabic discourse in this age or the centuries which preceded it has done what it did in the way of touching the seat of emotion in the heart and persuasion in the mind.[2]

Rida became a devoted disciple of Abduh from 1894 until his death in 1905. In 1897 he joined Abduh in Cairo, and in 1898 the first edition of their journal, *al-Manar*, was published. It remained the primary vehicle for Salafiyya reformist thought. The contents of the many volumes of *al-Manar* reflect the broad range of its concern for Islamic reform: doctrine and spirituality, Quran and *Tafsir* (commentary), political and legal modernization.

The departure point for Salafiyya thought was the legacy of Afghani and Abduh. Islamic reform was a sine qua non for the revitalization of the Muslim community and the restoration of its lost political power and prosperity. Like Afghani, Rida attributed the decline in Islam to stagnation and blind imitation that impaired the ability of Islam to respond to changing needs through modern political and legal reform. Following Muhammad Abduh, Rida believed that the return of Islam to a central position in public life required the restoration and reform of Islamic law. The development of a modern Islamic legal system was a fundamental priority and starting point. He rejected the authority of medieval law and distinguished between matters of ritual and worship, which were fixed, and those related to social laws, which continue to be subject to adaptation and change by successive generations of Muslims where public welfare requires reform:

> Creed and ritual were completed in detail so as to permit neither additions or subtractions, and whoever adds to them or subtracts from them is changing Islam and bringing forth a new religion. As for the rules of *muamalat* [social laws], beyond decreeing the elements of virtue and establishing penalties for certain crimes, and beyond imposing the principle of consultation, the Law Giver delegated the affair in its detailed applications to the leading *ulama* and rulers, who, according to law, must possess knowledge and moral probity, to decide by consulting one another what is more beneficial for the Community according to the circumstances of the times.[3]

Therefore, Islamic legal reform requires an Islamic government, that is, the restoration of the caliphate. For Rida the true Islamic political system is based upon consultation between the caliph and the *ulama,* who are the guardian interpreters of Islamic law. However, like most modernists, he believed that the *ulama* were backward and ill equipped to reinterpret Islam in light of modern exigencies. Thus Rida advocated the development of a group of Islamic progressive thinkers who could bridge the gap between the conservative *ulama* and westernized elites.

The political realities of the post–World War I period forced Rida reluctantly to accept political compromises and to shift in his reformism to a more assertive conservative position. His long support of a universal caliphate gave way to a grudging acceptance of an Arab nationalism informed by Islam.

Turkey, the sole remnant of the former Ottoman Empire, emerged as a nation-state, led by Mustafa Kemal (Ataturk) who, in rapid succession, abolished the caliphate (1924) and set Turkey on a Western secular path of political, social, and legal development. Therefore, without a caliph/sultan and the Ottoman Empire, who was the just Muslim ruler? Where was the pan-Islamic unity of the *ummah*? Like Afghani, Rida proved a political pragmatist. Although he advocated the ultimate restoration of the universal caliphate and a transnational Islamic community, he also accepted the reality of the new separate Muslim states, the importance of Muslim unity, and the need to avoid anything which might weaken that unity and make Muslims even more vulnerable to continued European rule. While some of Abduh's disciples turned to an Egyptian nationalism, Rashid Rida linked Islam with a broader Arab nationalism. For Rida, as in its early formation, the revitalization of the community was dependent upon Arab Muslim leadership. God's revelation had been in Arabic, and the Arabs had constituted the vanguard of Islam, spreading and uniting all under the banner of Islam. So, too, Muslim unity would only be restored again through the Arabs.[4]

Although pragmatically accepting nationalism and the nation-state, Rida also reminded Muslims of the transnational identity of the Islamic community. His position on nationalism and its relationship to pan-Islamism, as well as the influence of the Salifiyya movement beyond the Middle East, are reflected in a legal ruling given by Rida in the 1930s in response to an inquiry from an Indonesian Muslim about whether patriotism and nationalism were un-Islamic. In it Rida stated:

> All the jurisprudents have declared that holy war is a duty incumbent on all individuals when an enemy commits aggression against Muslims or occupies any of their lands. . . . The contemporary notion of patriotism expresses the unity of the people of different religions in their homeland and their cooperation in defending the homeland they share. They cooperate to preserve its independence. . . . The type of patriotism that should adorn Muslim youth is that he be a good example for the people of the homeland no matter what their religious affiliation, cooperating with them in every legitimate action for independence. . . . In his service of his homeland and his people he must not, however, neglect Islam which has honored him and

raised him up by making him a brother to hundreds of millions of Muslims in the world. He is a member of a body greater than his people, and his personal homeland is part of the homeland of his religious community. He must be intent on making the progress of the part a means for the progress of the whole.[5]

Thus Rida accepted the reality of patriotism and nationalism provided that national unity not overshadow or replace Muslims' identity and solidarity as members of a transnational religious homeland and community which remained the Islamic ideal. In *The Caliphate or Imamate,* written in 1923 in response to the caliphate crises, he declared: "The Muslims consider in fact that their religion does not really exist unless an independent and strong Islamic State is established which could apply the laws of Islam and defend it against any foreign opposition and domination."[6]

Despite Rida's commitment to Islamic reform and the important role of *al-Manar,* after World War I his Islamic modernism gave way to an increasing conservatism. Reacting to the growing influence of Western liberal nationalism and culture in Egyptian life, Rida became more critical of the West. Unlike Abduh and many of Egypt's elites who were influenced by their studies and travel in Europe, Rida had had only limited contacts. He believed the threat to be both religious and political: "The British government is committed to the destruction of Islam in the East after destroying its temporal power."[7] He also saw how Abduh's moderate liberal reformism had led other disciples, like Qasim Amin, Lutfi al-Sayyid, and Saad Zaghlul, to espouse a secular, liberal Egyptian nationalism that restricted religion to private, moral life. Alarmed at what he perceived as the growing danger of westernization, Rida drifted toward a more conservative position.

He had also become an admirer and staunch supporter of Abd al-Aziz ibn Saud's revival of the Wahhabi movement in Arabia. As had Muhammad ibn Abd al-Wahhab and premodern Islamic revivalism in general, Rida emphasized the comprehensiveness and self-sufficiency of normative Islam. The fundamental sources of Islam provided a complete code of life. Thus Muslim reformers must not look to the West for answers but must single-mindedly return to the sources of Islam—the Quran, the *Sunnah* of the Prophet, and the consensus of the Companions of the Prophet. Rida's increasing conservatism was reflected in his restricted understanding of the term *salaf.* For Abduh it was a general reference to the early Islamic centuries. For Rida, however, as for premodern Islamic revivalism, *salaf* was restricted to the practice of Muhammad and the first generation of Muslims.

As Muslim politics unfolded in the post-World War I Arab world, Islam was a factor but not the dominant factor in the development of Egyptian and Arab nationalism. Rida's primary commitment to an Islamic state and society increasingly made him less amenable to more secular-oriented modernists than to the religious establishment whose backwardness he had earlier criticized. He feared that modernist rationalism would lead to the westernization and secularization of society as was occurring under Egyptian nationalism. Increasingly, he defended Islam against the westernizing Muslim intelligentsia, many of whom had been Abduh's disciples, rather than against the intransigence of the *ulama*. In the end, he became "an ideologist bound by traditional idealism rather than a practical reformer."[8] Ironically, he had come full circle from his early days with Abduh when the majority of the members of the *al-Manar* circle were young laity and the majority of the *ulama* were critics. From being an Islamic modernist, Rida had become an Islamic fundamentalist ideologue. His emphasis on the comprehensiveness and self-sufficiency of Islam and his more critical attitude toward the West would prove acceptable to Islamic movements like Egypt's Muslim Brotherhood and many Islamic activist organizations today.

Egyptian Nationalism

For much of Islamic history, Egypt had retained its sense of separateness and regional identity. Throughout the caliphate period and later under the Ottomans, Egypt's rulers paid homage to the caliph, but Egypt functioned as a semiautonomous state at some distance from the central imperial capital and its authority. This strong sense of separate identity was reflected in the development of Egyptian nationalism. Although Egypt has come to be viewed as a leader of Arab nationalism, the early development of the nationalist movement in Egypt focused on a local, territorial Egyptian patriotism that was influenced by Western liberal, secular nationalism and rooted in a sense of separate Egyptian history, identity, and therefore nationhood. Though many Egyptian nationalist leaders were early disciples of Afghani and Abduh, Islamic modernism gave way to a more secular-oriented nationalism. The relationship of Islam to state and society was reinterpreted so as to restrict religion to personal, not public, life. Ahmad Lutfi al-Sayyid, Taha Hussein, and Ali Abd al-Raziq, who were influenced by Afghani and Abduh, are representative of this understanding and approach.

Ahmad Lutfi al-Sayyid (1872–1963) was born in Lower Egypt and received an early traditional religious education. Subsequently, he undertook his modern secondary and legal education in Cairo, where he met Afghani and became a close associate of Muhammad Abduh. After a short stint in government, Lutfi al-Sayyid and a group of Abduh's followers formed the People's Party and founded a publishing house. In March 1907, he edited the first issue of their newspaper, *al-Jaridah*. In later life, he served as a professor and then as the rector of the Egyptian (Cairo) University. Although strongly influenced by Abduh, Lutfi al-Sayyid, like many other disciples of Abduh, espoused a more liberal secular response. He emphasized national identity, the separation of religion from politics, as well as a process of selective appropriation and accommodation of European political and social ideas.

For Lutfi al-Sayyid traditional notions of the Islamic community had no real relevance to the political realities of the modern Muslim world:

> Among our forefathers were those who maintained that the land of Islam is the fatherland of all Muslims, however, that is a colonialist formula used to advantage by every colonizing nation that seeks to expand its possessions and to extend its influence daily over neighboring countries. . . . In the present situation, the [traditional Islamic] formula has no raison d'être because it fits neither the present state of affairs in Islamic nations nor their aspirations. One option remains to replace this formula by the only doctrine that is in accord with every Eastern nation which possesses a clearly defined sense of fatherland. The doctrine is nationalism.[9]

Lutfi al-Sayyid believed that the reality of the modern Muslim world was neither that of a pan-Islamic community nor a pan-Arab nation but a local, territorial nationalism. Each nation must seek to preserve its very identity and existence to gain independence. The Egyptian nation was based on common love and loyalty for a territorial homeland—Egypt: "Their love for Egypt must be free from all

conflicting associations. . . . They suppress their propensity for anything other than Egypt because patriotism, which is love of fatherland, does not permit such ties."[10] For Lutfi al-Sayyid, as for many of
his contemporaries, primary emphasis or loyalty was shifted from the
community with its religious, Islamic, solidarity to the Egyptian fatherland, the country, and the nation: "our Egyptian-ness demands
that our fatherland be our *qibla* [the direction to which a Muslim turns
in prayer, i.e., Mecca] and that we not turn our face to any other."[11]
Islam, while not rejected as a religion, was restricted to private life
and to informing the moral life of society.

Taha Hussein (1889–1973), an associate of Lutfi al-Sayyid, reflected the European orientation of Egyptian nationalism. This was
especially evident in his attempt to establish the cultural roots of
Egyptian identity as well as to chart its future course, not in its Arab,
Islamic past, but in the West. Although a childhood accident had left
him blind, after an early education in his village's religious school,
Taha Hussein went to Cairo. He studied at al-Azhar University for
ten years, and attended the Egyptian (Cairo) University. He then
spent four years (1915–19) studying in France. A member of Lutfi
al-Sayyid's circle of intellectuals and politicians who had founded *al-
Jaridah*, Taha Hussein quickly became a dominant and, at times, controversial figure in Egyptian intellectual and academic life, serving as
a university administrator in Cairo and Alexandria and then as minister of education (1950–52). In 1938 Taha Hussein published *The Future
of Culture in Egypt*, which epitomized the Western orientation of many
emerging Middle East elites for whom the acquisition of strength and
prosperity was to be accomplished not by a return to an Islamic past
or by Islamic modernist reform but by a liberal, secular reform program drawn heavily from the West. To a great degree, their diagnosis
judged Islam as either the cause of Muslim decline or as incapable of
meeting the new demands of modern life. Their cure was modernization based in large part upon Western models of political, social, and
legal change.

In *The Future of Culture in Egypt*, Taha Hussein addressed the fundamental question: "Is Egypt of the East or the West?" He found the
two closely linked in both their political and their cultural heritages.
In contradistinction to both Islamic modernism and Arab nationalism,
Taha Hussein denied the uniqueness of Muslims' Arab-Islamic past
while acknowledging Egypt's Islamic past and her Arabic language.

He asserted that from very early times Islam and the state were separated: "Muslims have been well aware of the now universally acknowledged principle that a political system and a religion are different things, that a constitution and state rest on practical foundations."[12] Hussein closely aligned both Islam and Egypt with Christian Europe in the past and especially in Egypt's modern political, educational, and legal development.

According to Hussein, Islam and Christianity had shared the same essence and source; thus there are no cultural or intellectual differences among Mediterranean peoples. Similarly, he maintained that Egypt's modern renaissance was based upon Europe: "So far has the European ideal become our ideal that we now measure the material progress of all individuals and groups by the amount of borrowing from Europe" (p. 75). Egypt's system of government emulated European administrative and political systems; likewise, Egypt's entire modern education system had been based on European models. Dependence on European modernization had even penetrated the religious establishment. Islamic institutions, the *Shariah* Courts, and al-Azhar University itself had been so modernized, Hussein maintained, that if God were to resurrect al-Azhar scholars of the past "they would beg Him in all sincerity to return them to their graves so they would not have to look upon the great innovations, deviation, unorthodox practice that have already been introduced into the university" (p. 76).

For Taha Hussein, Egypt had become an integral part of Europe, and so he urged: "The world has struggled for hundreds of years to attain the present stage of progress. It is within our power to reach it in a short time, woe to us if we do not seize the opportunity" (pp. 76–77). Such enthusiasm completely overshadowed, both for his contemporaries and for his critics today, Taha Hussein's claim that he advocated "a selective approach to European culture, not wholesale and indiscriminate borrowing" (p. 77). Taha Hussein represented the very Western secular nationalism that Rashid Rida had reacted against. His Islamic critics, both then and now, saw him as an example of the excesses that resulted from many educated Muslims' infatuation with the West. This Western orientation is characterized by contemporary activists as "Westoxification."

Ali Abd al-Raziq (1888–1966) took the Western, liberal secular tendency to its logical conclusion. A disciple of Abduh, he was educated at al-Azhar and studied for a year at Oxford University. Abd al-Raziq was a religious scholar and a judge in the *Shariah* Courts. In 1925 he published *Islam and the Principles of Government*,[13] which became a political cause célèbre in Egypt and led to his condemnation by a council of al-Azhar *ulama*.[14] As a result, he was dismissed from his job as a judge and prohibited from holding any public office.

Abd al-Raziq's book was written in response to the crisis over the caliphate that surfaced after World War I (1914–18). With Allied occupation of Constantinople, worldwide Muslim concern for the future of the Ottoman Empire and its caliph had mounted. Whatever the difference in inter-Muslim politics, Christian Europe threatened the centuries-old center of Muslim power and the symbol of pan-Islamic unity. In the Indian subcontinent, the Caliphate (Khilafat) Movement (1919–25) was created to promote preservation of the caliphate. Rashid Rida wrote *The Caliphate*, advocating the necessity and restoration of the caliphate.[15] Abolition of the caliphate in 1924 by the newly established Turkish nation brought the caliphate issue to a head. Several Arab monarchs eyed the title for themselves, among them King Fuad of Egypt. In 1925, after Rida published an article on the importance of the caliphate in *al-Manar*, Abd al-Raziq's book appeared, denying that Islam required the fusion of religion and political power. Abd al-Raziq's repudiation of this traditional Islamic religiopolitical position became a lightning rod for orthodoxy.

In 1926 al-Azhar, the center of Islamic learning, convened a Caliphate Congress to address the problem. The congress reasserted the traditional mainstream belief that the caliphate is legitimate and necessary. However, it acknowledged that a caliph with both spiritual and temporal authority was not possible, given the prevailing political situation; and so the issue remained unresolved.

Abd al-Raziq denied the necessity and bases of Islamic government. He maintained that, contrary to traditional belief, there were no clear Quranic or Prophetic texts prescribing an Islamic government and that none had been established by Muhammad at Medina:

> Muhammad was solely an apostle. He dedicated himself to purely religious propaganda without any tendency whatever towards temporal sovereignty, since he made no appeal in favor of a government . . . the Prophet had neither temporal sovereignty nor government. He established no kingdom in the political sense of the word nor

anything synonymous with it; . . . he was a prophet only, like his brother prophets who preceded him. He was neither a king nor the founder of a state, nor did he make any appeal for a temporal empire.[16]

Abd al-Raziq argued that the Quran, *Sunnah*, reason, and the very nature of the Prophetic mission "forbids us to believe that the Prophet, besides his religious preaching, engaged in propaganda with a view to constituting a political government" (p. 33). He argued that the caliphate, even that of the first four caliphs, was simply a political phenomenon. Monarchs had used or exploited religion to protect their thrones. Flying in the face of what he acknowledged as Muslim dogma from its early days, Abd al-Raziq espoused a thoroughly secular revisionist position that completely separated Islam from the political order: "This institution [the caliphate] has nothing in common with religious functions, no more than the judiciary and other essential functions and machinery of power and state. All these functions are purely political; they have nothing to do with religion" (p. 36).

The controversy surrounding Ali Abd al-Raziq's book is significant not only within its limited historical context but also because it crystalized many of the issues that modern secularism raises regarding the nature of prophecy and the Prophet Muhammad's mission and, by extension, the meaning and purpose of Muslim life. It strikes at beliefs, practices, and institutions that have been integral to mainstream Islam from its earliest period: the religiopolitical nature of Islam (the nature of the community and its divinely mandated mission) and the fundamental importance of the *Shariah* in providing guidance and certitudes in social life. Abd al-Raziq's position, like liberal secularism today, was viewed by many as simply acquiescing to Western secularism. Emulating the secular West, it sacrificed the totality of the Islamic world view for the restricted vision of Christianity and contributed to the further weakening of Islamic power vis-à-vis the West. The secular option was then, as it is today, a religiopolitical issue for many Muslims.

Arab Nationalism

Within Egypt the Islamic modernist legacy of Afghani and Abduh had taken two major paths: the increasingly conservative reformism of Rashid Rida and the liberal, secular nationalism of Egyptian elites such as Lutfi al-Sayyid and Taha Hussein, who, though they demanded political independence from Europe, looked to her as the paradigm to be emulated in nation building. However, Arab nationalism proved to be the more enduring and pervasive Middle East ideology. Arab nationalists emphasized the Arab nation, a national identity and solidarity rooted in the common language, history, culture, and geography of the Arab peoples.

Although Arab Christians of the Ottoman Empire had fostered Arab nationalist identity and pride through their literary revival and secret societies in the late nineteenth century, it had failed to become a popular movement or ideology. For Arab nationalism to become a popular ideology, Arab nationalists had to address the question of the role of Islam in Arab nationalism. This issue was inescapable given the traditional role of Islam in providing the common ideology and legitimacy for the Middle East's sociopolitical order, the Islamic subculture of the Arab masses as distinct from that of the new Western-oriented elites. Arab history, identity, pride, and language had been closely linked to Islam. Historically, Arabism and Islam had been intimately connected: the language of the Quran, the Prophet Muhammad, early Islamic conquests and heroes all sprang from Arabia. Arab nationalist writers and organizations, whether from genuine conviction or political pragmatism, were inevitably forced to address the relationship of Arab nationalism to Islam. This need was accentuated by the rejection by most traditional religious leaders of any form of nationalism as a particularism contrary to the universal message, mission, and nature of the transnational Islamic community. Thus, for example, during the 1920s both the rector of al-Azhar University, Muhammad al-Jizawi, and the *mufti* of Egypt, Abd al-Rahman Qurrah, had condemned nationalism. Similar denunciations came from Muslim revivalist groups such as Egypt's Muslim Brotherhood and Pakistan's Jamaat-i-Islami. If Arab nationalism or indeed any ideology was to be effective, its positive relationship to Islam, and thus its legitimacy, had to be established. Among those who addressed the question of Islam and Arab nationalism were Shakib Arslan, Sati al-Husri, and Abd al-Rahman al-Bazzaz.

Shakib Arslan (1869–1946) was a close friend and associate of Rashid Rida. He devoted much of his life to the Arab nationalist cause in the Middle East and North Africa and remained a convinced

advocate of the Islamic nature of Arab nationalism. Born into a lead-
ing Lebanese Druze family, Shakib Arslan studied at the American
school in Shwayfat and then at al-Hikma in Beirut. A visit to Cairo in
1889 brought him into contact with Muhammad Abduh and his circle.
He was elected to the Ottoman parliament in 1913; but after World
War I, he spent much of his time in Europe, where he published *La
Nation Arabe* and was a proponent of Arab causes at the League of
Nations. He also served as a link between Middle Eastern and North
African Islamic nationalist movements in Algeria, Morocco, and Tunisia. For Arslan the strength and inspiration of the Arabs, their history and civilization, had been Islam. Their decline was owing to the
fact that the: "zeal of our ancestors, their fervor and their devotion to
their faith, has disappeared from among the Muslims."[17] Arslan condemned both "ultra moderns" and "conservative conventionalists"
for "ruining Islam between themselves" (p. 63). He castigated conservatives for their "blind obstinacy," "maintenance of hackneyed conventions," "reducing Islam to a religion of mere otherworldly
preoccupations," and because they had "declared war on natural science, mathematics, and all creative arts [and] condemned them as
practices of infidels and thereby deprived Muslims of the fruits of
science" (pp. 63–64). He characterized the "ultra moderns" as those
who, upon encountering a Muslim who advised holding fast to the
Quran, religious traditions, Arabic language, and ethics, "would yell
like lunatics 'Down with your traditionalism. . . . How can you progress like others with outworn traditions and customs of the Middle
Ages?'" (p. 63).

For Arslan Islam provided the basis for Arab nationalism, Muslim
nationalism, and Islamic reform. He moved easily from one to the
other. Islam had provided the unity, strength, and prosperity of the
past, so: "If Muslims will resolve and strive, taking their inspiration
from the Quran, they can attain the rank of the Europeans, Americans
and the Japanese . . . nay more . . . we would be better qualified for
progress than others" (p. 64).

Sati al-Husri (1880–1964) moved beyond the generalities of Shakib Arslan and addressed in a more specific manner the issues that
were generated by the formulations of Arab nationalism, Egyptian
nationalism, and pan-Islamism. He brought both wide learning and
years of practical experience in politics to this task. Although born in
Aleppo, Syria, Sati al-Husri was raised and educated as an official of

the Ottoman Empire in Istanbul. Here he became familiar with European political philosophy in the new Ottoman schools. He served in the Ottoman Ministry of Education; and after World War I, he became committed to the Arab nationalist movement, serving King Faisal in education posts in Syria and then Iraq until 1941. He went to Cairo, where he became director general of Cultural Affairs for the Arab League and then dean of the Institute of Higher Arab Studies.

For Sati al-Husri, nationhood was not simply based upon the will of the people in forming and identifying with a group. Rather, it had an objective basis in reality. First and foremost, nationalism was rooted in language, followed by shared history and culture. The Arab nation was an objective fact, reaching across regional territories and encompassing all those whose mother tongue was Arabic. Language then provided the primary national bond that history and religion could support and strengthen. Sati al-Husri argued against the separatism of Egyptian nationalists like Taha Hussein who looked to Europe rather than the Arab world. Without sacrificing their regional ties (such as Egyptian, Syrian, Iraqi), all Arabs constituted a single Arab union or nation: "the idea of Arab unity is a natural idea . . . a natural consequence of the existence of the Arab nation itself. It is a social force drawing its vitality from the life of the Arabic language, from the history of the Arab nation, and from the connectedness of the Arab countries."[18]

Sati al-Husri also addressed the problem of the relationship of Arab unity to Muslim unity, or Arab nationalism to Islamic universalism. He argued that, given the vast geographic expanse and the diversity of languages and races of the Muslim world, Muslim unity could not be realized (p. 66). Al-Husri maintained that a careful study of Islamic history showed that "the political unity which existed in the beginning of its life was not able to withstand the changes of circumstance for any length of time" (p. 67). In fact Muslim unity was more symbolic than real. He distinguished between "the principles of Islamic brotherhood, in its moral sense, and the idea of pan-Islamic political unity, in its political sense" (p. 68). Fidelity to the Arab nation did not exclude a more universal religious solidarity with a worldwide Muslim community.

Finally, although al-Husri did not accept the idea of Islamic unity, in order to counter conservative religious forces, particularly the *ulama*, he argued that acceptance of Arab unity did not preclude a continued long-range commitment to bringing about Islamic unity, which is wider and more inclusive. Arab unity would be a necessary stage in establishing any later pan-Islamic unity.

While Sati al-Husri tried to make secular Arab nationalism religiously acceptable by maintaining that there was no necessary contradiction between Arab unity and Islam, Abd al-Rahman al-Bazzaz (1913–72) argued that Arab nationalism and Islam were in perfect harmony because Islam is the national religion of the Arabs. Abd al-Rahman al-Bazzaz was born and raised in Iraq. Lawyer, historian, and man of politics, he became dean of the Law School at Baghdad in 1955 and was Iraqi prime minister 1965–68. After the Baath coup in 1968, he was imprisoned and died subsequently in exile.

As Sati al-Husri, al-Bazzaz had to address those critics who not only rejected Arab nationalism as un-Islamic but also denounced it as a Western secular ideology. For al-Bazzaz the Arab nation was not an artificial creation formulated in response to or as a result of European influence. Al-Bazzaz, like al-Husri, believed that Arabism was a natural objective reality based upon language, history, and culture. "Language, then, is the primary tenet of our national creed; it is the soul of our Arab nation."[19] As with Rida and Arslan, he also believed that the religious dimension was integral to Arab nationalism. Those who had missed this point were influenced by Western thinkers who confuse the "comprehensive nature of Islam" with the more limited nature of Christianity. Unlike Christianity, according to al-Bazzaz, Islam consists of more than devotional beliefs and ethical values: "Islam, in its precise sense, is a social order, a philosophy of life, a system of economic principles, a rule of government in addition to its being a religious creed in the narrow Western sense" (p. 84–85). Al-Bazzaz maintained that the dualism (spiritual vs. temporal) of Western Christendom is unknown to true Islam.

For al-Bazzaz, Arabism and Islam are inextricably intertwined because the Arabs have been the backbone of Islam—the Quran was first revealed to the Arabs, its language is Arabic, its heroes and early conquests were Arab: "In fact, the most glorious pages of Muslim history are the pages of Arab Muslim history" (p. 87). Islam is the "reflection of the Arab soul and its inexhaustible source" (p. 90). Although al-Bazzaz sounded like such Islamic reformers as Rashid Rida, in fact he shifted the primary emphasis from pan-Islamic unity to Arab-Islamic unity. His primary focus was on Arab nationalism as

informed by Islam, whereas he viewed pan-Islamism as a pious desire which was unattainable. Like al-Husri he courted the support of
pan-Islamic advocates by writing that if pan-Islamism was ever to be
attained, Arab nationalism was a necessary prerequisite.

The Arab West: North African Nationalist Movements

Colonialism, as did national independence, came to North Africa (Algeria, Morocco, and Tunisia) later than most other parts of the Muslim world. French control over the Maghreb (the Arab "West") was
established in the late nineteenth and early twentieth centuries—Tunisia in 1881, Algeria in 1830, and Morocco in 1912. If European imperialism had posed a threat to Islamic identity, French policies in North
Africa often exemplified its most extreme form. Through a concerted
and sustained program, total political and cultural assimilation was
attempted and promoted under the French policy of "naturalization,"
or naturalized citizenship. French was imposed as the official language and the language of instruction in schools. Arabic was reduced
to a foreign status. The most extreme expression of French policy and
their "mission to civilize" occurred in Algeria where they attempted
"to eradicate Islam and impose French culture. Most of the Quranic
schools and *madrasas* [high schools] were shut down. Mosques were
turned into churches. Those who wanted an education had to turn to
the French; and the French opened their schools only to a small number of Algerian children, who thus learned about the French cultural
heritage—their ancestors the Gauls, Corneille, Racine, and the French
Revolution."[20]
   Key issues in the struggle for independence in North Africa,
which transcended the traditional Berber-Arab rivalry, were identity
and authenticity. North Africa's Islamic heritage and past provided a
natural, indigenous starting point. Islam offered a common history
and a set of beliefs, symbols, and language, which Islamic reformers
and early nationalists required in order to restore identity and pride;
Islam was also an effective means for mass mobilization in opposition
to colonial rule. Islamic reform leaders and organizations played an
important role in North African independence.
   The initial reaction of the Muslim community to the French protectorate was varied. The *ulama* and Sufi brotherhoods, though resistant to the religious and ideological challenge of the West, made

their political accommodation with French rule. While the traditional religious elites held fast to their medieval world view and resisted reform, they accepted French governance and, at times, even cooperated with the government. In Algeria, for example, the head of the Sufi Tijaniyyah Order assisted the French in an attempt to legitimate their colonial rule by obtaining a legal ruling from al-Azhar University regarding the permissibility for Muslims to live in a Christian-ruled country.[21]

Given the acquiescence of traditional secular and religious elites, resistance to Western imperialism in North Africa tended to come from young, modern, educated reformers. In its early stages, it was an Islamic reform rather than a nationalist movement. Faced with a policy of total assimilation to things French, cultural as well as political, young educated Muslims saw the need to reassert their own, indigenous identity. Their Arab-Islamic heritage was a natural starting point. Their agenda was the defense of Islam, the preservation of Muslim identity and values in the face of the French policy, through the revitalization of Islam. Muslims must see that Islam and the modern world were indeed compatible. The primary method would be educational reform.

The inspiration for Muslim reformers in the Arab West was the Salafiyya movement of the Arab East. The influence of Afghani and Abduh upon the thought and outlook of reformers like Morocco's Bonchaib al-Doukkali and Allal al-Fasi, Tunisia's Abd al-Aziz al-Thalibi, and Algeria's Abdul Hamid Ben Badis was such that Islamic reformism in North Africa is often referred to as a Salafiyya or neo-Salafiyya movement. This designation is misleading if understood as an organic, organizational linkage with the Egyptian Salafiyya or a single, unified reform movement within North Africa. However, the ideological influence of Afghani and Abduh certainly had its impact and served as a catalyst for North African Islamic reform. While there was some direct contact between reformers in the Maghreb and those in Egypt, the more extensive influence came indirectly through the writings of Afghani and Abduh, in particular the Salafiyya journal, *al-Manar* (The Lighthouse). In addition, North African reformers were inspired to publish similar journals such as *al-Islah* (Reform), *al-Shihab* (The Meteor), and *al-Muntaqid* (The Critic).

Despite differences in each country's experience, Islamic reform in North Africa did display common features.[22] First, in opposition to

French cultural assimilation, the reassertion of a national identity was rooted in an indigenous Islamic heritage.

Second, in addition to the external threat from French imperialism, Muslim survival was also threatened by an internal decay of the Islamic community attributed in large part to Sufism. As in many other parts of the Muslim world, although the mystical orders of Islam were credited with the initial spread of Islam, Sufi eclecticism was blamed for the "vulgarization" of Islamic practice. Popular superstitions, beliefs, and practices such as saint worship, passivity, and fatalism had been incorporated and had undermined the purity and vitality of Islamic orthodoxy. The Sufi orders were also criticized for their acquiescence to and collaboration with the French protectorate.

Third, the restoration of the unity and vitality of Islam required not only a cleansing but a reappropriation of Islamic learning coupled with modern sciences. Muslims were exhorted to see and accept the modern world, learn from the West, and thus be better prepared to respond to the ideological challenge of the West. Educational reform became the common vehicle for the reformist movement. In an attempt to counter both the modern secular French lycée and the traditional Islamic system, modern Quran schools (free schools), which incorporated both Islamic studies and modern disciplines, were established. A network of schools that provided a modern Islamic alternative sprang up in major cities of the Maghreb. Within sixteen years of the establishment of the first modern Quran school in Fez in 1927, a network of schools extended to major cities and towns throughout Morocco. At the same time, attempts were made to reform the curriculum at major Islamic universities, such as Qarawiyin in Fez and Zaytuna in Tunis. A noteworthy aspect of reformist activity was its leadership, which tended to be modern, educated Muslims rather than the traditionally educated religious establishment.

A fourth aspect of Islamic reformism was its call for reform in Muslim personal life and practice. Following Afghani and Abduh, emphasis was placed on the dynamic progressive character of Islam; the presence of a "Protestant work ethic" in Islam was rediscovered. Hard work and social responsibility, abstention from alcohol, and the discipline of the Ramadan fast were reemphasized. Islamic values and morality were an integral part of Islamic reform.

During the post–World War I period, Islamic reformism was transformed into a nationalist movement as religion and nationalism were joined together. Concern to preserve a sense of identity in the face of cultural absorption and to reform the Protectorate gave way to formal calls for national independence. Islamic reformist groups that were relatively small organizations of dedicated elites became linked with emerging nationalist movements. As nationalists of differing political orientations sought to build a mass political movement capable of effectively mobilizing popular support, Islam provided the common denominator that transcended all other political and tribal differences. Their Arab-Islamic heritage was a source of basic identity, solidarity, pride, history, and values. Islamic symbols and language offered an alternative rallying point and ideology capable of reaching out to the masses of Muslims and their religious leaders to unite them with elites in an opposition movement. Morocco provides a vivid example of this process.

Morocco

At the turn of the century, most observers would have viewed Morocco as a country under foreign control with a weak monarch, quiescent religious elites, and a centuries-old division between Arab and Berber tribes. French attempts to exploit the adversary relationship between Arab and Berber Muslims provided the issue for political activists. Though religious elites were open to occasional collaboration with their colonial masters, they remained aloof from any attempts at cultural absorption, continuing to maintain their own schools, Sufi centers, and way of life. The fiercely independent Berbers had resisted Arabization and were deemed casual in their Islamic observances. French administrators viewed them as likely candidates for their policy of cultural assimilation as a means for dividing their Berber and Arab Muslim subjects. In 1930 the French-promulgated Berber Decree declared that Berber tribal areas would be under French and tribal law rather than Islamic law. The decree provided the event that Moroccan activists needed for political agitation, an issue which would join Arabs with their Berber coreligionists. Mosques and religious preachers were pressed into service to denounce the French policy as a direct threat to Islam and to the unity and identity of the Islamic community. The traditional Islamic rallying cry of "Islam in Danger" seemed most appropriate. The issue took on an international Islamic character when Shakib Arslan, a friend of Rashid Rida and a supporter of North African Islamic reformism/nationalism, used his journal *Le Nation Arabe* to spread an awareness and concern for the problem. Thus the Berber Decree and its opposition served to crystalize a nationalist movement whose programs and language continued within a religious framework.[23]

Islam also played an important role in the development of Morocco's major political party, Istiqlal (Independence), which was organized in 1931 by the Salafiyya leader Allal al-Fasi. It remained a small group of young, educated, Islamically reform-minded urbanites from Fez and Rabat until Istiqlal adopted the organization and nomenclature of Sufi orders. The result was the transformation of Istiqlal into a mass political movement whose membership grew to ten thousand by 1947 and to one hundred thousand by 1951. As John Waterbury has noted regarding the Islamic impact on Moroccan nationalism, "nationalism made no real and important progress until it took the form of a religious brotherhood, the 'nationalist *zawiya*,' and until Allal al-Fasi became Shaykh Allal."[24]

Algeria

Algeria's struggle for independence also displayed influences of neo-Salafiyya thought and the use of Islam in building a nationalist movement. During the 1920s, a number of Islamic reform groups were established by young educated Muslims influenced by Abduh and Rida. Their reformist ideas were presented in newspapers and journals such as *al-Islah* (Reform) and *al-Muntaqid* (The Critic).

Among the most important Islamic reformers was Abdul Hamid Ben Badis (1890–1940), a scholar at the Zaytuna Mosque University in Tunis. After *al-Muntaqid* was banned, he and others published *al-Shihab,* whose banner read: "Our goal is the reform of religion and all that relates to the things of this world." In 1931 reformers joined with some *ulama* and founded the Algerian Association of Ulama (AAU), whose motto was: "Islam is my religion; Arabic is my language; Algeria is my Fatherland." The AAU combined Islamic reformism and nationalism and disseminated its brand of Algerian Muslim nationalism through the creation of a network of schools and centers. The AAU escaped French suppression by avoiding direct political action. At the same time, through its educational work and the direct involvement of *ulama*, Algerian nationalism was firmly planted in the minds of a new generation. Modern reformers were able to gain support and Islamic legitimacy by joining with the traditional religious leadership in developing and spreading an Algerian nationalism that was not simply Arab but Muslim.

The Algerian nationalist use of Islam found fertile ground in popular culture. The Islamic consciousness of Algeria's non-elites was reflected in popular poems, especially those recited by wandering bards. The major themes found in these works are a celebration of the past glories of Islam: the portrayal of the enemy as a powerful demon, an unbeliever (Christian France) who violates the law of Islam; the belief that the current humiliation in Islam at the hands of the unbeliever will be avenged by the Prophet's son-in-law, Ali. The French historian Joseph Desparment concluded that such views "have nourished and brought to birth primitive impulses that accord with national consciousness that the *ulama* are today transferring into nationalism."[25] As Islam was integral to Algerian nationalism, so too it would inform the revolution: "The Revolution was to be a struggle both for entry into the modern world and for a revitalization of Islamic values."[26] The slogan of the revolution would be "Algérie Musulmane" not "Algérie Arabe." It was declared a *jihad*; its leaders were called *mujahidun* (holy warriors), and its journal *El-Moudjahid* (The Holy Warrior). Thus Islam was the basic impulse in Algerian Arab nationalism.[27]

Tunisia

Tunisian nationalism received a major impetus from the Islamic reformer Abd al-Aziz al-Thalibi, an early nationalist who organized the Destour (Constitution) Party in 1920. Al-Thalibi was influenced by Abduh and the Salafiyya; however, though he advocated Islamic reform, his energies were devoted more to political independence. The Destour emphasized a national identity based upon Tunisia's Arab and Islamic heritage, Arabic language, and Islamic values. Tunisia was to be modern but to resist French colonial cultural absorption. Nationalists used the fear of loss of identity to assert their role as the defenders of Islamic identity and culture. Islamic symbols became an important tool in mass mobilization of national identity and political agitation. French attempts in 1923 to absorb Tunisian Muslims by offering them citizenship ("naturalization") were rejected on Islamic grounds. To do so would be apostasy because such citizenship meant transferral from Islamic jurisdiction to French. In 1932 a Tunisian *mufti* issued a legal ruling prohibiting the burial of such French "naturalized" Tunisians in Muslim cemeteries. Similar French attempts to outlaw Muslim women's wearing of the veil were rejected by modernist as well as conservative Muslims as an encroachment on their Islamic way of life and a threat to a symbol of their national identity.

Throughout the independence movement in the Maghreb, Islam informed and complemented Moroccan, Tunisian, and Algerian nationalism. What had begun as neo-Salafiyya Islamic reform in the early decades of the twentieth century turned into a nationalist movement after World War I. Islam was a basic component of national identity and provided the ideological framework and symbols for mass politicization.

Iran: Shii Islam and Political Protest

The Iranian nationalist movement developed during the late nineteenth and early twentieth centuries (1870–1914). Whereas in the Ottoman Empire and Egypt the power of the *ulama* had steadily decreased with government modernization, the Iranian *ulama* did not experience a similar loss of power. The Qajar shahs (1794–1925) had not established a strong central government. Under the long rule of Nasir al-Din (1848–96), little effective modern reform had taken place: provinces remained relatively autonomous; tribal chiefs with their own standing armies remained strong; and the *ulama* enjoyed popular respect and power. They maintained their own private armies and their own sources of revenue (religious endowments and Islamic taxes). When necessary, they assumed an effective oppositional role in government politics.

To appreciate the role of the *ulama* in both Qajar and contemporary Iranian politics, the distinctive Shii religiopolitical ideology that informed the *ulama* attitude toward government, as well as their perception of their role and function in society, must be recalled. Shii belief maintained that the mantle of leadership of the Islamic community belonged rightfully to the family of the Prophet. The institution of the imamate meant the descendants of Muhammad, Ali, and his successors were to be the *Imams*, religiopolitical leaders of the Islamic community. However, the political aspirations of Ali's party had been consistently thwarted: first by the election of the first three caliphs and later by Umayyad and Abbasid dynastic rule and finally for Twelver Shiism by the "occultation" or seclusion of the Twelfth Imam. Shiism had divided into several communities based upon differences in recognition of the specific number of Ali's successors as *Imam*. Twelver (Ithna Ashari, "Twelve") Shiism, which constitutes the majority community in Shii Islam, accepted twelve *Imams*. The Twelfth Imam is believed to have gone into seclusion in 874. His return in the future as a Mahdi, or messianic guide, was awaited. He would return at the end of time to bring an end to corruption and tyranny and to initiate a reign of justice and righteousness.

However, until the return of the *Imam* as the Mahdi, how was the community to proceed? Who would lead the Islamic community during the absence of its infallible guide? Into the void created by the seclusion of the *Imam* stepped the *ulama* and the shah. Although they did not claim the infallibility or the esoteric knowledge of the *Imam*, the ulama asserted their leadership as deputies of the *Imams*. Contrary to Sunni Islam, the Shii religious scholars retained the right to interpret Islam. As official interpreters, they were the religious guides, charismatic leaders who served as a "source of emulation" for the community during the absence of the *Imams*. However, the shah also claimed to be the deputy of the *Imam* until his return from seclusion. Shah Ismail Safavi, founder of the Safavid dynasty, alleging descent from one of the *Imams*, asserted both religious and temporal authority.[28]

The establishment of the Safavid dynasty (1501–1742) had brought Shii Islam its first major realization as the official religion of an Islamic empire. The Safavids skillfully used Islam and were relatively successful in subordinating the religious establishment. In practice Shii *ulama* accepted the shah as a representative of the *Imam*, acquiesced to the royal title Shadow of God on Earth, and willingly accepted government appointments. Despite imperial success, Shii doctrine, unlike Sunni political thought, never developed a theological or juridical justification for the religious legitimacy of temporal rulers.[29] Though the religious scholars were co-opted by the state, Shii political theory continued to affirm the *Imam* as the only legitimate ruler and to maintain an ambivalent attitude toward the state and its representatives. While a temporal ruler might be accepted as necessary for public order until the return of the *Imam*, ultimate legitimacy was denied him.

Iranian nationalism developed during the nineteenth century both as a response to the increasing threat to Iranian independence and to Islam by the penetration of Western (non-Muslim) colonial powers and as an attempt to introduce formal constitutional limits on an autocratic and, at times, despotic Qajar government. Under Qajar rule (1794–1925), the relationship of the *ulama* to the government changed as they reappropriated their oppositional role as guardians, protectors, and defenders of Islam rather than as government advisers and administrators. The relative weakness of the Qajars, both internally and before the Western colonialist forces of Russia and Britain, fostered a reassertion of the Islamic religious establishment's independence, its role as a curb and a check on the state. Religious leaders joined with intellectuals and merchants in forming political opposition movements and in political action. They formed particularly strong ties. Both represented traditional classes with power and prestige and a certain independence from the government. The merchants looked to the *ulama* for religious guidance. In addition to religious endowments, donations and payments of religious tithes provided a major source of revenue and hence independence for the *ulama*. Both the traditional religious and the merchant classes found their self-interests threatened by European modernization that brought both new institutions and professional elites as well as European intervention and control of commercial markets. Two such European attempts at market monopolization, in 1872 and again in 1890, served as catalysts for early nationalist activity as Iranians united in resistance to foreign control.

The Tobacco Protest

In 1872 the Shah Nasir al-Din sold a concession to Baron de Reuter, a British citizen, which gave him exclusive rights in developing banking, railroads, irrigation works, and mining. Both Russian and popular Iranian opposition led to the cancellation of the concession. In 1890, however, Nasir al-Din again sold a concession to a British company that gave them a monopoly on the sale and export of tobacco.[30] Popular Iranian protest was initiated and religiously legitimated in 1891 when Ayatollah Hasan al-Shirazi, a leading spokesman of the *ulama*, issued a legal ruling against smoking tobacco. The Tobacco Protest (1891–92) received strong support from Jamal al-Din al-

Afghani, who was serving as an adviser to the shah. He wrote a letter appealing to the religious scholars to resist such economic concessions that could only be a prelude to foreign rule.[31] Afghani's role in popular political agitation led to his expulsion from Persia in 1891. The nationwide boycott was led by the religious scholars and the merchants. Smoking was prohibited, the bazaars were closed, and political opposition and demonstrations grew. In December 1891, widespread opposition and fear of Russian intervention, if civil war ensued, caused the shah to capitulate and cancel the tobacco concession.

The arbitrary actions of the shah and the success of the boycott inspired the constitutional movement through which Iranian nationalists sought to curb the power of their rulers. A combination of intellectuals, religious leaders, merchants, tribal leaders, and land owners demanded liberal reforms to control the abuses of the monarchy. The core of the movement came from Islamically oriented groups—intellectuals, merchants, artisans, and craftsmen. Shii ideology, symbols, and leadership played a central role in a movement that was both nationalist and Islamic and would become the constitutionalist revolt.

The Constitutional Revolution (1905–11)

After Shah Nasir al-Din's assassination in 1896 by an associate of Jamal al-Din al-Afghani, Iran continued to degenerate. Semisecret societies supporting liberal reform were established, drawing heavily from the *ulama* for membership and religious inspiration.[32] These societies sought religious legitimacy by claiming that the first such group was founded by the Imam Husayn, Ali's martyred son.[33] The *ulama* became leaders of a popular protest movement, with the mosque serving as a center for political organization. Sermons proclaimed the danger to Islam and compared the tyranny of the Qajars to that of the Umayyads, who had martyred the Imam Husayn.[34] Moreover, the alliance of religious leaders and merchants, the mosque and the bazaar, constituted the backbone of the opposition movement. Both took refuge or asylum in the Shah Abd al-Azim Shrine, demanding the dismissal of the Belgian customs director and the governor of Teheran and the establishment of a Ministry of Justice to assure legal equity. Although imperial promises of constitutional reform were forthcoming, implementation was not. The religious leaders once more denounced the government, riots broke out, and the bazaars were shut down. Once again religious leaders, merchants, and others took refuge. More than one thousand leading *ulama* from Teheran sought asylum in Qum, while merchants flocked to the British embassy in Teheran. On August 5, 1906, the shah capitulated; and an imperial order was issued establishing a National Consultative Assembly.

The *ulama* returned to Teheran from Qum in triumph. Because of the religious character of the constitutional revolution, the liberal reform measures achieved were seen as restoring a more Islamic government and system of laws. However, as the constitution movement passed from simply one of opposition to that of actually drafting a constitution, the differing visions of religious traditionists and modern Western-oriented reformers surfaced quickly. The majority of the religious scholars had expected a return to Islamic law in its entirety. Modern reformers, who included some *ulama*, offered a compromise: the establishment of a parliamentary committee of five *ulama* who would determine whether legislation was compatible with Islam. The essential incompatibility of religious traditionists' and modernists' positions and points of view opened a rift that would grow wider. Leading *ulama* were themselves divided on the issue of constitutionalism as religious leaders like Shaykh Fadlullah Nuri (1842–1909) withdrew their original support, denouncing it as an "innovation and a downright aberration because in Islam no one is allowed to legislate." Nuri concluded that "constitutionalism is against the religion of Islam. . . . It is not possible to bring this Islamic country under a constitutional regime except by abolishing Islam."[35]

The debate among the religious scholars produced one of the most influential defenses of constitutionalism, *An Admonition to the Community and an Exposition to the Nation Regarding the Foundations and Principles of Constitutionalism*, written in 1909 by Shaykh Muhammad Husayn Naini (1860–1936). Naini argued that, in the absence of the *Imam*, complete implementation of the *Shariah* was impossible. Care had to be taken to develop a means to limit and circumscribe the powers of the temporal or secular ruler and thus protect against the tyranny and oppression of an authoritarian despot: "This sort of rulership is called bound, limited, just, conditioned, responsible and authoritative." Its basis is the "performance of duties for the sake of public benefit."[36] For Naini the establishment of such a responsible government was based upon two principles—a constitution and a national consultative assembly. The constitution should set forth the rights of the people and establish the limits of government. The consultative assembly, composed of the "wise ones of the country and the good intentioned," should serve as guardians and overseers to guard against oppression. The constitution could have no law that was contrary to Islam; the assembly would include a number of leading *ulama* or their delegates to assure that no provisions or draft laws were un-Islamic. However, the *ulama* continued to be divided; the question remained unresolved.

The constitutional period was short lived. In 1907 Britain and Russia signed an agreement recognizing their mutual spheres of influence—Russia in northern Iran and Britain in the south. With Russian support, the new shah was able to close the National Consultative Assembly in June 1908. Although reopened later in 1908, it was disbanded in December 1911. The West's presence and threat to Iranian national identity and independence as well as indigenous demands for constitutional reform would reemerge during the Pahlavi period. Islam had played an important role in the formative development of Iranian nationalism. The issue of constitutionalism and the place of Islamic law in the state would resurface again after the Iranian Revolution (1979). The pattern of a religious-lay alliance under the banner of Islam would be resurrected in the late 1970s in Iran's Islamic revolution.

The Indian Subcontinent: From Indian to Muslim Nationalism

In the Indian subcontinent the development of an independence movement and Indian nationalism began during the nineteenth century. Both Shah Abdul Aziz's legal ruling that British rule made India an un-Islamic territory in which *jihad* or emigration were appropriate Muslim responses and the Mutiny of 1857 demonstrated Muslim engagement in anti-British politics. While Sayyid Ahmad Khan had preached loyalty to British rule in the aftermath of the 1857 Mutiny, it was not long before anti-British sentiments led to the development of an Indian nationalist independence movement. By 1885 the Indian National Congress had been founded, and in 1906 the Muslim League was established. Although some Muslim leaders had concerns about Muslim rights in a Hindu majority movement, in general, during the early decades of the twentieth century, Muslim elites joined with the

congress either formally or through informal cooperation in seeking
national independence.

The *ulama* traveled in differing directions from each other. In addition to the choices of emigration and holy war during the latter half
of the nineteenth century, a number of religious scholars, although
theologically at odds with Sayyid Ahmad Khan's modernism, had
adopted a somewhat similar attitude of political accommodation toward the British. The Deobandi School of religious scholars, although
descendants of Shah Wali Allah and Shah Abdul Aziz, nevertheless
eschewed politics and devoted themselves to educational and scholarly activities. In Lucknow scholars at the Nadwat-i-Ulama Seminary
went further when they accepted British patronage and even tried to
integrate Western disciplines into their traditional Islamic curriculum.

A series of events between 1911 and 1913 brought together Muslims of differing political orientations, Western educated and *ulama*,
against the British in a common concern for preservation of Muslim
identity and political rights. The first event occurred in Bengal in
1911. Under pressure from Hindu antipartition groups, the British re-
voked the partition of Bengal. As a result, the separate Muslim majority province of East Bengal and Assam was lost and with it a major
source of Muslim political influence and administrative jobs. During
the same period, the Balkan War of 1912 had broken out in the Ottoman Empire. For many Indian Muslims, the revolt of "Christian"
Balkans was an attempt to overthrow the Ottoman Empire and with it
the caliph of Islam. These events were seen as simply part of the
historic confrontation between Christianity and Islam, dating back to
the Crusades. This situation was further exacerbated by the Russian
bombardment of the Shii holy city of Mashhad in 1912 and an Italian
threat to bomb the Kaba in Mecca, which further stirred Muslim emotions and concern for the safety of Islam and its holy cities. Shawkat
Ali, the brother of the journalist Muhammad Ali, and Mawlana Abd
al-Bari, leader of the religious scholars of Firangi Mahal, the oldest
conservative religious school in India, established the Society for the
Servants of the Kaba to unite Muslims in defense of the holy cities of
Mecca, Medina, and Jerusalem.

It was the "Kanpur incident" of 1913 that sparked the real confrontation between a united Indian Muslim community and its British
colonial rulers. In realigning a road in the town of Kanpur, a corner of
the local mosque, used for ritual washing before prayers, was demol-

ished. Arguing that this area was part of the mosque, a group of *ulama* issued a ruling condemning the government's action as an act of desecration and, thus, a threat to Islam. After a gathering of Muslims was told by a prominent religious leader that Islam was in danger and that Muslims must be prepared to make whatever sacrifice was required, the group moved on to the Kanpur Mosque to pray. They were confronted by armed police who fired upon them, and a riot broke out in which several Muslims were killed.[37] This essentially local incident became a national Indian Muslim cause. Leading Muslim newspapers, like Abul Kalam Azad's *al-Hillal* and Muhammad Ali's *Comrade*, bitterly denounced the central government for permitting this infringement upon Muslim rights by the local municipality. Under pressure from a united Muslim front, the British viceroy traveled to Kanpur to resolve the issue.

The Caliphate Movement

The events and lessons of 1911–13 left their impact upon Muslim leaders like Azad, Ali, and the traditional *ulama*. First, they reinforced the distrust of European colonial powers and stirred anti-British sentiments. Second, the effectiveness of both the Hindu agitation in Bengal and the Muslim political action at Kanpur confirmed the belief that the British were more responsive to action than to acquiescent accommodation. Third, these incidents and the appeals to Islam succeeded in the uniting and mobilization of modern Western-oriented Muslims along with traditional *ulama*. Finally, Kanpur strengthened the resolve of many Muslims to join with Hindus in pressing demands for more political autonomy. In 1916 the Muslim League and the Indian National Congress formed an alliance with the signing of the "Lucknow Pact." Muslim cooperation in the Indian nationalist movement was accompanied by a growing pan-Islamic sentiment after World War I that culminated in the Khilafat (Caliphate) Movement (1919–25). Indeed the two movements became intertwined in Muhammad Ali and Abul Kalam Azad.

Muhammad Ali (1878–1931) was educated in India and then at Oxford. After a brief career as a civil servant, he turned to journalism, founding and editing *Comrade* (English) and later *Hamdard* (Urdu). When Turkey entered World War I on the side of Germany in 1914, Ali wrote a provocative article, "The Choice of the Turks," for which he was arrested by the British and, like Abul Kalam Azad, imprisoned for the remainder of the war.

Abul Kalam Azad (1888–1958) was born in Mecca, where his Indian father, Mawlana Khayruddin, had emigrated from Delhi at the time of the Mutiny. In 1890 the family returned to Calcutta, where Azad received a traditional religious education. Despite his father's objections, he secretly learned English in order to study modern subjects. Azad began writing newspaper articles at eighteen and quickly gained recognition. At the age of twenty-two, he founded his own weekly *al-Hillal* (1912) which soon encountered problems with the British government for its criticism of Muslim loyalist attitudes toward the British. In 1914 with the outbreak of World War I, *al-Hillal* was confiscated. Azad then published *al-Balagh* which was closed down by the government in 1916. Azad was interned in 1919 and again sporadically from 1920 to 1945 for his political activities.

Despite Muslim-British clashes, the majority of Indian Muslims had remained pro-British during World War I while the Ottomans sided with Germany. However, after Germany's defeat, fear of the European allies (in particular Britain and France) and dismemberment of the Ottoman Empire and its consequent threat to the institution of the caliphate, a last symbol of Muslim power and unity, provided the seeds for mass politicization of Indian Muslims. The caliphate issue was used by Muhammad Ali and Abul Kalam Azad to develop a political movement that reached beyond Muslim elites to the masses. Because the Caliphate Movement appealed to pan-Islamic sentiments, it attracted religious leaders who otherwise remained aloof from Indian politics. Muslims rallied to the preservation of the caliphate and the protection of the holy places. Early support came from the Jamiyyat i-Ulama-i-Hind (the Organization of Indian Ulama). They were followed by others. Azad, like Muhammad Ali, recognized the need for the religious scholars to join with westernized modernists if an effective mass political organization was to be formed. This did not blunt Azad's criticisms of both segments of Muslim leadership:

> It drives me mad to see the deplorable sight that today among the Muslims there are only two kinds of leaders. For the traditionalists there are the *ulama;* for the modernist group, the Western-educated intellectuals. Both are ignorant of religion and both are paralyzed limbs of the community. . . . The first group is beset by religious

superstitions, prejudices and stagnancy while the other is caught in atheism, imitation of the West and love of power and position.[38]

Nevertheless, given the place of the *ulama* in Muslim society, Azad was convinced that mass mobilization and the political revitalization of Indian Muslims was dependent upon the assertion of the *ulama's* traditional right to lead the community politically as well as religiously.

The Caliphate Movement eclipsed the Muslim League, and it became a means for mass politicization of the Indian Muslim community both for the survival of the caliphate against European imperialism and in the struggle against the British for national independence. Muhammad Ali and Abul Kalam Azad brought Muslims into both the Caliphate Movement and the political alliance with the Indian National Congress under the leadership of Mahatma Gandhi. But the Caliphate Movement was short lived. The European Allies ignored Muslim concerns and partitioned the Ottoman Empire.

The Treaty of Sèvres (August 1920) set up a mandate system: Britain controlled Iraq and Palestine (including Transjordan); France governed Syria (and what is now Lebanon); the Hijaz was to be independent. The Ottoman Empire ceased to exist. Ataturk, who had emerged as the leader of an independent Turkey, set the new nation on a Western secular path. In 1924 the Turkish National Assembly abolished the caliphate and effectively removed the raison d'être of India's Caliphate Movement. While the battle for the caliphate had been lost, the struggle for independence continued. Islam and the movement had served Muslim leaders like Ali and Azad as a symbol for mass political mobilization and participation of the *ulama* and the Muslim masses who were thus drawn into India's independence movement. Once in, they would remain so. Moreover, the Caliphate Movement served as an example to Muslim League politicians of the strength of Islamic symbols in politics.

Islam and the Birth of Pakistan

The Central Caliphate Committee lingered on until the early 1930s working in concert with Gandhi and the Indian National Congress. Its demise coincided with the progressive withdrawal of major Muslim involvement in the Indian National Congress. Renewed ten-

sions and communal fighting between the Hindu and Muslim communities resurrected Muslim separatist sentiments. Leaders like Muhammad Iqbal and Muhammad Ali Jinnah of the Muslim League
became increasingly concerned about the future of a Muslim minority
in an independent, Hindu-dominated secular state. Given a long history of communal differences and distrust, could Muslims be sure
that communal rather than national identity and concerns would not
become an overriding factor in Indian politics? The provincial elections of 1937 seemed to confirm the worst fears of many Muslims.
The Congress Party routed Muslim League candidates in a landslide
victory and refused to establish coalition governments in Muslim majority areas. By the late 1930s, both Muhammad Iqbal and Muhammad Ali Jinnah of the Muslim League would call for the creation of a
separate Muslim state. At this point, three differing Muslim positions
regarding independence and nationalism had crystalized.

More traditional religious leaders like Sayyid Abul Hassan Ali
Nadwi of the Nadwat-i-Ulama Seminary in Lucknow; Mawlana Abul
Ala Mawdudi, who later founded the Jamaat-i-Islami in Pakistan; and
the majority of India's *ulama* argued that nationalism and Islam were
antithetical ideologies. Nationalism was condemned as a particularism that conflicted with Islamic universalism. It was a Western-bred
phenomenon rooted in "a narrow national feeling, racial prejudice,
and an exaggerated regard for geographical division [which] are the
characteristics of the Western mind."[39] In contrast, Islam, they maintained, teaches that all belong to a single, universal community governed by God's law: "Be it in the sphere of economics or politics or
civics or legal rights and duties or anything else, those who accept the
principles of Islam are not divided by any distinction of nationality, of
class, or country."[40] Therefore, any form of nationalism, even Muslim
nationalism, was rejected.

A second Muslim position was that of Abul Kalam Azad (1888–
1958) who had been the major theoretician of the Caliphate Movement and remained a staunch supporter of the Congress Party,
serving as its president. With the abolition of the caliphate and the
end of the Caliphate Movement, Azad's political philosophy shifted
to a "composite nationalism," based upon the Hindu and Muslim
communities' shared history and experience in the subcontinent.[41] Although for different reasons, he would later agree with Nadwi,
Mawdudi, and the majority of the religious scholars in their opposi-

tion to the establishment of Pakistan as a separate Muslim state. To the end, Kalam Azad remained committed to Indian nationalism.

Finally, a third position, Muslim nationalism, evolved in the Muslim League under the influence and leadership of Muhammad Iqbal, the Islamic reformer, and Muhammad Ali Jinnah, the politician. As noted, communal conflicts had led to a growing concern that the historic divisions between the Hindu and Muslim communities would seriously affect the rights of Muslims in a Hindu-dominated state. At the same time, the dismal failure of the Muslim League in the elections of 1937 convinced Jinnah and the leadership of the Muslim League that if they were to obtain mass support from the Muslim populations, a formal appeal to religion was the only effective means for building a national, all-India, Muslim movement. Islam provided a common denominator that bridged tribal, linguistic, provincial, regional, and class differences that otherwise divided Muslims and competing Muslim parties. It was the one element that had proven effective in uniting Muslims—modern elites, *ulama,* and the masses in the Caliphate Movement.

Muhammad Iqbal (1875–1938) embodied much of modern Muslim India's dilemma. Iqbal's early Islamic education was followed by years of study in England and Germany at Cambridge and Munich, where he earned a doctorate in philosophy and a law degree. He was enough of a religious romantic to revere the glories of his Islamic past but was also a realist who could appreciate the necessity and desirability for change and Islamic reform. Iqbal was a product of Indian Islam and could celebrate both the Islamic and the Indian aspects of his heritage equally. He was India's leading poet-philosopher, respected and admired by Hindu and Muslim alike. Yet his realism moved him to turn from the dream of a united India; espouse Muslim nationalism; and join with Jinnah, the secularist, in calling for a separate Muslim state. Iqbal provided the political philosophy and Jinnah the political leadership. They would come to be viewed by later generations as Pakistan's poet-philosopher and politician-founder respectively.

For Iqbal questions posed by secular nationalism for the Islamic world took on special significance, in India, where Muslims were a minority: "Is it possible to retain Islam as an ethical ideal and to reject it as a polity in favour of national politics in which religious attitude is not permitted to play any part?" Iqbal believed such a nationalist

option was impossible because the revealed "religious ideal of Islam
. . . is organically related to the social order which it has created."[42]
That Islamic social order included a state and a law, the *Shariah*. Any
nationalism that challenged Islamic solidarity and life was unacceptable. Iqbal was convinced that attempts in India to discover a principle of internal Hindu-Muslim communal harmony had failed and that
the object of Hindu political leaders was Hindu dominance in India.
Standing before the All-India Muslim League in Lahore in 1930,
Muhammad Iqbal issued a call which was progressively to dominate
Muslim politics in India, to subside only in 1947 with the establishment of Pakistan: "I would like to see the Punjab, North-Western
Frontier Province, Sind, and Baluchistan amalgamated into a single
state. Self-government within the British Empire or without the British Empire, the formation of a consolidated Muslim state is in the best
interests of India and Islam."[43]

Muhammad Ali Jinnah (1876–1948), like Iqbal, had initially been
an Indian nationalist. He began his political career as a member of the
Indian National Congress and later joined the Muslim League in 1913,
influenced by Muhammad Ali. Jinnah remained active in the Indian
nationalist movement until the 1930s. However, he left the Congress
Party and the Indian nationalist movement in 1932 disillusioned by
communal strife and the inability of Gandhi and Nehru to control
Hindu militancy. Jinnah turned to Muslim separatism and nationalism, sharing Iqbal's concern for the future of Muslims at the hands of
a Hindu majority. Although a secularist, he revived the Muslim
League during the late 1930s by consciously turning to religion as a
primary tool in the mass politicization of Muslims in the subcontinent. Religious language, symbols, and slogans, such as "Islam in
Danger" and the traditional battle cry *"Allahu Akbar!"* became an integral part of the Muslim League's political ideology and rhetoric. Local
religious leaders and mosques played an important role in bringing
the mass of Muslim peasants and artisans into the Pakistan Movement. Though religious leaders like Abul Kalam Azad, Mawlana
Mawdudi, and the *ulama* of the Jamiyyat i-Ulama-i-Islam (JUI) did not
support the call for Pakistan, they were soon a minority voice.

By 1940 the Muslim League, with its popular appeal to Islam,
emerged as the major Muslim political party, displacing competing
Muslim organizations. In that year, Jinnah set forth his "Two Nation
Theory" in which he argued that Islam and Hinduism were two sepa-

rate and distinct cultures. Jinnah espoused a theory of religiocultural nationalism, which maintained that, despite centuries of coexistence, there had never been a single nation in India but, instead, many nationalities and peoples. While Hindus and Muslims lived side by side, they neither "intermarry nor interdine together . . . they belong to two different civilizations which are based on conflicting ideas and conceptions. Their aspects on life and of life are different. . . . [They are] different and distinct social orders, and it is a dream that the Hindus and Muslims can ever evolve a common nationality."[44]

For Iqbal and Jinnah, the religious reformer and the secular politician, the path of national independence had shifted from a united India to a separate Muslim state. On March 20, 1940, the Muslim League held its annual meeting and passed a resolution calling for the creation of Muslim states in the northwest and eastern (Bengal) Muslim majority areas. By 1947 Pakistan was established as a Muslim nation-state, encompassing the areas of present-day Pakistan and Bangladesh.

As in many other parts of the Muslim world, Islam played an important role in the modern political development of the subcontinent. Its vitality was reflected in the Indian nationalist movement and, in particular, the use of Islam to legitimate a Muslim nationalism led to the creation of Pakistan as a modern nation based upon Indian Muslims' common Islamic identity and cultural heritage.

Conclusion

The evolution of nationalism in the Muslim world provides forceful examples of the role of Islam in mass mobilization and sociopolitical change. The Islamic world reached a political crossroads in the twentieth century. After a long period of colonial rule, Muslims mounted a series of efforts to respond to the political and cultural dominance of the West. Given the centuries-long history of Islamic power as well as its continued presence and strength in the lives of the Muslim masses, Islam played an important role in Muslim reaction and response to Western imperialism. It inspired the development of Islamic modernism and contributed to Muslim independence and nationalist movements. Appealing to their Islamic legacy and heritage, reformers attempted to restore Muslim pride and self-confidence, to revitalize the community politically and socially. Their brand of Islamic reform called for a new interpretation—a reformulation of Islam that reasserted the compatibility of Islam and modernity and reaffirmed the comprehensiveness and relevance of Islamic ideology to politics, law, and society.

Despite Islam's role during independence movements and its influence on the early development of nationalism, for younger generations of modern, educated nationalists, religion had been a means, not an end in itself. Once political independence had been achieved, Islam tended to recede from public life as political elites set about the process of nation building.

... *4* ...

The Modern State

*T*he pattern of modern political nation building in the Muslim world reveals three general orientations in the governments of Muslim countries: secular, Islamic, and Muslim. Turkey chose a totally secular path, separating Islam from the state and thus restricting religion to private life. States like Saudi Arabia and Pakistan formally proclaimed the Islamic character of their governments and the primacy of Islamic law; this Islamic commitment was used not only to legitimate domestic rule but also to strengthen foreign policy with other Muslim countries. The vast majority of Muslim countries emerged as Muslim states. While indebted to Western models for their political, legal, and social development, they incorporated certain Islamic constitutional provisions. For some Islam is declared the state religion, and the *Shariah* is said to be a source of law whether or not this is true in reality. Most require that the head of state be a Muslim and provide some state control over religious affairs. Countries such as Tunisia, Algeria, Egypt, Syria, Iran, Jordan, and Malaysia reflect this approach.

Islam was not only a factor in modern state building but also a catalyst in the formation of modern Islamic movements or organizations. Two of the most important were the Muslim Brotherhood of Egypt and the Jamaat-i-Islami (Islamic Society) of Pakistan. Both offered Islamic alternatives to what they viewed as an increasingly westernized and hence un-Islamic society. Both organizations have played significant roles within their countries of origin and internationally. The Brotherhood's Hasan al-Banna and Sayyid Qutb and the

Jamaat's Mawlana Abul Ala Mawdudi have become ideologues of contemporary Islamic revivalism.

Turkey

Once the heart of the Ottoman Empire, Turkey provides the sole example of an attempt to establish a totally secular state in the Muslim world. Turkey's war of liberation in 1919, led by Mustafa Kemal (Ataturk), sought to create in the Turkish fatherland a nation-state. Although Kemal initially appealed to Islam, his goal was to counter Western imperialism and to establish a modern secular state, not to restore an Islamic empire. Islamic religion and culture were not denied, but the foundations of the new state of the "People of Turkey" was to be the "national will," "national sovereignty." The dismemberment of Ottoman territory and the flight of Ottoman minorities had left a culturally and ethnically homogeneous culture of 97.3 percent Turkish Muslims; thus common language, culture, and territory could provide the ingredients for Turkish nationalism.[1] From 1924 to his death in 1938, Mustafa Kemal implemented a series of secular reforms that progressively created a state characterized by the institutional separation of religion from politics. In 1922 the sultanate was abolished; in 1924 the Turkish National Assembly also abolished the caliphate. At the same time, the chief religious office of the state, *Shaykh al-Islam,* and the Ministry of Religious Affairs and Pious Endowments were terminated. Passage of the Law on the Unification of Education made all education secular, thus eliminating the state's traditional Islamic educational system. The ultimate purpose and orientation of Mustafa Kemal's program was formalized in 1928, when a constitutional amendment deleted the phrase, "the religion of the Turkish state is Islam," as well as other references to Islam. Moreover, the constitution declared that the Turkish republic was a secular state.

In terms of classical political thought, the movement to the secular state was effected with the displacement of the *Shariah* by civil or man-made law. In April 1924, the *Shariah* court system was abolished, its judges retired, and its jurisdiction absorbed by the secular court system. In February 1926, Islamic law was totally replaced by a Swiss- and Italian-based legal system. The centuries-long practical criterion for the existence of an Islamic state—governance according to the

Shariah—had been removed. The radical nature of this change was reflected in the new laws affecting women and the family. The Quranically permitted and traditionally sanctioned practice of polygamy was simply abolished. A husband's unilateral right to divorce his wife was radically restricted by the requirement that all divorce was subject to the courts. Women received the right to vote and to be elected to public office. In addition, they were given greater access to education and the professions.

Kemalist reforms effectively controlled and suppressed the traditional religious establishment of the *ulama* and the heads of Sufi organizations. The secularization of law and education and state control of religious endowments struck at the very heart of the power and authority of the *ulama* who had served as judges, legal experts, and as advisers, educators, and administrators of religious endowments with their related social services. Most of these jobs were now abolished and their revenues sharply curtailed. In addition seminaries were closed, the use of religious titles forbidden, the wearing of ecclesiastical clothing prohibited outside mosques, and religious education in state schools was discontinued.

The Sufi brotherhoods had long provided popular religious leadership and guidance, enjoying great support and influence among the masses. However, if the religious scholars were seen as medieval obscurantists, the Sufi leaders were perceived by the government as purveyors of superstition and backwardness, the causes of passivity and fatalism. Moreover, Sufi brotherhoods, especially the Naqshbandi and Tijaniyyah, had joined in opposition movements against Ataturk's secularization of the state. When two shaykhs of the Naqshbandi order organized tribes in the Seyh Site Rebellion in 1925, the government responded by outlawing all Sufi brotherhoods. The net result of Turkey's new secularism was the disestablishment of the two major wings of the religious establishment, the *ulama* and Sufism.

The attempt to establish a Turkish nation-state also extended to the Turkification of Islam. The purpose was to replace Arab Islam, which was viewed as conservative and backward and more interested in a romanticized past than in the present, with a modern Turkish Islam. Reforms were introduced to have Turkish replace Arabic as the language of religion. Having rejected its Ottoman pan-Islamic past, Islam in Turkey was to be a *national* religion. Ataturk encouraged the translation of the Quran into Turkish. Turkish replaced Arabic in the muezzin's five daily calls to prayer as well as the Friday congregational prayer and sermon in the mosque.

The creation of modern Turkey included a broad attempt to purify its history and culture of foreign influences by cutting itself off from much of its Ottoman past. An attempt was made to start afresh and root Turkish identity and nationalism in a reclaimed, if not at times rewritten or fabricated, past. Turkey's capital was changed from Istanbul to the heartland of Anatolia-Ankara. Arab and Persian influences were rejected as backward and conservative. Perhaps the most radical reform was the replacement of Arabic script with the Latin alphabet. This change effectively cut off younger generations of Turks from the religious and literary heritage of their Islamic, Ottoman past, which was preserved in its official, religious, and literary language, Arabic. The change in script required a massive program of reeducation in order to read and write in Turkey's new script. Turkish was the only language taught in the schools and in which official documents and publications could be printed. An attempt was even made to purge Turkish of its many Arabic and Farsi loan words.

The fez and turban were outlawed as symbols of the decadent social class system of an Ottoman past. Instead, wearing a brimmed or visored hat was made compulsory because, for Mustafa Kemal, the hat symbolized the modernization of Turkey. For traditional Muslims, however, this "Western or European hat" symbolized apostasy, cooperation with foreign, infidel powers. Kemal made wearing of the hat a constitutional provision and, therefore, compulsory. Villagers objected that the brim interfered with their religious duties because the prostration in the performance of prayers required that the forehead touch the ground. Kemal toured the villages wearing a straw Panama hat to introduce and impose his new system. When traditional religious opposition took the form of violent disorder in the village of Rize, several of its religious leaders who had preached against the hat law were executed.[2]

To strengthen the sources of national identity and pride, the Turkish Historical Society (1925) and Turkish Language Society (1926) were established to assist in the process of rooting and buttressing Turkish nationalism. Turkish history was rewritten to foster Mustafa Kemal's theory that Central Asia, the original homeland of the Turks, was the origin of man, the cradle of human society and civilization and, thus, Turkish was the mother of all languages. Kemal's concern was less with historical accuracy than with providing a pre-Ottoman and pre-Islamic past upon which a strong Turkish nationalism might rest.

Kemal's ambitious program of political and social transformation owed much of its success to his total political control of the parliament and government. Only one political party was permitted—the Republican Peoples Party (RPP), which Kemal created in 1922. This situation did not change until 1946. Then the introduction of a multiparty system and consequent greater competition for votes strengthened sensitivity to the power of Islam in the lives of most Turks: "a kind of rediscovery of the continuing attachment of the peasant majority to traditional Islamic values and rituals."[3] Many middle-class Muslims had also remained religiously observant. Although committed to the secular, nationalist ideals of the Turkish state, many Turks were concerned that the pendulum had swung too far, inhibiting Islam from playing its role in personal life and from providing the basis for social morality. While modern nationalism and secularism were the cornerstones of public political life, Islam still remained the "practical criterion for Turkishness," commanding loyalty and providing internal unity.[4] The continued strength of Islam in the majority of Turkish Muslims' lives made politicians and political parties more open to concessions that eased restrictions on religious practice. For the political opposition, religion offered an effective appeal to a strong, widespread popular sentiment.

During the post–World War II period, when the Democratic Party came to power, the restrictive secularist policies of the state were somewhat loosened. Religious education was reintroduced in Turkish schools first as an elective (1949) and then as a requirement unless parents objected (1950). The faculty of divinity was restored at the University of Ankara to train religious leaders. New mosques were built and old ones repaired. By 1960 some fifteen thousand new mosques had been erected.[5] Mosque attendance and participation in the pilgrimage to Mecca increased to the extent that today Turkey ranks among the leaders (third in 1982) in the size of its delegation to the annual pilgrimage to Mecca. The prayer leader-preacher training schools, which had ceased to exist in 1932, were revived. Their number grew rapidly from seven in 1951 to 506 by 1980. Indeed, voluntary associations that support such activities as Quran courses and

mosque building grew from 237 in 1951 to 2,510 in 1967.⁶ Restrictions
on Sufi brotherhoods and their activities were lifted. Public performance of Sufi rituals were permitted as were visits to tombs of saints.
The growth of Sufi organizations and religious gatherings quietly increased. However, these concessions did not mean that the state had
departed from its secular commitment. When Naqshbandi and Tijaniyyah Sufi leaders became politically disruptive, the government
responded quickly by passing a law that forbade the use of "religion
to obtain political or personal gain."⁷

The easing of religious restrictions after World War II was also
accompanied by the increased involvement of religious groups in politics. The Democratic Party, having found religious appeals useful in
its defeat of the Kemalist RPP in 1950, forged an alliance with an
Islamic group, "The Followers of Light," led by Said Nursi (1867–
1960). Nursi favored the reestablishment of an Islamic state based
upon the *Shariah* and guided by the *ulama*. At the same time, a number of religiously oriented political parties began to appear. In 1948
the Nation Party was created, advocating private enterprise, economic planning, and a greater role of Islam in the state. Outlawed in
July 1953 for using religion to attempt to subvert the republic, it was
later restored as the Republican Nation Party.

In response to Sunni Muslim activity, the Alawi (Shii) organized
their own political party, the Party of Union, in 1966, to protect their
rights as a religious minority. After receiving only 3 percent of the
vote in the 1969 elections, they broadened their platform and base of
support to include other minority groups as well as the Turkish left.
Shortly thereafter, a Sunni political party, the National Order Party,
was established in 1970 by Doctor Necmettin Erbakan. Outlawed for
its antisecular religious and political activities, it was replaced by the
National Salvation Party in 1972. The NSP argues that the failure of
Turkey's modern secular identity to provide a sense of history, pride,
and values for society can only be rectified by a reappropriation of
Turkey's Islamic heritage. Its ultimate goal is an Islamic state. Critical
of Turkey's Europeanization, it emphasizes Turkey's more independent, authentic Islamic past. The NSP advocates the Islamization of
Turkish life: politically, economically, and socially and closer political
ties with Middle East countries.

During the 1970s, Turkish public life was often dominated by political extremism, pushing the state toward anarchy. Ethnic separa-

tism, terrorism (attributed to both radical secularists and Islamic fundamentalists), and religious sectarian conflicts between Sunni and Shii increased dramatically. The Iranian Revolution of 1979 fueled religious tensions and secularist apprehensions. Demonstrations by supporters of Erbakan's National Salvation Party increased along with demands for an Islamic state. In September 1980, a military junta seized power. The generals, committed to Kemalist secularism and to heading off political anarchy, moved quickly, clamping down on all "radical" elements. Erbakan was arrested and imprisoned for violating Turkey's law prohibiting the use of Islam for political purposes.

The impact of Turkey's secularist program under Mustafa Kemal cannot be underestimated. The abolition of the caliphate and the rapid modernization of the new Turkish state through a fairly comprehensive policy of secularization and Turkification brought substantive change. Yet despite Kemalist secular reforms in politics, law, and society, during the post–World War II period Turkey's secular path was somewhat modified, reflecting its political, religious, and social realities. In a state which is 99 percent Muslim and in which Islam retains its vitality among the majority of the population, Turkish governments, though committed to a secular republic, have often judged some accommodation with Islam desirable.

Saudi Arabia

Saudi Arabia has long provided the example of a modern self-proclaimed Islamic state. The Saudis proudly affirm and their history and practice mirror an Islamic character.

During the post–World War II period, the discovery of oil enabled Saudi Arabia to be transformed from an underdeveloped shaykhdom into a rapidly developing modern state with international status. Although the kingdom of Saudi Arabia was officially established in 1932, its origins date back to the eighteenth century. Modern Saudi Arabia is a product of an alliance struck in Central Arabia between the Islamic revivalist Muhammad ibn Abd al-Wahhab and a local ruler, Muhammad ibn Saud of Dariyah in the Najd (near modern-day Riyadh). In 1744 the religious reformer and the prince wedded spiritual vision and temporal ambition, producing a successful religio-political movement that occupied Mecca and Medina in 1802 and united the disparate tribes of Arabia in what seemed to its followers a re-creation of Islam's seventh-century beginnings under the Prophet Muhammad.[8]

Once again there was a unified Islamic community that included the holy cities of Mecca and Medina and was commanded by Imam Muhammad ibn Saud. Muhammad ibn Abd al-Wahhab provided the religious guidance and legitimation. They called themselves Unitarians, followers or believers in the unity of God. Affirming the absolute unity of God, a radical monotheistic position, they rejected the veneration of all else as polytheism or idolatry, which is the only unforgivable sin according to the Quran. Local religious practices, especially those of Sufism, were repudiated. Wahhabi armies destroyed saints' shrines and tombs, sacred temples, and trees. Strict observance of prayer and Quranic laws and punishments were enforced.

However, for many other Muslims, Wahhabi expansion and establishment of centralized rule over Arabia was cause for alarm rather than thanksgiving to Allah. Local tribal leaders within Arabia resented the Saud clan's infringement on their power. Shii, incensed at the destruction and desecration of their holy site at Karbala in 1802, struck back through a series of assassinations. The Ottoman sultan, threatened by these "upstarts" who challenged Ottoman control of the Meccan pilgrimage, sent Muhammad Ali of Egypt at the head of an army to drive the Wahhabis out of Mecca and Medina. They razed Dariyah, the Saudi capital, in 1819. Prominent members of the Saud and al-Shaykh (descendants of Muhammad ibn Abd al-Wahhab) families were exiled, and thus the core of Saudi power in the Najd was destroyed in 1819–22. Although the House of Saud reestablished itself at Riyadh, by the end of the nineteenth century the continued Ottoman opposition in the Hijaz and Eastern Province, the assertion of British influence in the Arabian Peninsula, a successful challenge by the rival Arabian dynasty of Muhammad ibn Rashid, and fraternal rivalries within the House of Saud seemed to spell the end of Saud fortunes. The Saud family fled to Kuwait for refuge. At the turn of the twentieth century, Abd al-Aziz ibn Saud (1879–1953) reasserted the Saud family's claims and undertook the reconquest of Arabia. Appealing once more to Islam, he led a religious and political movement that rapidly captured and established control over the Najd (1906), al-Hasa (1913), Asir (1920), and the Hijaz (1925). By 1932 the territorial state now called Saudi Arabia had superimposed a central government upon the tribes of Arabia.

Abd al-Aziz had used Islam skillfully to legitimate his claims and achieve his goals. First, the banner of Wahhabism enabled him to justify his seizure of Mecca and Medina from fellow Muslims as well as his battles with other Muslim tribal leaders. By the standards of the Wahhabi upholders of God's unity, or monotheism, the practice of the other Muslim communities could be denounced as polytheism; such un-Islamic behavior constituted unbelief. They were no longer brothers in faith but enemies; *jihad* was not only permissible but also obligatory in order to reestablish a true Islamic territory. Second, appeals to Islamic unity and solidarity were grounded in orthodox belief and symbols; the establishment of a unified Islamic state was reminiscent of the creation of the Medinan state by Muhammad and his early followers. As in the days of Muhammad, the religious solidarity of the Islamic community provided the one basis for uniting otherwise fiercely independent Arab tribes. It was this Islamic rationale that enabled Abd al-Aziz to recruit a Bedouin army. Islamic symbolism was employed to describe the process by which nomadic tribes were convinced to join in a brotherhood of believers. As Muhammad and his companions had had to emigrate to establish the first Islamic community at Medina, tribesmen emigrated to sedentary agricultural communities where they might better live as members of a virtuous Islamic community under their rightly guided leader. Here they trained militarily and religiously. By 1930 there were as many as two hundred brotherhood settlements that provided as many as thirty thousand warriors. Like their seventh-century predecessors, they were committed to spread Islamic rule in Arabia. Often this took the form of armed conflicts as missionary zeal and military might were combined in what were viewed as holy wars approved or legitimated by the religious authorities. To die in battle was to become a martyr and thus gain paradise; victory meant not only the triumph of virtue but also the rewards of plunder and booty.

Controlling his Bedouin forces proved difficult for Abd al-Aziz as intertribal attacks among the brotherhoods of believers broke out during the mid-1920s. Rebels mounted an ideological attack, repudiating Abd al-Aziz's dealings with the infidel British army, his curbing of their right to wage *jihad* (and thus gain booty) against British protected tribes, and his introduction of such Western devices as the automobile and telegraph. Abd al-Aziz crushed the revolt, eliminating his brotherhood opposition in 1929–30; tribal stability was restored.[9]

The traditional Islamic world view had been used to buttress and give meaning to the Saud movement. Through force, statesmanship, and ideological mobilization, the tribes of the Arabian Peninsula were united by the Saud tribe, and in 1932 the kingdom of Saudi Arabia was proclaimed. The union of the twin forces of Islam and the Saud family was vividly symbolized in the Saudi flag, which combines the confession of faith with the crossed swords of the House of Saud and ibn Abd al-Wahhab.

Islam has continued to provide the ideological basis for Saudi rule and its legitimacy. Although kingship is not an Islamic institution, the monarchy has been rationalized by the claim that all, even the king, are subservient to Islamic law. The Quran and *Shariah* provide the basis and fundamental structure of the state—its constitution, law, and judiciary. Moreover, this policy has also provided great flexibility because the royal family is free to regulate all areas that are not specifically covered by the Quran and *Shariah*. The Saud attitude toward the complete adequacy of the *Shariah* and thus superfluousness of a written constitution was reflected in a speech of Prince Faisal in 1963, one year before his becoming king: "What does a man aspire to? He wants 'good.' It is there, in the Islamic *Shariah*. He wants security. It is there also. Man wants freedom. It is there. He wants remedy. It is there. He wants propagation of science. It is there. Everything is there, inscribed in the Islamic *Shariah*."[10]

In many ways, the king symbolizes the union of sacred and secular power. He is head of the Saud family of some four thousand princes; the leading shaykh in a tribal society; leader of the *ulama*, who serve as his religious advisers; Protector of the Holy Cities of Mecca and Medina, and head of state. Unfettered by a constitution, legislature, or political parties, the House of Saud enjoys political power exceeded only by its oil wealth. The executive, legislative, and judicial activities of the state are overseen by the king, assisted by the Council of Ministers (created in 1953) and the bureaucracy.

A Consultative Council was created in 1926 on the basis of chapter 42 of the Quran, which commands consultation. In fact little happened. It was not until the early 1950s that oil revenue and the consequent growth of development projects made the creation of a modern administrative infrastructure critical. Government agencies proliferated. However, no national assembly or parliament was created prior to 1992. In times of grave crisis, talk of a national assembly has surfaced, only to recede in time. For example, during the early sixties when the House of Saud faced internal dissent from elements demanding liberalization as well as the external threat of radical Arab nationalist condemnations of "feudal Arab monarchies," Prince Faisal spoke of national and regional assemblies. Nevertheless, once Faisal became king in 1964, nothing happened.

Despite his power, the king is not an absolute monarch because he is ultimately subject to the *Shariah*. He does not rule by divine right but is informally elected by a council of Saud princes. Deviation from the *Shariah* is grounds for his removal from office, as exemplified by the case of King Saud. Saud ibn Abd al-Aziz ruled from 1953 to 1964. He proved an inept ruler given more to indulging his extravagant tastes than to governance. In 1964 a council composed of senior princes, *ulama,* and government officials forced the king to resign. They obtained a legal ruling from the *ulama* that Islamically justified the deposing of Saud and the transferral of power to his brother Faisal, who ruled until 1975. This judgment cited the Islamic legal principle of "public interest."

Islam has also been used to validate many other government actions and policies. The *ulama* serve as advisers in the drafting of royal decrees; their legal opinions are sought to justify, on Islamic principles, important political actions. Where official religious opposition to aspects of modernization has occurred, appeals to Islam have been used by the Saud family to win over the religious establishment and the masses. For example, Prophetic history and traditions concerning the employment of non-Muslims in early Islam were cited by Abd al-Aziz to justify the importing of oil technicians in the 1940s. Furthermore, Kings Abd al-Aziz and Faisal advanced Islamic rationales to gain religious support for such innovations as radio, telephone, automobiles, television, and women's education.

Although Saudi rulers have differed from time to time with the *ulama,* they have generally taken great care to court the support of these guardians of Islam, who serve as the consciences of the community. From the early alliance of Muhammad ibn Abd al-Wahhab and Muhammad ibn Saud, the Saudi monarchy has cultivated and maintained close ties with its religious establishment, especially the al-Shaykh family, the descendants of ibn Abd al-Wahhab. Intermarriage between the Sauds and the al-Shaykhs and royal patronage of the *ulama* have resulted in a close, supportive working relationship. In general Saudi monarchs have been careful to consult with and establish a basic agreement with the *ulama* on religious affairs as well as on those political matters that require or benefit from religious sanction. As Muhammad ibn Saud had always consulted with Muhammad ibn Abd al-Wahhab, so in the twentieth century Abd al-Aziz obtained legal opinions from the *ulama* whenever he led his warrior Brotherhood into a battle. Saudi monarchs' deference to Islam and religious scholars was dramatically evident in 1944, when Abu Bahz, an old member of the Brotherhood, publicly criticized Abd al-Aziz for importing oil technicians (Americans) who were unbelievers. The king brought Abu Bahz before a group of leading *ulama* at his royal court in Riyadh. After Abu Bahz repeated his denunciation, insisting that a good Muslim ruler's duty before God was not to aid nonbelievers in the making of profit from Muslims:

> the King left his throne seat and stood beside Abu Bahz and said, "I am now not the King, but only a Muslim, like you a servant of the Prophet, Abdul Aziz [Abd al-Aziz], appealing for judgment to the *ulama*, the judges of the Islamic law which binds us both equally." . . . Showing a thorough knowledge of the Prophet's life and traditions, the King cited several well-attested cases when the Prophet employed non-Muslims individually and in groups. "Am I right or wrong?" The judges replied unanimously that he was right. "Am I breaking the *Shariah* law, therefore, when I follow in the footsteps of the Prophet, and employ foreign experts to work for me? The Americans at El Kharj, and the other foreigners who operate machines, are brought here by me and work for me under the direction to increase the material resources of the land, and to extract for our benefit the metals, oil and water placed by Allah beneath our land and intended for our use. In so doing, am I violating any Muslim law?" The judges returned a verdict of not-guilty.[11]

The basic law of Saudi Arabia is the *Shariah*, which is administered by *Shariah* Courts, whose judges and legal advisers are *ulama*. Just as the use of the Quran in the place of a formal constitution has allowed the royal family great leeway in most areas that are not covered by scripture, a similar flexibility has existed in the Saudi judicial system's use of Hanbali legal tradition. Hanbali law is the strictest, most rigid of the Islamic law schools; yet where the written law is silent, change is possible. Moreover, though clearly circumscribed, unlike other Sunni law schools, reinterpretation has remained open in principle for Hanbali jurists. Thus the Saudi government has claimed the right to introduce modern regulations in areas not covered by Hanbali law.

The history of Islamic jurisprudence provides vast resources that a shrewd Saud leadership has used in rendering legal and social change. A judicious use of Islamic legal principles of jurisprudence, such as independent reasoning or interpretation, selection or the right to select from varying teachings of accepted law schools, and the public interest or welfare of society, have provided the rationale and means for substantive legal modernization where the Quran and *Sunnah* are silent. Furthermore, while the *Shariah* is the law and thus human legislation is technically proscribed, classical Islamic jurisprudence recognized Muslim governments' power to enact "regulations" by administrative decree in areas not covered by Islamic law. The result is an Islamic rationale that has enabled the Saudi government to promulgate various modern codes in the form of royal decrees, such as The Regulation on Commerce (1954), The Mining Code (1963), The Labor and Workman Law (1970), The Social Insurance Law (1970), and The Civil Service Law (1971).

Shariah Courts constitute the basic judiciary of Saudi Arabia. As in classical Islam, the judges have had full jurisdiction to apply *Shariah* law. However, this has not prevented change in the judicial system. Reforms have been introduced that resulted in the creation of a Ministry of Justice, in place of the traditional religious office of *Shaykh al-Islam,* which supervises the administration of the judiciary and a tiered system of *Shariah* Courts. A complementary judicial body handles extra-*Shariah* matters. The Board of Grievances, or *Mazalim* (Complaint) court was established by royal decree in 1955 to hear complaints against government officials. It found its Islamic rationale and justification in a similar system, the Complaint court, which had been established during the Abbasid period. Originally created to hear grievances against senior government officials, the Complaint court soon became a system of courts whose scope and functions were determined by the caliph. Saudi Arabia has adopted a similar rationale. Just as the early Complaint court system enabled the ruler to establish an alternative judicial body alongside the *Shariah-qadi* system to hear cases involving extra-*Shariah* areas (such as ruler-initiated laws or regulations), so too Saudi Arabia's Board of Grievances handles disputes resulting from royal decrees or modern legislation. Thus Saudi Arabia's legal system is a combination of Hanbali and modern law, of *Shariah* and grievance courts.

Finally, Saudi Arabia uses another traditional but informal Islamic institution for law enforcement—the religious police. Originally created during the Abbasid caliphate as inspectors of markets charged with checking on equitable business practice, these officials developed a broad jurisdiction roughly the equivalent of a supervisor of public behavior and morality. Saudi Arabia introduced this institution in 1929 when the Committee for Encouragement of Virtue and Suppression of Vice was established. Its members check on public Islamic behavior to confirm that business establishments close during prayer periods, that the Ramadan fast is publicly observed, that alcohol is not consumed, that people are modestly dressed.

Islam has also played a role in Saudi Arabia's foreign policy. The House of Saud's emphasis on its position as guardian of Islam's holy cities and overseer of the pilgrimage provided a basis for prestige and leadership in the Islamic world. The challenge of Arab revolutionary regimes, particularly that of Egypt's charismatic leader, Gamal Abd al-Nasser, served as an impetus for Saudi Arabia to expand its role in international Islamic politics. The late 1950s and early 1960s had been a troubled time for Arab monarchs. Egypt and Iraq's monarchies had been toppled by military coup in 1958; radical socialist governments had also come to power in Syria and Algeria. In 1962 Yemeni Republican forces, inspired and aided by Nasser, staged a successful coup d'état defeating the royalists and deposing the *imam* of Yemen, a country which borders Saudi Arabia.

In the early 1960s, Nasser sought to extend his influence beyond Egypt and assert his leadership of a pan-Arab movement. Espousing Arab socialism, Nasser bitterly condemned conservative Arab countries, like Saudi Arabia, charging them with cooperating with Western imperialism and distorting Islam in order to perpetuate their feudal regimes. He presented his socialist brand of Arab nationalism as an "Islamic socialism" that embodied the true revolutionary spirit of Islam, with its emphasis on solidarity, equality, and social justice. The fiscal irresponsibility and official corruption that had led to King Saud's forced abdication in 1964 had provided fuel for Nasser's propaganda. King Faisal responded to the threat of Nasser's pan-Arab challenge by advancing the cause of pan-Islam. Faisal sought to give an Islamic alternative to Nasser's Arab socialism. Thus Egypt and Saudi Arabia were pitted against each other in an ideological war in which both appealed to Islam.

Faisal's pan-Islamic leadership took several forms. First, during the 1962 pilgrimage, Faisal persuaded a group of leading *ulama* to condemn socialism. At the same time, the Muslim World League was organized with support from forty-three countries. The league sponsored Islamic conferences and programs and was a mouthpiece for the Saudi interpretation of Islam. It emphasized the universal Islamic community and Islamic unity over any form of nationalism: "the Islamic world forms one collectivity united by Islamic doctrine. . . . In order for the collectivity to be a reality, it is necessary that allegiance will be to the Islamic doctrine and the interests of the Muslim *ummah* [community] in its totality above the allegiance to nationalism or other isms."[12]

Second, in 1965 King Faisal joined with the shah of Iran in calling for an Islamic summit, or conference, of heads of Muslim states in Mecca. Nasser, viewing this as a threat to his pan-Arab nationalism, denounced this "Islamic Pact" before his own Supreme Council of Islamic Affairs as the plan of "reactionary governments which are imperialist agents exploiting and falsifying Islam."[13]

In March 1970, Faisal convened the first Islamic conference of foreign ministers in Jeddah. The result was the formation of a permanent body, the Organization of the Islamic Conference (OIC), with its secretariat in Jeddah. This body constituted the first official pan-Islamic institution of intergovernmental cooperation among Islamic governments. Since that time, Saudi Arabia has served as a catalyst for the creation of many other transnational Islamic organizations, such as the International Islamic News Agency, the Islamic Development Bank, the International Center for Research in Islamic Economics, and the Institute for Muslim Minority Affairs. All have their headquarters in Saudi Arabia and receive major funding from the kingdom. Saudi Arabia has also used its oil wealth to fund Islamic conferences, subsidize the publication and massive distribution of Islamic materials, encourage and assist Muslim countries in the Islamization of their governments and societies, and support Muslim organizations such as the Muslim Brotherhood in Egypt and Syria and Pakistan's Jamaat-i-Islami.

A third and major part of King Faisal's pan-Islamic policy centered on Saudi leadership in calls for the liberation of Jerusalem. The quick and decisive rout of Arab (Egyptian, Syrian, and Jordanian) forces and the loss of Jerusalem, Islam's third holiest city, in the Arab-Israeli war of 1967 offered the opportunity for Faisal effectively to counter Nasser's bid for transnational leadership and to enhance Saudi prestige in the Islamic world.

The ignominious Arab defeat of 1967 dealt a heavy blow to Arab pride and caused a great deal of soul-searching regarding the causes of Arab weakness and decline. It challenged the credibility of radical Arab nationalism and socialism in general and Nasser's claim to pan-Arab leadership in particular. Faisal seized the opportunity. Saudi Arabia led other Arab oil countries in providing financial aid to the defeated Arab countries, successfully pressured Nasser to remove his troops from Yemen, and committed itself to the liberation of Jerusalem. Whereas before the war Saudi Arabia had been wary of the Palestine Liberation Organization (PLO), from 1967 onwards the kingdom became a major source of its financial support.

The liberation of Jerusalem and the creation of a Palestinian state became a major component of Saudi foreign policy and an Islamic issue to which Faisal rallied worldwide Muslim support. When the al-Aqsa Mosque in Jerusalem was burned in 1969, Faisal called for a *jihad* against Israel and organized an Islamic summit conference, which was attended by representatives of twenty-five Muslim states. Faisal managed to combine his pan-Islamism with Arabism and establish Saudi Arabia as a leader for both Islamic and Arab world interests.

When Faisal died in 1975, King Khalid was quick to assert Saudi Arabia's Arab-Islamic leadership, reiterating commitment to its first pillar, Islam, and its second pillar, Arab solidarity.

If Saudi Arabia's Islamic ideology has proven flexible and viable thus far, its use of Islam may prove to be a mixed blessing. The appeal to Islam can be a two-edged sword. The strong identification by the House of Saud with Islam to validate the monarchy also invites its use by critics as a standard for judgment. Indictment of the government in the name of Islam by an Islamic opposition occurred dramatically on November 20, 1979. As Muslims prepared to celebrate a New Year's Day that ushered in the fifteenth Islamic century, the kingdom was rocked by the seizure of the Grand Mosque in Mecca by a group of militants, one of whom declared that he was the long-awaited Mahdi: "The Mahdi and his men will seek shelter and protection in the Holy Mosque because they are persecuted everywhere until they have no recourse but the Holy Mosque."[14]

Juhayman ibn Muhammad al-Utaybi and Muhammad ibn Abdullah al-Qahtami led a group of several hundred followers who repudiated the House of Saud for impiety and the unwarranted innovation of modernization, condemned the *ulama* for having been coopted by the government, and sought to establish a true Islamic state. The siege lasted two weeks and was finally terminated after the government obtained a legal ruling from the *ulama*, calling upon government forces to rescue the mosque and restore order.

While reeling from the Meccan turmoil, the kingdom was rocked by a second eruption that occurred at the same time. Riots broke out among the 250,000 Shii Muslims living in the oil-rich Eastern Province. Although Sunni Islam predominates throughout Saudi Arabia, Shii constitute a significant minority in the Eastern Province, where they make up 35 percent of the workers in the oil fields. The Shii minority have long felt that they have been discriminated against by their Sunni rulers in terms of their share in the country's economic prosperity and development projects. Pent-up feelings had exploded earlier in the year in response to the success of the Iranian Revolution and the Ayatollah Khomeini's triumphant return to Iran. These new riots occurred on Ashura, the tenth day of the annual mourning period commemorating Husayn's martyrdom at Karbala and the tyranny, injustice, and slaughter of Shii forces at the hands of their Sunni (Umayyad) oppressors.

Both the seizure of the Grand Mosque and the Shii disturbances focused attention on the question of pockets of dissatisfaction and political unrest within Saudi Arabia. Despite the successes of the Saudi monarchy in economic development and modernization and a social policy that provided housing, education, and health care services for all its citizens, did these disruptions signal serious potential problems?

While the use of arms and violence in the sacred area of the Grand Mosque alienated many, criticism of the government and the royal family in particular had been mounting. For many, rapid modernization undermined Saudi Arabia's Islamic way of life. In particular, questions of public morality became increasingly sensitive.

Reports regarding the un-Islamic personal behavior of the royal family were as common within the kingdom as they were in the media abroad. Drinking, gambling, and living ostentatiously—all ran counter to the Puritan-like spirit of Wahhabi reform. Stories of official corruption in government and business contracts leading to enormous windfalls and "billionaire princes" were common. There were signs in the late 1970s of government recognition of these problems. Regulations were hastily passed banning women from working alone and from working with men, enforcing dress regulations, and restricting members of the royal family from vacationing abroad during Ramadan (and thus avoiding the month-long fasting period). In the much publicized incident reported in the film *Death of a Princess*, a member of the royal family was executed for adultery.

After resolving the mosque incident, King Khalid announced plans for a consultative assembly in 1980. Historically, when the Sauds have felt challenged, talk of a consultative assembly has resurfaced. In 1982 King Fahd, the successor to King Khalid, reiterated a commitment to an assembly; it materialized only in 1992. Faced with the continued growth of religious revivalism and activism among students at university campuses and pressure from the *ulama* to preserve Saudi Arabia's traditional (Wahhabi) Islamic way of life, Fahd also announced the formation of a committee to develop a uniform code of Islamic law for the Gulf states.

From the inception of its state, the House of Saud effectively employed Islam to assert its traditional political and moral authority. As a result, it remained vulnerable to criticism and judgment by that very Islamic yardstick to which it appealed. Thus its legitimacy and support will depend upon its responsiveness to charges of royal corruption and conspicuous consumption, undermining Islam by rapid modernization/westernization, and failure to expand political participation in a system based upon royal patronage.

Pakistan

While most nations are based primarily on a common territory, ethnic background, or language, Pakistan was expressly founded in 1947 as a homeland for a people who shared a common religious heritage—it was to be a Muslim nation. Though juridically one nation, Pakistan was in fact a composite of people who were divided by many spoken languages (five major linguistic families with thirty-two distinct languages), strong regional sentiments, and distance (the two major provinces of West and East Pakistan were separated by more than one thousand miles of Indian territory).

During Pakistan's first decade, questions of national identity and ideology were overshadowed by basic issues of national survival. The process of nation building was severely constrained by the harsh practical realities of the postpartition period: settlement of vast numbers of Muslim refugees who had migrated from India, conflict with India over Kashmir, Muslim-Hindu communal rioting in the Punjab, and, as a result, mass migrations of Hindus from West Pakistan to India—these were political and social upheavals that caused vast carnage, destruction, and a breakdown of law and order. Such events rendered the situation of the new state precarious at best. Thus it is not surprising that the energies of the first years were devoted not to a realization of Islamic identity but rather to practical concerns assuring the survival of the state.[15] Early attempts at the consolidation of political power and the establishment of a viable political and economic system were further frustrated by the untimely death of Pakistan's founder-architect, Muhammad Ali Jinnah, in 1948, barely one year after independence, and the assassination of Jinnah's protégé and Pakistan's first prime minister, Liaquat Ali Khan, in October 1951—events that further intensified the fragile condition of the new state.

Although religious ideology and symbols had been used by the Muslim League to mobilize and unite Muslims during the independence movement, there was no clear understanding or consensus about the positive content of Pakistan's ideology and its application to the new state's structure, programs, and policies. Put quite simply, the ideological questions faced by the new nation were: What does it mean to say that Pakistan is a modern Islamic or Muslim state? How is its Islamic character to be reflected in the ideology and institutions of the state?

During the first decade of Pakistan's existence, two major events— the drafting of the Constitution of 1956 and the anti-Ahmadiyya disturbances—provide insight into the problems and issues associated with the quest to articulate Pakistan's Islamic identity. The process of framing the first constitution lasted about nine years. The constitutional debate provided an arena for a protracted battle between conservative religious leaders and modern secular factions—the former were inclined to a revival of a past ideal, the latter to modernization and reform through the adoption of Western-based models of development. The Constitution of 1956 reflected the long years of debate and the sharp differences between religious traditionalists and modernists.[16] The resulting document was substantially that of a modern parliamentary democracy to which several Islamic clauses or provisions were added in response to the expectations and demands of religious leaders. Among the principal Islamic provisions were: the title of the state was the Islamic Republic of Pakistan;[17] Pakistan was a democratic state based upon Islamic principles (Preamble); the head of state must be a Muslim (Part IV, Art. 32); an Islamic research center was to be established to assist in the "reconstruction of Muslim society on a truly Islamic basis" (Part XII, Art. 97); and finally, the so-called repugnancy clause, the stipulation that no law contrary to the Quran and *Sunnah* of the Prophet could be enacted (Art. 198).

The Constitution of 1956 demonstrated the early failure of the government to articulate and implement Pakistan's distinctive ideology, a Muslim nationalism that transcended ethnic ties and provided a sense of national unity and solidarity. It skirted the question of the Muslim or Islamic character of the state for it lacked any systematic statement and implementation of an Islamic rationale. Modernists had a document whose few Islamic provisions caused a minimum of difficulty. While religious leaders had called for an Islamic state based upon the full implementation of Islamic law, they had settled for a legal system in which no law could be repugnant to Islam. The relationship of modern constitutional concepts, such as democracy, popular sovereignty, parliamentary political party system, and the equality of all citizens to Islamic principles, was asserted but not delineated. These unresolved constitutional questions and inconsistencies illustrate the ideological quandary that has continued to resurface throughout Pakistan's subsequent history.

A second event during Pakistan's formative period also concerned the issue of the Islamic identity and character of the state, the 1953 anti-Ahmadiyya disturbances. During the constitutional debates, religious leaders had sought to have the Ahmadiyya, a modern Islamic sect, declared a non-Muslim minority maintaining that their founder, Mirza Ghulam Ahmad (1835–1908), had claimed the mantle of prophethood and had thus denied an essential Islamic belief—that

Muhammad was the final or last of the prophets. Furthermore, these religious leaders demanded that Zafrullah Khan, Pakistan's foreign minister, and other Ahmadi government officials be dismissed from office. They argued that a non-Muslim minority could not be fully committed to the state's Islamic ideology; and so non-Muslims should not hold key policy-making positions. The tragic result of this agitation was widespread rioting and murder of Ahmadis in the Punjab province.

A national court of inquiry was established to investigate the causes of these disturbances, and in 1956 it issued a report, commonly referred to as the *Munir Report,* named after Justice Muhammad Munir, president of the commission. This report is significant because it provides insight into several problems that have been and continue to be central to Pakistan's quest for its Islamic identity. Although the religious leaders could join in declaring the Ahmadis non-Muslims, those interviewed by the commission were unable to agree on the most fundamental questions: What is Islam? Who is a Muslim? What constitutes a believer? What is the nature of an Islamic state? As in the past, agreement could be reached in resisting a perceived deviation or threat to Islam, but consensus about the positive content of Pakistan's Islamic ideology, even the most fundamental questions of Islamic belief, seemed to be beyond those who were the self-proclaimed experts and the strongest advocates of an Islamic state. The commission addressed itself to the inherent danger of this situation for Pakistan in the future, identifying two key issues: the lack of any clear understanding or consensus regarding Islamic belief and ideology and the absence of a centralized teaching authority; and the necessity for a bold reorientation, through a process of reinterpretation and reform of Islam, to meet modern needs and demands.[18]

Discussion among the religious leaders regarding Pakistan's identity had existed from prepartition days. As previously noted, before the Partition of 1947, the *ulama* of the Indian subcontinent had been divided in their political responses to the Muslim League and the Pakistan Movement. Abul Kalam Azad had remained a staunch supporter of a joint, or composite (Muslim-Hindu), nationalism. Other *ulama*, such as those at Deobandi and the organization of Indian Ulama (Jamiyyat i-Ulama-i-Hind), also supported a political alliance. A second group of *ulama* who supported the Pakistan Movement created the Organization of the Ulama of Islam (Jamiyyat i-Ulama-i-Islam).

These religious leaders had joined with the Muslim League in the struggle for Pakistan. A third position was represented by men like Mawlana Mawdudi of the Islamic Society (Jamaat-i-Islami) and Abul Hasan Ali Nadwi of the Nadwat-i-Ulama Seminary, who objected to any form of nationalism, even Muslim nationalism. Their conviction that nationalism was antithetical to Islamic revivalism resulted in opposition to both Indian and Pakistani Muslim nationalists like Azad and JUI as well as the Muslim League.

After the creation of Pakistan, all religious leaders accepted the political reality, and a number of religiopolitical parties became active, providing organized outlets for the *ulama*. Among the three most important Islamic parties were the Jamaat-i-Islami (JI), Jamiyyat i-Ulama-i-Islam (JUI), and the Jamiyyat i-Ulama-i-Pakistan (JUP). Although Mawlana Mawdudi and his Jamaat-i-Islami were not an *ulama* organization, they were often joined by the *ulama* in demanding and working for full implementation of an Islamic ideology and state in Pakistan.

Moreover, the religious landscape remained further divided. Unity of faith did not mean a common interpretation or understanding of Islamic belief and practice. In addition to a sizable Shii minority, the Sunni Muslim community included many schools of thought—the Deobandi, Brelevi, Wahhabi, and Ahl al-Hadith. Although most might agree on the non-Islamic status of the Ahmadiyya or might unite in opposition to modernist innovations, their individual theological orientations constituted a form of sectarianism and remained an obstacle to any consensus on an Islamic vision and program for state and society. These differences in thought, exacerbated by the differing and competing personalities of their leadership, have remained a continuing problem.

The conflict between religious leaders and the government in defining Pakistan's ideology continued during the Ayub Khan era. In October 1958, Muhammad Ayub Khan led a military coup d'état. Although Ayub Khan's government sought primarily to rebuild a strong centralized national government and to foster rapid socioeconomic reforms, Islam continued to be a factor in Pakistan's political development. Ayub Khan was himself a Western-oriented modernist Muslim in understanding and approach. He stressed the need to "liberate the spirit of religion from the cobwebs of superstition and stagnation which surround it and move forward under the forces of modern

science and knowledge."[19] Ayub Khan's modernist outlook was reflected quite clearly in the new Constitution of 1962, the establishment of the Advisory Council on Islamic Ideology and the Islamic
Research Institute, as well as the reforms embodied in the Muslim
Family Laws Ordinance (1961). Once again, however, the struggle between modernist and traditionist factions resulted in minimizing the
potential of these mechanisms of reform.

Although the new Constitution of 1962 generally adopted the Islamic provisions of the 1956 constitution, there were some significant
changes. The new document omitted *Islamic* from the official name of
the republic and the divine sovereignty phrase, which limited the
power of the state, "within the limits prescribed by Him." However,
under strong public pressure, these Islamic provisions were again restored by the First Amendment Bill of 1963.

Perhaps the most notable Islamic provisions of the new constitution occurred in "Part X. Islamic Institutions," which, following the
lead of the Constitution of 1956, called for the establishment of an
Advisory Council of Islamic Ideology and a Central Institute of Islamic Research, the former concerned with legislation and the latter
with research, especially on Islam in the modern world.

The functions of the Advisory Council of Islamic Ideology were:
to make recommendations to the government regarding provisions
that may better enable Muslims to lead their lives in conformity with
the tenets of Islam; and to advise the government about whether proposed legislation is repugnant to Islam.

The Central Institute of Islamic Research had been mandated by
Article 197 of the Constitution of 1956. Its charter reflected a modernist approach, emphasizing its role as defining Islamic fundamentals in
a "rational and liberal manner" so as to "bring out the dynamic character in the context of the intellectual and scientific progress of the
modern world."[20] A connection between the Research Institute and
the Ideology Council existed because the council could request the
institute to gather materials and submit an opinion on a particular
legislative proposal.

The effectiveness of these Islamic institutions was compromised,
however, by their status as strictly advisory bodies. For example, in
addition to the fact that the legislature could ignore a recommenda-
tion from the Ideology Council, it could even pass new legislation
before consulting the council. Furthermore, both the Ideology Council

and the Research Institute were government-sponsored and supported, and their directors and members served at the pleasure of the executive.

Resistance to Ayub Khan's attempts to define Pakistan's Islamic identity in liberal modernist terms can be quite forcefully seen in two events: the agitational politics that forced the director of the Central Institute of Islamic Research from office and the bitter debate surrounding passage of the Muslim Family Laws Ordinance.

Fazlur Rahman, a scholar educated both in Pakistan and at Cambridge University, was appointed director of the Central Institute of Islamic Research in 1962 by Ayub Khan. He also served as a member of the Advisory Council on Islamic Ideology. The research conducted under his leadership and many of the publications in the institute's journal, *Islamic Studies,* reflected modernist, reconstructive themes that alarmed many traditionalists. Opposition intensified with the publication of Rahman's book, *Islam,* which contained several modernist interpretations objectionable to traditional religious leaders, who seized this opportunity to rally their forces against the government of Ayub Khan. Throughout Pakistan, the religious leaders directed mass demonstrations against Rahman. These demonstrations eventually led to his resignation. Their struggle, however, was more with Ayub Khan than with his appointee, Fazlur Rahman.

Traditionists took strong exception not only to Ayub Khan's modernist positions but also to his methods. Because Ayub viewed the *ulama* as chiefly responsible for the retrograde state of Islam and as generally ill prepared to meet the demands of modernity, he had severely limited their powers and participation in government. Although the *ulama* were, according to tradition, the protectors of the law and therefore advisers to the government, Ayub minimized their role within the Ideology Council, the Research Institute, and the Commission on Marriage and Family Laws, which were all dominated by laypeople. The tension between Ayub Khan and traditionist religious leaders was especially evident in the debate surrounding the reform of Muslim Family Law. In many ways, it crystalized two major questions associated with the long struggle to articulate Pakistan's Islamic identity: "Who shall have primacy in this process?" and "How shall change be brought about?"

The Commission on Marriage and Family Laws was established in 1955 and issued its report in 1956 with recommendations for reforms in the laws governing marriage, divorce, and inheritance. The commission had consisted of seven members: three men, three women, and one representative of the *ulama*. From its inception, the work of the commission was surrounded with controversy. The religious establishment bitterly resented the government interference in their province; they objected to the "lay dominance" of the commission; they denied the need for substantive change in the *Shariah*. Moreover, given the centrality of the family in Islamic society, Muslim family law had enjoyed pride of place as the heart of the *Shariah*. While other areas of Islamic law had been replaced in many Muslim countries as part of the process of modernization, family law had remained relatively secure. Therefore, potential changes affecting such areas as polygamy, divorce, and inheritance rights were viewed with great dismay by most traditional religious leaders. Moreover, family law reform also became politicized because it provided a major test case: confrontation concerning Ayub Khan's policy of imposing his modernist interpretation of Islam with little regard for a religious establishment whom he viewed as part of the problem rather than integral to the solution.

Predictably, the Commission on Marriage and Family Laws split between its modernist lay majority and its single religious leader, Mawlana Ihstisham-ul-Haq. The arguments advanced in the majority and minority reports reflect basic differences in outlook between modernists and conservative religious leaders. Moreover, these differences regarding the authority of traditional law, the need for social change, and the sole authority of the *ulama* as official interpreters of Islam remain contested issues throughout much of the Islamic world today. The modernist majority of the commission argued that because the Quran and *Sunnah* of the Prophet had not, indeed, could not, "comprehend the infinite variety of human relations for all occasions and for all epochs, the Prophet of Islam left a very large sphere free for legislative enactments and judicial decisions. . . . This is the principle of *ijtihad* or interpretive intelligence working within the broad framework of the Quran and *Sunnah*."[21] Echoing Islamic reformers like Jamal al-Din al-Afghani, Muhammad Abduh, Ahmad Khan, and Muhammad Iqbal, the modernists advocated an ongoing legal process freed from simple dependence upon medieval legal interpretations and open to continued development in light of changing historical and socioeconomic conditions. Of equal significance, the report rejected the *ulama*'s monopoly of Islamic learning and interpretations, maintaining that all informed Muslims have the right to exercise interpretation because "Islam never developed a church with ordained priests as a class separate from the laity . . . some may be more learned in the Muslim law than others, but that does not constitute them as a separate class; they are not vested with any special authority and enjoy no special privileges" (p. 202).

In his minority report, Mawlana Ihstisham-ul-Haq questioned the competence, motives, method, and recommendations of his colleagues on the commission. How could the commission's majority "whose members have neither the detailed knowledge of Islamic teachings and injunctions nor are . . . versed in the interpretation and application of those laws" assume "the position of an expert authority on the *Shariah* and an absolute *mujtahid* [one who practices interpretation]" (p. 205). He accused the modernist majority of "contravening the Holy Quran and the *Sunnah* and . . . ridiculing Muslim jurisprudence" (p. 205). He reasserted the role of the *ulama* as religious guides, for it is the "pious *ulama* who possess knowledge of *Shariah* and act upon it" (p. 206). Finally, Mawlana Ihstisham-ul-Haq rejected the reform recommendations of the modernist report as an effort to copy the West blindly, portraying the attempt to limit polygamy as caused by an "inferiority complex against the West and a desire to copy it blindly" (p. 206).

In many ways, Mawlana Ihstisham-ul-Haq's minority report served as the religious establishment's indictment of the government's legislative attempt to reform Muslim family law. Strong religious opposition forced a national debate that lasted five years. But with support from the Ayub government and women's organizations, led by the All Pakistan Women's Organization, the Muslim Family Laws Ordinance of 1961 was finally enacted. The religious opposition did affect the final draft of the law, which had been weakened by a series of deletions and qualifications of the original commission majority report.

The year 1971 marked a turning point in Pakistan's history. As previously noted, although a sovereign state, Pakistan lacked many of the characteristics of a nation—common language, ethnic background, or geography. Nowhere was this more evident than in Pakistan's eastern wing. East Pakistan was Bengali, ethnically and linguistically. The sole rationale for national unity between East and West Pakistan had been their common bond, Islam. However, for many Bengalis this ideal was far from the reality. A persistent complaint of less developed East Pakistan was the belief that their interests were subordinated to those of West Pakistan. As the capital remained in the West (first in Karachi and later in Islamabad), so, too, West Pakistan dominated the government, the military, and the economy. In such a situation, Mujibur Rahman was able to mobilize Bengali support for his Awami Party on the basis of Bengali ethnic nationalism. The disastrous civil war of 1971, with its brutality and carnage, shocked West Pakistan as it had the world community. With assistance from India, Pakistan's erstwhile enemy, East Pakistan seceded and was reconstituted as an independent nation, Bangladesh.

The loss of the eastern wing and 55 percent of the population stood as a direct challenge to Pakistan's very raison d'être. What had happened to that common Islamic bond, which was the basis of national unity and solidarity? What then was the source of Pakistani identity?

As one reviews the first two decades of Pakistan's existence and quest to give shape to its Islamic aspiration, several conclusions emerge. First, while there was general agreement regarding the need for a Muslim homeland, what that meant was far from clear. For some it was simply a nation of Muslims, for others it was an Islamic state. Second, profound differences in education, outlook, and approach between modernists and traditionalists presented formidable obstacles, as witnessed in the drafting of the 1956 Constitution and the Muslim Family Laws Ordinance of 1961. Third, as a consequence of unresolved differences, ad hoc, piecemeal approaches were taken to reach an acceptable compromise. No systematic attempt had been made to define and implement Pakistan's Islamic identity and ideology. The net result of this approach is exemplified by constitutions for an Islamic state whose Islamicity was established by the inclusion of a few Islamic provisions; by Islamic institutions (the Advisory Council on Islamic Ideology and the Central Islamic Research Institute) whose independence and effectiveness were seriously hampered by their excessive dependence upon the executive and whose power was at best advisory; and finally by a major piece of family law reform legislation whose passage was surrounded by controversy and whose final form was compromise both in its substantive provisions and in its legal methodology.[22]

Iran

Nothing could be further from our present-day views of Iran than prerevolutionary Pahlavi Iran. Before the Khomeini era, Iran seemed to be an oasis of stability in an otherwise volatile Middle East—a staunch political ally and a seemingly insatiable market for the products of the American military-industrial complex. In fact the reality was far more complex than its façade, which was the product of both Western ignorance and imperial public relations.

Muhammad Reza Shah Pahlavi ascended the peacock throne in 1941, succeeding his father Reza Khan Shah, a military commander who had taken control of Iran's government in 1925. Reza Khan, an admirer of his Turkish contemporary, Mustafa Kemal, had moved quickly to modernize the Iranian state and society. However, unlike Ataturk, he did not single-handedly attempt a total secularization of society. As in Egypt, Reza Khan sought to modernize Iran politically, militarily, economically, and socially. Rather than eliminating traditional institutions, he sought to limit or control them. Politically, he built a strong central government, a dynastic monarchy rather than a republic. His choice of Pahlavi, the language of pre-Islamic Iran, and the adoption of symbols such as the lion and the sun were proof to his religious opponents of the non-Islamic (equated with anti-Islamic) character of the Pahlavi dynasty. Zoroastrianism was reestablished with Islam as the state's religions. Streets and public places were renamed in honor of pre-Islamic heroes such as Cyrus the Great. Furthermore, while Reza Khan Shah paid lip service to Islam and Iran's Islamic heritage, his modernization program progressively alienated many of the *ulama*. Two areas, law and education, are indicative of Reza Khan Shah's approach.

Western-based legal codes were enacted. Though incorporating some *Shariah* regulations, they were essentially secular laws applied by state, not religious courts, and administered by a Western-oriented bureaucracy. Even the *Shariah* Court, which continued to apply Muslim family law, came under the Ministry of Justice. In effect much of the power and revenue of the *ulama* as judges, legal experts, notary publics, and registrars of deeds was now under government control and in the hands of modern judges and lawyers and civil servants.

A second area in which the power of the *ulama* was eroded was education. The modern secular school system received strong royal patronage and thus was greatly expanded while the religious educational system was taken out of the administrative hands of the *ulama* and brought under state control. The Ministry of Education set the curriculum, oversaw examinations, and certified teachers.[23]

A special irritant to the *ulama* and traditional classes in general was passage of the Uniformity of Dress Law (1928), which mandated Western dress for men and shedding of the veil by women. In addition to these state-enforced modernization reforms, "the regime sustained a day-to-day harassment concerning efforts to conduct moralistic passion plays, public homilies, pilgrimage to shrines, etc."[24] This, then, was part of the legacy of Reza Khan Shah to his twenty-two-year-old son, Muhammad Reza Shah, in 1941, a legacy that had alienated most of the religious establishment and traditional classes in society and had effectively weakened the *ulama*.

During the first decade of Muhammad Reza Shah's reign, the young monarch was less a ruler than a survivor. Because of Reza Khan Shah's strong ties with Nazi Germany, Britain and Russia had reoccupied Iran in 1941 and forced Reza Khan Shah to abdicate in favor of his son. For the remainder of World War II, Iran was occupied and controlled in great part by England, the Soviet Union, and the United States. During the early post–World War II period, the young shah was caught between Western colonial powers and domestic opposition forces. Anglo-Soviet occupation forces were reluctant to leave owing to Iran's vast oil wealth. However, in 1946 the Soviets withdrew from northern Iran because of pressure from the United States and United Nations. At the same time, the American presence in Iran grew as the United States began to develop its close ties with Muhammad Reza Shah's regime.

Within Iran there were many who, as in the nineteenth-century Tobacco Revolt, objected to foreign presence and control. Muhammad Mosaddeq organized a coalition, the National Front, and mounted a campaign to nationalize the British-owned Anglo-Iranian Oil Company (AIOC). Britain's presence and the shah's protection of the foreign (non-Muslim) economic domain proved a popular cause. Mosaddeq's coalition included support from "the traditional middle class—the *bazaari*—formed of small merchants, clerics, and guild elders; and the modern middle class—the intelligentsia—composed of professionals, salaried personnel, and secular educated intellectuals."[25]

By 1951 religious leaders who had been politically subdued by Reza Shah were issuing decrees calling for the nationalization of the Anglo-Iranian Oil Company. With passage of the Nationalization Bill in 1951, Britain and the West boycotted Iranian oil. Mosaddeq emerged as a popular hero, a symbol of national unity and independence in the face of foreign intervention. The shah could not prevent his becoming prime minister. When the shah did try to dismiss Prime Minister Mosaddeq in 1953, popular reaction and support for Mosaddeq resulted in the shah's flight from Iran. Within six days, however, the continued loyalty of the army and strong U.S. support, including that of the Central Intelligence Agency, enabled the shah to return.

Reestablished on his throne, the shah sought to consolidate his power. Aware of his weak position and more sensitive to the religious and traditional classes in Iranian society, he realized the need for greater cooperation with the clergy. The religious leadership had been divided over the question of direct involvement in politics. Although some had been issuing rulings on political matters and other religious leaders had been among Mosaddeq's staunch support in parliament, a majority, under the leadership of Ayatollahs Muhammad Musavi Bihbihani (d. 1965) and Muhammad Husayn Burujirdi (d. 1961), had been against political activism. In 1949 Ayatollah Burujirdi had held a conference of two thousand *ulama* in Qum and issued an injunction banning clergy from joining political parties or acting in politics. Disturbed by secularist and leftist extremism, in particular that of communism, Burujirdi and Bihbihani followed a policy of political quietism while the shah crushed the Fidaiyan-i-Islam, a militant Islamic organization that had often been critical of the religious leaders as well as of the Communists. Similarly, they did not voice objections to Iran's reinvolvement with the Western oil companies. In exchange the shah made religious concessions: more coverage of Islamic topics in the state-run press and media, observance of the Ramadan fast in government offices, greater funding for mosques and schools. Moreover, Qum, under Ayatollah Burujirdi, emerged as the center of Shiism, to which even the government was careful to pay deference. Its religious schools thrived as student enrollment rose sharply from thirty-two hundred in 1952 to five thousand in 1956. However, the shah was walking a tightrope. The *ulama's* attempt to ban the Bahai provides a primary illustration of the complexity of clergy-state relations.

In 1955 the *ulama* mounted a campaign against the Bahai, a nineteenth-century Iranian religious movement whom the Shii regarded as heretics and enemies of the state. A bill was introduced in parliament declaring the Bahai faith illegal, stipulating imprisonment for its members and seizure of Bahai property and its distribution by the government to Islamic religious schools and activities. The army chief of staff and the governor of Teheran had participated in the destruction of the main Bahai center in Teheran. Although communicating sympathy for the concerns of the *ulama*, the shah finally side-stepped the legislation, fearful of international repercussions. However, the uneasy tactical alliance between the shah and the clergy was broken in 1959 over two issues—women's suffrage and land reform.

In January 1959, a government draft bill for women's enfranchisement drew heavy criticism from the religious establishment, causing the regime to back down. But it was a bill concerning land reform that proved to be a turning point in state-clergy relations as well as a catalyst for broader-based opposition politics.

The Land Reform Bill, which called for the redistribution of large tracts of land to peasants, drew strong criticism from the religious establishment. Indeed Ayatollah Burujirdi issued his only decree against the regime's policy on this issue. Objection to the bill was based less on its economic merits than on its religious and political implications. Land reform affected religious endowments as well. The revenue from these endowed lands provided for support of mosques, schools, seminaries, and the salaries and income of religious personnel as well as students. Withdrawal of this revenue would seriously undercut the independence of the clergy from the state—an independence that was to prove crucial during the revolution of 1978. In addition the *ulama* charged that the bill violated the *Shariah*-mandated principle of private property. Although ratified in 1960, the law remained inoperative.

In 1961 the shah suspended the parliament and announced his decision to rule by royal decree. Under pressure from the U.S. government, he moved to implement land reforms. His edict drew fire from a coalition of religious and secular leaders. Critical of his growing authoritarianism, they demanded the reinstatement of parliament. Antigovernment street demonstrations culminated in riots at Teheran University in January 1962. Demonstrators were brutally crushed by the army and police; several protestors were killed and scores were arrested.

In 1963 subservience to the West was added to the bill of indictment against the shah as Iran contracted a $200 million loan with the United States for military equipment. In addition the government proposed to grant diplomatic immunity to U.S. personnel (military and nonmilitary advisers) in Iran. Amidst the renewed political agitation, the Ayatollah Khomeini emerged as a leader in Iranian politics.

After the death of the Ayatollah Burujirdi in 1961, no single individual proved capable of succeeding him as the country's Shiite leader. Instead people were guided by a number of respected ayatollahs. From among the more prominent, Ruhollah Khomeini of Qum emerged in 1963 as a leading critic of the shah's regime. Although considered a junior colleague to men like Ayatollah Muhammad Kazim Shariatmadari of Qum and Ayatollah Hadi Milani of Mashhad, Khomeini became a symbol of resistance to the shah. Khomeini delivered a series of provocative sermons at the principal seminary of Qum, Madrasah-i-Fayziyah, in which he criticized "the shah's autocracy, corruption, social inequity and injustice, foreign domination, the regime's enfranchisement of women and the Family Protection Law, and the government's land tenure policies."[26]

In March 1963, the shah's secret police (SAVAK) arrested Khomeini. Released within several days, he again spoke out, criticizing Iran's close ties with America, which he denounced as an enemy of Islam for its imperialist control over Iran and its support of Israel.[27] By June 1963, the situation came to a head. On the tenth of Muharram (the anniversary of Husayn's martyrdom at Karbala), Khomeini was arrested for his continued fiery attacks against the shah. In response to the shah's accusation that the *ulama* were parasites on society, Khomeini had retorted: "Am I a parasite . . . Or are you, O Shah, the parasite, who have erected towering palaces and filled foreign banks with your untold wealth.[28] As news spread, the religious processions commemorating Husayn's martyrdom turned into political protest marches. During the following days, demonstrations (led by religious leaders) spread from Qum to other provinces. The government responded swiftly and harshly: thousands were killed; in Qum, seminarians were thrown from the roof of the seminary to their death. Khomeini proved an indefatigible critic. Upon his release from prison in August, he denounced the shah's plans for elections and called for a boycott. He was again imprisoned and finally in 1964 deported to Turkey.

During the late 1960s and early 1970s, the shah consolidated his power with major military assistance from the United States both in weapons sales and in training for his military and secret police. The economic and selective social reforms of the shah's "White Revolution" were pursued with great fanfare. They were often plagued by corruption and mismanagement. They seemed to benefit the cities more than the rural areas and the new entrepreneurial, industrial, and bureaucratic classes rather than the traditional merchants and artisans. For the more traditional populace, the impact of a rapid and often indiscriminately imposed modernization policy meant enduring the trauma and dislocation engendered by the urbanization, industrialization, and westernization of their traditional way of life and values. Another kind of burden was borne by religious leaders and liberal intellectuals. Although friends of the regime were rewarded lavishly and enjoyed the good life, its critics were silenced through surveillance, harassment, arrest, torture, and even death. The government also harassed the *ulama:* defaming religious leaders like Khomeini; monitoring sermons; attempting to control seminaries and schools; introducing a corps of state-certified, secular, university-trained teachers to fill positions in rural elementary religious schools, which were the province of the clergy. From his exile in Turkey and later in Iraq, and France, the Ayatollah Khomeini denounced the monarchy and became the primary symbol of political protest.

By the 1970s, Muhammad Reza Shah Pahlavi had gone from a figurehead in an Allied-occupied nation during World War II to an autocratic monarch who had stilled many of the voices of dissent and ruled what appeared to many outsiders as a modern, progressive, stable society in the Middle East. Though charges of authoritarianism, political oppression, and corruption could be found, the voices of dissent had been silenced. In October 1971, a Muslim ruler, the second generation of a dynastic monarchy in which Islam was the state religion, held the celebration of the twenty-five hundreth anniversary of his Pahlavi dynasty at Persepolis, Persia's ancient pre-Islamic Zoroastrian capital!

Egypt

Unlike Saudi Arabia and Pakistan, Egypt has never proclaimed itself to be an Islamic state. From the nineteenth-century reforms of Muhammad Ali and the Khedive Ismail, Egypt pursued a Western secular path in its political, military, and socioeconomic development. Although Islam was acknowledged as a source of Islamic law, Egyptian law, its constitution, and system of government were Western in origin and outlook. When the Free Officers overthrew King Farouk on July 20, 1952, Egypt continued, under Gamal Abd al-Nasser (1918–70), along its secular path, respecting Islam but generally separating religion as far as possible from the state. The agenda of the July Revolution was summarized in the preamble of the Constitution of 1956. "The eradication of all aspects of imperialism; the extinction of feudalism; the eradication of monopolies and the control of capitalistic influence over the system of government; the establishment of a strong national army; the establishment of social justice; and the establishment of a sound democratic society."[29] Nowhere was Islam mentioned in this early statement of the goals of Nasserism. When referred to, as in his *Philosophy of the Revolution*, published in 1955, Islam meant simply Egypt's Islamic heritage, which constituted one of the three geographic historical circles to which she belonged: "Arab, African, and Islamic."[30]

During the late 1950s and early 1960s, radical Arab regimes had come to power in Syria, Iraq, and Algeria as well as in Egypt. Western-inspired liberal governments were indicted for the continuance of feudal societies in the Middle East. The failure of liberal nationalism and the influence of Western capitalism and imperialism were denounced by the new regimes with promises of a social revolution to redress the profound socioeconomic inequities of their societies. Rejecting a "feudal past" and a Western capitalist present, the Baath Party in Syria and Iraq, the Front de Liberation Nationale (FLN) in Algeria, and Nasser in Egypt advocated an Arab nationalist/socialist future—Arab socialism. From the mid-1950s, Nasser merged Egypt's local nationalism with the broader identification of Arab nationalism and, in the process, sought to be both president of Egypt and an Arab leader. In 1956 Nasser seized control of and nationalized the Suez Canal. His "victory" in the Suez War of 1957 over British and French colonial forces made him a popular hero throughout the Islamic world and enhanced his bid for Arab leadership. Egyptians were both children of the Nile Valley and members of the Arab family/nation. Article 1 of the Constitution of 1956 described Egypt as a "sovereign independent Arab state . . . part of the Arab nation."

Nasser's bid for leadership in the Arab world led to his progressive use of both the Arab and the Islamic aspects of Egypt's heritage. These twin aspects of Egyptian identity often were intertwined as important components of "Nasserism," its ideology and politics. Although Nasserism had been an essentially secular movement in its early stage, internal and external political realities led Nasser to selectively employ Islam to legitimate his Arab socialist ideology and to muster popular support at home and abroad. Thus Islam increasingly became a factor in Egypt's domestic and foreign policy. During the 1960s, Nasser had competition from several Arab socialist regimes: Syria, Iraq, and Algeria, in addition to the newly emerging, oil-rich, conservative Arab monarchy in Saudi Arabia.

Domestically, Nasser faced the disruptive challenge of the Muslim Brotherhood, an Islamic movement that rejected the Western secular path of modern Egypt and advocated a return to Islam and the *Shariah* in charting Egypt's future. Although originally supportive of the Free Officers Revolution, the Brotherhood felt alienated from Nasser when it became clear that he was not going to join with them in the creation of an Islamic state. The Brotherhood increasingly became an opposition movement that resorted to violence in achieving its goals. After several assassination attempts had been made against him, Nasser suppressed the Brotherhood. Nasser's need to counter the Muslim Brotherhood's Islamic appeal and its challenge to his legitimacy and to mobilize the Arab masses behind his Arab socialist revolution at home and abroad influenced him to turn to Islam to achieve his political goals: "The regime seemed to recognize more and more that Islam remained the widest and most effective basis for consensus despite all efforts to promote nationalism, patriotism, secularism, and socialism."[31]

Although he had refused to acquiesce to the demands of religious leaders that the Egyptian Charter of 1962, which set forth Nasser's socialist blueprint for society, include a clause declaring Islam the state religion, by 1964 the clause was placed in Egypt's constitution. Nasser also involved the government in Islamic affairs when he nationalized al-Azhar University, the oldest Islamic university and a major center of religious authority. Key administrative positions went to government officials, and curriculum reform was imposed by the government. The justification given was the need to counter a reactionary conservatism and train a new generation committed to and capable of contributing to modernization and development. As a result, the university lost much of its independence both academically and politically.

Government control of al-Azhar as well as those mosques whose *imams* (prayer leaders) were appointed and paid by the Ministry of Awqaf (Endowments, Religious Affairs) enabled Nasser to marshal religious support for such socialist policies as land reform and nationalization of public utilities. For example, the rector of al-Azhar, Mahmud Shaltut (1892–1963), declared that Islam and socialism were completely reconcilable because Islam was more than just a spiritual religion; it regulated "human relations and public affairs with the aim of ensuring the welfare of society."[32] Basing his interpretation upon the Quran, Shaltut justified government policies such as the religious acceptability of expropriation of land in the public welfare because "If worldly possessions are the possessions of God . . . then wealth, although it may be attributed to a private person, should also belong to all the servants of God, should be placed in the safekeeping of all, and all should profit from it."[33] Shaltut could conclude: "Can man find a more perfect, more complete, more useful, and more profound socialism than that decreed by Islam? It is founded on the basis of faith and belief, and all that is decreed on that basis participates in the perpetuation of life and doctrine."[34]

The government obtained *fatwas* from religious authorities to support programs such as birth control or land reform.[35] Moreover, the Supreme Council of Islamic Affairs, a government-created and funded agency, published such decrees in its journal *Minbar al-Islam* (The Pulpit of Islam), which also included articles written by lay intellectuals on Arab socialism and Islam, with such topics as "Socialism in Islam," "Arab Socialism Is in the Spirit of Islamic Belief," and "The Cause of the National Charter Is the Cause of Islam." *Minbar al-Islam* became "the single most important attempt by a group of writers to lay out the major concepts of a socialist ideology drawn from Islamic principles."[36]

The use of Islam to legitimate Arab socialism also enhanced Nasser's foreign policy because the vast majority of Arabs to whom he was appealing were Muslim. Moreover, as indicated earlier, in the rivalry that developed between Egypt and Saudi Arabia, Islam became important because Faisal used Islam to condemn Arab socialism and to advocate a pan-Islam that countered pan-Arabism. When Faisal obtained a decree from his *ulama* condemning socialism, Nasser obtained decrees from Egyptian *ulama*, especially leading scholars of al-Azhar, legitimating his ideology and programs. While Faisal argued that pan-Islam included Arabism, Nasser proclaimed that Arab socialism was rooted in Islam: "Islam is the first religion to call for socialism, the first religion to call for equality." Countering his conservative Arab critics, Nasser declared: "Our enemies say that socialism is infidelity. But is socialism really what they describe by this term? What they describe applies to raising slaves, hoarding money and usurping the people's wealth. (Nasser's criticism of the Saudi regime.) This is infidelity and this is against religion and Islam. What we apply . . . is the law of justice and the law of God."[37]

Many forces during the 1950s and 60s resulted in the reemergence of religion in Egyptian politics. Nasser's use of Islamic politics was a testimony to the widespread presence and influence of Islam in the lives of the majority of the population—in all classes of society and across educational levels—and a testimony to the capacity of Islamic history and belief to include political and socioeconomic aspects of life within its normative boundaries.

The Egyptian experience challenged underlying assumptions of modernization and development theories. Despite the century-long commitment of Egyptian leaders to modernization, reforms imposed from above did not guarantee their acceptance by the vast majority of the people. The orientation of the state—its institutions, laws, and policies—revealed more about the ideals and goals of Egyptian rulers than about the realities of Egyptian society. Modern elites constituted a small fraction of an otherwise tradition-oriented majority. Thus, if modernization is equated with the beliefs, values, and attitudes— with the total world view of a people—then Egypt, like most Muslim countries, was not truly a modern (secular-oriented) state. The institutions of a modern state had been transplanted from the West to a society whose historical experience and values were not the same. These differences account for the failure of political institutions (parliaments, political parties, free elections) to function despite their official existence in constitutions. The continued presence and importance of religion was reflected both in the politicizing of religion under Nasser and in the activities of the Muslim Brotherhood. Indeed, as Muslim states in nation building had tended to ignore, downplay, or control religion in their general pursuit, two major Islamic organizations—the Muslim Brotherhood in Egypt and the Jamaat-i-Islami in Pakistan advocated a return to an Islamic alternative to Western-inspired political systems. Their influence would in time extend beyond their national origins as they became international Islamic organizations that have had a major impact on contemporary Islamic politics from Algeria to Indonesia.

Islamic Alternatives

The Muslim Brotherhood

Hasan al-Banna (1906–49), the founder of the Muslim Brotherhood, was born in Mahmudiyya, a small town northeast of Cairo in the Nile Delta. His early traditional religious education was combined with some exposure to modernist thought through his father, Shaykh Ahmad Abd al-Rahman al-Banna, who had been a student at al-Azhar during the time of Muhammad Abduh. After study at a local teacher training college, al-Banna went to Cairo to study at Dar al-Ulum College. In Cairo he came into contact with Rashid Rida and his Salafiyya movement. An avid reader of *al-Manar,* he absorbed the reformist spirit of Afghani and Abduh. He was, however, particularly influenced by Rida's writings on the political and social aspects of Islamic reform, the need for an Islamic state, and the introduction of Islamic law. It was the later, more conservative Rida that al-Banna knew. He was attracted by Rida's emphasis on the complete and total self-sufficiency of Islam and the dangers of westernization.

In addition to the influence of al-Banna's father and early teachers, two other factors played a significant role in his formation: the anti-British revolt of 1919 and membership in several Islamic associations. Although al-Banna had become deeply involved in Sufi mystical practice, he responded immediately to the political crisis of 1919: "Despite my preoccupation with Sufism and worship, I believed that duty to country is an inescapable obligation—a holy war."[38] The aborted revolt and British occupation of al-Banna's hometown reinforced his sense of British hegemony in Egypt and the political as well as cultural threat of Western colonialism. The conclusion he drew as a thirteen-year-old regarding the relationship of religion to politics would become a foundation stone of the Muslim Brotherhood.

During his school days, Hasan al-Banna belonged to a number of Islamic associations, such as the Society for Ethical Education and the Society for the Prevention of Prohibited Actions. These associations emphasized individual religious and moral reform and a commitment to preach and spread the message of Islam to other Muslims in coffee-houses and other public gathering places as well as in mosques. Al-Banna would comment later: "There is no doubt that such an association has more influence in forming character than twenty theoretical lessons."[39] Both the political and the religious moral activities of his youth were major influences on the formation of his own Islamic society, with its emphasis upon organization and its religious rationale for political and sociomoral reform.

After completing his studies in 1927, Hasan al-Banna accepted a teaching post at a primary school in Ismailiyya. Convinced that only through a return to Islam (by following the Quran and *Sunnah* of the Prophet) could the Muslim world be awakened from its lethargy and decline, he organized religious discussion groups and committed himself to Islamic renewal. A man of great religious zeal and charisma, al-Banna quickly attracted followers and, in 1928, established the Muslim Brotherhood, or Muslim Brethren (al-Ikhwan al-Muslimun).

During his studies in Cario and in Ismailiyya, which was at the heart of the British occupied Suez Canal zone, Hasan al-Banna experienced both Western political presence, or occupation, and its religious and cultural challenge to traditional Egyptian society. The threat of westernization came both from the British and from westernized Egyptian elites who sought to implement Western-based models in political, social, and economic development. Hasan al-Banna, like Rashid Rida, concluded that westernization was a major threat to Egypt and Islam, the source of much of Egypt's political, social, and economic problems. Thus, as he viewed the political disunity, the profound socioeconomic disparities, the social dislocation, and the growing indifference to religion in Egyptian society, Western secularism and materialism stood out as major causes of Muslim impotence and decline. The cure for this "disease"—a return to Islam. But unlike Islamic modernists, who looked to the West and provided an Islamic rationale for the appropriation of Western learning, Hasan al-Banna emphasized the perfection and comprehensiveness of Islam and hence its self-sufficiency. Following the methodology of nineteenth-century Islamic revivalism, al-Banna called for a return to the Quran and *Sunnah* of the Prophet as the primary sources for the reestablishment of an Islamic system of government. In addition to rejecting Western sources, he also differed from the general tendency of the *ulama* to rely on their medieval formulations of Islam. Like Muhammad ibn

Abd al-Wahhab and other revivalists, al-Banna believed that Muslims must go back beyond all historical accretions and return to the early normative period of Islamic history—the time of the Prophet and the first caliphs of Islam.

During the first decade of its existence, the Muslim Brotherhood concentrated on moral and social reform, attracting popular support for their educational and social welfare projects. They ran small hospitals, built neighborhood mosques and schools, established cottage industries, and opened local social clubs. By 1949 the Brotherhood had some two thousand branches spread across Egypt, with an estimated membership of five hundred thousand and an equal number of sympathizers. Each branch consisted of a center, mosque, school, and a club or home industry.

In 1933 Hasan al-Banna decided to move the center of activities to Cairo, where he devoted himself to the organization and communication of the Brotherhood's mission and message. The comprehensive nature of the Brotherhood's organization and program was reflected in his description of the movement as "a Salafiyya message, a Sunni way, a Sufi truth, a political organization, an athletic group, a cultural-educational union, an economic company, and a social idea."[40] It was in Cairo that the Muslim Brotherhood's weekly magazine, *Majallat al-Ikhwan al-Muslimun* (Journal of the Muslim Brothers), and its press, which would play an important role in the development and dissemination of Muslim Brotherhood ideas throughout the Muslim world, were established.

Under the leadership of its charismatic guide, the Brotherhood developed into a well-knit religious and political organization with a network of branches that were further divided into secret cells. Its members underwent a program of training and ideological indoctrination emphasizing moral and physical fitness in order to defend Islam. Membership spread beyond its rural, lower-class origins to the urban middle class. It attracted merchants, teachers, physicians, lawyers, judges, civil servants, the military, and university students.

The Brotherhood became progressively embroiled in politics, in particular through its anti-British and anti-Zionist activities. Its goal was the establishment of an Islamic state in Egypt. The situation came to a head in December 1948 when the government of King Farouk, reacting to a series of violent incidents, including the assassination of Cairo's chief of police, banned the Brotherhood and imprisoned many of its key leaders, excepting Hasan al-Banna. Shortly afterward Egypt's prime minister, Nurashi Pasha, was murdered by a twenty-three-year-old veterinary student and Muslim Brother. Although al-Banna denied either his or the Muslim Brothers' involvement, the government blamed the Brotherhood and the estimated one million members of the Brotherhood were driven underground or into exile. On February 12, 1949, in retaliation, Hasan al-Banna was himself assassinated by Egypt's secret police as he left his Cairo office.

When martial law was finally abolished in May 1952, the Brotherhood reemerged. As noted, the Brotherhood's initial support of Gamal Abd al-Nasser's July 1952 "Revolution" was withdrawn when it became clear that Nasser was not going to establish an Islamic state or share power with the Brotherhood. The conflict between the Brotherhood and Nasser's government climaxed in 1954 with an abortive assassination attempt against Nasser by several of its members. Although there was no proof that this was anything more than the act of several individuals, the government used it as a pretext to crush the entire Brotherhood organization. Its headquarters in Cairo and the provinces were sacked, thousands of members arrested, and a number of its leaders executed.

The Muslim Brotherhood's understanding of the nature of Islamic state and society has been particularly influenced by the teachings of Hasan al-Banna and the writings of Sayyid Qutb (1906–66). Like Hasan al-Banna, Sayyid Qutb graduated from Dar al-Ulum and was a schoolteacher. He then became an inspector in the Ministry of Education. In 1948 he published *Social Justice in Islam*, after which he spent two years in the United States studying educational organization. On his return to Egypt, Sayyid Qutb joined the Muslim Brothers and became its major ideologue. Qutb was a prolific author, writing some twenty-four books and a host of articles primarily on religion but also on literary criticism and education. Among his religious writings were *Islam, This Religion of Islam, Islam the Religion of the Future, Signposts on the Road*, and a commentary on the Quran.

Although initially attracted to the West, like many Egyptian intellectuals, Sayyid Qutb became disillusioned during the 1940s. Western complicity in the establishment of Israel and his stay in the United States convinced him of the moral decadence of Western civilization and its anti-Arab bias. Qutb's increasingly militant Islamic writings and activities catapulted him into a position of leadership in the

Brotherhood and made him a target in Nasser's crackdown in 1954. He was sentenced to fifteen years in prison, where he continued to write. Released in 1964 through the intervention of Iraq's president, Abd al-Salam Arif, Qutb was again arrested only a few months later and executed with two other Brothers suspected of plotting against the government. Like Hasan al-Banna, Sayyid Qutb is often referred to as the martyr of the Islamic revival. Both their writings not only have had a formative influence upon the Muslim Brotherhood but also have been a major influence upon Islamic revivalism today.

Sayyid Qutb's thought was strongly influenced by Hasan al-Banna and the writings of Pakistan's Mawlana Mawdudi. He borrowed frequently from Mawdudi in his exposition on such themes as God's governance, *jihad,* and the revolutionary character of Islam. Because he wrote more extensively than al-Banna, he provided more of a blueprint for the Muslim Brothers. Although Qutb drew from Mawdudi, he took many of these beliefs to their more literal, militant conclusion. Qutb himself moved from an early phase which spoke of an Islamic alternative to Western systems to a latter stage in which an Islamic alternative became *the* Islamic imperative that all Muslims were obligated to implement, for which the true believers should be willing to live and die.[41] As a result, he appealed to the more radical elements among his contemporaries in the Brotherhood and has been a strong formative influence on militant Islamic organizations today, including Egypt's Takfir wal Hijra (Excommunication and Emigration) and al-Jihad (the Holy War Society), the assassins of Anwar al-Sadat.

Like premodern revivalists and modern Islamic reformers, for al-Banna and Qutb the early Islamic state of Muhammad and the first four caliphs constitute the ideal period. After that time, pure Islam declined as kingship was introduced by the Umayyads, and tribal factionalism reemerged and wracked the history of the Islamic empires. Despite political and cultural success, the Islamic ideal was not being fully realized; and, therefore, the Islamic community remained vulnerable to outside attack and penetration from the Crusades to European colonialism. Internally, un-Islamic practices infiltrated Islamic belief and practice. This degeneration was evident in medieval Islamic law and the extremes of Sufism. The net result was a weakened, disintegrating Islamic community, whose decayed state made it an easy victim of European imperialism. Muslim governments succumbed politically, militarily, intellectually, spiritually, and culturally to the West.

Muslim leaders had failed their community. Sufism had become corrupted through its absorption of superstitious practices. The *ulama*, clinging to their medieval ways, had become irrelevant as they proved incapable of responding to the demands of modernity. Islamic modernists had also failed. Primarily concerned with charting an Islamic response to the West through religious, intellectual, and educational reform, they sought an Islamic rationale for learning from the West. As a result, they were too Western-oriented. More importantly, they did not undertake mass political organization and action. Finally, the most influential and destructive force among the Muslims was its secular, elite leadership. Islamically uncommitted, they turned to the West in politics, economics, law, and education. Secular elites constituted indigenous, domestic colonizers, responsible for the westernization of Muslim society. As Muhammad al-Ghazzali, a Muslim Brother, wrote: "The faction which works for the separation of Egypt from Islam is really a shameless, pernicious, and perverse group of puppets and slaves of Europe."[42]

Yet the Brotherhood charged that faith in the West was misplaced; the West had failed miserably. Parliamentary government and democracy were simply manipulated by the upper class to control the masses. Concentration of political power was accompanied by that of wealth and resources. Western democracy had not countered but contributed to continued economic exploitation, corruption, and social injustice by landlords, as well as by new "modern" elites. Western secularism and materialism undermined religion and morality and thus weakened the fabric of society in general and the Muslim family in particular. Finally, despite Egypt's uncritical dependence upon and subservience to the West, the West had betrayed the Arabs in its support for Israeli occupation of Palestine.

The Brotherhood believed that neither Western capitalism nor atheistic communism could cure the diseased condition of the Muslim community. The only answer was a return to Islam, which provided the revealed ideological alternative for Muslims.

There are two huge blocs: the Communist Bloc in the East and the Capitalist Bloc in the West. Each disseminates deceptive propaganda throughout the world claiming that there are only two alternative views of the world, Communism and Capitalism, and that other nations have no alternative but to ally themselves with one bloc or the other. . . . We have recently experienced in Palestine that neither the Eastern Bloc nor the Western Bloc give any credence to the values they advocate, or consider us ourselves as of consequence. . . . We will receive no mercy from either bloc.[43]

The Islamic alternative is "a divine vision that proceeds from God in all its particularities and its essentials. It is received by man in its perfect condition. . . . He is to appropriate it and implement all its essentials in his life."[44]

Implementation of the Islamic model is an imperative that demands the restoration of Islam through a return to the Quran and the *Sunnah* of the Prophet. For both Hasan al-Banna and Sayyid Qutb, the task of modern Muslims is nothing less than a great *jihad* against the enemies of Islam to reestablish a true Islamic territory, or rule, which is the prerequisite for following the Islamic way of life. Such an Islamic revival would assure the restoration of Islamic ascendency in the world. Any other form of government, whether foreign dominated or under Muslim control, is illegitimate and thus a non-Islamic territory, an object of holy war. Muslims who stand in the way of implementing an Islamic government are themselves unbelievers and therefore enemies of God and the state, objects of *jihad*.

Ideologically, the Brotherhood emphasized the union of religion and society in Islam. This belief was grounded in the unity of God and his supreme sovereignty over all His creation: "If Islam is to be effective, it is inevitable that it must rule. This religion did not come only to remain in the corners of places of worship. It has come that it may govern life and administer it and mold society according to its total image of life, not by preaching or guidance alone but also by setting of laws and regulations."[45]

God's will for his creation is embodied in the *Shariah*, which provides the comprehensive blueprint for Muslim society. Emphasizing the universality of the Islamic community and its mission, the Muslim Brotherhood rejected nationalism, whether liberal nationalism or Arab nationalism, and called for an Islamic state governed by the *Shariah*. While open to modern science and technology, the Brotherhood renounced the dependence of Muslim intellectuals and of Muslim governments upon the West. Instead of westernization and secularization, the renewal of Muslim society must be rooted in Islamic principles and values: "Until recently, writers, intellectuals, scholars, and governments glorified the principles of European civilization . . . adopted a Western style and manner. . . . Today, on the contrary, the wind has changed. . . . Voices are raised . . . for a return to the principles, teachings, and ways of Islam . . . for initiating the reconciliation of modern life with these principles, as a prelude to a final Islamization."[46]

For many the Brotherhood critique of both the West and the Egyptian society rang true and seemed a ray of hope in a society gripped by disillusionment and cynicism. They appealed not only to the religiously devout but also to those Egyptian elites whose initial faith in liberal nationalism had been deeply shaken. The disastrous defeat of the Arabs in Palestine, the establishment of the Israeli state with U.S. support, the continued failure of the Egyptian government to rid itself of its British occupiers, the massive unemployment and poverty of post–World War II Egypt, and the rampant political corruption moved many former protagonists of Western culture to reassess their position, so much so that by the 1940s "the whole Egyptian literary endeavor came to be dominated by works on Muslim subjects."[47] In particular, authors looked to Muhammad and the heroes and the victories of early Islam for inspiration and values. Native rather than foreign soil became the source for historic identity, pride, and values. In this climate of disillusionment and disaffection, the Muslim Brotherhood offered a well organized and politically mobilized viable opposition movement.

Traditional Islamic categories were used to describe the two options open to mankind today: ignorance and Islam. The former, which had been used by Muslims to describe pre-Islamic Arabian society, was extended to apply to the blind condition of non-Muslims and Western-oriented Muslims who had compromised themselves. They uncritically emulate everything they see. The other option, Islam, is the divinely mandated alternative to Western capitalism and Eastern communism: "Islam alone has remained preserved in its principles. Its sources have not been polluted, nor has its truth been superimposed on falsehood."[48] The Islamic vision is divinely ordained and unique: "of such comprehensiveness and breadth, of precision and depth, of authenticity and integratedness that it rejects every foreign element."[49]

The Muslim Brotherhood called for an Islamic revolution; it offered a theology of liberation. If Muslims were to restore Islamic ascendency, they must return to Islam, to the straight path of a comprehensive way of life. The task at hand required nothing less than a holy war against the enemies of Islam. These included both the forces of Western Christian imperialism and of Muslim westernizers—both were the oppressors, both were guilty of unbelief. The faithful Muslims, the true soldiers or holy warriors of Islam must band together in groups or societies for the struggle to implement Islam. Such Islamic societies or organizations are the leaven that will bring about the Islamization of the community.

The Brotherhood believed that, given the un-Islamic and anti-Islamic condition of modern Muslim societies, Islamic societies or organizations at first would, of necessity, be small vanguards of true believers. Like the early Muslims who were forced to withdraw from Mecca and emigrate to Medina, they also would experience oppression and would be compelled to withdraw from modern-day un-Islamic society. During this interim period of struggle, the Islamic societies must form their own separate community or family where, in a true, Islamic milieu, members could study and be formed to constitute the saving remnant, the nucleus of actors who were the agents of change, the implementers of the Islamization process. The true soldier of God must expect adversity as seen in the example of Muhammad and of all God's prophets. *Jihad* was a necessary component in the struggle against the enemies of God. Indeed Qutb came to divide society into two camps: the party of God and the party of Satan, those committed to the rule of God and the remainder who followed all other, un-Islamic, systems. Qutb was critical of Islamic modernists as well as those members of the religious establishment who downplayed *jihad* as armed struggle preferring to restrict it instead to moral self-discipline. Qutb reminded Muslims that the Quran mandated the waging of war where God's enemies prevented Islamic governance. Though they experienced persecution and martyrdom because God governs all creation, ultimate victory would be realized, that is, a new Islamic political order would be established based upon Islamic brotherhood and social justice and governed by God's law.

The Brotherhood believed that the introduction of the *Shariah* makes a government and society Islamic; therefore, implementation of Islamic law was a primary goal. The Muslim Brotherhood's understanding of *Shariah* was quite flexible. Muslims were not restricted to the formulations of the four Sunni law schools. These interpretations were themselves conditioned by their historical context and therefore open to revision. Sayyid Qutb distinguished between the eternal principles of the *Shariah* and the law regulations contained in the law books that were made by men, who applied the *Shariah* to specific historical and social situations. True renewal was not based on blind imitation of tradition but was open to fresh interpretation to meet the needs of the community. Thus, although eternal in nature and universal in scope, Islamic law remains flexible and open to development.

A guiding principle in Islamic legal reform is the general welfare of public interest. In addition the ruler can enact regulations to assure Islamic government. What assures the authenticity of Islamic law is its reference point, God, as opposed to temporal social needs or desires, as in the human legislation of secular societies. The *Shariah* of God provides the guiding principles that check all new interpretations. Moreover, the restoration of Islamic law will overcome the alienation from law that necessarily results from the adoption of Western codes, which were "inspired in an alien environment, with a different history, religion, conditions and needs. Unless the law is a response to the ethos and need of the masses, they will not be led by it nor will they be faithful to it."[50]

Because the Muslim Brotherhood is often characterized as a fundamentalist movement, it has been depicted as desiring to re-create a seventh-century Islamic state or government. In fact this is a gross distortion. The Brotherhood is fundamentalist in the sense that it called for a return to Islamic principles, which are timeless, but it did not necessarily advocate adopting a specific form of government. In its conception of both government and law, due recognition was given to the fact that specific institutions and regulations were created to meet particular sociohistorical situations. "The Islamic system is not restricted solely to a replica of the first Islamic society. . . . The Islamic system has room for scores of models which are compatible with the natural growth of society and the new needs of the contemporary age as long as the Islamic idea dominates these models in its expansive external perimeter."[51] Thus whether a particular form of government is Islamic is determined by implementation of the *Shariah*, which provides the framework for state and society.

In general the Muslim Brotherhood gave little attention to the specific form of an Islamic state. Rather, it provided general principles. Discussions of Islamic government tend to be theoretical, marked by a moral idealism, rather than practical. God is the sovereign ruler of the universe, the only true legislator. The Quran, therefore, is the fundamental constitution of the state. The temporal ruler receives his authority and power from God and is to administer and supervise, that is, to assure that society is governed by the *Shariah*. The ruler must be Muslim, male, sane, virtuous, and knowledgeable in Islamic jurisprudence. The method by which he is chosen by the people (direct or indirect selection or election) is not fixed, nor is his tenure in office, which may be for a fixed term or for life. In governing the ruler must follow the Quranic principle of consultation of the people (3:159). Thus there is a covenant, or social contract, between the ruler and the ruled, who have delegated authority to him. In this sense, Islamic government is democratic. The form that such consultation would take has not been given and therefore may vary. The consultative assembly may consist of a select number of Muslims or all Muslims, directly or indirectly selected or elected. Obedience is due a Muslim ruler who governs according to the *Shariah*. If he does not do so, then the covenant between the ruler and the people ceases. Such a ruler becomes an unbeliever and, according to the Quran (5:44), must be resisted.

Islam's comprehensive system includes the social as well as the political and legal aspects of life. While affirming that there is an Islamic social system, again the Brotherhood offered guidelines or limits rather than detailed models, principles rather than specific institutions.

At the heart of Muslim society is the family. The Brotherhood believed that the strength of the nation begins with the individual, is nurtured in the family, and blossoms into a strong and powerful nation. The central importance of the family was based upon the attention given to the Prophet's family and that of Ali as a paradigm for society and in the historic primacy of Muslim family law as the very heart of the *Shariah*. Given the family's role as the cornerstone of Muslim society, the Brotherhood viewed the status and role of women with special concern. It espoused the traditional Muslim position that

Islam had improved the status of women in Arabia, giving her marriage, divorce, and inheritance rights. Women were viewed as equal to men before God, but different. Because they believed men to be generally endowed with superior mental ability and emotional stability, men exercise political and social leadership and are responsible for women and the family. Women's primary sphere of activity is home and family. Therefore, education is important but with emphasis on those areas that best prepare Muslim women for their roles as wives and mothers. With this view of human nature, the Brotherhood deemed separation of sexes rather than coeducation preferable. Women may have careers in engineering, medicine, and law, where necessary; but special care must be given to a woman's dignity and modesty. Most importantly, career development should not obscure or hinder the realization of woman's natural and primary role: "The woman's natural place is in the home, but if she finds that after doing her duty in the home she has time, she can use part of it in the service of society, on condition that this is done within the legal limits which preserve her dignity and morality."[52]

For the Muslim Brotherhood, economic reform was imperative, both to assure Islamic social justice and to repel the forces of imperialism. Muslims, caught between the twin fallacies of capitalism and communism, must turn to the creation of an Islamic economic order. An Islamic economic system is based neither on unfettered individualism and conspicuous consumption nor on state socialism but upon Islam's integration of the material and the spiritual aspects of life. As in politics, so too in economics—God is the point of origin. All wealth, as all power, belongs to God. Man has a Quranic-mandated role as God's steward, or trustee. Muslims do not enjoy an absolute, unfettered right of ownership and wealth. This belongs to God alone. Individual rights are limited by God's law and the broader needs of the Islamic community. Certain means of acquiring wealth, such as usury and gambling, are prohibited, as are hoarding and the monopoly of natural resources. The Brotherhood strongly affirmed the right of private property in Islam as well as differences in wealth based upon personal initiative, hard work, and an individual's natural endowments and skills. However, wealth involves social duties as well. Muslims have a social obligation to assist fellow Muslims who are in need. The *zakat*, that is, wealth tax on capital as well as profits, is "the social pillar of Islam," the fundamental principle of Islamic social justice. Payment of the wealth tax is not simply a discretionary, charitable act but is based upon the right of the poor to assistance from their more fortunate cobelievers. Where social justice demands, the state may even limit the individual's right of private ownership in the public interest through government land reform and nationalization of public utilities, banks, and mineral resources. Thus the Muslim Brotherhood maintained that Islam provided its own distinctive approach and basis for a social revolution that would bring about true social equity.

The political and social program of the Brotherhood, however, was never realized. Indeed the ruthless suppression of the Brethren by Nasser in 1965 led many to believe that the movement had been effectively extinguished. Few would have anticipated its return and revival in Egypt nor its influence upon contemporary Islamic activists throughout the Muslim world.

The Jamaat-i-Islami

In South Asia a second major Islamic organization, the Jamaat-i-Islami (Islamic Society), developed under a contemporary of Hasan al-Banna, Mawlana Mawdudi (1903–79).[53] Mawlana Abul Ala Mawdudi was born in Aurangabad, in central India. His early upbringing and education were dominated by his father, who supervised his son's traditional religious education (Quran, *hadith*, *Shariah*, Islamic languages, and history). Modern education was assiduously eschewed, so that it was only later that Mawdudi learned English and studied modern subjects. Mawdudi pursued an early career as a journalist, and at twenty-one he became editor of *al-Jamiah* (1924–27), the newspaper of India's Jamiyyat i-Ulama (Association of Ulama). Like many other Indian Muslims, Mawdudi was active in the Khilafat Movement and the All-India National Congress. However, he progressively became convinced that the future of Indian Muslims was threatened not only by British imperialism but also by Hindu and Muslim nationalism.

Two particularly important events served as catalysts that motivated Mawdudi to assume an independent role as an Islamic leader and attempt to be a spokesman for an Islamic alternative for state and society. In 1925 Swami Shradhanand, leader of a Hindu revivalist movement (the Shudhi) was assassinated by a Muslim extremist who claimed it was a religious duty to kill nonbelievers. In the public controversy that followed, there were charges that Islam was a religion of the sword. As Ahmad Khan had responded to similar claims after the war of 1857, Mawdudi came to the defense of Islam. He wrote a series of articles that were published as a book, *War in Islam*, in 1927. Mawdudi not only discussed the Islamic attitude toward warfare but also presented in seminal form many of the themes that he would develop and explicate in his later writings on the Islamic state and society.

A second formative influence on Mawdudi was the Indian independence movement and, in particular, the question of Indian or Muslim nationalism. As previously discussed, during the 1930s when Hindus and Muslims strongly pressed for independence from Britain and the establishment of a separate state, Mawdudi had become increasingly critical of the options presented to Indian Muslims by both the Gandhi-led Congress Party and the Jinnah-led Muslim League. Aware of the reality of religious communalism in India, he shared the growing concern of most Muslims for the survival of their identity and way of life in a Hindu-dominated, albeit secular, state. He regarded Mahatma Gandhi's increasing reliance on Hindu beliefs such as truth-force and self-rule to express the ideology of the Indian nationalist movement as well as the Hindu communal approach to the 1937 elections as proof of fundamental Hindu-Muslim differences. In language strikingly similar to the "Two Nation Theory" of Muhammad Ali Jinnah, Mawdudi asserted that Muslims were a permanent community "based on specific moral and civic rules. We have some basic and inherent disagreements with the majority [Hindu] *qawm* [community] . . . so it is not possible to join ourselves into a single whole. . . . Their path and ours can run parallel, and can even come together in places, but they can never coincide."[54]

Mawdudi was equally critical of the Muslim nationalism of the Muslim League. As noted, he viewed nationalism as an imported ideology from the West, alien to Islam and ill suited as the basis for a so-called Muslim state. Muslim nationalism was ultimately idolatrous because nationalism emphasized popular sovereignty rather than divine sovereignty as well as secularism, or the separation of religion from the state. Moreover, its narrow particularism was contrary to the universalism of Islam and would further divide an already fragmented Islamic community. In addition Mawdudi objected to the potential Muslim League leadership of the proposed Muslim state because he regarded Jinnah and his associates as secular, westernized Muslims incapable of true Islamic leadership. Thus neither in its ideology nor in its leadership would the proposed Muslim state be Islamically acceptable. Mawdudi's convictions placed him at odds with most of India's leadership: secularists as well as Hindu and Muslim nationalists. He rejected the two dominant positions in the Indian subcontinent: Congress's call for an independent, united, secular Indian state as well as the Muslim League's proposal to partition India and establish Pakistan as a separate Muslim state.

Judging the nationalist options offered Indian Muslims unacceptable, Mawdudi believed that an Islamic revolution was necessary to establish an Islamic state and society. He advocated a gradual societal, rather than a violent, political, revolution. The Islamization of society was a prerequisite for establishing a true Islamic state. From the late 1930s onwards, Mawlana Mawdudi committed himself to the task of Islamic revivalism, in particular the training of Islamic leaders who might bring about the transformation of society. He developed and disseminated his interpretation of an Islamic alternative in the journal *Tarjuman al-Quran* (Exegesis of the Quran), whose editorship he assumed in 1934. The journal remained a major vehicle for his thought during subsequent years. Mawdudi's purpose and vision were reflected both in his exposition and interpretation of Islam in that journal and in his founding of the Jamaat-i-Islami (the Islamic Society). In the former, he set forth the principles of Islamic state and society; through the latter, he hoped to produce a band of committed and well-trained Muslims, a righteous society capable of implementing true Islam in the Indian subcontinent.

Mawdudi had moved from India to the Lahore area of what is now Pakistan in 1938 at the invitation of Muhammad Iqbal to establish the Dar al-Islam Academy at Pathenkot. In 1941, joined by seventy-five followers, he founded the Jamaat-i-Islami. Like the Muslim Brotherhood, the Jamaat was an ideological rather than a political party. Membership was strictly limited to those "righteous" Muslims whose understanding of Islam and religious integrity were proven and acceptable. Major emphasis was placed upon the formation and indoctrination of members. Mawdudi's interpretation of Islam provided the basis for instruction and guidance. In the prolific writings of Mawdudi, one finds the authoritative source of the Jamaat's Islamic ideology and its program. He was in every sense the *amir* (leader) of the Jamaat.

Although Mawdudi had objected to the establishment of Pakistan as a separate Muslim nation, after the partitioning of India, he accepted political reality and remained in what had become Pakistan. The Jamaat proceeded almost immediately to assert a position of leadership in the debate (1948–56) surrounding Pakistan's first constitution. As the new country's leaders sought to define and institutionalize Pakistan's ideology and system of government, the Jamaat pressed for the establishment of an Islamic state. In this effort, Mawdudi shared a common cause with most of the *ulama,* in particular, with their organization—the Jamiyyat i-Ulama-i-Pakistan (the Association of Pakistan's Ulama)—and with the general public for whom Jinnah's Muslim homeland and an Islamic state were interchangeable terms. From 1948 to the present, the ideas of Mawdudi and the Jamaat-i-Islami have remained active in Pakistan's politics, often, as we shall see in the next chapter, in opposition to the government, pressing for its vision of an Islamic state. At the same time, the Jamaat's mission and influence has extended beyond Pakistan. Through distribution of its literature and its widespread activities, it has advocated and disseminated its message internationally. Mawdudi, like Sayyid Qutb, who borrowed extensively from Mawdudi, has been a major influence on contemporary Islamic revivalism.

Mawdudi's outlook and method differed from that of both Muslim secular elites and Islamic modernists. Unlike the former, he did not look to the West for the models of modern political and social development; in contrast to the latter, he did not seek an Islamic rationale for the appropriation of Western science and technology. Rather, like Rashid Rida and the Muslim Brotherhood, he asserted the self-sufficiency of Islam as the source for Islamic renewal and reform. Mawdudi emphasized the universalism of Islam and the comprehensiveness of Islamic life. This position was at the heart of his rejection of nationalism and secularism. Unlike the Muslim Brotherhood, the Jamaat-i-Islami, through the writings of Mawdudi, has attempted to provide a theoretical blueprint for what Mawdudi saw as a revival or "Islamic revolution" in Muslim society. The character and extended parameters of this blueprint are reflected in the titles of such works as *The Process of Islamic Revolution, Nationalism in India, The Islamic Way of Life, First Principles of the Islamic State, Islamic Law and Constitution,* and *Economic Problem of Man and Its Islamic Solution.* Mawdudi's writings have been translated and distributed across the Islamic world and may be found in bookshops and stalls from Cairo to Jakarta.

Given the propagation of Mawdudi's Islamic vision and its impact on contemporary Islamic revivalism, an understanding of his interpretation of Islam is essential.

For Mawdudi the foundational principle of an Islamic state and society is the doctrine of the unity and universal sovereignty of God. "The belief in the Unity and the sovereignty of Allah is the foundation of the social and moral system propounded by the Prophets."[55] As the creator, sustainer, and ruler of the universe is one, so too is God's law which governs all creation. All of reality—all areas of life—come from God and are subject to his sovereign law, *Shariah:* "The *Shariah* is a complete scheme of life and an all-embracing social order."[56] Thus the comprehensiveness of the Islamic way of life is rooted in the unity and totality of God's law revealed in the Quran and the example (*Sunnah*) of the Prophet. It is this organic relationship between religion, politics, and society that distinguishes Islam and the Islamic community from the West. Separation of religion from the state for Mawdudi represents the inherent fallacy of Western secularism, where the withdrawal of divine guidance has been the basis for its moral decline and its ultimate downfall. Western culture and all who do not follow Islam, God's revealed straight path, exist as did pre-Islamic society in a state of ignorance and darkness.

Mawdudi emphasized that Muslims' vocation must be to live within the limits and according to the precepts of the *Shariah* in its entirety. A *Shariah*-governed community constitutes an Islamic state. While Muslims such as the great Islamic jurists of the law schools may discern and apply God's law, God alone is the supreme lawgiver, the source of all authority and law. Thus there can be no human lawgiver. However, despite an interdict on human legislation, Mawdudi does acknowledge the role of the state not only to enforce but also to create laws in areas not covered by the *Shariah*. The state can do this by virtue of its role as God's agent, or vicegerent. For Mawdudi the Quranic teaching regarding man's vicegerency (Quran 24:55) encompasses both the individual and the communal Muslim mission on earth. All Muslims are God's vicegerents or representatives (caliphs). Thus an Islamic state may quite accurately be called a "caliphate." The ruler (caliph, *imam*, *amir*) is the one whom the community has delegated as their leader. The head of state, or *amir*, receives his authority from God and exercises his power on behalf of the people. As with the Rightly Guided Caliphs, he may be elected or selected by the people, directly or indirectly, through their representatives. He is the representative of both God and his fellow Muslims: "answerable to God on the one hand and on the other to his fellow caliphs who have delegated their authority to him."[57] The ruler oversees the conduct of state: the executive, legislative, and judiciary. His power would include that of both the president and the prime minister of a modern state. Yet, because the ruler is bound to observe and enforce God's law, he does not have an absolute power and authority. He is neither monarch nor dictator.

According to Mawdudi, the legal qualifications for head of state are that he must be Muslim, male, adult, sane, and a citizen of the Islamic state. More importantly he should be the best man, that is, the most committed and virtuous Muslim. The idealism of Mawdudi's approach is further reflected in his assertion that this "best man" can neither seek office nor undertake a political campaign. Rather, suitable candidates will be identified by some kind of election or selection committee. The utopianism of Mawdudi's thought is strikingly evident in his assertions that in the time of the early caliphs there was no dissension, only complete harmony: "the Ministers and the Head of State were all along working in complete cooperation and harmony and the question of anybody resigning in protest never arose at all."[58]

Mawdudi's Islamic idealism also gave rise to an "Islamic totalitarianism." Given the comprehensive nature of the Islamic state's divinely revealed law, "no one can regard any field of his affairs as personal or private."[59] Is this not totalitarianism? Mawdudi answered with a qualified yes. The totalitarianism of an Islamic state is a good form of totalitarianism because it requires and enforces God's precepts. Unfortunately, Mawdudi did not indicate how Muslims can safeguard against rulers who falsely use the banner of Islam to legitimate their rule, impose their will, and stifle dissent.

The Islamic state was viewed by Mawdudi as the "very antithesis of secular Western democracy."[60] Western democracy is based upon popular sovereignty, with the people or nation enjoying absolute powers of legislation and thus able to make laws which are even contrary to religion and morality. For this reason, "Islam has no trace of Western democracy. . . . [It] repudiates the philosophy of popular sovereignty and rears its polity on the foundations of the sovereignty of God and the vicegerency (*khilafah*) of man" (p. 160).

Mawdudi concluded that the Islamic system might best be called a theo-democracy. He used this term to distinguish the Islamic state as the "Kingdom of God" from the Western meaning of theocracy, which also implies rule by a religious class or clergy. Here Mawdudi rejected any notion of *ulama* governance of the state. Furthermore, as a theo-democracy, while affirming the political role of all Muslims, the state was protected from, what Mawdudi called, the "tyranny of the masses" permitted by Western democracy. Because Islamic democracy must function within the limits of God, no law that is contrary to the *Shariah* may be passed, even though it may enjoy mass support. Mawdudi was skeptical about the ability of most people to transcend their narrow self-interest: "the great mass of the common people are incapable of perceiving their own true interests" (p. 134). He cites the repeal of the Prohibition Act in America as an example. Despite alcohol's proven danger to physical and mental health, those who voted for prohibition subsequently revolted against it and so, Mawdudi asserted, the law was finally repealed by the very people who had voted for it (p. 137). Mawdudi believed that this problem could not occur in an Islamic state, which is governed by religious norms, not societal whims.

Popular vicegerency in an Islamic state is reflected especially in the doctrine of mutual consultation (*shura*). Because all sane adult Muslims, male and female, are vicegerents (agents of God), it is they who delegate their authority to the ruler and whose opinion must also be sought in the conduct of state. This may be done, directly or indirectly, through an elected representative body, or assembly. Thus the head of an Islamic state is not free to do as he likes. According to Mawdudi, the consultative assembly, or parliament, should consist of adult Muslim males who are good Muslims and sufficiently Islamically trained to interpret and apply the *Shariah* as well as to draft laws that are not contrary to the Quran and *Sunnah* of the Prophet.

The functions of the parliament are fourfold: (1) to enact legislation that embodies the explicit directives of God and Muhammad as well as regulations that will assure their proper enforcement; (2) where differing interpretations of the Quran and *Sunnah* exist, to decide which interpretation is to be enacted; (3) when no explicit directives exist, to deduce rules from the Quran and *Sunnah* or where previously enacted laws are found in the legal manuals to adopt one of them; (4) finally, where "even basic guidance is not available," to formulate laws provided such legislation is not contrary to the letter and spirit of the *Shariah*.[61]

Given the ideological nature of the state and the functions of the parliament in an Islamic state, Mawdudi believed the vast majority of its members should be Muslim. While non-Muslims may elect their own representatives, this should be done through a system of separate electorates so that non-Muslims would be excluded from the selection of Muslim representatives. Mawdudi suggested another possible alternative for both non-Muslims and Muslim women, who were not eligible for election. Each might have their own consultative assembly; each could then advise the ruler and the parliament on those issues that affected their lives and welfare.

Mawdudi's notion of citizenship in an Islamic state and the rights of non-Muslims followed rigorously from early Islamic practice and medieval Islamic political theory. There are two categories of citizenship in a modern Islamic state: Muslim and non-Muslim. Non-Muslims are "protected people" (*dhimmi*). In return for payment of the poll tax, they enjoy protection and have certain rights and duties. They may worship but not proselytize. In religious matters, they are governed by their religious leaders. However, in all other areas of life, Islamic law prevails because it is the "Law which commands the approval of the majority alone [which] has the right to become the Law of the Land."[62] Because an Islamic state is an ideological state, only those who accept that ideology should run the state. Therefore, non-Muslims would be barred both from key administrative positions and from policy-making posts. Moreover, they should not serve in a standing army because, as nonbelievers, they could not be expected to defend Islam.

For Mawdudi herein lies the difference between a national state and an Islamic state. For the former, citizenship is based upon belonging to a nation, race, ethnic group. For the latter, citizenship is determined by ideology (belief or unbelief). Therefore, citizenship is not equal and the same for all. Rather, citizens are classified as Muslim or non-Muslim and, as a result, differ in their rights and duties.

Preservation of an Islamic state may necessitate and even require a holy war. Mawdudi believed that *jihad* is an obligation for the faithful Muslim citizen. He began with the broad definition of *jihad* as the duty of all Muslims to strive or struggle to actualize God's will. "Those who believe fight in the cause of God, and those who disbelieve fight in the cause of force" (Quran: IV:76). He viewed two kinds of warfare as permissible: defensive *jihad* and corrective *jihad*. These became necessary when Islamic belief and practice were threatened by an external enemy, by disruptive internal forces, or by non-Muslim rulers in a non-Islamic state. While many modern Muslims prefer simply to emphasize the meaning of *jihad* as an internal struggle to lead a virtuous Muslim life, Mawdudi did not shrink from affirming the continuing division of the world into Islamic and non-Islamic territory and the right, indeed duty, of a good Muslim to wage war when Islam and the Islamic way of life were threatened.

For Mawlana Mawdudi and the Jamaat-i-Islami, as for the Muslim Brotherhood, the Islamic community in the twentieth century was at a critical crossroads. Like secular modernists and Islamic reformers, they acknowledged the internal weakness of the Muslim community, the external threat of Western imperialism, and accepted science and technology. However, unlike secularist and Islamic reformers, the Brotherhood and the Jamaat were more sweeping in their condemnation of the West and their assertion of the total self-sufficiency of Islam. While secularists might reject Western political hegemony, they looked to the West in charting their future. Islamic reformers sought to provide an Islamic rationale for a selective borrowing from the West. However, Islamic movements like the Brotherhood and the Jamaat tend to view their options more clearly and simply. Both capitalism and Marxism represented man-made Western secular paths that were alien to the God-ordained, straight path of Islam. If Muslims were to remain faithful to God and His divine will, they must reject Western secularism and materialism and return solely to Islam, whose perfection assured guidance in all aspects of life.

Conclusion

During the postindependence period, newly emergent Muslim states faced a formidable task. For most the process of modern nation building followed a long period of colonial political and military domination and economic dependence. Their recent colonial experience by the West had been preceded by a centuries-long Islamic imperial past. For modern elites, their Islamic heritage was, though perhaps still valid for spiritual life, no longer relevant to the needs and requirements of modern politics and society. Because modernization and industrialization had originated in the West, Western nations had had several centuries to grapple with questions of religious reform and modern nation building. Issues of national identity and ideology, the development of appropriate institutions of government and law had been hammered out, if not fully then at least adequately. Despite the strains of post-Enlightenment rationalism and the industrial revolution, change had occurred within the context of Western history and tradition. Muslim leaders were faced, however, with a compressed time frame of decades rather than centuries and with models for modern development that were indeed "alien," of foreign origin. Ataturk's secular path and Saudi Arabia's "Islamic" path provided polar solutions, enforced by autocratic rulers. For many other Muslim countries such as Egypt, Syria, Libya, or Pakistan, the inherited colonial patterns were carried over and augmented by those alterations that suited the state's needs or the personal preferences of their rulers. Though heavily indebted to Western models, Islam was selectively employed where deemed necessary or useful. But for Islamic organizations like the Muslim Brotherhood and the Jamaat-i-Islami, modern states in the Muslim world were doomed to failure as long as they looked to the West and failed to root their identity and sociopolitical development directly in Islam. Thus they spoke of the third Islamic alternative, indeed as if it were an imperative. Few people would have guessed that, in the decade of the 1970s, Islam would reemerge in Muslim politics across the Islamic world to such a marked degree that scholars, journalists, and government analysts would employ phrases like "Islamic resurgence," "Islamic revival," and "the rise of militant Islam" to describe this new and unexpected phenomenon.

$\cdots$ *5* $\cdots$

Contemporary Politics

*P*olitical events in the Muslim world during the final quarter of
the twentieth century dramatically draw attention to the political and social potential of Islam. Contrary to accepted norms of political development, with its secular presuppositions, and the expectations
of many analysts, religion did not recede in the Muslim world but
rather reemerged in the politics of countries such as Iran, Pakistan,
Egypt, Afghanistan, Saudi Arabia, Syria, and Malaysia.[1]

Islamic ideology, symbols, slogans, and actors became prominent
fixtures in Muslim politics. Iran established an Islamic republic, and
Pakistan recommitted itself to the implementation of a more Islamic
system of government. Islamic laws, dress, taxes, and punishments
were introduced in many Muslim countries. Both incumbent governments and opposition movements often competed with one another
in declaring their allegiance to Islam and their commitment to a more
Islamic way of life. Islamic politics, economics, law, and education
became hotly contested issues. But amidst the diverse manifestations
of Islamic revivalism, with its common sociopolitical concerns and
themes, there prevails a general consensus that Muslims have failed
to produce a viable political and social synthesis that is both modern
and true to their history and values. Among the shared concerns of
Islamic activists' sociopolitical thought were the continued impotence
of Muslim society (i.e., the failure and ineffectiveness of Muslim governments and nationalist ideologies), a disillusionment with the West,
and the desire to articulate a more authentic identity.

If Islam's glorious political and cultural past had been reversed by European colonial rule, political independence had not significantly improved the political and socioeconomic condition of Muslim countries. Most continued to be subservient to the West both politically and culturally. European colonialism was replaced by American neocolonialism as represented by America's foreign policies, military presence, and multinational companies. Moreover, political leaders failed to establish a legitimate, effective public order and to address adequately the profound socioeconomic disparities in wealth and class in most Muslim countries. This sense of disillusionment and failure was reflected in Muslim literature in the late 1960s, in its growing criticism of the West and its concern to reclaim historical and cultural identity.[2]

For the religiously oriented, the problem had always been clear — departure from the straight path of Islam was doomed to failure. For Western-oriented intellectuals and elites, the disillusionment was more unsettling. They had embraced the West as both an ally and a model for modern development. The establishment of Israel, continued massive American economic and military aid for Israel, support for regimes like that of the shah of Iran, and the failures of Muslim governments posed a direct challenge to those Muslims who had espoused Western-oriented positions.

The complete and decisive nature of the Arab defeat at the hands of Israel in 1967 shattered faith and confidence in the West and in Arab nationalism. The defeat in 1967 was the most vivid confirmation, in Muslim eyes and before the world, of political and military impotence. Despite national independence, the centuries-long decline of Muslim power and prestige had not been reversed but, in fact, seemed to have reached its nadir. From the establishment of Israel, Arab forces had lost in a series of military confrontations. However, Egyptian and Syrian forces were now defeated with lightning speed by Israel's preemptive strike that destroyed much of the Arab forces before they could even respond and left Egypt and Syria in a state of debilitated paralysis. The trauma of the 1967 war in the Arab world was vividly reflected by its common reference in literature as the "disaster."

The result was a protracted period of soul-searching self-criticism: What had gone wrong? Why did Muslim countries remain weak and subservient to the West and Israel, its "Middle East colony." For the

Islamically oriented, there were two questions: "What had the Muslims continued to do wrong that Divine guidance seemed so absent?" and "Could it be that Islam was the cause of Muslim backwardness, that it was unable to respond to modernity?" For Western-oriented Muslims, the questions were different but no less troubling: "Despite their confidence in the West, why had they remained so impotent?" and "Why did the West continue to favor Israel over the Arabs?"

The self-criticism and disillusionment with the West was accompanied by an increased emphasis on the need for greater self-reliance, a desire to reclaim one's past and to root individual and national self-identity more indigenously, to find pride and strength in an Islamic past and cultural tradition that had once been a dominant world civilization. This quest for greater authenticity was reflected in popular and intellectual as well as religious literature, where there was a confluence of concerns on such topics as religion, tradition, and values, politics and ideology, language and education.[3] All became part of a general call for a religiocultural revival, reform, or renaissance.

The year 1973 proved to be decisive, providing a sign that Muslim fortunes were indeed changing. The Arab-Israeli war of 1973 and the Arab oil boycott became major sources of Muslim pride. The Arab defeat of 1967 was reversed by the "Islamic victory" in the October War of 1973 with Israel. For Arabs the ability and success of Egyptian forces were established even if final victory had been thwarted by massive American assistance to Israel. The war and thus the "victory" had been placed in an Islamic context. Islamic symbols and slogans were emphasized; from its name, the Ramadan War; its battle cry, *Allahu Akbar!* ("God is Most Great"); and its code name, *Badr,* Muhammad's first victory over his Meccan opponents. For many the victory, coupled with the oil boycott's demonstration of Arab (Muslim) economic power, instilled a new sense of pride and strengthened a commitment to their Islamic identity. The return of power and wealth, lost during the colonial period, seemed a sign from God and the revival of Islamic ascendancy.

Although there are distinctive differences among Islamic revivalists, they share both a common Islamic heritage and confrontation with Western political and cultural imperialism. Common themes in Islamic politics and sociopolitical thought may be identified as (1) the failure of the West—that is, the inappropriateness of transplanted, imported Western models of political, social, and economic develop-

ment—and the need to throw off Western political and cultural domination, which fosters secularism, materialism, and spiritual bank-
ruptcy; (2) the need to "return to Islam" in order to restore a lost
identity, moral purpose, and character; (3) an emphasis on the unity
and totality of Islam, rooted in the doctrine of the unity of God (*tawhid*), which is the belief that religion is integral to politics and society
because Islam is both religion and government; and (4) a call for the
reintroduction of *Shariah* law as the sine qua non for establishing a
more Islamic state and society.

Despite the unity of faith and commonality of general concerns,
the character and manifestations of the Islamic resurgence have varied significantly, reflecting each country's specific history and politics.
The examples of Libya, Pakistan, Iran, Egypt, Sudan, and Lebanon
amply illustrate the complexity of contemporary Islamic politics. Islamic vision is translated into reality. Differences in context as well as
understanding and interpretation have resulted in divergent experiences.

Libya

On September 1, 1969, the government of King Idris (1890–1983) was
overthrown by a clique of junior military officers headed by a young
army lieutenant. Since that day, Muammar al-Qaddafi (b. 1942) has
been the principal architect of modern day Libya.[4]

Libya had been a monarchy ruled by the grandson of Muhammad Ali ibn al-Sanusi (1787–1859), founder of the Sanusiyyah Sufi
Order. As discussed in chapter 2, the Sanusiyyah, like other eigh-
teenth- and nineteenth-century Islamic reform movements such as the
Wahhabi in Saudi Arabia and the Mahdi in the Sudan, had united
tribes in what today is Libya, Chad, and western Egypt into a movement that sought to purify Islamic practice and establish an Islamic
state and society. During the early twentieth century (1911–30), however, Italy progressively extended its colonial rule over Libya. Under
Idris, the grandson of the Grand Sanusi, the Sanusiyyah led the resistance to Italian forces, with encouragement from Great Britain. Although Italy had effectively subdued Libya by 1930, the Sanusiyyah
fought on as an Islamic resistance movement. To counter their Islamic
opposition, the Italians cultivated the non-Sanusi religious establishment, providing generous government support for the *ulama* and for
Islamic education. Moreover, in 1937 Benito Mussolini even pro-

claimed himself "the protector of Islam."[5] The *ulama*, who had fared less well under their Sufi Sanusi competitors, cooperated with the Italians.

After Italy's defeat in World War II, its hold in Libya came to an end, and Libya gained its independence in 1951. Idris, who had been living in exile in Cairo, returned as Idris I, king of an independent Libya. Although King Idris was a descendant of the founder of the Sanusiyyah, Libya was in fact more a Muslim than an Islamic state. And although the legitimacy of the monarchy and its Islamic character rested upon King Idris's position as head of the Sanusiyyah Sufi Order, yet with few exceptions, Libya's law and its government were inspired by the West. Libya's legal system was based upon French and Italian legal codes, not on Islamic law. The Islamic courts were absorbed under a united national judicial system. Only Muslim family law remained in force. The *ulama*, who were viewed as having collaborated with the Italians, were incorporated within the bureaucracy and thus controlled by the state. The royal family was assisted by a small coterie of prominent families and Sanusi religious leaders in governing Libya.

Libya's modern development has been profoundly affected by two events. In 1959 oil was discovered, and so this poor nation of one million inhabitants, which had been economically dependent upon Britain and America, became a leading oil producer within a decade. The second dramatic event was the coup d'état in 1969 that brought Muammar al-Qaddafi to power. As with similar revolutionary movements during the late 1950s and early 1960s in Egypt, Syria, Iraq, and Algeria, the rationale for seizure of power was socioeconomic reform necessitated by the failure of Libya's liberal, Western-influenced monarchy. Under Muammar al-Qaddafi, three interrelated ideas were woven into Libya's ideological identity: pan-Arabism, socialism, and Islam.

Qaddafi had long been strongly influenced by Egypt's Gamal Abd al-Nasser. For Qaddafi Nasser was the hero of Arab nationalism who rejected Western imperialism, called for Arab unity, reestablished Egyptian and Arab pride and identity on its own cultural foundations, and tried to right the socioeconomic inequities of Arab feudalism through planned socialism. Nasser and Egypt provided a model for the early stages of the Libyan revolution as seen in its self-designation as the "Free Officers" revolution; its Nasserite slogan of "free-

dom, socialism, unity," its provisional constitution; and its single
party, the Arab Socialist Union. It was not long, however, before Qaddafi, at the head of the Revolutionary Command Council, turned to
Islam for popular support and legitimation. Given Qaddafi's personal
piety and the religious revivalist (Sanusi) character of Libya's national
history, such a move was not surprising.

In late 1969, Qaddafi announced his intention to reinstitute Islamic law as a first step in what appeared to be the Islamization of
state and society. Qaddafi seemed to be placing Libya on a path of
Arabization and Islamization. In addition Nasser's untimely death in
1970 at the age of fifty-two created a void that Qaddafi tried to fill.
Qaddafi combined Arab nationalism and socialism with his own
brand of Islamic fundamentalism:

> Our socialism is both Arab and Islamic. We stand midway between
> socialism and communism and socialism and capitalism. Our social-
> ism springs directly from the needs and requirements of the Arab
> world, its heritage, and the needs of society. It consists of a social
> justice which means sufficiency in production and just distribution.
> These principles are to be found in the Islamic religion, and partic-
> ularly in the law of *zakat* (alms).[6]

Qaddafi took up the banner of Arab socialism and relied heavily
upon an Islamic rationale both to legitimate his domestic reforms and
to assert his pan-Arab as well as pan-Islamic leadership. During the
1970s, both within Libya and abroad, the new "Arab Republic of
Libya" was viewed as an Arab-Islamic state. The early statements of
the new government placed Libya on an Islamically legitimated, Arab
socialist path. Distinguishing itself from Marxism, the state's social
policy, Qaddafi declared, was the socialism of Islam: "a socialism emanating from the true religion of Islam and its Noble Book."[7] Though
strongly influenced by Nasser, Qaddafi went beyond his hero in emphasizing the Islamic component of his ideology.

Qaddafi's Appeal to Islam

A series of well-publicized reforms implementing Libya's Arab-
Islamic identity and orientation were instituted. In reasserting Libya's
heritage, vestiges of a Christian European colonial past were suppressed. Churches and cathedrals were closed; foreign missionary

activities were banned. Arabic was required in all government transactions, and Arabic names and street signs replaced their Western counterparts. Islamic measures prohibiting gambling, nightclubs, and alcohol were introduced. Islamization of state and society seemed near in October 1971, when a law commission was established to review all Libyan law in order to bring it into conformity with Islam. In 1972 several Islamic laws were introduced. Canonically mandated criminal penalties (the *hudud*, "limits" of God) were reinstated: amputation for theft, stoning for fornication and adultery. Several other Islamic regulations that affected the collection of the alms tax and the banning of banking interest were announced. Despite the rhetoric and activity, however, their implementation was limited. In fact if closely examined, despite much fanfare by the Libyan government and the Western press, Islamic law remained relatively peripheral to Libyan society.

Islam became an important element both in domestic and in foreign policy. Like Saudi Arabia, Libya under Qaddafi combined appeals to Islamic solidarity with oil wealth to promote its role as a leader in the Islamic world. He did this within a context in which a number of events in the Muslim world had led to greater emphasis upon Islamic identity, brotherhood, and solidarity. Reeling from their humiliating defeat in the 1967 Arab-Israeli war and loss of Jerusalem, Muslims throughout the world were stunned and outraged in 1969 by the desecration of the al-Aqsa Mosque in Jerusalem. A deranged European Christian tourist had set fire to the mosque, one of the holiest shrines in Islam; however, many Muslims believed the Israelis were responsible or could have prevented it. In response to the al-Aqsa fire, the first Islamic summit was held in Rabat, Morocco, in 1969. This was followed in 1970 by the first Islamic Foreign Ministers' Conference in Jeddah, Saudi Arabia, which resulted in the formation of the Organization of the Islamic Conference (OIC) in 1972.

Within this international context of renewed emphasis upon Islamic identity and solidarity, Libya's Revolutionary Command Council established the Islamic Call Society. Its goal was not simply the preaching and promotion of Islam domestically but its spread internationally as an integral part of Libyan foreign policy. Mass media, religious publications, missionary activities, mosque building as well as medical and social welfare services were among the main tools for the spread of Libyan political and religious influence. Combining diplomacy with the activities of the Islamic Call Society, Libya in the 1970s and early 1980s competed with Saudi Arabia in its use of Islam, using its petrodollars to extend its influence from Muslim student groups to liberation movements. Thus, for example, in the early 1970s Libya provided one of the first and the strongest supports for separatist Muslim groups in the southern Philippines by expanding aid for religious activities and refugees to military and diplomatic support.[8] Libya gave sanctuary to leaders of the Bangsa Moro Liberation organization (BMLA) and the Moro National Liberation Movement (MNLF). Along with the Saudi-based OIC, it successfully pressured the Philippine government to negotiate with Muslim leaders; the result was the Tripoli Agreement of December 1976.[9]

By the 1980s, many governments in Africa, which had been a major focus area of Libyan activity, no longer regarded Libya and the Islamic Call Society as welcome sources of development funds and greater Islamic solidarity; instead, because of their political involvement and support for militant Islamic activists and revolutionary groups, they were considered a threat to security and stability.[10] Thus Libya's influence and its effective export of Islam waned in the 1980s in many parts of the world as governments and Islamic organizations became leery of its tactics and as its oil revenues dried up.

Qaddafi's reliance upon Islam in domestic and foreign affairs was rooted in his own distinctive brand of Islam. By 1975, with the publication of *The Green Book*, it had become clear that Libya's Islamic character and Qaddafi's world theory or "Third Way" were owing neither to Sanusi (Sufi) Islam nor to the Islam of the *ulama* but rather to Colonel Qaddafi's own idiosyncratic interpretation of Islam and the world. The title of Qaddafi's tract relied on a number of religious and historical considerations to broaden its appeal. Green is traditionally regarded as the color of the Prophet and of Islam. Islamic belief lays great emphasis on peoples who possess a book, that is, God's revelation as a guide for society. Muslims have their book, the Quran, as do Jews and Christians who are regarded as "People of the Book." Thus the title *The Green Book* gave it an aura of Islamic legitimacy. It also pointedly contrasted its blueprint for society and cultural revolution with that of Mao Tse-tung's Red Book and cultural revolution in China.

The Green Book is a series of three small volumes: "The Solution to the Problem of Democracy" (1975), "Solution of the Economic Problem: Socialism" (1977), and "Social Basis of the Third International Theory" (1979). It is taught in the schools, required reading for all Libyan citizens, and propagated through the innumerable wall posters that seem to dominate the Libyan landscape. It is in *The Green Book* that Qaddafi presented his alternative to Western imperialism. In contradistinction to capitalism and communism, Qaddafi offered his "Third Way" or "Third International Theory" that was to provide the blueprint for Libyan society, an example to the Arab world, and more broadly to the Third World. As he stated in a *New York Times Magazine* interview with Oriana Fallaci (December 16, 1979), "*The Green Book* is the guide to the emancipation of man . . . the new gospel. The gospel of the new era, the era of the masses."

For Qaddafi colonialism caused the Arabs to forget and doubt their cultural identity and values, to become like the pagans to whom God had sent his messengers—peoples for whom religion and morality are dismissed as fables and reactionism. Both the Soviets and the West are the culprits: "Both the East and West want to corrupt us from within, obliterate every distinguishing mark of our personality and snuff out the light [religion] which guides us."[11]

To counter this threat, Qaddafi set forth a theory whose focus, he claimed, was the Quran, the perfect book and comprehensive guide: "We must take the Quran as the focal point in our journey in life because the Quran is perfect; it is light and in it are solutions to the problems of man . . . from personal status . . . to international problems."[12] Qaddafi asserted a continuity between Libya's new social revolution and Islam's glorious past. Though the bulk of *The Green Book* is not overtly Islamic, he drew upon the major themes of Islamic renewal and reform, similar to those found in the eighteenth- and nineteenth-century reform movements. As a result, Qaddafi's experiment also provides a bridge to the contemporary political revival of Islam.

Qaddafi's assessment of the Arab world's plight is cast in the categories of traditional Islamic revivalism: the decline of the community caused by departure from religion and cured by a return to the true path of Islam. Thus, again, the backwardness of the Arab-Islamic world is likened to the "pagan" pre-Islamic period when prophets were rejected and revelation was likened to fables. It is a time of social injustice characterized by exploitation and corruption. The cause of this backwardness is departure from the true path of Islam by blindly following the dictates of Western imperialism. Muslims stand torn between two extremes: capitalism, with its unbridled emphasis on wealth and power, and communism, which seeks violently to uproot and reshape everything. Like the revivalists of old, Qaddafi called the community to its historic, divinely mandated mission: "The time has come to manifest the truth of Islam as a force to move mankind, to make progress, and to change the course of history as we changed it formerly."[13]

But who is to undertake this grand Islamic struggle (*jihad,* in its fullest sense)? In the first volume of *The Green Book,* Qaddafi maintained that "the details of the theory, its component parts and its elucidation are not my specialization . . . [but lie within the understanding of] . . . every learned person, every thinker, every *mujtahid* [one capable of interpreting *ijtihad*]."[14] This position was indicative of Qaddafi's break with the *ulama,* who had initially supported his regime. Traditionally, they alone had claimed to have the proper training and expertise to qualify as interpreters of Islam. This belief had been the basis for their status and power as guardians and interpreters of Islam. In declaring that all learned Muslims could interpret Islam, Qaddafi undermined the authority of the *ulama* as a religious establishment and set the stage for his authoritative religious leadership. The state had already intervened in another area traditionally the province of the *ulama* and the Sufi orders: the propagation of the faith; for the government had created its own Islamic missionary organization, the Islamic Call Society.

Having opened wide the door of interpretation, Qaddafi proceeded in subsequent years and in the later volumes of *The Green Book* to delineate the "Third Way." In so doing, he radically redefined traditional Islam and Arab socialism, stamping them with his own distinctive interpretation. Although Qaddafi had appealed to the Quran as the source of his revolutionary theory, "in it are solutions to the problems of man," and maintained that Libya's socialist program emanates "from the true religion of Islam and its Noble Book," specific references to Islam are conspicuously absent from the last two volumes of *The Green Book.*

As noted, *The Green Book* displaced the *Shariah's* governance of the political and social order. Mixing populist ideological statements with a broad range of political, social, and economic experimentation, Qaddafi undertook nothing less than his own "Islamic revolution," a cultural revolution based, not on the divine guidance of the Quran or the example of the Prophet but, upon the thought of Muammar al-Qaddafi. Libya's new identity and ideology of popular authority were symbolized in March 1977 when the General People's Congress, which replaced the Revolutionary Command Council, changed Libya's name from the Libyan Arab Republic to the Socialist People's Libyan Arab Jamahiriya. Qaddafi resigned his position as president to become the philosopher-ideologue of the revolution. Al-Jamahiriya ("the masses") was to be a peoples' state. Libya became a decentralized, populist, participatory government of people's committees that controlled government offices, schools, the media, and many corporations. Qaddafi encouraged people's committees to take over Libya's embassies and to seize control of its mosques. The socialist economic policy of *The Green Book* includes the abolition of private land ownership, wages, and rent in favor of worker control and participation in the means of production. Implementation of the new socialist experiment began in 1978, with Libyans who owned more than one home or apartment being forced to choose which one they wished to retain and live in. Those who were renting became owners of these dwellings. Factory workers seized their factories and overnight became partners in this workers' revolution.

Qaddafi responded to Islamic critics of his socialist policy by condemning the status quo in the name of Islamic social justice and by resorting to a creative interpretation of Quranic texts. In addition the continued use of Islam for legitimation and popular support were reflected in the innumerable billboards whose slogans extolled and exhorted the masses, such as: "Al Fateh ["the beginning," i.e., of Libya's Revolution, 1969] is an Islamic Revolution" and "The Glorious Quran Is the Shariah of our New Socialist Society."[15]

Qaddafi's "Third Way"

Although Islam is involved, Libya's socialist experiment was certainly a departure from the past. Even though Qaddafi is generally characterized as an Islamic fundamentalist, his use of Islam could more properly be described as modern revisionist. Indeed for some Muslims, his substantive deviations from Islamic tradition are seen as heresy. A major example of Qaddafi's innovative interpretation of Islam is the place of the *Shariah* in the state. As noted in chapter 1, Sunni jurists had accepted acknowledgment of the *Shariah* by the ruler or *Shariah* governance as the practical criterion for an Islamic state. Traditional Islamic law was based on the Quran and the *Sunnah* (Example) of the Prophet and provided the ideal blueprint for state and society. In contrast Qaddafi distinguished between the Quran alone as revelation and declared that all other sources and beliefs were human in origin and thus subject to error and change. He denied the authoritative role of Prophetic traditions, claiming many are not authentic. As a result, the Quran and *The Green Book*, which Qaddafi maintained was rooted in the Quran, became the ideological foundation of Libyan society. Contrary to his earlier claims in *The Green Book* regarding the economic, military, and sociopolitical aspects of scripture, the Quran was restricted to religious observances (prayer, fasting, almsgiving) while *The Green Book*, not the *Shariah*, governed politics and society. Thus *The Green Book*, the message of Muammar al-Qaddafi, replaced the traditional, comprehensive role of the *Shariah*. Qaddafi set aside the traditional formulations of Islamic law, distinguishing between the immutable Quran and those formulations or interpretations (*fiqh*) that are historically and humanly conditioned. Here he adopted the position of many Islamic modernists. However, rather than reforming the law, he replaced much of it with *The Green Book*. Such a position was bound to earn the ire of the *ulama*, whose predecessors had formulated the law and whose status and authority were undermined by these innovations.

Qaddafi's confrontation with the *ulama* was forewarned in an article "No *mufti*, no marabouts, no shaykhs" that appeared in the official government daily newspaper *al-Fajr al-Jadid* in October 1977. Although written under another name, the article was believed to have come from Qaddafi himself. A major contention of the article is the rejection of traditional religious leaders and the authority of the *mufti* as contrary to "popular authority." In April 1978, religious leaders, at an international conference on *The Green Book*, publicly criticized its socialist doctrine as incompatible with Islam, specifically its assertion that "land is not private property," which had been the pretext for the state's nationalization of religious endowments or trusts, a source of revenue and power for the *ulama*. Qaddafi defended his interpretation as consonant with Islamic social justice. Within one month, people's popular committees were "instructed to 'seize the mosques' to rid them of 'paganist tendencies' and of *imams* [religious leaders] accused of 'propagating heretical tales elaborated over centuries of decadence and which distort the Islamic religion.'"[16] Having rejected the *ulama's* authoritative role as the guardians and interpreters of Islam, Qaddafi freely reinterpreted Islamic belief and practice. As he had questioned the authenticity of many of the Prophetic traditions, so too he changed the dating of the Muslim calendar from the *hijra* to the death of the Prophet; declared that the pilgrimage to Mecca was not obligatory; equated the alms tithe (*zakat*) with social security; and, contrary to tradition, maintained that the rate of the tithe could be a variable rather than a fixed (2.5 percent) tax.[17]

Though Muammar al-Qaddafi skillfully used Islam to legitimate Arab socialism and his radical populist state and maintained the right of all learned Muslims (not just the traditional religious leadership) to interpret Islam, he has not tolerated alternative Islamic voices and visions. His personalized, innovative interpretation of Islam generated a significant, though often muted and silenced, opposition that incorporated a broad spectrum of Islamic orientations. Traditional religious leaders, the Sanusi and the *ulama*, resent his attack on their authority and interests as well as his reinterpretation of Islamic doctrine. The *ulama* have condemned Qaddafi's "innovative" interpretations of Islam—his rejection of the binding force of Prophetic traditions, his substitution of *The Green Book* for *Shariah* governance, and his abolition of private property—for their deviation from the Islamic tradition. Popular reform-minded *ulama*, heirs of Afghani and Abduh's (Salafiyya) modernist movement, attracted Libyan youth to their mosques, preaching their own Islamic alternative to Qaddafi's brand of Islamic socialism. They were silenced, however, by government regulations prohibiting the discussion of politics in religious gatherings and, more effectively, by the state's security force. Thus, for example, Shaykh al-Bishti, a popular preacher and critic of the regime who drew large crowds to his Friday sermons, disappeared in 1980.

Qaddafi's authority and legitimacy have also been challenged by the Muslim Brotherhood and the Islamic Liberation Party (ILP). Qaddafi regards the Brotherhood, a strong religiopolitical movement in Egypt and neighboring Sudan, as a political organization whose ideology, goal, and organization (antisocialist, pan-Islamic, hierarchical) are a direct threat to his populist, socialist, Arab nationalist vision. The ILP, active in Jordan, Tunisia, and Egypt as well as Libya, has from time to time infiltrated the military and been implicated in attempted coups. In 1983 ILP members of the Libyan armed forces were reported to have been arrested, and in 1984 two students reputed to be members of the ILP were hanged.[18] Both the Brotherhood and the ILP regard Qaddafi as a military opportunist who has simply manipulated and distorted Islam for his own ends.

Although the Libyan government has been able to control or silence much of its opposition, it has from time to time imprisoned and executed Muslim Brothers or Islamic fundamentalists. Reports of militant Islamic opposition persisted in the late 1980s. Members of groups referred to as Jihad and Hizballah were executed in 1987. Muslim student activism became more noticeable in 1989 with greater numbers of women wearing head scarves on campus, student demonstrations at Tripoli's al-Fatah University that were attributed to the Muslim Brotherhood, and a resumption of political discussions at mosques.[19] In the fall of 1989, Islamic militants participated in bloody confrontations with security forces and were denounced by Qaddafi as a "cancer, the black death, and AIDS."[20]

During the time that Muammar al-Qaddafi has been in power, Libya has undergone a series of changes as Qaddafi has put his theories into practice. Although varying in degree of intensity, Qaddafi has used Islam, throughout his rule, to buttress his Arab socialism. The process has moved from what appeared to be a fundamentalist implementation of traditional Islamic law to the more radical revisionist program of *The Green Book*. Qaddafi's reforms have been condemned both within Libya and in the greater Muslim world as heresy. His experiment in redefining Libyan identity with his populist, socialist "Third Way" alienated both landed and business classes as well as the religious establishment. Although signs declaring "This Is an Islamic Revolution" may be found in Libya and many in the West view Qaddafi as an "Islamic" leader governing an Islamic state, for many Muslims, in Libya and throughout the world, Qaddafi's experiment in redefining Libyan identity has been regarded as far from Islamic.

Pakistan

When Zulfikar Ali Bhutto was elected head of state in 1971, few expected that this secularist, who was representing the socialist platform of his Pakistan People's Party (PPP), would be the initiator of Islamization in Pakistan. Most observers believed that, although religious sensitivities had to be respected, Pakistan would generally continue in its political and social development along a de facto Western secular path. Several factors caused a significant revival of Islam in Pakistan's politics, however: a post-Bangladesh identity crisis, Arab oil, and domestic politics.[21] As a result, Islam became a major theme in Pakistan politics; indeed, by the end of Bhutto's rule, it had become the dominant theme.

The loss of East Pakistan, after a bloody civil war that led to the formation of an independent Bangladesh in 1971, caused a crisis in Pakistan. This experience resulted in a renewed concern with questions of national identity and unity as Pakistan's founding and early history were reexamined to understand better the basis for its existence.[22] Amid the soul-searching and deliberations in national conferences, publications and the media, Pakistan's establishment as a Muslim homeland was reexamined. The popularly perceived, though vaguely defined, commitment to Islam resurfaced in politics. For many Islam was the reason and only means to create a sense of unity that transcended Pakistan's ethnic and linguistic divisions.

Internationally, Bhutto determined to draw closer to the Arab oil countries for aid and, toward this end, progressively emphasized the common Islamic identity and bond of Pakistan with the Arab world. He embarked upon a shuttle diplomacy with the Arab oil countries. This new initiative was strikingly symbolized in 1974 by Pakistan's hosting of an Islamic Summit in Lahore. The summit, attended by heads of state from around the Muslim world, provided a forum for Col. Muammar al-Qaddafi, who addressed throngs of Pakistanis at the Badshahi Mosque in Lahore. Bhutto permitted Anwar al-Sadat's mediation between Pakistan and Bangladesh and a restoration of diplomatic relations in the name of Islam. The Bhutto government also initiated programs to encourage the study of Arabic and fostered an increasing number of religious conferences to which representatives from other Muslim countries were invited.

Despite all of his efforts in the name of Islam, the Jamaat-i-Islami and other religious parties led a concerted effort to defeat Bhutto. Their tactics included the raising of a substantial campaign fund—the Fund for the Protection of the Ideology of Pakistan—and the issuing of decrees against Bhutto's socialism by 113 *ulama*. In reacting to this internal political pressure from religious critics, Bhutto increasingly responded to them on their own ground—through appeals to Islam to legitimate his programs and policies. The Pakistan People's Party

(PPP) had established itself as a mass political party with such populist, socialist slogans as "roti, kapra, aur mikan" (bread, clothing, and
shelter) and "zamin kashtkaron ko" (land to the tiller). Its socialist
orientation and social reform policies such as nationalization and land
reform were progressively equated with Islamic social justice. Phrases
like "*Musawat-i-Muhammadi*" (the Equality of Muhammad) and "*Islami Musawat*" (Islamic Equality) became part of the PPP's political
rhetoric. A new journal *Musawat*, (Equality), was founded that, somewhat like *Minbar al-Islam* in Nasser's Egypt, provided an organ for
the Islamic justification of the PPP's policies appealing to the Quran,
the *Sunnah* of the Prophet, and the practice of the early Rightly
Guided Caliphs.[23]

In addition, in 1974 Bhutto yielded to the decades-long campaign
of religious leaders to have the Ahmadiyya declared a non-Muslim
minority. As discussed in chapter 4, many religious leaders had long
maintained that the Ahmadiyya recognized their founder, Ghulam
Ahmad, as a prophet and thus rejected a pillar of Islam—that
Muhammad was the final Prophet of God. As seen in the discussion
of the anti-Ahmadiyya riots of 1953, religious leaders viewed the
Ahmadiyya as non-Muslims and especially objected to their holding
important positions in government and the military. Bhutto approved
provisions in the 1973 Constitution that required that both the president and the prime minister be Muslims; the oath of office was
amended to require an affirmation of the finality of Muhammad's
Prophethood.

The politicization of Islam reached its zenith in the general elections of March 1977. Nine political parties joined under the umbrella
of Islam to form an opposition block, the Pakistan National Alliance
(PNA), which included the Pakistan Muslim League, National Democratic Party, and Tehrik-i-Istiqlal. Its direction and leadership, however, came from the Islamic religious parties: the Jamaat-i-Islami, the
Jamiyyat i-Ulama-i-Pakistan (the Organization of the Ulama of Pakistan), and the Jamiyyat i-Ulama-i-Islam (the Organization of the
Ulama of Islam). Although member parties spanned the political
spectrum, the PNA's symbols and slogans were Islamic: "Islam in
Danger" and "The System of the Prophet" (i.e., an Islamic system of
government). Criticisms of the Bhutto regime were carefully couched
in Islamic terms. Both Bhutto's personal life-style and his government
were denounced as anti-Islamic. The PNA pledged itself to the intro-

duction of an Islamic system of government. The vast network of *ul-ama*, mosques, religious schools, and seminaries were employed as centers for political organization and communications.

The strength of Pakistan National Alliance support came primarily from the middle class (traditional and modern): urban intellectuals who had supported Bhutto's early socialist platform and were now alienated by his purge of the more leftist elements in his cabinet in 1974; and small traditional businessmen and merchants and members of the "new" middle-class professions (teachers, doctors, clerical workers, university students, and other professionals) for whom Bhutto's political and economic reforms resulted in an increased sense of powerlessness and alienation. Bhutto's political reforms had resulted in tighter control by the Pakistan People's Party of government and district level officials, as primary emphasis was placed on party loyalty and connections rather than on merit. Moreover, Bhutto's autocratic rule was reflected in a government that increasingly resorted to media censorship, the "policing" of its own security force, political harassment, arrests, and imprisonment.

The middle-class nature of the Pakistan National Alliance movement was reinforced by the presence and leadership of the religious parties whose traditional base of support has always come primarily from among the urban and town-based middle class. This was particularly true of Mawlana Mawdudi's Jamaat-i-Islami, whose ideological and organizational input in the PNA was of major importance.

Mawdudi and most of the religious leadership had, from the start, rejected Bhutto's socialism as un-Islamic. To this objection they added a critique of political and social corruption, the breakdown of law and order. In place of socialism, they called for national unity rooted in Pakistan's Islamic raison d'être, in which Islamic brotherhood and solidarity would transcend regional, linguistic divisions. They emphasized that the only means to achieve this form of government was a return to Islamic law, which provided the blueprint for a democratic, egalitarian society based upon Islamic social justice. Such a system of government would avoid the extremes of corporate capitalism and state socialism, substitute Islamic values for their excessive materialism and secularism, counter the corruption and spiritual malaise of the Bhutto years, and thus realize for the first time Pakistan's destiny as an Islamic state and society.

The Pakistan National Alliance manifesto reflected the concerns of a religious and middle-class alliance. It called for the introduction of an Islamic system of government, the elimination of political and moral corruption, and support for small industry and business interests. Thus, in the 1977 election campaign, the lines of battle were drawn between a broad coalition of political parties (PNA) enjoying strong middle-class support and the new alliance of the upper and lower classes that supported Bhutto's Pakistan People's Party.

In order to counter the growing Islamic opposition with its popular appeals to Islam, Bhutto and his PPP increasingly placed themselves under the banner of Islam. As their emphasis shifted toward Islamic slogans like the equality of Muhammad or Muhammad's egalitarianism, their use of the term *socialism* had now receded into the background. The new Pakistan People's Party manifesto included provisions that promised greater Islamization of society, such as a commitment to center community life more firmly upon the Quran and to have Friday replace Sunday as the weekly holiday.

Despite their appeals to Islam, the Pakistan National Alliance clearly did not have the votes of the people, and Bhutto and the Pakistan People's Party scored what appeared to be an impressive victory in the general elections of March 1977. Amid charges of widespread poll irregularities, however, the PNA boycotted the provincial elections of March 7 and renewed their agitational politics. The mosques of the country became the centers not only for Friday communal prayer but also for political agitation. The sermons concerned Islamic politics, and a community gathered for prayer was easily transformed into a political rally and march. Responding to widespread disturbances, the Bhutto government imposed martial law and curfews. As PNA activities increased, Bhutto sought to diffuse their appeal by announcing further Islamization measures, such as the prohibition of alcohol, gambling, and nightclubs. These Islamic provisions and promises to introduce other *Shariah* laws served to reinforce the Islamic character of the conflict. Most importantly, a turning point had been reached. Islam and Pakistan's Islamic identity had reemerged as the dominant theme in Pakistani politics in a manner and to a degree that had not been seen since Pakistan's establishment.

The Martial Law Regime of Zia ul-Haq

The anti-Bhutto movement came to an abrupt halt with the bloodless military coup d'etat that brought Gen. Zia ul-Haq to power on July 5, 1977. As chief martial law administrator and president, Zia ul-

Haq appealed to Islam to legitimate his coup and subsequent rule, based upon a commitment to implement the Nizam-i-Mustapha (System of the Prophet) or, as it was more commonly called, Nizam-i-Islam (System of Islam). Zia not only seized the Pakistan National Alliance slogan but attempted to forge an alliance with the PNA. Some, like the Jamiyyat i-Ulama-i-Islam (organization of Ulama of Islam), refused to participate. Others, especially the Jamaati-Islami (the Islamic Society) and Jamiyyat i-Ulama-i-Pakistan, accepted the opportunity to advise and assist a government that had taken up the banner of the system of Islam. Individuals noted for their strong commitment to Islam, especially members of Mawlana Mawdudi's Jamaat-i-Islami were appointed to key cabinet positions in the ministries of law, religious affairs, information, production, and planning. Zia skillfully legitimated his seizure of power by both co-opting the PNA's Islamic banner and eliminating Bhutto. Bhutto's downfall was attributed to his "un-Islamic" behavior. He was progressively discredited and, after a controversial trial, executed for murder on April 4, 1979, amid worldwide appeals for clemency.

Gen. Zia ul-Haq, in many forums, declared his commitment to "transform the country's socioeconomic and political structure in accordance with the principles of Islam."[24] Toward that end, the Islamic Ideology Council was reconstituted, and its scope broadened to serve as the president's chief advisory council for introducing a more Islamic system of government, for the Islamization of state and society. Three areas of immediate concern were targeted: the Islamic taxes (*zakat* and *ushr*), an interest-free economy, and an Islamic penal code.

In December 1978, the time of the Islamic New Year, Zia proclaimed Pakistan's new beginning in an address entitled "Measures to Enforce an Islamic System [Nizam-i-Islam]." In addition to declaring the intention of his government to introduce reforms in the areas that were under study by the Islamic Ideology Council, Zia announced the creation of *Shariah* Courts to determine whether specific existing laws were repugnant to Islam. In February 1979, Zia formalized the commitment of his government to the system of Islam with his promulgation "Introduction of Islamic Laws." Appealing to the traditional Islamic belief that Islam is a total way of life, this document announced a series of reforms in worship, law, economics, and education. Islamization became a prominent part of Pakistan's politics and life, and Islamic measures and proposals affecting politics, law, economics, education, and culture were introduced. Islamic symbols and criteria were invoked so successfully that Zia's opposition often felt constrained to cast its criticisms and policies in an Islamic mold.

Politics

Throughout Zia's rule, Islam was used politically as the source of legitimation and a rationale for the continuation of martial law. Although Zia had originally promised elections within ninety days of his July 1977 coup, elections in Pakistan were postponed and political parties were disbanded. The primary reason or excuse cited was doubt about whether Pakistan's political system with its Western-inspired democracy and political party system was compatible with Islam. In October 1979, Zia announced that elections would be postponed indefinitely as the government searched for an Islamic form of democracy. These questions were referred to the Islamic Ideology Council, a government-appointed body, which included religious leaders as well as experts in banking, economics, and law. Zia's actions produced a broad-based opposition in the Movement for the Restoration of Democracy (MRD), which included not only Bhutto supporters but also many of the Pakistan National Alliance members who found themselves disenfranchised, their political parties declared "defunct." Both secular and religiously oriented parties joined together in demanding the end of martial law and the restoration of the political process through elections. Even religious leaders like Mian Tufail Muhammad, successor to Mawlana Mawdudi as amir of the Jamaat-i-Islami, declared that martial law rule was not Islamic. They argued that the government could not claim to be an expression of the System of Islam because the head of an Islamic state should be chosen or elected by the people and is, himself, subject to the Shariah or sovereignty of God's rule. Although the Jamaat-i-Islami had always been considered close to Zia's government and had not joined the MRD, by spring 1984 it called for a united political front to oppose martial law and campaigned for the restoration of democracy.

Zia ul-Haq was criticized for placing his martial law regulations above even the Shariah. Whereas the only criterion, or norm, guiding the Shariah Courts should be the Quran and Sunnah, General Zia exempted his martial law regulations as well as matters of taxation and banking from the courts' purview.

To blunt his critics, in 1982 Zia created a Federal Advisory Council, an interim parliamentary assembly using the Islamic designation *majlis al-shura* (consultative council, a term originally used to refer to those who selected/elected the early caliphs and, more recently, used by some governments for parliament). Members were appointed, not elected; it was a consultative body with no legislative powers. Their mandate to "create conditions in which the country could attain a democratic Islamic polity" did not allay critics who charged that it was not Islamic and was but another tactic to delay elections.[25] Many religious leaders asserted that Islamic government was not military rule and that in an Islamic state members of the parliament should be elected, not appointed by an unelected military ruler.

Law

Zia ul-Haq's Islamization program included the introduction of Islamic measures affecting substantive law and the judiciary. The 1973 Constitution was "augmented" by a series of martial law regulations such as MLR 48 and 49, which banned political parties and prohibited newspapers from political commentary and criticism. In effect, with the dissolution of the National Assembly, these martial law ordinances constituted the only legislation possible; thus Zia ul-Haq, as chief martial law administrator, remained the sole lawmaker. Islamic laws were introduced through a series of proclamations in the areas of fasting, prayer, penal law, and economics.

Public observance of fasting during Ramadan, one of the Five Pillars of Islam, had always been expected in Pakistan. Actual observance had varied significantly, subject to personal conscience and to peer pressure. The state now assumed the power of public enforcement. Public consumption of food or drink and smoking during Ramadan were punishable by a sentence of up to six months in jail. In addition dance and musical productions were also curtailed during Ramadan. As noted previously, under Bhutto's government, Friday replaced Sunday as the weekly holiday. The Islamic system of Zia continued this practice. The government also issued ordinances requiring that workers be provided with the time and a suitable place to perform their daily prayers. Companies were required to close during the noon hour on Friday to permit workers to attend communal prayers at a mosque.

The most prominent and, at times, controversial area of legal reform occurred in Pakistan's penal code—in particular the imposition of Quranically or Prophetically prescribed punishments for drinking, theft, adultery, and false accusation (i.e., bearing false witness regarding sexual crimes). The Pakistan Penal Code was amended so that punishments of imprisonments or fines for Quranically prescribed crimes were replaced by amputation of the hand for theft, stoning for adultery, and flogging for fornication and drinking. Nevertheless, public flogging for drinking violations and other Quranically prescribed crimes were restricted because of both internal criticisms and to adverse publicity in the international media. Although amputations were ordered by the court, none occurred because physicians refused to perform them. A sharp controversy surrounded the imposition of stoning for adultery. Although ordered by the courts, such verdicts were appealed to the Federal *Shariah* Court, which set them aside. The government reorganized the *Shariah* Court to include three *ulama* among its members and expanded its jurisdiction so that the court could review its previous decisions. Subsequently, the Federal *Shariah* Court reversed itself, with conservative members arguing that stoning, although not based on a Quranic text, is rooted in Prophetic tradition. Defenders of this provision argued that this severe punishment is to serve as a deterrent to the most blatant violations of public morality and that conviction would be rare because Islamic law requires four eye witnesses to the act itself.

Shariah Courts

In 1978 the government announced the creation of *Shariah* Courts. These courts differ from the traditional Islamic legal system where judges applied *Shariah* law. Pakistan's *Shariah* Courts were essentially courts that determined whether a specific law was contrary to the *Shariah*. The courts' jurisdiction were to review petitions from individuals and from the federal or provincial governments that challenged any law as repugnant to Islam (i.e., the Quran and the *Sunnah*.) The court was barred, however, from reviewing laws in three areas (the constitution and martial law ordinances, family law, and fiscal laws) for a period of three years. *Shariah* Bench decisions could be appealed to the Appellate *Shariah* Bench of the Supreme Court. Laws or provisions found to be un-Islamic were to be amended through legislative action taken by Gen. Zia ul-Haq.

The *Shariah* Courts reviewed a broad spectrum of suits ranging from challenges to the legitimacy of Pakistan's constitution and law to the acceptability of cinema, from government-enforced land reform to the stoning of adulterers. Moreover, the court continued the work of the Islamic Ideology Council in reviewing all of Pakistan's legal codes to identify and rectify those aspects, or provisions, that were un-Islamic. Islamization of law is not seen as totally replacing Pakistan's Anglo-Muhammadan legal system with classical Islamic law or developing a new system but rather purifying its current system of un-Islamic provisions.

Other changes were subsequently introduced in the judiciary: the introduction of *qadi* (judge) courts and the establishment of a Department of Public Morality (*Ihtisab*). A bill (Qadi Courts Ordinance, 1983) establishing *qadi* courts was approved February 20, 1983, by the Federal Advisory Council. *Qadi* courts were to replace local and district courts, that is, existing civil and criminal courts. They were to be a further step in the establishment of an Islamic system of justice. Because judges were to apply Islamic law, many were to be recruited from the traditional religious schools and from the graduates of the Islamic University. Such measures were targeted by Zia ul-Haq to curry the favor and support of the *ulama*.

As with the *Shariah* Courts, critics of the proposed system included the legal profession as well as certain women's organizations. The Bar Councils' Convention held in September 1982 rejected the Qadi Courts Ordinance.[26] The Department of Ihtisab reinstituted the traditional Islamic institution of the supervisor of public behavior and markets, who investigates charges of maladministration against government ministries, agencies, and corporations.[27]

Economics

Islamic economic measures were an integral part of Zia's Islamization program, affecting questions of private property, taxation, and interest. The introduction of an alms tax (*zakat*), and an agricultural tax, and interest-free banking were the more substantive and controversial measures. A *Zakat* Fund was created in 1979 with substantial financial assistance from Saudi Arabia and the United Arab Emirates.

Collection and distribution of the alms tax was managed by a multi-tiered elected administrative (organization) system. A wealth tax of 2.5 percent was levied on all income and assets in excess of two hundred dollars and deducted directly at the source, that is, directly from bank accounts and other financial assets, such as investment shares, annuities, and insurance.

Criticism of the alms tax and agricultural tax measures came from various quarters. Some resented the government's taking over what was regarded as a private obligation before God that enabled Muslims to look after needy family and friends. The *zakat* system was perceived as the government's bureaucratization of a personal, charitable duty, which was now subject to mismanagement and misappropriation. The Shiah community objected vociferously to the alms tax order because, according to their law, the alms tax is not compulsory on capital and trading money. The government yielded with legislation that permitted a Muslim to obtain an exemption if he states that the alms tax is not enjoined by his faith and law.

The agricultural tax on productive land, finally implemented in May 1983, was set at 5 percent.[28] The tax, while compulsory, was paid voluntarily and monitored by committees that randomly sampled the landowners in their districts.

The most potentially far-reaching Islamic economic change was the abolition of interest. Early in his administration, Zia ul-Haq committed himself to the abolition of the "curse of interest."[29] In January 1981, interest-free banking accounts were introduced on a voluntary basis in all seven thousand branches of Pakistan's nationalized commercial banks. Under a system called "Profit/Loss Sharing," the depositor and the bank enter into a partnership in which both share in the profits or losses. Money was invested in a selective portfolio, some of which consisted of government-owned companies that were secure and whose profitability was known. The Profit/Loss Sharing System was optional and applicable to savings and fixed deposit (time-deposit) accounts.

Introduction of an interest-free economy proved more difficult than the implementation of individual economic measures. Indeed, as early as May 1980, a special Committee on Islamization appointed by the finance minister had cautioned in its report, "An Agenda for Islamic Economic Reform" (issued by the Pakistan Institute of Development Economics), that "the Islamic rejection of interest is in effect a rejection of the entire capitalistic system: an interest-free economy is in fact an exploitation-free economy" (p. v). The committee stressed that the abolition of interest must be part of a far more comprehensive and complex process, the development of a complete economic system without which an interest-free economy would neither be possible nor effective: "The abolition of interest is part of a fundamental restructuring of the whole spectrum of production, consumption, and distribution relationships on the Islamic lines. However, the search for such a system must be gradual to let the interaction between theory and practice . . . produce an economic system which corresponds to the overall vision of an Islamic economic system (p. vi)."

Zia ul-Haq's government did not adopt this more comprehensive outlook. Instead it continued to advocate and pursue a fragmented, ad hoc gradualist policy of Islamic economic reform, often more rhetoric than substance, which satisfied none of its critics.

Education

Education and cultural reforms provided the final area of Zia ul-Haq's Islamization program. They were an attempt to resolve Pakistan's decades-long identity problems, to overcome ethnic and regional factionalism by establishing a common national identity and ideology firmly based on the twin pillars of Islam and Pakistan. A series of changes, real and symbolic, were introduced to underscore the government's commitment to strengthen Pakistan's national identity through a reaffirmation of its Islamic-Pakistani identity and to produce what Zia ul-Haq called a new generation wedded to the ideology of Pakistan and Islam. An ever-burgeoning series of regulations and programs involving areas ranging from language and dress to mass media and education were introduced and enforced. Urdu, Pakistan's national language, replaced English as the medium of instruction in schools and assumed a more prominent place in public life and in the government and media.

General Zia called upon all Pakistanis to wear national attire during working hours. Civil servants, university professors, and businessmen were to trade their suits for traditional attire. While there was initial compliance, especially in government offices and schools, there was also widespread resistance. Increased emphasis on Pakistani and Islamic identity and fraternal ties with Arab-Muslim countries resulted in an expanded use of Arabic in education and in the renaming of cities, streets, and public facilities: Iqbal Open University, Quaid-i-Azam ("the Great Leader," a reference to Muhammad Ali Jinnah) University, and Feisalabad (a city named for Saudi Arabia's King Faisal).

Government literature on Islamization—as used in the ordinances promulgated by Zia ul-Haq, the Islamic Ideology Council, the *Shariah* Courts, and in reports by special committees such as the Panel on Islamic Economics and Banking—emphasized the importance of Islamizing society because an Islamic outlook and attitude would assure awareness and appreciation of and compliance with Islamic regulations. The mass media and education have become major foci for traditional religious forces as well as for the implementation of the Islamization of society by government. Critics viewed such actions as simply religious censorship and obscurantism. Virtually all television and radio broadcasts were in Urdu, programs on national/Islamic history and culture were prominent in radio, television and in print. At the same time, censorship of movies, television commercials, and restrictions on coverage of "un-Islamic" activities sharply increased. Ironically, the emphases on Islam and Pakistani identity sometimes came into conflict. For example more traditional religious leaders attacked public performances and media coverage of national dance and music programs as un-Islamic activities.

Islamization of the informal means of education was accompanied by reforms in Pakistan's formal educational system as well. Courses in Islamic Studies were required at the university level as well as in preuniversity education. The Department of Education had for several years been engaged in reviewing curricula and textbooks both to eliminate un-Islamic materials and to revise and develop curricula and books that fostered Islamic-Pakistani values.

No single institution better symbolized the Islamization of education than the Islamic University, established in 1980 in Islamabad. Its faculties and their curricula were to assist in the implementation of the religious and cultural program of Islamization: "Islam enjoins upon the *Ummah* [community] to establish a just and humane world order . . . the purpose of education is to produce people who are imbued with Islamic learning and character and capable of meeting economic, social, political, technological, physical, intellectual, and aesthetic needs of the society." The purpose and goal of the new Islamic University were to fuse Pakistan's dual or parallel systems of secular and religious learning "so as to provide an Islamic vision for those engaged in education and to enable them to reconstruct human thought in all its forms on the foundations of Islam."[30]

Women

A final area affected by Islamization was the status of women. Islamization had caused increased apprehension among many professional women. Fearing that government policies and the growing vocal protestations of conservative religious leaders would lead to more restrictions and a loss of any gains in women's rights, organizations such as the Women's Action Forum in Karachi were created. Viewed by conservatives as simply a small westernized elite, professional women's associations organized conferences, led public demonstrations, and lobbied for women's rights. Increased emphasis on national dress and on covering the head with a veil or scarf are viewed as symbolizing a reinforcement of traditional, regressive attitudes and customs toward women that have rendered Muslim women second-class citizens. Veiling and seclusion, although often a practiced norm in Pakistani society, were rejected as un-Islamic historical accretions that are contrary to the reformist spirit of the Quran and Muhammad.

Pakistan, like many other Muslim countries, is a society in which seclusion as well as the wearing of the long veil covering the body (*burqa*) have been very much in practice. Until a few years ago, public separation of the sexes in buses, in banks, in education, and in many offices was commonplace. The continued strength of "purdah [seclusion] mentality" regarding women's modesty among lower and middle classes was witnessed by newspaper debates concerning whether wearing a sari was Islamic, by incidents in which women with uncovered heads were publicly reprimanded and even accosted, by the banning of women's hockey before mixed audiences, and by the issuing of legal opinions (*fatwas*) by religious leaders declaring that women may not hold political office. Moreover, the example of the postrevolutionary Iranian Islamic government's actions regarding women's status—from dress to employment to the repeal of Iran's Family Protection Act with its reforms in marriage, divorce, and inheritance—reinforced women's fears that Pakistan's *ulama*, who have been vocal in their public mosque and media statements, would follow a similar path. Conservative religious leaders have called for the repeal of Pakistan's Muslim Family Laws Ordinance of 1961. The Islamic Ideology Council itself found that three provisions in the Family Laws Ordinance were un-Islamic and had recommended their repeal.

Three other government measures concerned women's groups: proposals for separate women's universities, the introduction of *qadi* courts, and the revision of Pakistan's Law of Evidence Act. Women's universities were viewed as acquiescing to conservative religious pressures for separation of the sexes in society. Critics feared that women's universities would lend credibility to the belief that Islam required such separation of the sexes. Indeed women were originally excluded from the new Islamic University. When finally admitted to the university, they were educated in separate facilities. Thus many women found reason for concern that Islamic education would be equated with separation of the sexes.

The establishment of *qadi* courts reconstituted religious courts manned by judges drawn from the *ulama*. Given the conservative character of the majority of religious authorities and their tendency to turn to the world view of classical Islamic jurisprudence, with a minimal recognition of the need for reinterpretation, serious difficulties on women's issues were anticipated. For many women, the revision of Pakistan's Law of Evidence Act confirmed their worst fears. The draft submitted by the Islamic Ideology Council, supported by the vast majority of religious leaders and finally passed, implemented the traditional Islamic legal point of view that the evidence of two Muslim women equals that of one Muslim male.

Transition to Civilian Rule

By 1984 Zia ul-Haq initiated a series of events that would end martial law and move Pakistan slowly, at times almost imperceptibly, toward civilian rule and a more democratic order. In December 1984, Zia called a surprise national referendum: "To approve policies to conform the nation's laws with Islam and the peaceful transition of power to elected representatives." Although ostensibly to ask voters if they approved of his Islamization program, Zia linked a yes answer with his retention of the presidency until 1990. Despite an opposition boycott, led by the Movement for the Restoration of Democracy

(MRD), charges of election irregularities, and a low voter turnout (the government claimed a 50 percent turnout; unofficial estimates were 15–20 percent), a majority voted in the affirmative. Thus martial law was lifted after seven years, but not before amendments were passed to the 1973 Constitution to preserve Zia's ultimate power as president, to incorporate many of the martial law regulations promulgated during Zia's rule, and to exempt from future prosecution those associated with the martial law system.

In February 1985, national and provincial elections were held on a nonparty basis. Zia continued to maintain that his version of Islamic democracy, "shuracracy" (government by consultation, *shura*), was more faithful to Islam, which was based on divine sovereignty and thus did not recognize Western democratic notions of popular sovereignty and political parties. By the end of 1985, martial law had been terminated and civilian rule restored. In January 1986, a civilian government headed by Prime Minister Muhammad Khan Junejo, whom Zia had selected the previous March, took office. Press censorship was lifted and political parties were permitted to function with some restriction. Nevertheless, the return to civilian rule did not bring stability. The MRD continued to press for free elections on a political party basis and for General Zia to resign as army chief of staff in order to be a true civilian president.

Benazir Bhutto

In April 1986, Benazir Bhutto, the daughter of Zulfikar Ali Bhutto, returned to Pakistan to challenge Zia's regime. Zia and the military did not miss the message in the record crowds that greeted Benazir Bhutto, many of whom were there to voice opposition to Zia's rule rather than solely to support Bhutto. The Zia/Junejo government was also challenged by serious ethnic and religious conflicts: Baluchs and Pathans clashed in Baluchistan, Sindi nationalism erupted, battles raged between Pushtu-speaking Pathans and Urdu speaking Muhajirs (Urdu-speaking Muslims who immigrated after the creation of Pakistan) in the Sind province, and Sunni-Shii conflicts often led to confrontations in Karachi, Lahore, and Islamabad.

At the same time, many of the *ulama* and traditional religious parties had become more vocal in their criticisms of the government's failure to adequately and expeditiously implement an Islamic system of government. In July 1985, two Jamaat-i-Islami members of the Senate introduced the *Shariah* Bill, which was to require that all laws be brought within the purview of the *Shariah*. The move proved unpopular to both the government and to many nongovernment organizations including the Women's Action Forum and Shiah organizations. More serious was a proposed amendment (the Ninth Amendment) to the constitution that would have extended the jurisdiction of the Federal *Shariah* Court to include family laws. While conservative religious organizations favored the bill, more liberal leaders worried that such a change could lead to repeal of or changes in Pakistan's Family Laws ordinance of 1961 and to the passage of laws discriminatory against women, especially because the *ulama* would play a greater role as judges on the *Shariah* Court.

The return to civilian government moderated the pace of Islamization programs but increased calls for democratic national elections. Though unable to mount a unified movement, Benazir Bhutto remained Zia ul-Haq's most formidable critic and political opponent. The situation changed abruptly on August 17, 1988, when Zia ul-Haq, accompanied by the American ambassador and many of Pakistan's military leaders, died in a suspicious plane crash. Eleven years after the imposition of martial law, Pakistan held its first party-based national elections in November 1988. Benazir Bhutto, at the helm of her father's Pakistan People's Party, defeated the reputed heirs of Zia ul-Haq's legacy, the Islamic Democratic Alliance (IDA) and Islami Jamhoori Ittehad, a coalition of nine parties that claimed the banner of Islamization and included the Jamaat-i-Islami, the Muslim League, and the Jamiyyat i-Ulama-i-Pakistan. Pakistan and the Muslim world had its first woman prime minister.

Although religion was not a central issue in the elections, given the political realities of Pakistan, political Islam provided a platform for the IDA while the PPP pledged to repeal the Hudud Ordinance of 1979 and discriminatory laws against women as well as to raise women's rights on a par with those of men. Thus the election of Benazir Bhutto was certainly seen by many as a referendum on the religious politics of the Zia era.

Benazir Bhutto's first years in office were characterized less by effective leadership than political survival. She entered office with only a small margin of victory; the PPP polled 39 percent to the IDA's 32 percent. Indeed, with the exception of her home province, Sind, the PPP and IDA garnered the same number of votes in all provinces. Thus Benazir Bhutto came to power with only a bare plurality of votes at the national level. Moreover, the IDA in provincial elections gained control of the Punjab, Pakistan's most populous (60 percent of the population) province. Benazir was also dependent on support from two long-time supporters of Zia, the United States and the pro-American Pakistani military. Moreover, she was not able to make significant inroads in dismantling or countering Zia ul Haq's "Islamic legacy." Indeed she herself found it necessary to project a profile that reflected Pakistan's Islamic religiocultural heritage. Shortly after Bhutto's election, she went on a much-publicized pilgrimage (*umra,* the lesser, or individual, pilgrimage) to Mecca, an act that has been repeated annually. She was careful to show deference to customs: she covered her head in public, had an arranged marriage, and began to raise a family. Although she had distinguished between a correct interpretation of Islam and Zia ul-Haq Islamization program, political realities prevented any substantial changes in Islamic laws or the initiation of substantive women's reforms.

Domestically, Benazir Bhutto had to contend with ethnic and regional conflicts. The central government in Islamabad had to cope with demands for greater provincial autonomy in Baluchistan, Punjab, Northwest Frontier Province and Sind; the growth of regional political parties; and an epidemic of violence and lawlessness. Ethnic battles, bombings, and killings among Baluch and Pathan in Baluchistan and Sindhi and non-Sindhi and Sindhi nationalists and Muhajir in Sind were devastating in their human and political consequences. The consequences of what Pakistan's interior minister called "the culture of Kalashnikov and heroin" have threatened the very fabric of society.[31]

By late 1990, the Sind province seemed at times to be a lawless area on the brink of disintegration. Bombings, kidnappings, riots, looting, and the massacres of hundreds of people had become commonplace. Prime Minister Benazir Bhutto, pledged to the restoration of democracy, sent twenty thousand army troops into the Sind to restore order at a time when within a single week the death toll from political and ethnic violence rose to more than 250. Although the PPP had formed a coalition with the Muhajir Qaumi (Nationalist) Movement (MQM), it unraveled as Muhajirs became more militant and their battle with Sindhi nationalists escalated. The MQM had risen to power rapidly. Founded in 1986, it successfully mobilized the younger Muhajir generation and scored resounding victories in elections in major cities in Sind. More ominously, the initially improved relations with India collapsed, and Pakistan once again faced another war with India over the independence movement in Kashmir.

The New Government of the IDA

Amid civil strife and charges of corruption in her government and family, Benazir Bhutto's attention and energies, as said earlier, increasingly seemed to be focused more on political survival than institution building. As one analyst observed at the time, because Benazir and the PPP lacked a coherent strategy and political program, they "failed to make an impact on any of the country's pressing problems. . . . Not only is democracy clearly set on no firmer foundation than before, but there is an absence of statesmanship in evidence and even of basic honesty on all sides of the political spectrum."[32]

On August 6, 1990, President Ghulam Ishaq Khan, closely associated with Zia ul-Haq and strongly supported by Pakistan's powerful military establishment, dissolved the National Assembly and dismissed Prime Minister Benazir Bhutto's government on charges of corruption and incompetence. New elections were scheduled for October 24, 1990. The continued perception of the importance of Islam as a potential force in mobilizing political support was reflected in several ways. While neither side seemed concerned to present a detailed platform, both felt constrained to pledge themselves to the implementation of an Islamic society in Pakistan. Benazir and the PPP headed a coalition, the Pakistan Democratic Alliance, that included the Nifaz-i-Fiqah-i-Jafari, a clerically led Shii party. Benazir's chief opposition was organized under the banner of Islam in the Islamic Democratic Alliance, which was led by the Muslim League and included the Jamaat-i-Islami.

To the astonishment of many and amidst charges by the PPP of ballot fraud, the IDA swept both the federal and provincial elections in what most observers expected to be a close race. The IDA enjoyed a clear parliamentary majority; control of three of Pakistan's four provinces; and support from the bureaucracy and, most importantly, the army. The victory of the IDA (with its campaign promise of a "*Shariah* Bill" that would in effect subordinate civil law to traditional

Islamic law) and Pakistan's new prime minister, Nawaz Sharif, a protégé of Zia ul-Haq, promised a visible, though selective, use of Islam
in Pakistan's politics and policies. Nawaz Sharif's primary concerns
were in fact bread-and-butter issues: a failing economy whose bal-
ance-of-payments deficits were compounded by the effects of the Gulf
crisis of 1990, escalating oil prices, and loss of remittances from workers in Kuwait and Iraq; the suspension of American military and economic aid owing to a continued dispute over Pakistan's nuclear
program; and higher defense spending required by Pakistan's conflict
with India over Kashmir.

   During the period from 1990 to 1997, a seesaw process of politics
occurred as power passed back and forth between Benazir Bhutto and
Nawaz Sharif. This was a period marked by democratic elections and
the subsequent dismissal of prime ministers by the presidents of Pakistan. On April 18, 1993, President Ghulam Ishaq Khan, a former associate of both Zia ul-Haq and Nawaz Sharif, dismissed Prime Minister
Nawaz Sharif. Nawaz's privatization of the economy neither jump-
started the economy as he had hoped nor mobilized the broader base
of support from the defecting religious parties or the lower classes.
Nawaz Sharif's struggles with a failing economy, sectarian and ethnic
violence, and an intransigent bureaucracy were compounded by his
power struggle with the president who intervened in national and
provincial politics. Rather than working cooperatively, the prime minister and the president jockeyed for position and for the support of
Pakistan's military, long a powerful force in Pakistani politics. After
months of contention over who had the right to appoint the chief of
the army staff, Ghulam Ishaq Khan, supported by the military, dismissed Sharif, dissolved the parliament, and called for new elections.
However, on May 26, 1993, Pakistan's Supreme Court restored the
prime minister, charging that the president had failed to remain neu-
tral and had undermined the stability of the government.

   In July 1993 both the president and the prime minister resigned
and new elections were scheduled. In October 1993 Benazir Bhutto
and the PPP defeated Nawaz Sharif and the IDA and returned to
power. Benazir's second term as prime minister ultimately proved no
more successful than her first. She, like her predecessor, struggled
with a stagnant economy, seemingly endemic corruption, and lawlessness. Rampant ethnic and sectarian violence were exacerbated by
a growing culture of drugs and arms, the result of the war in Af-

ghanistan, Pakistan's role as a base for *mujahideen* operations, and the massive settlement of refugees. Benazir used the threat of Islamic radicalism to strengthen relations with the United States. After the apprehension of Ramzi Yusef, who had been apprehended and extradited in a joint Pakistan-U.S effort, she asked for U.S. assistance in 1995 to contain the threat of radical Islamic fundamentalism to Pakistan and the region. The rift between Bhutto and the Islamic parties was strained to the breaking point in October 1995 when the government claimed to have foiled a coup by "fundamentalist military officers" supported by Islamic groups.

The Benazir Bhutto government's inability to stem the breakdown of law and order, the recurrence of charges of rampant corruption (especially of her husband and close associates), and the deteriorating relations with Sardar Leghari, president of Pakistan, provided sufficient grounds for Sardar Leghari on November 5, 1996, to dismiss Bhutto's government on grounds of corruption and mismanagement, dissolve the National Assembly, and schedule elections for February 3, 1997.

During the 1990s the role of Islamic parties in the political process, especially the Jamaat-i-Islami, had shifted dramatically. The Jamaat-i-Islami, which had joined the Muslim League-led Islamic Democratic Alliance in 1988, broke with Nawaz Sharif prior to the elections when he rebuffed their claim to several prominent cabinet positions. Nawaz, like Zia, had proven willing to accept Jamaat support and thus, for example, approve a *Shariah* bill but not to have them dictate or significantly determine state policies. The defection of the Jamaat and the decision of the Islamic parties to contest elections on their own in 1993 weakened both the IDA's performance and that of the Islamic parties themselves. The Jamaat-led Islamic Front failed miserably. Islamic parties won a total of nine seats; the Jamaat took only two and its leader, Qazi Hussein Ahmad, failed to win a seat. In the 1997 elections, the Jamaat and the Jamiyyat i-Ulama-i-Pakistan (the Party of Pakistan's Ulama) boycotted elections. They, like the PPP, were blindsided by the results—a sweeping victory in national (136 of 217 seats vs. the PPP's 19) and provincial elections for the Pakistan Muslim League. The representation of Islamic leaders fell to its lowest in history due to the boycott by Islamic parties and the poor showing (two seats in the National Assembly) of the Jamiyyat i-Ulama-i-Islam (Party of the Ulama of Islam).

The popularity and relative success of the new government was due to a number of factors: Nawaz Sharif's PML majority, the fact that for the first time in history a political party controlled 75 percent of the National Assembly, the belief by many that time was running out for Pakistan to gain control of its destiny, and finally Nawaz's early policies. In addition, the low voter turnout (estimated at between 30 and 35 percent) and the continued threat of the Jamaat to engage in agitational politics against what it termed an unrepresentative government weakened the government's claim to legitimacy and made its successful performance in restoring economic and political stability that much more important.

Summary

For two decades, Islam progressively moved from the periphery to the center of Pakistan's politics, first under Zulfikar Ali Bhutto and then under Gen. Zia ul-Haq. Zia's Islamization program traveled a rocky road. When he assumed power in July 1977, both because of his own religious belief and because of the climate of Pakistani politics, he committed his regime to the implementation and enforcement of an Islamic system of government to legitimate his rule and to provide a basis for national identity and unity. Greeted with skepticism by some and with enthusiasm by many, the process led to frustration, disillusionment, and opposition.

The political aspirations of both secularists and traditional religious factions were thwarted. The parties of the Pakistan National Alliance soon discovered that they had won a Pyrrhic victory. National and provincial elections were postponed as rule by martial law was extended; and within two years the Pakistan National Alliance parties, like all political parties, were banned. All of this had been done in the name of Islam. Perhaps the most fundamental questions raised by Pakistan's experiment in Islamization are: "Whose Islam?" and "Why a negative Islam?"

Religious leaders, in particular, who initially applauded and supported the government's commitment to the establishment of an Islamic system of government, became increasingly disillusioned. Participation in the government gave way to opposition. Many religious leaders criticized the slow pace of Islamization. They expected and demanded full and immediate implementation of Islamic measures such as Islamic taxes and interest-free banking.[33] Of equal importance, Zia ul-Haq, not the *ulama* nor religious parties, was the final interpreter of Islam. Islamic regulations had but one source—Zia ul-Haq; even the *Shariah* Court's authority was circumscribed by the chief executive. Zia's martial law regulations were not subject to its jurisdiction. The court's decisions had to be endorsed by Zia before they could take effect.

"Whose Islam?" was for many tied to a related question: "Why a negative Islam?" The Islam that Zia ul-Haq's regime implemented was criticized as simply one of restrictions, Quranically prescribed punishments, taxation, and political control—all carried out in the name of Islam. Broad criticism from many quarters focused on the government's "manipulation" of Islam to postpone elections, to outlaw political parties, and to censor and suppress dissent. This quandary underscored a dual problem that has confronted Pakistan (and many other Muslim countries) throughout its existence: an inability to agree on the content of Islamic belief and the need for substantive reinterpretation and reform. Pakistanis have found it easier to rally under the umbrella of Islam in opposition movements—for example, against British and Hindu rule or, more recently, against Zulfikar Ali Bhutto's regime—than to agree upon what Islam and an Islamic state are.

A continuation of Pakistan's inability to achieve any consensus in theory or practice regarding the Islamic nature and character of the state was demonstrated by a debate in the media in which more than one hundred religious leaders, politicians, military officials, and intellectuals discussed the nature of an Islamic state. The positions ranged from advocating dictatorship to popular democracy, from a one-party to a multiparty political system.[34]

Islamization also exacerbated problems of religious sectarianism—both between Sunni and Shia and among Sunni Muslims themselves. Although no statistics are kept, the Shia constitute perhaps 25 percent of the population (estimates range from 5 percent to 25 percent). Historically, religious differences have resulted in clashes between the two communities. Zia's Islamization program underscored religious differences and their ability to split society. Initial Islamic measures like the alms and agricultural taxes and the imposition of Quranically prescribed penalties brought objections from the Shii community, who complained that their school of law, Jafari, differed in its prescriptions from the Sunni, Hanafi-based draft laws. Thus Islamization did not simply mean the implementation of Islamic law in their lives but of Sunni legal interpretations in particular. In July 1980, some fifteen thousand Shii marched in a demonstration in Rawalpindi against compulsory alms taxes. Although the government amended the *zakat* ordinance to exempt those who believed compulsory deduction of alms tax was against their school of law, it did not end communal conflicts.[35] Shii activism in building religious edifices, taking out religious processions, demonstrating for their rights, establishing their own activist student organization (the Imamia Student organization) on campuses, and the emergence of militant reformist Shii political movements and party (influenced by the Ayatollah Khomeini) brought a Sunni backlash that led to counter demonstrations, mutual vilification by militant preachers from each sect, violence, riots, deaths, and government-imposed curfews in major cities.[36]

Of equal significance are the religious differences among Sunni Muslims that have often been overlooked by analysts more familiar with the Arab world. Pakistani Sunni Muslims distinguish themselves according to their schools: Deobandi, Brelevi, Wahhabi, Ahl al-Hadith, and so forth. If anything, the resurgence of Islam in Pakistan meant not only greater emphasis on its Islamic character but also a proliferation of religious literature, much of which emphasized sectarian differences in belief and practice. The Pakistani Sunni Muslims' individual theological orientations constitute a form of sectarianism and remain an obstacle to any consensus on an Islamic vision for state and society. In addition they often represent differing class and religious interests. Provincial governments were directed to prohibit mosque sermons "against the faith of one sect or the other."[37] These differences, coupled with the lack of hierarchical structure in Sunni Islam, have historically been a major factor in the failure of religious groups to unite and work constructively in addressing Pakistan's Islamic identity.

The post-Zia period has been dominated by its concerns to strengthen national unity and democracy in a country torn by ethnic and regional differences and conflicts. At the same time, Benazir Bhutto's style of governance and the decision of her main opposition to mobilize under the banner of the Islamic Democratic Alliance demonstrate the extent to which any government must remain sensitive to Pakistan's Islamic identity. The post-Zia period (1986–98) was remarkably fluid. Although characterized by the rapid turnover of governments, economic stagnation, corruption, violence and sectarian warfare, yet, unlike the first four decades of Pakistan's history, change was accompanied by democratic elections and the unwillingness of the military to intervene directly and seize power. The Bhutto-Sharif periods also demonstrated the extent to which Islamic parties developed and changed as a result of their ability to exist and function within the political process. In contrast to more repressive Arab experiences, Pakistan's Islamic parties have become part of the political mainstream, institutionalized participants in political and social change. Over time they have come to accept democratic processes and participate in elections. While they did abstain from participation in the 1996 elections, the boycott was a political tactic, not a rejection of democratic elections.

Islamic parties in Pakistan, although subject to control and at times suppression, have not experienced systematic repression and have not evidenced the radicalism and extremism witnessed in many Arab countries. Participation in the political process has meant compromise and tactical and strategic changes that have become internalized over time. At the same time, a political environment that permitted alternative religious and nonreligious parties prevented any single Islamic party from becoming the sole voice and rallying point for opposition. As a result, while Islamic parties like the Jamaat-i-Islami have proven effective in oppositional politics and influenced government Islamization programs, they have never dominated electoral politics. Indeed, their performance at the polls has become weaker rather than stronger over time. The Jamaat was established as an ideological organization, elite rather than populist in membership and orientation. It has drawn support heavily from the urban middle class, whose interests it has represented, over the impoverished masses. Ideology without a sufficient popular base has proven effective in influencing religious discourse and politics but not in garnering the votes necessary to come to power or to significantly change the political and economic institutions.

The issue of Pakistan's Islamic identity has existed ever since the Muslim League chose to appeal to Islam to mobilize popular support during the independence movement. Governments from that of Jinnah to Nawaz Sharif have had to contend with this question to varying degrees, especially after a prolonged period in which Islam had dominated political discourse. While many might differ in their Islamic or non-Islamic orientations, dismantling the Islamization process of the 1970s and 1980s can be a political minefield if it is seen as undermining Pakistan's Islamic identity, however amorphous that might be. While there are many aspects to a Pakistani's identity, there remains an underlying belief or yearning among many for some kind of Islamic order or dimension to their life and society.

Iran

Although the anti-shah movement in Iran in 1978 startled Western observers, beneath the seemingly secure surface upon which Iran's ship of state sailed, there had long been strong currents of discontent and opposition. Oil wealth, an ambitious modernization program administered by an enormous bureaucracy, the largest and best-equipped army in the Middle East, and an effective secret police (SAVAK) were the foundations of Pahlavi power and security. Yet development programs, royal patronage, repression, and official corruption proved incapable of containing growing discontent with an increasingly authoritarian state. The much-touted success of the Muhammad Reza Shah's White Revolution proved less impressive upon closer examination. Despite considerable gains in health, education, and agricultural reform, a disproportionate amount of the benefits from Iranian reforms went to the elites of the society. Modernization had perhaps increased their number, but it also continued the pattern of concentration of wealth at the top. At the same time, the real improvements and gains of socioeconomic development did not meet rising public expectations or significantly change the lot of many. While the literacy rate rose from 26 to 42 percent, "fewer than 40 percent of the children completed primary school, the teacher-student ratio in public schools deteriorated, only 60,000 university places opened each year for as many as 290,000 applicants, and the percentage of the population with higher degrees remained one of the lowest in the Middle East."[38]

The fruits of modernization were visible in major cities and in the lives of the upper and middle classes. Its impact upon village life was more problematic. Ninety-six percent of the villages remained without electricity. Iran had once been agriculturally self-sufficient; by the mid-1970s, more than $1 billion was spent per year on imported products. As in many parts of the Middle East, modernization and urbanization resulted in the migration of villagers to the city and the proliferation of urban slums. The potential advantages of migration to the city were often offset by the breakdown of the extended family and by a deterioration in the quality of life—shortage of housing, overcrowded dwellings, congested streets, and unemployment. As Ervand Abrahamian has perceptively observed: "For these millions, most of whom had been forced out of the villages into the new shantytowns, the oil boom did not end poverty; it merely modernized it."[39] The socioeconomic realities of the shah's modernization program were exacerbated by the regional and ethnic tensions that grew out of resentment over the unequal distribution of development projects to preferred major cities like Teheran. Finally, many in the new middle-class professions were frustrated by a system that made them totally dependent upon the government. Despite their education, professional positions, and favorable economic status, most remained politically powerless under a monarchy that had become progressively autocratic. Constitutional rights and protections, parliamentary rule, and a political party system were subverted by a government of decrees and secret police.

Both liberal democrats and leftists were equally threatened by a growing monarchical absolutism. Discontent with the fast pace of modernization and imperial autocracy contributed to the expansion of a religiocultural alliance of traditional religious leaders and lay intellectuals that had developed during the 1960s and early 1970s. For the religious classes, Pahlavi rule had come to mean the erosion of their status and sources of revenue; the undermining of their ideology, institutions, and values; and the imposition of an alien (Western, Christian, or secular) way of life. At the same time, even among those who had benefited from Western-style educations, many had become gravely concerned about the influence of the West, especially of the United States, upon Iranian politics and society. America through its CIA had orchestrated the shah's return from exile to Iran in 1953. Since that time, American advisers had played a major role in the training and development of Iran's military and secret police as well as in its economy.

Military and economic dependence were matched by the progressive westernization of Iranian education and society. Religious and lay people shared a common concern about cultural alienation caused by what the secular intellectual Jalal al-Ahmad called "Westoxification" or "Weststruckness," the indiscriminate borrowing from and imitation of the West. The danger of Western cultural imperialism was joined to fear of Western political domination. By 1978 there were forty-one thousand Americans in Iran. The growing American diplomatic, military, and corporate presence and the very nature of development programs, which were based upon Western models of socioeconomic change, fueled fears of a loss of national autonomy and identity. The preservation and revival of Irano-Islamic culture became a common concern and rallying point. Iran's Shiite Islamic religious and cultural heritage provided an ideal framework for both a meaningful critique of the status quo and an authentic source of pride and identity, a sense of history and values. Interpretations of the meaning and implications of reclaiming Irano-Islamic identity, however, varied greatly.

The prevailing mood among the regime's opposition before 1978 had been one of reformism, not revolution. Progressively confronted by a political order that enforced its will and countered its opposition not by constitutional means but by military and police force, the coalition broadened its membership as well as its goal and became a political revolution. Reform of a corrupt system was seen to necessitate removal of its source or foundation, the Pahlavi monarchy. The religious-lay alliance included a diversity of positions. Although the opposition shared a common concern and diagnosis of the disease ("Weststruckness" and authoritarian rule), their understanding of the nature of the cure—symbolically represented as a return to Islam— varied markedly.

Jalal al-Ahmad was a leading intellectual and literary figure in Iran. The son of a religious scholar, his studies at a local religious school were followed by an urban university program where he learned and was influenced by Western thought. He had been a member of the Tudeh (Communist) Party for several years. His acceptance of the scientific and technological aspects of modernization became tempered, however, by his wariness and finally bitter criticism of the cultural danger of Western influence: "I say that *Gharbzadegi* ["Weststruckness"] is like cholera . . . It is at least as bad as sawflies in the wheat fields. Have you ever seen how they infest wheat? From within. There's a healthy skin in place, but it's only a skin, just like the shell of a cicada on a tree."[40]

Like most countries influenced by colonialism, Iran had become the blind progeny of the West: relying on Western sources, judging by

Western standards, dependent upon foreign advisers and consultants. Jalal al-Ahmad believed that the result of this total dependence on the West was loss of identity: "We're like a nation alienated from itself, in our clothing and our homes, our food and our literature, our publications and, most dangerously of all, our education. We effect Western training, we effect Western thinking, and we follow Western procedures to solve every problem."[41]

Iranians were cut off from their historical roots: the core of their society, culture, and tradition. For Jalal al-Ahmad, Iranian options were not simply limited to either the westernization of society or the rejection of modernization by retreating to the past; instead he advocated a third alternative that stressed the country's Irano-Islamic cultural tradition. Islam was the unifying force in Iran. Though a secularist, he had become convinced that Iranians must turn to their Islamic heritage for the foundation stones of national identity: ideology, sense of history, and values. It alone enjoyed wide public acceptance and appeal and could be used effectively to mobilize the populace. Similarly, though critical of the conservatism of the clergy, he recognized the role they might play in mass mobilization given the respect they received from the great majority of the public. As we shall see, the potential that Jalal al-Ahmad saw in Islamic ideology and religious leadership for mass mobilization later became the basis for the broad-based religiopolitical opposition movement that dethroned the shah.

The secular intellectual indictment of westernization and the call for a continuity of modern Iran's identity and culture with its past was a primary agenda for religiously oriented lay and clerical ideologists as well as for men like Mehdi Bazargan, Ali Shariati, and of course the Ayatollah Khomeini.

In 1962, the same year that Jalal al-Ahmad's *Gharbzadegi* appeared, Mehdi Bazargan (b. 1907) delivered a lecture entitled "The Boundary Between Religion and Social Affairs," on the relationship of religion to politics. Bazargan, a French-trained engineer with a strong Islamic commitment, had been jailed in 1939 for his opposition to the shah's religious policies. In 1961 he and the Ayatollah Taliqani (1910–78), who had both been active members of Prime Minister Mosaddeq's National Front, organized the Liberation Movement of Iran. It sought to bridge the gap between modern, secular, and traditional religious Iranians in working toward a more Islamic state and society.

Arrested once again in 1962 for his opposition to the shah, Bazargan was released in 1969. In 1979 he became the provisional prime minister of the Islamic Republic of Iran. He is viewed as a founder of modern Iran's Islamic movement.

Bazargan's political activism was inspired by his Islamic commitment. His orientation is reflected in the titles of his speeches and booklets: "The Causes of the Decadence of Muslims," "Islam, the Dynamic Religion," "Mission and Ideology," "The Relationship of Religion to Politics." Bazargan was especially effective because he combined a traditional religious outlook and vocabulary with modern concerns. He appealed to the integral relationship of religion to politics and society in Islam as embodied in the unity of God, the Muslim belief that Islam is a way of life, the combined role of Muhammad as prophet-statesman, and the activities of the early Shii *Imams*. He spoke the language of the *ulama* and could use his credibility with them to criticize the political neutrality of many religious leaders. Bazargan argued that recognition of the interrelatedness of religion and politics in Islam should prompt the *ulama* to become actively involved in politics in order to bring about the renewal of Islamic society in Iran.

The socialist inclinations of Jalal al-Ahmad and the Islamic reformist spirit of Bazargan were combined in Ali Shariati, whose revolutionary Islam was at once more appealing to secularists, leftists, and, in particular, Iranian students who often found the traditionism of their religious leaders unconvincing and the secular modernism of many professors disorienting. Ali Shariati (1933–77) incorporated many of the reformist currents of his times: opposition to the shah, rejection of westernization, religious revivalism, and social reform. Shariati was born in a village near Mashhad, in eastern Iran. His father, Muhammad Taqi Shariati, was a scholar-preacher, traditionally trained but reformist in outlook. The father served as the model and formative influence upon his son's religious and sociopolitical outlook: "My father fashioned the first dimensions of my spirit. It was he who taught me the art of thinking and the art of being human . . . I grew up and matured in his library, which was for him the whole of his life and family."[42]

Shariati received his early education in Mashhad. During his high school years, he became active in his father's youth center, the Center for the Spread of Islamic Teachings, which sought to propagate Islam among Iranian youth and to communicate the relevance of Islam to contemporary Iranian life.

There was an educational vacuum in Iranian society. Traditional religious leaders and their seminaries had developed a siege mentality in the face of the shah's modernization reform with its imposition of Western secular curricula. At the same time, many of the university professors had adopted a Western secular outlook. Young Iranian students were caught between their traditional religious upbringing and a modern educational world view. It was this segment of Iranian society, in particular, to which Shariati devoted his life's work. In the late 1940s, Shariati and his father joined the Movement of God-Worshiping Socialists, which attempted to synthesize Shiism with European socialism.[43] Father and son were also active in Mosaddeq's nationalist movement and in the abortive coup of 1953.

After graduation from the Teacher Training College, Shariati taught elementary school. It was during this time that he discovered a second hero, or model, for Islamic life—Abu Dharr al-Ghiffari. Abu Dharr had been a companion of the Prophet Muhammad who later denounced the wealth and corruption of caliphal court life and championed the rights of the poor. As such, for Shariati and indeed for many contemporary activists who emphasize Islamic social justice or Islamic socialism, Abu Dharr was a model to be emulated in present-day Muslim societies.

From 1959 to 1965, Shariati was in Paris, where he studied Islamic history and sociology and earned a doctorate from the Sorbonne. His knowledge of traditional Islamic sources was now supplemented by the ideas of Emile Durkheim, Max Weber, Che Guevara, Albert Camus, and Frantz Fanon. As had his early years in Iran, the years in France contributed to his development both intellectually and politically. It was the time of the Algerian and Cuban revolutions. Shariati was attracted by and translated the writings of Guevara and Fanon. During the early 1960s, he was active in the Liberation Movement of Iran, founded by Bazargan and Taliqani, and also edited *Free Iran*.

From his return to Iran in 1965, Shariati was viewed by the shah's government as a threat. He was imprisoned for his anti-government activities in Paris and then, after his release, was denied a teaching post at Teheran University. Although he finally obtained a position at the University of Mashhad, his popularity with students and his inno-

vative ideas brought him into conflict with both the conservative
ulama and the promonarchist administrators at the university.

In 1967 Shariati moved to Teheran, where, in 1972, he became a
leader at the Husayniyah Irshad Religious Center. Husayniyahs were
places for the commemoration of Husayn's martyrdom. As such the
center symbolized Husayn's righteous struggle and martyrdom
against the oppression and social injustice of the Umayyad caliphs.
For Shariati it also symbolized the contemporary situation of the Iranian people. The impact of Shariati's lectures was almost immediate.
Thousands came to hear him speak; six thousand students attended
his summer classes. The original center had to be expanded, and
plans were made to establish similar centers outside Teheran. More
than one hundred thousand copies of his lectures and writings were
published and distributed.[44] The enormous success of his lectures in
winning a wide following among students, intellectuals, and the Left
caused the shah to denounce him as an "Islamic Marxist" and finally,
in 1973, to imprison him and close down the Husayniyah Irshad. After eighteen months in solitary confinement, Shariati was released
and restricted to his village, Mazinan, under close surveillance. Finally, in 1977 the government permitted him to leave Iran for England. Shortly after his arrival in England, he died of an apparent
heart attack at the age of forty-four. His supporters suspected SAVAK
of foul play.

Shariati was an innovative Islamic thinker who stood in sharp
contrast to the traditional religious intepretation of the *ulama* and the
westernized secular outlook of many university professors. Influenced by modern Islamic reformers such as Jamal al-Din al-Afghani
and Muhammad Iqbal, he emphasized the dynamic, progressive, scientific nature of Islam and the need for a thoroughgoing reinterpretation of Islam to reverse the retrogressive state of Islam and to revitalize
the Muslim community. Shariati combined Islamic thought with Western social-scientific language in trying to provide an indigenous Shii
ideology for sociopolitical reform. In doing this, he risked and confronted the wrath of the shah, as well as the criticism of many religious leaders who viewed his syncretistic, innovative interpretation of
Islam as an unwarranted departure from tradition.

Shariati's lectures and publications reflect the Irano-Islamic issues
of his time: "Reasons for the Decline of Religion," "The Machine and
the Captivity of Machinism," "Man Without Self—Two Concepts of

Alienation," "A Revolution in Values," "Tawhid, A Philosophy of History." He began with the denunciation of "Weststruckness": "Come, friends, let us abandon Europe; let us cease this nauseating, apish imitation of Europe. Let us leave behind this Europe that always speaks of humanity, but destroys human beings wherever it finds them."[45] His "return to Islam" was not based upon the medieval Islamic world view of conservative *ulama*. He distinguished scholastic, institutionalized Safavid Islam from Alid Islam—the true, dynamic, revolutionary message of Shii Islam—of which he wrote: "original Shiism was an intellectually progressive Islamic movement as well as a militant social force, the most committed, most revolutionary Islamic sect."[46] The doctrine of Divine Unity (*tawhid*) provides the intellectual foundation for all the affairs (religious, political, economic, social) of society. Shariati preached what may be termed a liberation theology that combined a reinterpretation of Islamic belief incorporating modern sociological language with the Third World socialist outlook of Frantz Fanon and Che Guevara. But he differed with Fanon's rejection of traditional religions and instead insisted that the defeat of Western imperialism in Iran required the reclaiming of her national, religious, cultural identity—a reclaiming of Iran's Islamic roots.

For Shariati the revolution in Iran had two fundamental aspects: national identity/unity and socioeconomic justice. Only this dual program could address a politically subjugated and economically exploited Iran, caught in the grips of "world imperialism, including multinational corporations and cultural imperialism, racism, class exploitation, class oppression, class inequality, and *gharbzadegi* ["Weststruckness"]."[47] But who was to lead such a movement and what Islamic ideology should be followed?

Although Shariati, like Khomeini, spoke of the *Imam* as the guide of the community, he believed the leadership for the reassertion of Iran's political and social revolution would come primarily from religiously minded lay intelligentsia rather than from the *ulama*. In general Shariati criticized the religious leaders for having been co-opted by the Safavids in allowing the dynamic, revolutionary ideology of Shiism to become an establishment religion, bureaucratic and supportive of the status quo. As a result, Islam's dynamic ideology had become institutionalized, leading to the gap between Islam and the social realities of Iran. Traditional Islam under the *ulama* had become mired in a fossilized past and scholastic manuals; and it had become the popular, fatalistic opiate of the masses. It had ceased to be a social force, effectively addressing the changing realities of society. Thus the decline of Muslim society was caused not only by Western imperialism but also the retrograde state of the religious establishment.

Shariati called for a "scientific" approach to Islam in order to recover the spirit of early Islam, which was a socially revolutionary movement. His call for a scientific examination of Islam and his use of modern sociological terminology appealed to modern, educated Iranians, especially the younger generation who felt caught between past upbringing and contemporary Western ideas. It restored cultural pride and confidence. At the same time, his anti-Western critique and use of Islamic sources and beliefs resonated with the world view and vocabulary of the majority of Iranians—traditionists as well as modernists. Shariati's methodology, however, was clearly reformist.

Influenced in particular by Muhammad Iqbal's *Reconstruction of Religious Thought in Islam,* Shariati emphasized the dynamic character of Islam as it related to individual Muslims and the Muslim community. Islam is progressive, scientific, and revolutionary. Starting with the doctrine of the unity of God, he maintained that this was not only a theological statement about the monotheistic nature of God but the unity of all creation. God's rule and guidance extends to politics and society. This fundamental Islamic belief had been compromised by the Safavids' co-opting of religion and the religious establishment's cooperation with Safavid rule. Islam had become an establishment religion supporting oppressive governments rather than in continual revolt as it should be. Too often the *ulama* had become government advisers or succumbed to political quietism rather than protectors and activist leaders of the people, guarding against compromise, denouncing the oppression of rulers, and being true warriors of Islam.

Shariati's social doctrine began with the belief that the ideal social order established by the Prophet Muhammad was a system based on the unity of God, *nizam-i-tawhid.* This, too, had been subverted by imperial governments with their feudal systems based on class consciousness and economic exploitation. As such Iranian society was not the society envisioned by Islam but was rather one based upon polytheism (i.e., giving ultimate allegiance to anything other than God). For Shariati true Islamic society was to be a classless society, which rejected distinctions based upon tribal, economic, or personal status.

Nowhere was Shariati's innovative method of intepretation and his revolutionary, sociopolitical understanding of Shiism more evident than in his explanation of the meaning and significance of the expectation *(intizar)* of the *Imam* as the Mahdi, the rightly guided one. With the absence or seclusion of the Twelfth Imam, religious leaders had acquiesced to the de facto separation of religion and politics because they had accepted the legitimacy of temporal rulers, or monarchs, during this absence. Political quietism resulted as the community passively awaited the future coming of the Mahdi and the messianic age of justice. Shariati believed that such a depoliticized Shiism subverted its true revolutionary character. True expectation is an active striving *(jihad)* to realize social justice, motivated by the messianic hope and promise of the Mahdi. This is the sense in which all Muslims are called to be holy warriors. Muslims find themselves "plundered, tortured, hungry, oppressed and discriminated against." *Intizar* is God's promise of victory to Islam: "He had promised the wretched masses they would become leaders of mankind; He had promised the disinherited they would inherit the earth from the mighty." Shariati concluded: "Belief in the final Saviour, in the Shii *Imams* and the Twelfth Imam, means that this universal Revolution and final victory is the conclusion of the one great continual justice-seeking movement of revolt against oppression."[48]

Ali Shariati did not establish or lead a specific activist organization. Instead he influenced a broad range of Islamically oriented reform-minded Iranian youth, some of whom established their own organizations. Among the more prominent was the Mujahideen-i-Khalq (the People's Soldiers), a secret revolutionary organization often denounced by the shah as "Islamic Marxists." Shariati's interpretation of Shii Islam as a revolutionary ideology whose goal was a socially just society was adopted by the Mujahideen as the basis for a social revolution to create a *Tawhidi*, an Islamic socialist system. Although originally part of the united Islamic opposition to the shah, after the revolution the Mujahideen's initial cooperation with the Ayatollah Khomeini would give way to active, violent opposition to conservative *ulama* power and government control. Assassination of government officials by the Mujahideen would be countered by Khomeini's denunciation of the Mujahideen as non-Muslims and an equally violent purge by government forces.

Khomeini

If Shariati was the ideologue of the Iranian Revolution, Ayatollah Khomeini was its living symbol and architect. As discussed earlier, Khomeini was not among the most senior ayatollahs; nevertheless, he had vigorously spoken out against the shah's policies during 1963–65, had been imprisoned several times, and had finally been exiled. From his exile, Khomeini continued his criticism of the monarchy. During the 1970s, as the shah became increasingly autocratic and used the military and SAVAK to silence his critics, only the religious establishment was able to remain relatively intact. Although the shah had moved against individual religious leaders and his educational and land-reform policies had weakened the religious establishment, still the religious establishment retained its independence. First, the sheer number and distribution of religious scholars and local religious leaders, as well as the more than twenty thousand mosques scattered throughout every village and city, made effective government control impossible. Second, the religious establishment retained a good deal of financial independence. In addition to religious endowments, they received the *zakat* (2.5 percent wealth tax for the poor) and *khums* ("one-fifth" religious tax on annual income), which Shii Muslims are expected to contribute to religious authorities.

Khomeini shared with Mawlana Mawdudi of the Jamaat-i-Islami and Hasan al-Banna of the Muslim Brotherhood a condemnation of westernization, Western imperialism, and Israel: "the foul claws of imperialism have clutched at the heart of the lands of the people of the Quran, with our national wealth and resources being devoured by imperialism . . . with the poisonous culture of imperialism penetrating to the depths of towns and villages throughout the Muslim world, displacing the culture of the Quran." The shah's recognition of Israel and Iran's shipment of oil to Israel came under blistering attack as well: "The sinister influence of imperialism is especially evident in Iran. Israel, the universally recognized enemy of Islam and the Muslims, at war with the Muslim peoples for years, has, with the assistance of the despicable government of Iran, penetrated all the economic, military, and political affairs of the country; it must be said that Iran has become a military base for Israel which means, by extension, for America."[49]

Throughout his exile in Iraq and then in France, Khomeini became the symbol of opposition to the shah. He continued to function as a guide to his followers in Iran and thus to receive revenue for his activities from religious taxes. With such support from his Iranian followers, Khomeini continued to speak out and finance a movement against the shah's regime. Copies of his writings and speeches as well as tape cassettes were smuggled into Iran and circulated. Khomeini had several advantages over other opposition leaders or groups: Because he was outside Iran, he had the freedom and independence to say exactly what he thought without fear of intimidation or imprisonment, and his appeal to religion could attract a more broad-based constituency than the nationalists whose opposition was based upon secular principles.

During the 1970s, Khomeini's position moved sharply from that of a critic calling upon the shah to reform his government to that of an opposition leader, denouncing an illegitimate, un-Islamic government. In Islamic terminology, Khomeini ceased to call upon the shah as a Muslim ruler to repent, that is, to stop his wayward behavior and return to a more faithful following of God's path; instead he increasingly condemned the shah and his government as anti-Islamic, as a regime based upon unbelief, and thus the object of *jihad*. In the 1940s, in *Revealing of the Secrets*, Khomeini had attacked the autocratic policies of Reza Shah but had given a qualified acceptance to monarchy. By 1971 in a message to those on pilgrimage at Mecca, he stated unequivocally: "Islam is fundamentally opposed to the whole notion of monarchy." In that same message, Khomeini denounced Iran's monarchy: "God only knows what disasters the Iranian monarchy has given rise to since its very beginning and what crimes it has committed. Crimes of the kings of Iran have blackened the pages of history. It is the kings of Iran that have constantly ordered massacres of their own people and had pyramids built with their skulls."[50]

During 1970, Khomeini had occasion to lecture on the nature of government in Islam and the role of the *ulama*. These lectures, delivered at the seminary in Najaf, Iraq, were later published under the title of *Islamic Government*. Rejecting monarchy, Khomeini argued for the supervision of the government by religious authorities and even their direct rule. Like Ali Shariati, Khomeini believed that absence of the *Imam* did not mean Shiite political quietism. Muslims were not to wait for the return of the *Imam* in order to live in an Islamic state and society. Islam and politics were inseparable, and so there should be an Islamic government. Such a government could take a number of forms. In the case of a temporal ruler, the Islamic character of the government is determined by *Shariah* rule. Islamic law provides the blueprint for state and society, which the executive is to protect and safeguard and the judiciary is to apply. The legislative branch of government is not necessary because only God can legislate and Muslims already possess His law. What is necessary is the *Shariah's* implementation in place of the man-made foreign codes that they have adopted. Khomeini differs sharply here from Mawlana Mawdudi and the Muslim Brotherhood, for they both maintain that Muslim society must first be made truly Islamic before Islamic law (especially its penal laws) can be fully implemented. In contrast Khomeini maintained that the immediate implementation of Islamic law is the means to bring about the reformation or renewal of Islamic society. In this Khomeini's position was similar to that of Islamic revolutionaries in Iran and Egypt who advocate the overthrow of corrupt, unIslamic governments, and the Islamization of society through the imposition of Islamic law.

Khomeini's view on Islamic government would have remained academic had the political situation in Iran not deteriorated so rapidly and had the shah's repressive policies not only silenced but also provided a common cause for a broadly based resistance movement. With the widespread suppression of the shah's critics, including intellectuals, journalists, politicians, liberal nationalists, socialists, and Marxists, Shii Islam provided the most viable banner for a united opposition. Khomeini, who had been asked to leave by the Iraqi government, once again sought exile—this time in Paris. While there, he became the symbol and center of opposition not only because of his increasingly vitriolic condemnation of the shah, who had originally forced him into exile, but also because of his call for a new political order that included a constitutional government and socioeconomic reform. Iranian dissidents who were studying or living in Europe and America, such as Abol-Hasan Bani Sadr, Sadeq Ghotbzadeh, and Mansur Farhang, gathered around him.

Khomeini believed that the establishment of Islamic governments faced formidable obstacles: "the imperialists, the oppressive and treacherous rulers, the Jews, Christians, and materialists are all attempting to distort the truths of Islam and lead the Muslims astray."[51] In 1970 Khomeini had spoken of an Islamic revolution whose realization might take centuries; even he could not foresee the events that would rapidly bring about the revolution of 1977–79, the downfall of the shah, and his triumphant return to Iran to establish the Islamic Republic of Iran.

An "Islamic" Revolution

As opposition mounted within Iran in the late 1970s, Shii Islam emerged as the most viable vehicle for an effective mass movement. Islam provided a common set of symbols, a historic identity, and a value system that was non-Western, indigenous, and broadly appealing. It offered an ideological framework within which a variety of factions could function. Moreover, the religious leadership had remained untainted, having not cooperated with the government. It also provided some hierarchical organization and leadership in its charismatic ayatollahs. A number of them—the Ayatollahs Khomeini, Taliqani, and Shariatmadari—had suffered under the shah for their opposition to the government. Moreover, Islamic lay reformers like Shariati and Bazargan enjoyed the respect of many, especially of an alienated and increasingly militant younger generation. The *ulama*-mosque system provided a natural, informal nationwide communications network. Thus the thousands of mosques in Iran, became the foci for dissent, centers for political organization and agitation. Mosques offered a sanctuary, the Friday sermon became a political platform, and religious figures represented a vast reservoir of grassroots leadership. Shii Islam offered an ideological view of history that gave meaning and legitimation to an opposition movement. Shii Islam is a religion with an ideology and symbolism well suited for protest and opposition.

Unlike Sunni Islam, with its sense that early success and power were signs of God's favor, for Shii Islam, history documents the persistent denial or frustration of God's will regarding leadership of the Islamic community. As noted previously, the Shii ("the Party" of Ali), believe that Ali, the cousin and son-in-law of Muhammad, had been designated by Muhammad as his successor. His right of succession as leader, however, was denied by the Sunni majority of the Islamic community who accepted the selection of Abu Bakr as successor to the Prophet. The martyrdom of Husayn at Karbala in A.D. 680 was of special significance, providing the paradigm for the Iranian Revolution. It symbolized the role of Shii Islam as a protest movement in which a small righteous party struggled against the overwhelming forces of evil. Thus Shii Islam, the religion of the vast majority of Iranians, provided the ideology and symbols for a popular revolutionary struggle. For many Shii, the shah and his overpowering military army, like Yazid's army, represented the evils of corruption and social injustice. Like Husayn and his forces, the righteous had a religious duty to revolt against this modern Satan and to undertake a holy war to restore the reign of goodness, equity, and social justice to make Iran a true Islamic territory. Toward this end, self-sacrifice and even death were to be freely accepted, for to die in God's struggle was to become a martyr and to win eternal reward.

Under the umbrella of Islam, heterogeneous groups in the political spectrum, from secularists to Islamic activists, from liberal democrats to Marxists, joined together. They marched behind banners that symbolically declared their three options: USA (West), hammer and sickle (USSR), and Allah. Crossing out the first two options on their banners, they rejected the West and the Soviet Union and chose the third, more authentic, Irano-Islamic alternative. But although there was a common purpose—opposition to the shah and a desire for a more indigenously rooted modernity—the religious and political outlook and agenda of the various groups were quite diverse. Some wished to reclaim their Iranian identity, or selfhood, through a more conscious incorporation of their cultural heritage, its history, and its values, within Iran's modernization. For many the Islamic alternative, symbolized by the name Allah, meant a return to Islam, the establishment of an Islamic state and society.

Among the Islamically committed, there were sharp and distinctive differences in their interpretations of Islamic identity and ideology. Nowhere was this clearer than in the juxtaposition of banners depicting the Ayatollah Khomeini and Ali Shariati in street protests and homes. The former emerged as the leader of the revolution and the latter served as its ideologue. Khomeini, the conservative religious authority, looked to Islam's traditional past, the manuals of medieval Islam. Shariati and other Islamic modernists represented a far more innovative, reformist approach, viewing Shiah Islam in a more radically creative, revolutionary manner.

The year 1977 was a turning point in contemporary Iranian history, the onset of the revolution of 1977–79. Like the uprisings in 1963, the high point of political agitation in 1978 would occur during the holy month of Muharram. Several events in particular caused the tumultuous but contained forces of political opposition to erupt into mass, public demonstrations in the streets that were to spread across Iran and eventually to bring down the government. In November 1977, the police tried to break up a session of what had been a series of peaceful poetry readings at Aryamehr University, sponsored by the Writers' Association, an organization of leading writers and intellectuals who were critical of the regime. The more than ten thousand students and participants poured out of the packed hall into the streets, shouting antiregime slogans. In the clash that followed, one student was killed, seventy injured, and one hundred arrested.[52] This police action precipitated a mass of student strikes that shut down major universities in Iran.

Two months later, two additional incidents occurred that brought public political protest to a climax. In January 1978, a seminarian who had been granted sanctuary was killed by government forces. As in the Tobacco Revolt, religious sanctuary was used to publicize political protest as well as to seek protection. Although the regime had often chosen not to respect religious sanctuary during the previous decade, the climate had changed. The government's ability to control or repress its opposition had been weakened both because of external pressures regarding human rights and, much more importantly, because of the growing galvanization of diverse groups and factions, united by their common opposition to the monarchy. Moreover, given the Islamic identification of anti-shah forces, the violation of sanctuary took on an added religiopolitical significance.

The event that sparked a long round of demonstrations and violence was the government's attack in January 1978 upon the *ulama*, particularly Khomeini. On January 7, a newspaper article entitled "Iran and the Black and Red Reactionaries" denounced the religious leaders as "black reactionaries" in league with international communism. Moreover, "the article also charged that Khomeini was really a foreigner who in his youth had worked as a British spy, led a licentious life, and to top it all, had written erotic Sufi poetry."[53] The pattern of protest was one that became familiar. The *ulama*-merchant leadership closed down their establishments, and four thousand demonstrators took to the streets, chanting "We don't want the Yazid government" and "We demand the return of Ayatollah Khomeini."[54] The police moved in, and, in the ensuing clash, students were killed and injured. What became known as the Qum Massacre was followed by a series of public demonstrations that were originally called to commemorate peacefully events such as the massacre, especially on the fortieth day of its anniversary, by closing down the universities and the bazaars and attending mosque services.

While most demonstrations remained peaceful, in Tabriz (February 18, 1978), Yazd (March 29), and again in Qum (May 10) demonstrators rioted when fired upon by police, army tanks, and helicopter gunships. Protestors attacked symbols of the royal family and its "modernized-westernized state: police stations, statues of the Pahlavi monarchs, luxury hotels, liquor stores, movie houses. Increasingly, the chanting slogans of the crowds became more militant: "Death to the shah," "Glory to Husayn," "Husayn is our guide, Khomeini is our leader," "Cast out America," "We desire an Islamic Republic." The shah was the new Yazid, the devil incarnate; Khomeini was the representative of the martyred Imam Husayn. The battle had been struck between the "pagan" Pahlavi usurper regime and the "forces of Islam." On September 7, 1978, more than five hundred thousand demonstrators had gathered to protest the imposition of martial law by royal decree. The following day, events came to a head in Teheran; on "Black Friday" (September 8), approximately seventy-five thousand people staged a sit-in demonstration in Jaleh Square. When the military and police were unable to break up the crowd, the crowd was directly fired upon by helicopter gunships as well as by tanks and soldiers on the ground.

Black Friday was a turning point in the revolution. It united the opposition and radicalized and mobilized the masses. The opposition, secular and religious, regardless of political outlook and orientation, united to an unprecedented degree with Khomeini as its symbol. Islamic ideology, symbols, and the *ulama*-mosque infrastructure formed the core of the revolution; and in this sense, Iran's revolution became an Islamic one, cast in an Irano-Islamic mold and idiom. This development was demonstrated by the use of Islamic symbols. Believer and unbeliever, liberal constitutionalist and radical, traditionist and modernist could be heard by the hundreds of thousands throughout the major cities and in villages proclaiming in defiance throughout the night *"Allahu Akbar!"*—the traditional Islamic battle cry—"God is most Great." Similarly, women who had worn modern attire now joined with their more traditional sisters in donning the veil as a symbol of protest against a monarch whose modernization program had once attempted to ban the veil.

During the months that followed Black Friday, a wave of strikes swept across the country, threatening to paralyze the government. Schools, universities, banks, railroads, airlines, mass media, government offices, oil fields, mines and many industrial plants were affected as white- and blue-collar workers, traditional and modern members of the middle class, city dwellers and rural peasants swelled the ranks of the opposition and engaged in political action. In December 1978, the month of Muharram, the religious symbolism and emotions that surround the commemoration of Husayn's martrydom were once again fused with contemporary political realities as religious processions became protest demonstrations. In Teheran the Ashura procession drew almost two million people who called for the overthrow and death of the shah, the creation of an Islamic government, and the return and leadership of Khomeini. On January 6, 1979, the shah, buffeted by widespread dissent and violence, unable to count on a military whose soldiers were defecting, and finding his American patrons wavering in their support, left Iran.

The Islamic Republic of Iran

Iran's revolution brought together a diverse cross-section of religious and secular lay leadership, social classes, and political parties as well as guerilla movements. For historical and cultural reasons, Islam had emerged as the most effective means for mass organization and mobilization. Thus the revolution occurred under the umbrella of Islam: employing a Shiite ideology, religious symbols, and a mosque-centered organization and communications network. Though the anti-shah forces were many and varied in religious and political orientations, the Ayatollah Khomeini had emerged as both the symbol of resistance and, in time, its principal leader and spokesman. Yet many Iranians were not prepared for what was to unfold during the first days and years after the establishment of the Islamic Republic of Iran. Most were unaware of Khomeini's views on the nature of government and politics and their relationship to Iran. His criticisms and denunciation of the shah and his call for a new, just political and social order had been in religiocultural categories not unlike those of many other critics of the shah. His advisers in Paris and in the early days after he returned to Teheran included men like Bani Sadr and Sadeq Ghotbzadeh, Mansur Farhang, and Ibrahim Yazdi—modern laymen influenced by the outlook of Ali Shariati. Moreover, although the opposition had a common enemy (the shah, Pahlavi despotism, and foreign control) and a common purpose (a more just and egalitarian government), there had been no agreement upon the particular form of government or even its leadership. These were revolutionary times. Few, other than Khomeini's colleagues and students, were familiar with his writings on the nature of Islamic government and the rule of the *faqih,* an expert in Islamic law. Indeed few foresaw the control that he and the *ulama* would exert in their creation of a "clerical" Islamic government.

In his writings on Islamic government, Khomeini argued from the position of requiring that the true Muslim ruler must be noted for his "comprehensive knowledge, justice, and moral character" to the possibility of direct rule by jurists themselves. This could be accomplished either by a group of jurists *(faqihs)* or even by a single individual. He also asserted that such guardianship or government by a jurist *(vilayat-i-faqih)* is similar to that exercised by the Prophet Muhammad. The jurist would have the same authority to govern and administer though, of course, not the same status as Muhammad. Few had taken much note of Khomeini's interpretation of Islamic government and the rule of the legal expert. The implications of this doctrine were only to be realized during the post–1979 period, when Khomeini asserted his role as guardian, or overseer, of Iran's government.

Khomeini, like Mawdudi and the Muslim Brotherhood, did not provide a detailed model of an Islamic government. Instead he spoke of general principles and specific traditional Islamic institutions that provided the basis for an Islamic state. For Khomeini both revelation and reason made it clear that if an Islamic state was necessary in the time of the Prophet for the realization of God's will, it would continue to be so until the end of time. Further, the very nature of God's revealed law (the *Shariah*) "furnished additional proof of the necessity for establishing government, for they indicate that the laws were laid down for the purpose of creating a state and administering the political, economic, and cultural affairs of society."[55]

From its inception in February 1979, the provisional government of the new Islamic Republic of Iran reflected the impending struggle between moderates and militants. The former represented by lay Islamic moderates, such as Mehdi Bazargan, Abol Hasan Bani Sadr, and some religious leaders, and the latter dominated by conservative *ulama*. Institutionally, the moderate/militant split was embodied in Iran's "dual government"—the Bazargan cabinet and the clerically controlled Revolutionary Council. The *ulama* prevailed. Their dominance of the political system was symbolized by the resignation of Bazargan in November 1979 and by executive rule of the Revolutionary Council.

In the meantime, the *ulama* dominated the Council of Experts and drew up a constitution (ratified in November 1979) calling for the "Rule by the Jurist," the Ayatollah Khomeini, assisted by a Council of Guardians to be chosen by Khomeini and the Supreme Judicial Council.[56]

Elections followed a similar course. Although Bani Sadr was elected Iran's first president in January 1980, the *ulama* controlled the Islamic Republican Party, which won the majority of seats in the parliamentary elections. They were able to consolidate their power by controlling the new cabinet, which replaced the Revolutionary Council, and by impeaching Bani Sadr (June 1981). Since that time, the *ulama* have maintained control of the government: executive, legislative, and judicial.

Overseeing Iran's government was the Ayatollah Khomeini as its guardian. Upon his death, a successor was to be selected by the clerically dominated Council of Experts. The *ulama* controlled the cabinet and the president of parliament. The Islamic Republican Party held most of the seats in parliament. Most importantly, because Islamic law had been declared state law, the *ulama*, as the traditional interpreters and guardians of the *Shariah*, controlled the Supreme Judicial Council, which oversaw the judiciary. They filled political posts or appointed those committed to their theocratic, ideological interpretation. A Ministry of Islamic Guidance oversaw the press and media.

Iran in the early 1970s had appeared to be a state well on the way to becoming a modern, powerful, stable nation under an enlightened

Pahlavi ruler. A corps of modern elites appeared to be growing rapidly and assisting in achieving the economic, social, educational, and military transformation of traditional Iranian society as symbolized by Reza Shah's White Revolution. But by the late 1970s, Iran's Western secular path to a modernized future came to a dead end. Pahlavi's reign was abruptly terminated as Iran's peacock throne fell before a popular revolutionary movement led by a bearded Islamic cleric. The monarchy, with its political and social corruption and its puppet-like ties to the United States and Israel, was to give way to an independent, Islamic republic that was to implement a more democratic and socially just society.

Postrevolutionary Iran witnessed the replacement of the shah and his secular elites by the Ayatollah Khomeini (the *Imam* as Guardian) and his conservative religious colleagues. The coalition that brought about the revolution disintegrated as not only Pahlavi officials but all who differed with the new "clerical autocracy," Islamic and Marxist dissidents alike, were silenced. Women and religious minorities as well as a wide variety of political and intellectual dissidents felt the swift arm of Islamic justice as meted out by revolutionary guards and courts. Prisons were again filled, trials and executions often occurred in such summary fashion that the Ayatollah Khomeini himself felt constrained to intervene and warn against such excesses. The Islamic republic's first prime minister, Mehdi Bazargan, resigned in disgust; Bani Sadr, its first elected president fled to exile in France; Sadeq Ghotbzadeh, who had held a number of government posts, including that of foreign affairs minister, was executed for his participation in an alleged plot to assassinate Khomeini.

All had been protégés of Khomeini and brought into office with his blessings. Those religious leaders who had not accepted Khomeini's doctrine of "Rule by the Jurist" were hounded and harassed by fellow clerics. The Ayatollah Shariatmadari, a senior ayatollah revered for his learning and piety, was himself "defrocked" in the spring of 1982.

The *ulama* and their supporters consolidated their power and control of the government, parliament, the judiciary, the media, and education. Iran's revolution was successfully institutionalized. Purges (of political organizations, the military, the judiciary, educational institutions, and government bureaus), control of the media, and intimidation of dissident clergy severely restricted the opposition. Similarly, the cultural revolution was promoted and institutionalized while alternative points of view were restricted or suppressed. Iran's pre-Islamic heritage was denigrated while Islamic history, belief, and revolutionary themes were promoted in the media, movies, schools, and the arts. The Council for Cultural Revolution was established to oversee higher education, from its curricula to the revolutionary/Islamic credentials and knowledge of its faculty and students. Islamic dress codes were enforced on the streets, in government offices, and in the universities.

Clerical and lay voices of dissent were offset by a critical mass of committed clergy and laity. The Society of Militant (Combatant) Clergy was charged with identifying and confirming true, as distinct from dissident, clergy. The government exercised careful attention to the appointment and control of Friday mosque preachers who served as the *imam's* representatives in cities, towns, and villages and whose Friday congregational prayer and religiopolitical sermons were an important means to reinforce the regime's brand of Islam and to mobilize the people. The militant clergy were supported by the "lay stratum of the Islamic republic" who accepted clerical rule, served in the government, and filled many key positions in the bureaucracy.[57] Most shared a common social (lower middle-class and merchant [*bazaari*] families) and educational (first-generation university graduates in the sciences and medicine) background.[58] Thus the Islamic republic was based upon a clerical-lay alliance, committed to the *Imam* and the revolution, though with differences of vision and policy.

The institutionalization of the revolution was accompanied by a twin goal, the export of "Islamic" revolution. The promotion and spread of Islam was a primary foreign policy objective. The Ayatollah Khomeini espoused a nonsectarian universalist Islamic revolution to liberate all oppressed Muslims. This goal—rooted in the Quranic mandate to spread the rule of God, in the example of the Prophet, and in the spread of Islam during the early conquests—was reflected in the Constitution of the Islamic Republic of Iran's exhortation: "to perpetuate the revolution both at home and abroad."[59] Traditional distinctions between the *dar al-Islam* (Islamic realm) and the *dar al-harb* (realm of warfare) were combined with that of the oppressor and the oppressed. Both peaceful means, preaching and propaganda, and confrontation and armed struggle were employed. The Ministry of Islamic Guidance was responsible for providing preachers and pub-

lications, conducting conferences for *ulama* from overseas, and distrib-
uting propaganda abroad. At the same time, the Ayatollah Khomeini
and broadcasts of Iran's "Voice of the Islamic Revolution" called upon
Muslims of the Gulf and throughout the world to rise up against their
governments.

Iran's revolution occurred at a time when the revivalist spirit was
alive and active in other Muslim countries. There was much in Iran's
revolutionary experience and ideology that resonated with the problems and concerns (sociopolitical discontent, cultural alienation, economic grievances, and a quest for identity and authenticity) of Muslims
in other societies. The success of the Iranian Revolution fired the
imaginations of many throughout the Muslim world and made Muslim governments nervous. The Sunni Gulf rulers, with their proximity
to Iran and their large Shii populations, were especially concerned.
Khomeini was particulary critical of "un-Islamic" monarchies and
their close ties with the United States, "American Islam." Riots in
1979 in Saudi Arabia's oil-rich Eastern Province (al-Hasa), where 35
percent of the population is Shii; an aborted coup in Bahrain in 1981;
Shii unrest in Kuwait and the subsequent car bombings there of the
American and French embassies in 1983; and Iran's intervention and
aid to Shii militants in Lebanon fueled fears of other Iranian-inspired
and -instigated Islamic revolutions. But these pockets of Shii militancy
did not translate into successful revolutionary movements as most
states practiced a carrot-and-stick response, addressing socioeconomic
inequities and then cracking down on militants.

While the leadership in Iran had remained united in its desire for
a victory in the war with Iraq, two differing tendencies, or factions,
emerged within the political elite concerning power, policy, and ideology on issues such as relations with the West, promotion of revolution
abroad, land reform, and nationalization. Pragmatists/realists and
revolutionary purists/radical hard-liners vied for power and influence with the Ayatollah Khomeini. The former were represented by
Ali Akbar Hashemi Rafsanjani, Speaker of the Parliament, Ali Akbar
Velayati, the foreign minister, and Ali Khamenei, then president
(now the Ayatollah Khomeini's successor as *faqih*). The latter were
led by Prime Minister Mir Hussein Musavi, Minister of the Interior
Ali Akbar Mohtasheimi, and Attorney General Musavi Khoeiniha,
who in 1979 had convinced Khomeini to support the seizure of the
American embassy. Two events reflect this rivalry, as each sought to

discredit the other. The arrest and execution in October 1986 of Mehdi Hashemi, head of the bureau charged with exporting Iran's revolution, was a sign of internal differences and political jockeying for power. Hard-liners countered by leaking to the press in November 1986 that former U.S. National Security Adviser Robert McFarlane had met with Rafsanjani and that the United States had exchanged arms with Iran for the release of American hostages held in Lebanon.

Likewise, while the leadership in Iran remained committed to the revolution, significant differences of opinion and policy existed between rival factions over domestic and foreign policy issues. For supporters of Iran's revolution, the goals were not only political and cultural but also social and economic. Social justice, the redressing of the oppression of the poor and the disinherited, were popular revolutionary themes. Although criticism of the shah's Western-inspired modernization program had once provided a common ground, post-revolutionary attempts to implement an Islamic model for socioeconomic development revealed substantial differences of opinion among clergy. Islam was used to justify both state control of the economy and freedom of private sector. Competing Islamic interpretations resulted from differences in juristic interpretation and conflicting class interests. Although all accepted the authority of Islamic law, some insisted that answers must be found or based upon explicit texts in traditional Islamic jurisprudence, that is, upon past legal interpretations or regulations. Others argued that new problems require new interpretations of God's revelation.

Confusion and indecision characterized much of the attempt to institute substantive social reform. A majority in parliament attempted to implement a social revolution to improve the lot of the urban poor, farmers, and villagers through state control of the economy and thus through restriction of the private sector and free enterprise. A series of laws were passed to limit the private sector: to control prices and markets; to nationalize many industries and banks, as well as foreign trade; to expropriate urban land for use by the poor and homeless; and to undertake major land reform through the redistribution of the agricultural lands of absentee landlords to peasant farmers. Merchants, who had been a major source of financial support for the revolution, and landowners (including clerical leaders) were among those who were strongly opposed to such measures and lobbied politicians and senior clerics. The Council of Guardians (a committee of clerical experts in Islamic law who determined whether a parliamentary law is Islamically acceptable) rather consistently vetoed much of the reform legislation. The Ayatollah Khomeini appointed a committee to mediate between the parliament and the council; however, the issue was not resolved. Although Khomeini could have broken the deadlock, he did not.

Post–Iran-Iraq War

The truce in the Iran-Iraq War in 1988 refocused attention on domestic problems and ideological differences. The war and the charismatic guidance of Khomeini had deferred serious popular examination and consideration of deteriorating conditions in Iran. Iran's population had grown from thirty-five to fifty-one million during the first decade of the Islamic republic. Urban areas like Teheran had tripled their population, while the city's infrastructure remained unchanged; if anything it had deteriorated. Years of Iraqi bombing had destroyed plants, factories, oil refineries. The Iran-Iraq War, while devastating in its human and economic tolls, had provided an excuse for Iran's serious economic problems, had minimized criticism of the government, and had mobilized support for the regime. Failure to achieve victory, an economy drained by the war, a general deterioration in the quality of life, and growing public disaffection were exacerbated by ideological differences within the government over strategies for national reconstruction and export of the revolution.

The pragmatist camp espoused a policy of national reconstruction and normalization of relations with the West; though the United States remained a special problem. Iran's export of the revolution was to be through example rather than violent revolution. As a result, between August 1988 and February 1989, diplomatic and economic contacts and missions from the West increased. Iran seemed intent upon improving its international image at the United Nations and in other international contexts. The tide abruptly turned in February 1989, however, with the storm created over the publication of Salman Rushdie's *Satanic Verses* and the denunciation of his portrayal of Islam as blasphemy. In the midst of Iran's official celebration of the revolution's tenth anniversary, demonstrations in neighboring Pakistan and India resulted in riots and death.

The Rushdie affair provided the radical camp with an issue to counter the influence and ascendancy of the pragmatists. The Ayatollah Khomeini's condemnation and call for the execution of Salman Rushdie for apostasy precipitated an international crisis and became an opportunity for Khomeini to reassert his Islamic leadership internationally, to rekindle and mobilize militant fervor for the defense of Islam, and thus to distract attention from Iran's pressing socioeconomic problems and growing social discontent. The reassertion of a more radical profile could be seen not only in the return to hard-line political rhetoric and condemnation of the West but also in the dismissal of a number of moderates in the government and the forced resignation of Ayatollah Montazeri (March 1989), Khomeini's designated successor, who had criticized the regime's human rights' excesses and had called for reconciliation with liberal elements such as Mehdi Bazargan's Freedom Party.

Despite the expectation of some, the death of the Ayatollah Khomeini in June 1989 did not create a power vacuum or precipitate a catastrophic power struggle between pragmatists and radicals. The contending forces closed ranks to assure a smooth transition that would foil the hopes of their enemies. Within a brief period, Rafsanjani and Khamenei emerged as the key players. The Council of Experts, whose charge it was to select Khomeini's successor, elected President Khamenei as Iran's "guardian" jurist by a two-thirds majority; and in July 1989, with 85 percent of the vote, Rafsanjani was elected the new president of Iran, a post whose powers were considerably broadened. President Rafsanjani was then able to gain approval for his cabinet, which noticeably dropped a number of key hard-liners, like Interior Minister Mohtasheimi, from the cabinet.

Iran's new leadership steered a more flexible course. Rafsanjani and Khamenei worked together for economic reconstruction and normalization of diplomatic and economic ties with the international community. Thus, for example, Rafsanjani cut back on Iran's support for more radical Shii factions in Lebanon, sought to mediate between AMAL and Hizballah, worked for the release of American hostages in Lebanon, and accepted disaster assistance from Western countries, including the United States, when Iran was devastated by an earthquake that claimed forty thousand lives in June 1990.

More militant, isolationist voices and factions continued to exist—bent on the preservation of their revolutionary purity, less able to learn from Iran's postrevolutionary experience, and afraid of the negative consequences of renewed international relations and the following danger of dependency on the West. For these groups, any cooperation between Iran and the United States, whether it be to free hostages or to aid Iranian victims of an earthquake, is unacceptable. While the balance of power seems to be in the hands of more pragmatic ideologues like Rafsanjani and Khamenei, their credibility and power will be sorely tested by their ability to redress significantly Iran's deep-seated economic and political problems and to offer an alternative vision for the development of Iranian society that is capable of incorporating diverse religious and political positions.

Reconstruction

The history of the Islamic Republic in the 1990s, although dominated by two leaders, Hashemi Rafsanjani and the Ayatollah Sayyed Ali Khamenei, continued to be plagued by factionalism, shifting alliances, and contention among multiple centers of power. As a result, Iran's politics and policies have often vacillated between authoritarianism and popular participation, censorship and dissent, internationalism and militant extremism.

Rafsanjani's position as president (1989–97) had been strengthened by a constitutional amendment in 1989 that eliminated the position of prime minister and increased the powers of the presidency. The Ayatollah Khamenei, although he did not enjoy the same level of respect and personal authority as Khomenei, exercised the constitutionally recognized powers of the Spiritual Guide (*faqih*), enabling him to challenge, counter, or check initiatives from the executive, legislative, and judicial branches. However, domestic policies and foreign affairs were often subject to the ebb and flow of factional rivalries based upon ideology, class, and self-interest.

While difficult to categorize, the political spectrum in the 1990s increasingly revealed three general tendencies (conservative, pragmatist, and hardliner) rather than the two (pragmatist and hardliner) of the late 1980s.[60] The conservative faction was dominated by traditionalist clergy who rigorously maintained the right of the clergy to govern and adhere to traditional Islamic jurisprudence. The clergy's (*ulama*) historic association or alliance with the traditional merchant (*bazaari*) class resulted in a strict interpretation and application of Islamic law and values, including a restrictive code of dress and public behavior for women, and firm limits on entertainment and the arts (music, dance, singing). They strongly support private enterprise and private property and believe in a limited role for the state in the economy. Their foreign policy emphasizes Islamic solidarity and relations with Muslim countries and is guarded in its approach to the West, wishing to improve relations but resisting Western culture.

Hard-liners retain a more revolutionary, antiestablishment posture. Drawing support from the younger militant clergy, the lower classes, students in Islamic associations, private revolutionary organizations and foundations, they emphasize Islamic social justice and the redistribution of wealth to improve the lot of the oppressed masses or *mustazafin* (the poor, laborers, peasants). They emphasize economic self-sufficiency, more state ownership or control over the economy (foreign trade, banking, major industries), and social welfare reform. Their foreign policy stresses closer ties with Muslim and developing nations and a commitment to export of revolution, and it is visceral anti-American/Western. They rule out any attempts to normalize relations with the West, fearing its cultural penetration and hegemony as well as an increased influence of Westernized technocrats. Hard-liners receive substantial support and exercise influence through nongovernmental revolutionary organizations and foundations. Their control of the third Majles was swept aside in the 1992 parliamentary elections which saw conservatives take control of parliament.

Pragmatists or moderates balance their commitment to an Islamic republic and its religiously guided government with an appreciation of limited popular sovereignty. With support from the modern middle class, technocrats, government officials, professional and intellectuals, their domestic, foreign, economic and cultural policies are more open and flexible. They advocate a dynamic view of Islam and Islamic law, one that is capable of adaptation and change. They support greater political participation and the strengthening of civil society, initiatives that permit greater pluralism, freedom, and tolerance. Their economic policies affirm economic liberalization and privatization at home and stronger economic trade/ties abroad. Rafsanjani epitomized the pragmatist approach in his quest to reconstruct Iran through national mobilization, strengthening its international economic linkages, and liberalizing regulations affecting free speech, political dissent, women, and the media. In the post-Khomeini period, he was able to advance the pragmatist position vis à vis the conservatives and hardliners.

However, pragmatist initiatives while sometimes successful are also challenged at other times by more conservative and hard-line factions on issues as diverse as resolving the Rushdie affair, liberalizing regulations regarding women, or permitting greater freedom of expression in the media and society. Thus, when attempts were being made to find an "honorable solution" to the Ayatollah Khomeini's *fatwa* sanctioning the killing of Salman Rushdie, author of the *Satanic Verses,* the Fifteenth of Khordad Foundation offered 2 million dollars to anyone who would assassinate Rushdie. Similarly, in 1992, Muhammad Khatami, minister of Islamic Culture and Guidance (1982–92), was forced to resign over his liberal cultural policies: legalizing music and chess, encouraging the revival of the cinema, and allowing a nongovernmental press. Moreover, while the hard-liners were marginalized after their defeat in 1992, the conservative dominated fourth Majles (1992–96) proved equally militant in resisting Rafsanjani's reform programs. They often enjoyed the support of the Ayatollah Khamenei who, in contrast to Ayatollah Khomeini, intervened in politics and took exception to the programs and policies of President Rafsanjani from greater state control or intervention in the economy to relations with the West.

Foreign policy, reflecting contending forces, continued to proceed on two tracks. On the one hand Rafsanjani and others emphasized export of the revolution by example (national solidarity, economic development, the cultivation and dissemination of religious knowledge) rather than force and the pursuit of trade and credit with the West. On the other hand, Iran continued to be accused of support for radical religious regimes (Sudan) that harbored and trained terrorists, militant organizations (Hizballah which continued to fight the Israeli occupation of South Lebanon), and death threats against, and assassinations of, Iranians abroad. The United States (and many of its European and Middle Eastern allies) continued to condemn Iran as a terrorist state. European countries, although desirous of expanding commerce, prosecuted militants who assassinated Iranian residents. The Clinton administration, viewing Iran and Iraq as destabilizing forces in the Middle East and as a threat to the Gulf oil producing states and to Israel, crafted a policy of dual containment, which included economic sanctions, to isolate Iran and Iraq politically and economically. It denounced Iran for its promotion of terrorism, clandestine nuclear weapons program, violation of human rights, and opposition to the Middle East peace process. The Republican dominated

Congress passed legislation to support the destabilization of Iran's Islamic government. Both the U.S. and Iranian governments vilified each other. The former charging that Iran was a primary sponsor of international terrorism and the latter charging that the U.S. was the enemy of Islam and of Muslims worldwide.

Iran's Islamic foreign policy has been complex. While it has close ties with the Islamic Republic of Sudan, it has distanced itself from the Taliban who established the Islamic Republic of Afghanistan. In 1997 Iran denounced the Taliban of Afghanistan, the Islamic student *(taliban)* militia group that had captured more than two-thirds of the country and harshly enforced its brand of Islamic public standards, for its un-Islamic behavior. While supportive of Islamic activists' struggle to create an Islamic state in Algeria, it condemned blind or mindless acts of violence by the Armed Islamic Group, charging that its wanton killing of fellow Muslims was anti-Islamic and could undermine the struggle of Islamic groups.

Iran also undertook new international initiatives towards the "Islamic establishment." Calling for Islamic unity, it sought to strengthen its ties with the Organization of the Islamic Conference (OIC) and, through quiet diplomacy, with Saudi Arabia and other Gulf neighbors.

Limited Liberalization

While at one level Iran remains a repressive authoritarian state, the 1990s saw an expansion of political participation and dissent. Both Rafsanjani's more moderate policies and the space created by rival factions and centers of power offered conditions that tolerated dynamic change. Although the process of credentialing candidates was controlled, presidential and parliamentary elections continued to occur without interruption and often with relative independence. Parliamentarians engaged in heated debates over government policies and proposals, feeling free to criticize, excoriate, and reject presidential appointments and legislative initiatives. Intellectual life and debate, the numbers of independent newspapers, magazines, and journals all increased significantly.

Iran often displayed a level of political diversity that contrasted sharply with many of its Arab neighbors. Despite limitations on women's freedom in public life, they still enjoyed more freedoms than many of their sisters in other Muslim societies, ranging from education and employment to voting, holding political office, and driving cars. Public discussion and debate between conservative and more liberal or feminist voices (religious and secular) occurred regularly in many magazines and books. At the same time, given the contending ideological visions and centers of power and the continued dominance of conservatives in some key government positions (in particular the support of Iran's Supreme Guide, the Ayatollah Khamenei) and parliament, reformers remained vulnerable to attacks by militants who disrupted classes in the university, silenced or sacked liberal professors and intellectuals like Abdul Karim Soroush, and destroyed offensive books, videos, and shops.

Perhaps the most stunning example of the diverse currents in Iran, its increasing though limited moderation and pluralism, was the presidential elections of 1997. Given the conservative dominance of the parliament and the role of the Ayatollah Khamenei, most observers expected Ayatollah Ali Akbar Nateq-Nuri, speaker of the parliament, to win handily. Nateq-Nuri, a former interior minister and standard bearer of the conservative clergy, had allied himself with Rafsanjani against the hard-liners in the elections of 1992. However, once elected he distanced himself from Rafsanjani in the conservative controlled parliament. Nominated for president by influential clerics in Qom close to Khamenei, he had criticized liberal reforms, called for greater Islamization of the universities and of society, and had been a strong critic of the West.

Ayatollah Muhammad Khatami, a cleric with strong revolutionary credentials as an early supporter of Iran's revolution and a *sayyid* (descendent of the Prophet Muhammad) had a record of moderation. As indicated above, his liberal views as minister of Islamic culture and guidance and his criticism of the failures and excesses of the regime had led to his being forced out of office. His emphasis on greater individual and collective freedoms, political tolerance, and respect for the people's will rankled conservatives who saw this as a threat to the authority of the Supreme Guide or *faqih* who was to stand above the constitution, law, and popular will. Many did not expect him even to be approved as a candidate. In a stunning victory on May 23, 1997, Khatami won with 69 percent of the votes cast by 67 percent of eligible voters. His victory demonstrated a broad-based appeal, winning support from the higher middle and upper classes, Iranian youth and women, intellectuals, professionals, and artists who preferred the moderate liberal message of Khatami to the conservatism of Natiq-Nuri. However diverse their backgrounds and motivations, one thing was shared among them: a desire for greater liberalization and change and a demand for more political and cultural space in society.

In the wake of Iran's elections, the issue of a cautious movement toward a rapprochement was raised and debated in both Iran and the U.S. President Clinton set preconditions such as halting Iran's support of terrorism, development of nuclear weapons, and opposition to the Middle East peace process. Iran countered that its support for groups like Hamas and Hizballah, which America regards as terrorist, are guerilla movements fighting Israel's illegal occupation of their lands (Palestine and southern Lebanon). It demanded that the U.S. make the first goodwill gesture by releasing the billions of dollars in Iranian assets that were frozen after the 1979 revolution. However, at the same time, Ayatollah Khatami, warning of the dangers of Samuel Huntington's theory of a clash of civilizations, called for a dialogue of civilizations and religions. Whether Khatami and others like Rafsanjani and counterparts in the United States would prevail against those who continued to advocate a hardline remained uncertain.

The Role of Muslim Militias

Accompanying the emergence of Islamic political and social movements has been that of militias. In contrast to underground clandestine movements, the militias have been associated with movements that exist and function in the public arena as resistance movements (although employing some degree of secrecy for reasons of security) and, depending on contexts, participate in the political system. Among the more prominent have been groups like Lebanon's AMAL, spawned by Imam Musa Sadr's Movement for the Dispossessed and the Iranian-backed Hizballah of Lebanon, Hamas in Palestine, the *mujahideen* and Taliban of Afghanistan. While some of these groups have a transnational character and message, they are primarily focused on local contexts and issues. Dismissed by opponents as radical extremists and terrorists, members and supporters claim they are armed resistance movements, responding to the violence and oppression of regimes or to armies of occupation, freedom fighters and liberators rather than "fundamentalist fanatics."

Hamas: The Islamic Resistance Movement

Hamas ("fervor") is the acronym for the Islamic Resistance Movement (Harakat al-Muqawama al-Islamiyya). An offshoot of the Palestinian Muslim Brotherhood, it was created in 1987 as a response to the *intifada* ("uprising"), the Palestinian uprising against Israeli occupation and rule in Gaza and the West Bank. Its organizers included a religious leader and prominent professionals. Sheikh Ahmad Yasin, the charismatic paraplegic leader of the Muslim Brotherhood, was the driving force behind its creation. He was joined by Abd al-Aziz al-Rantisi (a physician), Ibrahim al-Yazuri (a pharmacist), Issa al-Nashshar (an engineer), Abd al-Fattah (a schoolmaster), and others.

Islamic activism had existed in Palestine for decades. Its most prominent expressions were the Muslim Brotherhood and Islamic Jihad. The Muslim Brotherhood came to Palestine in 1935 when Abd al-Rahman al-Banna, the brother of Hasan al-Banna, founder of the Egyptian Muslim Brotherhood, visited Hajji Amin al-Husseini, the Mufti of Jerusalem. It formally established a branch in Palestine (Jerusalem) in 1945. The Egyptian Muslim Brothers actively participated in the Palestinian revolt and the Arab-Israeli war of 1948, increasing their popularity in Palestine. However, Gamal Abd al-Nasir's suppression of the Brotherhood in Egypt in the 1960s, the creation of Fatah, which initially emerged from within the Muslim Brotherhood but later severed all organizational and ideological ties, and the rise of Arab nationalism eclipsed the Muslim Brotherhood.

After the 1967 war, the Brotherhood confined its activities to religious, educational, and social services while the Palestine Liberation Organization became the chief spokesman and leader of Palestinian resistance to Israel. The Brotherhood saw its apolitical stance as strategically important to enable it to grow under the watchful eyes of Israeli security as well as to create and cultivate an Islamic society prior to establishing an Islamic state. The Israelis quietly supported its growth and activities on campuses as a counterbalance to the secular Arab nationalist oriented PLO. The Brotherhood's lack of involvement in the political struggle against Israel cost it support among many Palestinians, many of whom turned to Fateh and the PLO during the 60s and 70s. It also led to the emergence of Islamic Jihad in the 1980s, created by frustrated Muslim Brothers who saw militant action, armed struggle (*jihad*), as necessary in the war against Israeli occupation and aggression in Palestine. Fathi Shqaqi and Abd al-Aziz Audeh formed Jihad in 1980, an umbrella group whose clandestine cells mounted daring attacks against the Israeli military. During the first half of the 1980s, Islamic Jihad's quick effective strikes earned it the condemnation of Israel as a terrorist organization and the admiration of many in Gaza and the West Bank and set the stage for the intifada: "there is no doubt that the Islamic Jihad singularly contributed to the psychological preparation of the Uprising; it promoted among the population a conscieneness [*sic*] of its capacity to face up to the occupation and to challenge the political and military status quo."[61]

When the *intifada* occurred in December 1987, the Muslim Brotherhood realized that it had been caught off guard and needed to be seen as relevant and involved in the uprising against Israeli occupation. Hamas was the response, a wing of the Muslim Brotherhood, a resistance movement that would assume a leadership position in the *intifada*. Hamas filled a vacuum. Its success in attracting followers and its popularity completely overshadowed the Brotherhood and challenged the leadership of the PLO in the struggle against Israeli occupation.

For Hamas Palestine is a permanent Muslim territory, a land which has been and will continue to be in Muslim hands until the end of time. As its Charter of August 1988 declared: "The Islamic resistance Movement believes that the land of Palestine has been an Islamic Waqf (endowment) throughout the generations and until the Day of resurrection; no one can renounce it or part of it, or abandon it or part of it. . . . And this *waqf* will endure as long as heaven and earth last."[62]

The ideology of Hamas combines Islam and Palestinian nationalism, viewing the defense of Palestine as a *jihad* incumbent upon all Muslims: "The Hamas regards nationalism as part and parcel of the faith. Nothing is loftier or deeper in nationalism than waging *jihad* against the enemy and confronting him when he sets foot on the land of the Muslims. . . . When our enemies usurp some lands, *jihad* becomes a duty on all Muslims."[63]

Hamas has multiple aspects: religious, social, political, and military. It is at one and the same time a religious organization, a political organization, and a militia. Hamas recruits members from a network of mosques, schools, and charitable institutions. While its leadership has included religious officials (*imams*), the majority are professionals and technocrats trained in medicine, engineering, science, and business. Hamas has combined political action on the one hand and guerilla warfare on the other. Its popularity and effectiveness have been based on many factors. Hamas' blend of political action and social activism has won material and moral support from many Palestinians and their supporters in the broader Arab and Muslim world for an extensive network of community and charitable projects and programs. It provides kindergartens, schools, scholarships, support for students studying abroad, libraries, social and sports clubs, and other social welfare services (medical, legal, and financial aid). In a downtrodden and impoverished community where resources are scarce or inadequate,

> Hamas runs the best social services network in the Gaza Strip. . . . Structured and well organized, Hamas is trusted by the poor (Gaza's overwhelming majority) to deliver on its promises, and is perceived to be far less corrupt and subject to patronage than its secular nationalist counterparts, especially Fateh. . . . Some senior officials in UNRWA [United Nations Relief Works and Agency] in Gaza acknowledged that Hamas is the only faction they trust to distribute UNRWA food donations to the people.[64]

Both its social programs and charitable projects as well as its ability to confront Israel won significant grass roots support.

Politically, Hamas engages in political education, mobilization and protest. It challenges the legitimacy and platform of the PLO, claiming to offer a more authentic and equitable Islamic alternative. Hamas sponsors political forums, distributes pamphlets and cassettes, and organizes mass demonstrations and strikes. From the outset, Hamas offered an Islamic alternative to the PLO's secular nationalist agenda, vying with it for popular support. Its fortunes have often been contingent on the progress of the peace process. Attracting strong but a minority of support, its popularity and its performance in municipal, professional association, and university student elections have soared when relations between Israel and the Palestinians have deteriorated, as during the *intifada*. Thus, for example, when the first municipal elections in fifteen years were held in Hebron in 1992, Islamists sympathetic to Hamas won as they did in 1993 in Ramallah, a city with a large Palestinian Christian community. They took more than 40 percent of the vote in professional association elections (Medical, Accountants and Bar Associations, Engineers Syndicate, and the

Gaza Chamber of Commerce). Hamas fortunes in University elections have also reflected the ups and downs of the peace process. In 1993 Hamas and its allies won 52 percent of the vote at Bir Zeit University. In 1994 Hamas won overwhelmingly in strongholds like the Islamic University in Gaza and garnered 24 percent of the vote to Fateh's 64 percent at Al-Azhar University, a Fateh stronghold.

As a militia (the military wing of Hamas), the Qassim Brigade engages in military strikes or attacks against Israeli targets, military and civilian. While members of Hamas participated in the everyday confrontations with Israeli forces during the *intifada*, the Brigade engaged in well planned selective attacks against Israeli military and police. The Qassam Brigade focused on guerilla warfare, not random acts of violence. Members are organized into small clandestine cells who, for security reasons, remain in the shadows. Their identity is not known to the majority of Hamas members, and they often function with relative autonomy. Desirous of countering their image as a terrorist organization (they are on the American list of terrorist organizations), Hamas leaders insisted that they were a militant nationalist movement in a struggle against Israeli occupation and violence. Thus, they restricted their activities and attacks to the occupied territories and emphasized that they did not attack targets outside the occupied territories or in the West. That position changed dramatically after the Oslo Accords.

The Qassim Brigade undertook direct attacks outside the territories in the heart of Israel against civilian as well as military targets. In particular they introduced a new type of warfare in Palestine, that of suicide bombers. These deadly attacks increased exponentially after a Jewish settler (Baruch Goldstein) killed twenty-nine worshipers during the Friday congregational *(juma)* prayer at the Mosque of the Patriarch in Hebron on February 25, 1994. The Brigade promised swift revenge for the massacre and undertook five anti-Israeli operations within Israel itself in cities like Galilee, Jerusalem, and Tel Aviv. The most deadly occurred on October 19, 1994, in the heart of Tel Aviv with the bombing of a bus which killed twenty-three and injured nearly fifty people.[65] The Brigade again disrupted peace negotiations on July 30, 1997, when suicide bombers killed thirteen and wounded more than 150 in a Jerusalem market. These acts revealed deep cleavages within Hamas, many of whose leaders claimed that such actions were committed by members of the Brigade whom they were not able to control. They also struck fear in the hearts of many Israelis and created a backlash that some believe contributed to the election of Benjamin Netanyahu, a candidate who appealed both to the Israeli right wing, more hard-line Israeli voters, the religious right, and settlers. Netanyahu had been a critic of the Labor government of Rabin and Peres and its Oslo accords. He had long dismissed both the PLO and Hamas as terrorists. The new Likud government continued to move aggressively to eradicate Hamas, arresting or deporting many of its leaders, and insisting that the PNA government of Yaser Arafat move effectively to suppress or dismantle Hamas, which it portrayed not only as the principle perpetrator of terrorism but also the primary obstacle to peace.

The post Oslo period challenged Hamas on many fronts. The Oslo Peace Accords (or Gaza-Jericho agreement) of September 13, 1993, demonstrated the extent to which Yaser Arafat and the PLO had retained leadership of the Palestinian struggle and negotiated with Israel in the name of the Palestine people. Hamas, like many, had been caught off guard by the quietly and privately negotiated settlement. Hamas opposition to Arafat and the accords and its call to continue to wage the Palestinian struggle against Israel now put it at odds with both the PLO/PNA and Israel. Prior to the accords, both the PLO and Hamas were commonly dismissed as terrorist organizations. With the "rehabilitation" or legitimation of Yaser Arafat and the PLO by the international community, Arafat the "terrorist" now became the statesman. Hamas now became the common enemy (to both Israel and the PLO) or primary obstacle to peace, commonly denounced as extremist and terrorist.

Although Hamas boycotted the Palestinian National Authority elections, in fact the post-Oslo period saw divergent currents and growing divisions within Hamas. Younger militants, particularly those in the Qassim Brigade, wished to step up the armed struggle to strike further against continued Israeli occupation, undermine the peace process, and encourage a continuation of the *intifada.* The main political wing grappled with the issue of the elections. Some feared that nonparticipation in elections would further marginalize Hamas and thus spoke of participation in the political process. Others espoused an even more pragmatic response to the unfolding new realities, the formation of a political party to assure that Hamas' voice was present in the PNA government and Palestinian politics. Shaikh

Yasin in a series of letters from prison reflected upon these choices, cautiously opting for participation:

> Holding elections is now an issue for the Palestinians; the Islamists are divided between supporting participation and those opposing it; as far as I am concerned, but only God knows, I consider it is better to participate than to abstain, providing that the Council be empowered with legislative privileges *(tashri)*; as a matter of fact we are opposed to what is happening in the streets, so why not express our opposition within the legislative institution which will de jure become in the future the authority representing the Palestinian people? [This participation] will reassert the strength of the Islamic presence on the arena and will prevent it from losing ground because of its isolation.[66]

This pragmatism continued to be reflected by the general response of the Hamas leadership who accepted Arafat's election as president of the PNA and disassociated itself from militants whose radical rejection led to continued armed struggle. While rejecting the accords, the majority chose a pragmatism that adapted itself to the political realities. Some in Hamas advocated returning to the Muslim Brotherhood with its emphasis on Islamization of society and limited involvement in politics. Others called for adapting to the new political realities, renouncing violence and engaging in direct participation in politics. A small minority continued to espouse violence and confrontation to liberate the whole of Palestine.

The Taliban of Afghanistan

While the majority of Muslim militias have functioned and remained in opposition to established governments, Afghanistan witnessed the rise of a seemingly improbable militia that would go on to unite three-fourths of the country and establish the Islamic Republic of Afghanistan.

The liberation of Afghanistan from Soviet occupation in 1979 did not bring peace to this war-torn country. The struggle of brave Afghan *mujahideen*, Muslim militias, against the occupation of their country by an "atheist" Soviet army had captured the support and sympathies of many in the West and the Muslim world alike. In contrast to fear of the Islamic resurgence or "Islamic fundamentalism" in

Iran and the Middle East, Afghanistan's *mujahideen* were seen as freedom fighters whose *jihad* (holy war) received substantial aid from
America, Saudi Arabia, and other countries. However, the *mujahideen*
victory did not bring peace. The common Islamic identity, which had
served to mobilize and inspire, to unify the *mujahideen* in their *jihad*
against the Soviet Union, was now eclipsed by Afghanistan's age-old
tribal, ethnic, and religious (Sunni-Shii) differences and rivalries.

Afghanistan, a predominantly Sunni country, had always enjoyed
a fragile unity, offset by the realities of its multiethnic tribal society
(Pathans, Pashtuns, Uzbeks, Tajiks with Persian speaking Shiis in the
West). The leadership vacuum created by the Soviet defeat now unleashed a factional power struggle. Having driven out the Soviets in
1989 and then defeated the communist regime of Najibullah in Kabul
in 1992, the *mujahideen* Islamic government then fell prey to a bloody
internal struggle for power as *mujahideen* militia leaders (or perhaps
more accurately warlords) vied for supremacy, resulting in more
deaths and devastation than its liberation had cost. Two major groups
came to the forefront, Hizb-i-Islami, led by Gulbudeen Hekmatyar,
and Jamaiat-i-Islami, led by Burhanuddin Rabbani. Much of Afghanistan, like Kabul, was caught in the rivalry and crossfire between
these two groups.

After almost eighteen years of civil war, a seemingly endless state
of carnage and chaos was abruptly reversed. As if out of nowhere, a
band of *madrasa* students *(taliban)* appeared in late 1994 and within
two years swept across the country. Denouncing all the warlords and
representing no outside interests, they claimed the mantle of moral
leadership as representatives of the majority of Afghans who were
victims of the internecine warfare. Although initially portrayed as
young students from the *madrasas* with no military background, in
fact, they were a force of *mullahs* and *taliban*, religious leaders and
students. The former comprised veterans of the Afghan-Soviet war
who had returned to the *madrasas* after the departure of the Soviets.
The profile of their leader, Mullah Omar, reflected this older
generation.

Mullah Omar had been a student of Islam before joining the Islamic Revolutionary Movement (Harakat-i-Inqilabi-i-Islami) of Mohammad Nabi Mohammadi. During the 1980s, he fought against the
Soviet occupation, losing an eye and becoming deputy commander of
the movement. In 1994 he launched the *taliban* campaign to restore

stability and order and establish an Islamic state. Because little was known about them and they were portrayed simply as young students from religious schools, inexperienced in warfare and poorly armed, they were initially not taken seriously. However, in time they proved to be a formidable force, feared by warlords but welcomed by ordinary people, that captured Kabul and controlled three-fourths of the country.

Although initially hailed as liberators who secured towns, made the streets safe for ordinary citizens, and cleaned up corruption and graft, their strict form of Islam soon became an issue for some. The Taliban subscribe to a very conservative (puritanical) interpretation of Islam. Their doctrines are close to those of Saudi Arabia's Wahhabi religious establishment and Pakistan's Jamaat-i-Islami. As Sunni Muslims, they denounced their Shia opposition as infidels. When they captured the Afghan capital Kabul after a two-year battle, they not only restored law and order but also sought to create or impose a moral (*Shariah*-governed) society, mandating their brand of Islamic reform. They segregated the sexes outside the home, closed girls' schools, required that all women be fully covered in public, and banned women from the workplace. They also banned television, cinema, and music, ordered men to grow beards and pray five times a day, introduced the *hudud* punishments (amputation for theft, death for murder, stoning for adultery). If the United States, Saudi Arabia, and Pakistan saw them as a potential stabilizing force, China, India, Russia, and the CIS (Commonwealth of Independent States) were less sanguine.

Egypt

In 1981 Anwar al-Sadat, the self-styled "Believer-President," was assassinated by Muslim militants in the name of Islam. This was the climax of a turbulent period of "Islamic politics" during the Sadat years. Anwar al-Sadat had come to power in 1970, succeeding Gamal Abd al-Nasser. At first Sadat seemed content to rule in the shadow of Nasser, as was symbolized by the placement of his picture in public places and government offices alongside of, not in place of, Nasser's. By 1971, however, he began to assert his own policy and move against his Nasserite and socialist opponents with the inauguration of his Rectification program or "Corrective Revolution." The Arabic terms chosen to describe the twin bases for this new orientation had strong Islamic connotations—faith *(iman)* and knowledge, which was the traditional designation for religious disciplines *(ilm)*. In his own way, Sadat was continuing Nasser's use of Islam to enhance his political legitimacy.

Sadat's Use of Islam

Sadat had a reputation for personal piety; the callus on his forehead from repeated prostration in prayer attested to it. He also, at one time, had close ties with the Muslim Brotherhood. In cultivating a public image as a pious Muslim ruler, the president appropriated the title "The Believer-President," much as caliphs had once taken the title "Commander of the Faithful." As Hasan Hanafi, an Egyptian professor and Islamic activist, has observed:

> President Sadat has been given the title "the Believer-President." He is always called by his first name Muhammad. He is shown in the mass media in his white *jallabiya,* going to the mosque or coming out of it, with a rosary in one hand, Moses stick in the other, and with a prayer mark on his forehead . . . He murmurs in prayer, closes his eyes and shows signs of humility and devotion. He begins his speeches with "In the name of God," and ends them with Quranic verses signifying modesty and asking for forgiveness.[67]

All official pronouncements began with the traditional religious invocation, "In the name of God, the Merciful and Compassionate." Sadat also increased Islamic programming in the media and Islamic courses in the schools and universities. In Cairo, a city of some forty thousand mosques, the government built a thousand additional mosques. Sadat also cultivated his relationship with religious leaders of popular and official Islam. Sufi orders were permitted to function freely in public. The bastion of "official Islam"—al-Azhar University—became an object of special financial support, undertaking an expansion program that included new buildings and satellite provincial campuses. By the late 1970s, Sadat could count on support from leading Azhar religious scholars and the Shaykh of Al-Azhar (Abd al-Rahman Bissar) for many of his policies: the Egyptian-Israeli peace treaty, Muslim family law reforms, criticism of Islamic "extremist" movements. Sadat's control of religion was enhanced by the creation of the position of deputy premier for Religious Affairs and of the Ministry of Religious Endowments and al-Azhar Affairs, which administered religious endowments; paid salaries for some religious functionaries; and, in time, tried to control the topic and content of mosque sermons.

Anwar al-Sadat gave the Egyptian-Israeli war of 1973 a special and transcendent religious significance. It was waged during the holy month of Ramadan. Whereas Nasser had employed the secular motto "Earth, Sea, and Sky" in the 1967 war, Sadat used *"Allahu Akbar!"* the opening words of the call to prayer and the traditional Islamic battle cry. *Allahu Akbar!* was on the lips of Egyptian troops as they stormed across the Suez Canal. The Islamic character of the war and the miraculous nature of Egypt's success was strikingly attested to by military participants: "I swear '*Allahu Akbar*' was written in the sky. During the crossing as we looked up, *Allahu Akbar* was vividly written across the sky."[68] The war itself was in every sense portrayed as a *jihad;* religious language and symbolism were freely employed. As a result, Egypt's success in penetrating Israeli positions was seen as an Islamic victory. Sadat emerged a Muslim hero.

Sadat's encouragement of religious revivalism included a more liberal attitude toward Islamic groups, in particular the Muslim Brotherhood and Islamic university student organizations. This was done to counter the influence of pro-Nasser secular leftists. Shortly after Sadat assumed office, Muslim Brothers who had been imprisoned since the 1965 abortive coup were released; those in exile were permitted to return to public life in Egypt. In 1976 religious publications such as *al-Dawa* (The Call), run by Muslim Brothers, were permitted. Edited by Umar Talmassani, a Muslim Brother sentenced under Nasser to fifteen years imprisonment in 1965, *al-Dawa* soon achieved a circulation of one hundred thousand.

By 1974 the Sadat government had begun to feel the strains of politicizing religion, as seen, for example, in the debate over implementation of the *Shariah* and the antigovernment activities of Islamic militants. Also, the government's use of Islam did not necessarily solidify its control of Islamic issues or organizations. The greater profile of Islam in public life led to more discussion and agitation for increased application of Islam in state and society. The "Islamic euphoria" after the victory of 1973 had confirmed for many that Islam offered the strength, pride, and sense of history that should serve as the core of Egyptian national identity. The "return to Islam" had expressed itself in many ways: increased mosque attendance, adoption of Islamic attire by men and women, a proliferation of religious literature and tape cassettes of sermons, a burgeoning of Islamic organizations. A significant proportion of the younger generation (university students and recent graduates) became involved in this Islamic revival. Sadat encouraged the creation of Islamic student associations to challenge Nasserite leftist student organizations. Between 1975 and 1979, Islamic groups dominated student elections at major universities; however, they soon became more independent and critical of the Sadat government and in 1979 were outlawed by presidential decree.

During the 1970s, several committees of al-Azhar religious scholars had been established to facilitate the application of the *Shariah* in Egypt. As reported in *al-Jumhuriyah* (December 16, 1976), the legislative committee of the People's Assembly and the Committee on National Security had called for the introduction of *Shariah* law. In 1977 a resolution to that effect was introduced but then shelved. On December 15, 1978, *al-Ahram* noted that a joint committee of National Assembly legal authorities and al-Azhar religious scholars had been established to pave the way for the implementation of the *Shariah*. The net effect of the drawn-out discussion regarding implementation of the *Shariah* was years of debate and controversy in the National Assembly and especially in the press as secularists, Islamic modernists and religious conservatives argued about the feasibility of making the *Shariah* the law of the land. For the Muslim Brotherhood and younger Islamic militant organizations, introduction of the *Shariah* was the first and essential step in establishing an Islamic state in Egypt. From their point of view, Sadat's failure to do this for so many years was inexcusable.

Opposition Movements

From 1977 onward, Islamic criticism and opposition to Sadat grew. Anwar al-Sadat's appeal to religion and support of Islamic organizations began to backfire as these organizations took on a life of their own. They increasingly asserted their independence and pressed for substantive Islamic changes, condemning what they judged an opportunistic control and use of Islam by the Sadat government. In response the Sadat government became more autocratic. When food riots racked Cairo in January 1977, Sadat cracked down on the Left and Communists as well as other opposition groups, among them the Jamaat al-Muslimin (Society of Muslims), or as more popularly known Takfir wal Hijra (Excommunication and Emigration).

The Takfir was one of a number of militant Islamic organizations that had sprung up after 1967. The humiliating defeat in the war, the loss of Jerusalem (the third holiest city of Islam), and the occupation of the West Bank were taken as clear signs of a politically impotent, inept, and corrupt system of government. The Western secular model of government had failed; Muslims' only hope was a return to their Islamic alternative. While the older generation of Muslim Brothers had moderated their voices during the early Sadat years, this new generation of Islamic militants, some of whom had been younger members of the Brotherhood, espoused a more aggressive, antigovernment strategy. Because these groups developed as secret societies, little notice was taken until they began to engage in violent, antigovernment acts.

In April 1974, a group called Muhammad's Youth (Shabab Muhammad), or the Islamic Liberation Organization, attempted a coup d'état. It seized the Technical Military Academy/Military Engineering College in Cairo but was prevented by government forces from carrying out its plan to assassinate President Sadat. Eleven people were killed and twenty-seven wounded. The Takfir wal Hijra dramatically drew attention in July 1977 when they kidnapped Husayn al-Dhahabi, an Azhar shaykh and former minister of Religious Endowments, who had been a strong critic of Takfir. When their demands for the release of imprisoned compatriots were not met, al-Dhahabi was executed. In the nationwide crackdown that followed, 620 members were arrested and 465 were tried before military courts.[69] The leaders of both Muhammad's Youth and the Takfir were executed, and their members imprisoned by the Sadat government. Although the groups were suppressed, many simply went underground and became active in other militant groups such as the Jund Allah (Soldiers of God) and Jamaat al-Jihad (Holy War Society), which by late 1977 became very active. Despite government surveillance and prosecution, militant groups grew and their violent activities multiplied.

Ideologically, Islamic militants are heavily indebted to Sayyid Qutb and Mawlana Mawdudi. They interpret their call for an Islamic revolution and *jihad* quite literally. Force and violence are accepted as part of their liberation struggle. Although differences exist, there is a great deal of agreement in the ideological framework of Islamic militant organizations: Among their major beliefs are:

1. Muslims have a God-ordained purpose and vocation, that is, submission to and realization of God's will.

2. God's will governs both individual and community life.

3. The correct path or divine blueprint for society or *Shariah* is contained in the Quran and *Sunnah*.

4. Islam is a total way of life that embraces religion and politics, state and society.

5. An Islamic state, the rule of God on Earth, must be established.

6. It is imperative that the *Shariah* be implemented, replacing existing Western-inspired legal codes.

7. The westernization of Muslim society and its Western models for modernization are condemned because they have failed and are thus responsible for political corruption, economic decline, social injustice, and spiritual malaise, just like the pre-Islamic period of ignorance.

8. A crusader mentality, neocolonialism, and the power of Zionism have resulted in a Western Judeo-Christian conspiracy that pits the West against the East.

9. Because the legitimacy of Muslim governments is based on the *Shariah*, governments such as Egypt's that do not follow the *Shariah* are illegitimate. Those guilty of unbelief, "atheist states" are lawful objects of *jihad*.

10. Muslims are obliged both to overthrow such governments and to fight those Muslims who do not share the "total commitment" of militants. Like the Kharijites in early Islam, militants regard such "uncommitted" persons as no longer Muslims but rather unbelievers.

11. *Jihad* against unbelievers is a religious duty. The life and goods of an infidel are forfeit.

12. Non-Muslims are no longer considered "People of the Book" but rather "unbelievers." Thus non-Muslim minorities, such as the Copts, are persecuted.

13. The official *ulama* are rejected for their tendency to downplay the meaning of *jihad* as armed struggle and simply reduce it to striving to lead a moral or virtuous life. They have succumbed to the West and have been co-opted by the government.

14. The majority of mosques that are state supported and controlled are places of unbelief because God's will and the Prophet's teachings are not upheld there.

But who are these militants—uneducated peasants ignorant of the modern world, rejecting modernization in order to bury themselves in the past? The leadership of Takfir wal Hijra and Muhammad's Youth had combined an early traditional religious upbringing with a modern education. Salih Siriya, founder of Muhammad's Youth, had earned a Ph.D. in science education. Shukri Mustafa, founder of Takfir wal Hijra, held a B.S. in agricultural science. Both had been members of the Muslim Brotherhood and had been imprisoned. In fact Mustafa had been imprisoned from 1965 and was among those released in 1971 by Sadat. Though Siriya and Mustafa honored the memory of Hasan al-Banna and Sayyid Qutb, they believed that the Brotherhood had drifted away from its early commitment; many of its members had been broken, mellowed, or burned out. Therefore, each had begun to develop their own organizations during the late 1960s and early 1970s. The primary source for members was Egypt's younger generation. Religiously concerned students and recent university graduates were recruited from local mosques, schools, and universities and were then organized into secret cells. Most members had come from villages and towns and migrated to such cities as Cairo, Alexandria, and Asyut. Many were educated, highly motivated members of the lower middle and middle classes. As one investigator has concluded:

> The typical social profile of members of militant Islamic groups could be summarized as being young (early twenties), of rural or small-town background, from the middle and lower middle class, with high achievement motivation, upwardly mobile, with science or engineering education, and from a normally cohesive family. It is sometimes assumed in social science that recruits of "radical movements" must be somehow alienated, marginal, anomic, or otherwise abnormal. Most of those we investigated would be considered model young Egyptians.[70]

Separated from their families and village communities, these young Egyptians were exposed in heavy doses to the "new ways" of city life. Here they encountered vividly the realities of modern Egyptian life: the wealth and high life-style of the rich, which contrasted starkly with the overcrowded ghettos, the poverty, massive unemployment, and the Western dress and social (especially sexual) mores on the streets and in the media that contradicted their traditional Islamic values regarding women and the family. Although the freedom and delights of city life may have proved seductive for some young people, many Islamically minded young Egyptians, cut off from the identity and support system of their rural backgrounds, often reacted to modern Egyptian life with a sense of alienation. Islamic organizations, divided into cells called families, offered them a new sense of community. More importantly, this community was based upon an Islamic ideology that provided a critique of society and an agenda for radical change, rooted in the traditional religious world view of these young Egyptians.

The organization and leadership of Islamic organizations reflected the temperaments and styles of their leaders. Mustafa, the "commander of the society of believers," ran the Takfir as a highly disciplined organization, strictly controlled and "guided" by its *amir*. Like Muhammad's Youth, Takfir viewed contemporary Egyptian society as un-Islamic, a domain of unbelievers. So, like the Prophet Muhammad, who when faced with the unbelief of Mecca had emigrated to Medina, the Takfir set up its own "rightly guided" communities that worked, studied, and prayed together. Its goal was the establishment of a separate community of true believers in Egypt. Like the Muslim Brotherhood and Pakistan's Jamaat-i-Islami, there were gradations of membership. Full members in Takfir were expected to devote themselves totally to the work of the community, leaving their jobs, families, and former friends behind. Total commitment was expected. The ideal was martyrdom, that is, a willingness to give up everything even one's life, in the struggle for Islam. The *amir* demanded unquestioning obedience. Errant members might be excommunicated or punished. Although members of Muhammad's Youth were equally militant, well organized, and disciplined, they were governed more democratically by an executive council that relied on consultation rather than one-man rule. Thus, despite Siriya's personal belief that such an action was premature, in April 1974 the council decided to seize the Technical Military Academy and to assassinate Sadat.

During the late 1970s, Sadat's critics became increasingly more vociferous. The political, economic, and social tensions in Egyptian society were fast reaching the boiling point. In January 1977, Cairo was convulsed by food riots that the government blamed on Marxists and leftists. The government's response was swift and strong, arresting many opposition leaders, including members of Islamic militant organizations like the Takfir. Sadat undertook several new policies to bolster the Egyptian economy: an open-door *(al-infitah)* economic program and pursuit of a peace treaty with Israel (Camp David). Both proved unpopular. For many the open-door policy simply meant greater Western (especially American) economic involvement and influence that would line the pockets of multinational companies and Egyptian elites rather than address the basic economic and social problems in Egyptian society. As the best of Egyptian produce was shipped to Europe and the oil-rich Gulf states and Egyptian workers were offered subsidized imported foods, critics might well ask:

> How can the peasant, the hardworking Egyptian fellah, maintain his dignity when, after sweating in the hot sun all day long, he has to stand in line only to receive a frozen American chicken? . . . As he sits in the evening with the family to watch the television that his son has purchased from the fruits of his labor in Saudi Arabia, the intrigues of J.R. Ewing and Sue Ellen in Dallas strip him of what is left of his legitimacy as a culture bearer in his own culture. Between programs, he is told in English that he should be drinking Schweppes or in dubbed Arabic that he should use deodorant, and that all his problems are caused by having too many children—a total package of imported ideas.[71]

Camp David was viewed by Egyptian critics, as well as by most Arab Muslim governments who consequently broke diplomatic ties with Egypt, as a unilateral capitulation to Israel and, by extension, its American patron.

Sadat's foreign minister resigned, public criticism rose, and Islamic critics denounced the action as the treasonous act of an "unbeliever." The criticism of the government was not lessened by al-Azhar's endorsement of Sadat's peace initiative. Rather it confirmed the belief that the religious establishment had become a puppet of the regime. Throughout Egypt demonstrations were organized, especially by Islamic student associations at university campuses. Although the Muslim Brotherhood had initially been cautious in its responses, by March 1979 it published a call "to follow the example of Iran and to wage holy war against Israel."[72]

Islamic critics were further outraged by Sadat's unilateral implementation of controversial reform measures in Muslim family law by
presidential decree during a parliamentary recess. Similar reforms
had been attempted on numerous occasions, including the early
1970s, only to be shelved. The new measures, such as those expanding a wife's grounds for divorce and her maintenance rights, were
regarded as a pet project of Sadat's wife, Jihan al-Sadat. Islamic critics
viewed these reforms as representing a "Western model" of woman-
hood as inappropriate and objectionable as Western models of political and economic development. Family law reforms were viewed as
an attack on traditional Muslim family law that would weaken family
ties and lead to the sexual permissiveness of the West. The fact that
Sadat managed to obtain the support of his appointee, the rector of
al-Azhar, did nothing to assuage Islamic critics. The Muslim Brotherhood, through publications such as *al-Dawa*, and through other militant Islamic organizations, attacked the reforms as anti-Islamic.

As opposition to Sadat became progressively more widespread
and aggressive, he responded defensively and repressively. Sadat's
leadership style had been symbolized by his self-description which he
drew from two traditional titles: "the Believer-President" and "the
head of the family." As dissent mounted, Sadat became the authoritarian father who knew what was best for his family and community
and expected unquestioned support and compliance. Sadat demanded what he himself had been to Nasser, a yes-man, or syc-
ophant. He had silenced the Communists and leftists and now moved
against other critics—intellectuals, lawyers, and university professors.
His real battle, however, was with a burgeoning Islamic opposition.
The Muslim Brotherhood and Islamic student organizations, which he
had encouraged, had taken on a life of their own and had become as
outspoken as other Islamic militants.

Although the official Islamic establishment of al-Azhar could be
marshaled for public support and although the Western media portrayed an enlightened and popular Egyptian first family, preachers in
many of Egypt's mosques bitterly denounced the Sadat government
and its policies: open-door policy, Camp David, family law reform,
the admission of the shah of Iran, and Sadat's denunciation of the
Ayatollah Khomeini and Iran's Islamic revolution.

During 1979–80, Sadat took additional measures to silence his
critics. In February 1979, shortly after the shah's overthrow, in a
speech at Alexandria University, Sadat warned that religion and poli-

tics were separate spheres. Moreover, he declared to members of his National Democratic Party: "Those who wish to practice Islam can go to the mosques and those who wish to engage in politics may do it through the legal institutions," as reported in the *Egyptian Gazette*, February 2, 1979. This statement was taken by his Islamic critics as further proof that Sadat, "the Believer-President," was in fact an unbeliever. Sadat criticized the Muslim Brotherhood for becoming a "state within a state."[73]

As previously noted, university student Islamic organizations were banned by presidential decree in 1979. Finally, in September 1981, the government cast a wide net over its reputed opponents, arresting and imprisoning Muslim Brothers and other members of militant Islamic organizations, university professors, political opposition leaders, Muslim preachers, journalists, and writers. Approximately fifteen hundred people were detained. Both secular political and Islamic opposition publications were banned. Those imprisoned were as diverse in their religious and political positions as in their professions. Indeed the Islamic militants among them would have rejected many of their fellow prisoners as Marxists, atheists, leftists, and Muslim "backsliders." As the shah had done in Iran, Sadat combined autocratic rule and identification of Egypt with his personality and will: "Sadat the dictator was becoming the State itself and the Sadatization of Egypt was expressed in almost every song on radio and television . . . Two processes were at work: a Sadatization of Egypt on the one hand and a deification of Sadat on the other—the rebirth of the Egyptian pharoah."[74] Sadat's indiscriminate crackdown in September and his pharaonic style only served to broaden popular discontent and opposition among moderate Egyptians.

On October 6, 1981, while reviewing a parade commemorating the successes in the 1973 war, Anwar al-Sadat was assassinated. The leader of the assassins had cried out: "I am Khalid Islambuli, I have killed Pharoah and I do not fear death." While Sadat had enjoyed a favorable press in the West, where he was regarded as a peacemaker and an enlightened leader, his growing authoritarianism and suppression of dissent at home had resulted in a secular and religious opposition that increasingly referred to him as pharoah. Thus, for many in Egypt: "Khalid therefore appeared as a sort of 'right arm' of the popular will, and not merely as a militant exponent of an Islamicist group."[75]

Although the assassination was initially attributed to the Takfir wal Hijra, it soon became evident that the Jamaat al-Jihad (Holy War Society) was responsible. Al-Jihad had developed from the survivors of Muhammad's Youth's abortive coup in 1974.[76] Those who had escaped or were released had scattered and had taken up residence in Upper Egypt (Asyut, Minya, Fayyum) as well as in Cairo and Giza. In time separate groups grew up around a local leader. Members came primarily from the lower middle and middle classes, rural migrants who had come recently to the cities. The leadership could best be described as young, devout, educated, committed, but disillusioned and increasingly disaffected with Egyptian society, finding it politically corrupt, economically unjust, and spiritually lax.

Al-Jihad recruited its membership from those young people who were observed at both university mosques and private mosques. The latter had proved especially important in the development of Islamic movements by providing recruits and sympathetic supporters. During the 1970s, the number of private mosques had doubled from approximately twenty to forty thousand so that out of forty-six thousand mosques in Egypt only six thousand were controlled by the Ministry of Religious Endowments (*Waqfs*). Private mosques dotted the neighborhoods of cities and towns, where they served the vast majority of the Egyptian people. More importantly, such mosques and their preachers were independent, financially and politically, unlike the state-supported mosques whose staffs and sermons came under government control. As the situation in Egypt became more radicalized in the late 1970s, Sadat's support from the official Islamic establishment and the government-controlled media was often seriously undermined and offset by the fiery sermons delivered by his Islamic critics in private mosques. Such mosques provided natural meeting places and organizational centers for Islamic militants.

Al-Jihad also extended its influence through the establishment of religious societies, such as those for Quran study, and social centers. The latter provided food, clothing, and assistance in obtaining housing. In particular religious fraternities were created at universities to assist students with free books, tutoring, and housing.

During the late 1970s, al-Jihad's centers grew and its members often clashed with Egyptian security forces, especially in Asyut, Minya, and Alexandria. Despite arrests, government surveillance, and harassment, their strength was not diminished but rather increased. In 1980 a central consultative committee was established, bringing together, in a greater organizational unity, the leaders of the various factions. It was not until March 1981, however, that the leadership of al-Jihad moved beyond isolated attacks and confrontations with the government to plotting an overthrow of Anwar al-Sadat. Among the leading figures to emerge during this process were Muhammad al-Farag, Col. Abbud al-Zumur, Lt. Khalid Islambuli, and Shaykh Umar Abd al-Rahman. They reflected a civilian, military, and religious alliance and character. Al-Farag was in many ways the ideologist of al-Jihad. Colonel al-Zumur and Lieutenant Islambuli were primarily responsible for the recruitment, planning, and execution of the assassination.[77] And Shaykh Abd al-Rahman served as the religious adviser for al-Jihad. He issued decrees that provided religious legitimacy for al-Jihad's actions.

The assassination of Anwar al-Sadat followed quite logically from the ideology of al-Jihad. Like other militant groups, it was strongly indebted to the writings of Hasan al-Banna, Mawlana Mawdudi, and, most especially, Sayyid Qutb. This is clearly reflected in Muhammad al-Farag's brief tract, *The Absent Obligation* (i.e. *jihad*). As a former Muslim Brother who had become disaffected by the group's moderate posture, al-Farag drew heavily on the ideology and world view of al-Banna, Mawdudi, and Qutb, taking them quite literally and following their thoughts regarding the required Islamic revolution to their logical conclusion. At the heart of al-Jihad's message and mission was the call to "true believers" to wage holy war against Egypt's un-Islamic state and its leader, Anwar al-Sadat. Al-Jihad's goal was the establishment of an Islamic state, a society governed by the *Shariah*. But given the decadent state of Islamic society, they believed that *jihad* was required.

Because Muslims find themselves living in what is in effect a non-Islamic territory, an abode of war, armed struggle is necessary to establish once again an Islamic territory. Al-Jihad advocated a caliphal form of government in which the just leader (*imam*) would govern according to the *Shariah*. The *ulama* were faulted for their cooperation with the government and their encouragement of a quiescent Islam through their interpretation of *jihad* as being primarily a personal struggle to lead a virtuous life. The Muslim Brotherhood were also found wanting. Their moderate tone in working for the gradual Islamization of society in order to establish an Islamic state was seen as unrealistic. From al-Jihad's point of view, the depravity of Egyptian society required that power be seized immediately and that an Islamic state be established so that an errant Egyptian society might be Islamized.

The Mubarak Years

The persona of the Egyptian president, the policies of the government, and the nature of Islamic revivalism changed during the 1980s. Hosni Mubarak, in contrast to Anwar al-Sadat, is reserved, less flamboyant; his wife, though active in social welfare, is less westernized than Mrs. Sadat and assumes a lower public profile. In contrast to the repression of the late Sadat years, when Hosni Mubarak became president in October 1981, he balanced swift action and firmness with those who used violence to threaten the authority of the state and public order with a policy of political liberalization and tolerance of dissent. Mubarak did not shrink from executing Sadat's murderers, trying others arrested for complicity in the assassination, and using security forces and the military against militants. A revolt in the Upper Egyptian town of Asyut two days after members of al-Jihad assassinated Sadat was quickly crushed by government paratroopers.

The government's policy of distinguishing more carefully between religious and political dissent and direct threats to state security served as a safety valve in an explosive environment. Mubarak released the fifteen hundred political prisoners detained during Sadat's last month in office, consulted with opposition leaders, permitted open debate and criticism of government policies, eased government control and restrictions on the media, and prosecuted those accused of corruption and exploitation during the Sadat years. Mubarak accepted the court's acquittal of more than 170 defendants in the Sadat trials and released the prisoners. Religious critics of the government were given public outlets, permitted to voice their objections in the press and in the media, and allowed to publish their own newspapers. The government sponsored debates between militants and representatives of the religious establishment, or official Islam, particularly religious scholars from the government-controlled al-Azhar University. Mubarak's strategy was to align the state with official Islam and thus demonstrate the acceptability of both mainstream Islam and reasonable opposition. His purpose was to drive a wedge between the majority of Egyptians who did not rise up in revolt and the militant radicals and extremists, portrayed as "religious fanatics," who distorted true Islamic belief and practice.

Mubarak's liberalism was tested when Egypt's courts acquitted 174 of those militants tried for the Sadat assassination. The professions of those who were released revealed something of the nature and appeal of radical groups: members of the presidential guard, military intelligence, security, civil servants, radio and television workers, university students and professors. The militants' defiant chants from behind prison bars reflected their deep-seated fears and condemnation of Egypt's dangerous dependence upon a host of "enemies": "Holy war against lackeys, Jews, Christians and atheists" and "No to America and no to Israel."[78] These tensions in Egyptian society continued to be reflected in a number of incidents such as continued clashes between militants and Coptic Christians in which Coptic shops and property were destroyed, and the burning of an Israeli flag in February 1985 to protest the "normalization" of relations with Israel.[79]

By the mid-1980s, the government's flexible response to Islamic activism began to show signs of strain. In 1985, when a number of religious organizations and opposition parties resurrected the call for Islamic law, Mubarak's response was uncharacteristically harsh and reminiscent of Sadat's excesses. For Islamic activists, application of the *Shariah* was the litmus test for Islamic orthodoxy, one which Sadat had ultimately failed. More significantly, among the leaders of this initiative were not simply militant activists but prominent religious, political, and intellectual leaders who reflected a more general sentiment for implementation of the *Shariah*. Mubarak banned a mass march planned by its supporters, broke up subsequent rallies led by popular religious leaders like Shaykh Hafez Salama, and threatened to reinstitute Sadat's plan to nationalize all private mosques. Sadat's attempt to do this during the last month of his rule had been a clear indication of his recognition that these independent mosques and their preachers were often the centers and sources of popular criticism of the regime. In July 1985, the Mubarak government placed all private mosques under the aegis of the Ministry of Religious Endowments; this new authority also gave the ministry control over Friday sermons, which led to the arrest of Shaykh Salama and closed down his mosque, a center of dissent. Mubarak's more aggressive and confrontational policy emphasized his fear of religious extremism, united oppositional forces, and undermined his credibility with the general public.

The mood of Egypt's opposition, both nationalist and religious, and a growing anti-American sentiment were evident in December 1985 when a disturbed border policeman, Suliman Khater, killed several Israeli tourists in the Sinai. Opposition newspapers, political parties, and Islamic leaders like Shaykh Hafez Salama defended this action against the "enemies of the nation." Ibrahim Shukry, leader of the Socialist Labor Party, reflected the mood when he declared his support for "this young man who has removed the shame from Egypt after Israel has bombarded the PLO headquarters in Tunisia and after the Americans have hijacked the Egyptian plane" (referring to the Achille Lauro incident).[80]

The most important characteristic of Egyptian Islamic revivalism, as in many other parts of the Muslim world in the late 1980s and early 1990s, was the extent to which its impact had become broad based and institutionalized rather than restricted to small, clandestine groups on the periphery of society. A quiet rather than violent revolution had occurred. The strength of the resurgence of Islam, in numbers and outward signs of piety, was witnessed across the religious, political, and socioeconomic spectrum of society—in conservative establishment Islam, Sufi mysticism, moderate Islamically oriented organizations and voluntary social welfare associations, and radical underground groups. Islamic activism became normalized and institutionalized, a significant part of mainstream Muslim life and society.

The desire to lead a more Islamically informed way of life was found among middle and upper class, educated and uneducated, peasant and professional, young and old, women and men. These devotees were active in Quran study groups (conducted by men and women), mosques, Sufi gatherings, and social welfare organizations. Mosques abounded, built both by the government and by private individuals. They included not only the formal buildings but thousands of structures and rooms added on to hotels, hospitals, and private dwellings.

Religious programming and literature were not only more evident in the government-controlled media and in newspapers but also in bookshops and scattered among the popular secular magazines and books of street vendors. The popularity of preachers such as Shaykh Muhammad Mitwali al-Shaarawi and Abd al-Hamid Kishk, an outspoken government critic often regarded as an extremist and imprisoned by both Nasser and Sadat, made them into religious media stars in Egypt and the Arab world. Their voices were heard not only in mosques or religious gatherings but also on cassettes played in taxicabs, in shops, on the streets, and in the homes of the poor and the middle class alike. Even the book and audio/record stores in luxury hotels carried religious literature and audiocassettes of popular preachers interspersed among their more conventional luxury items. Islamic identity and values were expressed not only in religious literature and worship but also in the social services.

The growth and impact of revivalism showed its many faces. Although the National Assembly vetoed implementation of a codified Islamic law, it promised to review all laws to assure their conformity with the *Shariah* and to expand religious education. An unexpurgated edition of *A Thousand and One Nights* was banned under Egypt's pornography law as constituting a threat to the moral fabric of society. Alcohol was banned in most nontourist areas, and draft laws were submitted to ban alcohol completely as well as to fine all who ate or smoked in public during Ramadan. Islamic student organizations became more aggressive at campuses in Asyut, Minya, Cairo, and Alexandria. Their demands ranged from an Islamic revolution to the implementation of Islamic law, separation of the sexes in classes, and banning of Western music.

Islamically oriented organizations, voluntary or nongovernment associations, and activists proliferated and pursued a number of paths from apolitical activism to antiregime insurrection. Their growth was fed by the dismal socioeconomic realities of Egyptian life. Egypt remained a society that often seemed to be on the verge of economic collapse: unchecked poverty and illiteracy, high unemployment in a society in which more than half its 50 million citizens were below the age of twenty, the additional loss of jobs and remittances from the Gulf, the inability of the government to provide jobs for hundreds of thousands of university graduates, a bureaucratic infrastructure that was not able to deliver necessary goods and services, and a growing gap between rich and poor.

For the average (i.e., poor) Egyptian, government services were too few and too expensive. Islamic associations provided an alternative institutional infrastructure to fill the void created by the failures of the state bureaucracy. "Walk the back streets of Cairo, or the narrow, winding paths of the smaller towns bordering the Nile; people and poverty are everywhere, as are Islamic institutions."[81] Their range of activities included: educational facilities, which were often connected with a mosque; psychiatric, dental, and drug rehabilitation clinics; nurseries; legal aid societies; subsidized housing; food distribution; banking and investment houses. As the Egyptian sociologist Saad Eddin Ibrahim commented:

> This strand of Islamic activism has therefore set about establishing concrete Islamic alternatives to the socioeconomic institutions of the state and the capitalist sector. Islamic social welfare institutions are better run than their state/public counterparts, less bureaucratic and impersonal . . . They are definitely more grass-roots oriented, far less expensive and far less opulent than the institutions created under Sadat's *infitah* (open-door policy), institutions which mushroomed in the 1970s and which have been providing an exclusive service to the top 5 percent of the country's population. Apolitical Islamic activism has thus developed a substantial socioeconomic muscle through which it has managed to baffle the state and other secular forces in Egypt.[82]

Political Islam proved equally as diverse and textured as apolitical activism, ranging from the emergence of the Muslim Brotherhood as a mainstream political opposition to the violent activities of militant groups and individuals. The profile and fortune of the Muslim Brotherhood have changed considerably over the decades from the Brotherhood's original emergence as a religiosocial reform society to its suppression by Nasser for political extremism, from the militant, rejectionist ideological world view of Sayyid Qutb to its rehabilitation under Anwar al-Sadat. In the early Sadat years, the Brotherhood seemed the aged remnant of a once-vital past, often appearing guarded in its criticism of a government that had given the group its freedom or overshadowed by the religious righteousness and radical politics of new youthful extremist groups. However, in the 1980s, the Brotherhood leadership emerged from their imprisonment during the September 1981 crackdown by Sadat as a respectable opposition group that had demonstrated its ability to stand up to "pharoah" without resorting to terrorism. It had established its credentials as a moderate Islamic organization, publicly eschewing violence and working within the political system. The Brotherhood's ideology and political strategy were thus transformed to incorporate parliamentary democracy and political pluralism. The Brothers entered electoral politics, cooperating with secular parties when necessary.

In the national elections of May 1984, the Brotherhood formed an alliance with the New Wafd Party, which won 12.7 percent of the seats in the People's Assembly. In 1987 the Brotherhood formed a new coalition, the Islamic Alliance, with the Liberal and the Socialist Labor Party. Using the slogan "Islam is the solution" and calling for the implementation of Islamic law, they won 10 percent of the vote, emerging as the chief opposition in parliament to Mubarak's National Democratic Party. The Brotherhood has grown in numbers and in its institutions, ranging from publishing houses and medical clinics to financial houses.

The relatively quiet first years of the Mubarak era evaporated by the mid-1980s as Islamic militancy again challenged the government's authority and threatened the public order. Bars, nightclubs, cinemas, and video stores were attacked or bombed; and the shops of Coptic Christians were burned in major cities and towns. The continued growth of antiregime militant activism within the army and middle class was underscored in December 1986 when Egyptian authorities arrested thirty-three activists, including four military officers, charged with plotting to wage a holy war to overthrow the government. They were alleged to be connected to al-Jihad, Sadat's assassins. In 1989 there were reports that as many as ten thousand Islamic militants had been arrested. Thousands were held without charge, and the Arab Human Rights Organization accused the government of routine torture.[83] In August 1989, the Egyptian government arrested forty-one members of a clandestine Shii movement, reportedly trained in Iran and Syria to overthrow the government as well as to attack American and Israeli targets. One month later, members of a group called Salvation from Hell were sentenced for the attempted assassination of two former cabinet ministers and a journalist who had written articles condemning religious extremism. Having "agreed to form an illegal party and to declare Egypt's rulers and society infidel," they called for holy war and the establishment of an Islamic state.[84]

State Power and Civil Society

Throughout the 1990s Egypt, along with many governments in North Africa, identified "Islamic fundamentalism" as the major threat to state and regional security. In the post-Gulf period, Egypt's profile abroad was that of a U.S. ally playing a constructive role in the Middle East peace process and at home a moderate government beset by religious revolutionaries. This picture often obscured the complex struggle within Egypt.

In the 1990s Egypt provided a primary example of the dynamic and diverse relationship of religion to society, its challenge to the state, and its impact upon the democratization process. The Egyptian experience has witnessed: radical violent revolutionary Islamic activism as well as the institutionalization of Islam socially and politically; diverse state policies towards Islam in the struggle of government and ruling elites to maintain their legitimacy, power, and privileges; a growing polarization (as in many Muslim societies) between Islamists and government/secular elites; a commitment to democratization and the government's withdrawal of that commitment justified by the charge that "fundamentalists" were out to "hijack" democracy; and finally the widening of a confrontation between state security forces and Muslim extremists that included moderate activists (in particular the Muslim Brotherhood) as well as violent revolutionaries (the Gamaa Islamiyya).

The Jihad Continues

Radical violent extremists, more silent in the early Mubarak period, boldly and directly challenged the regime in the 1990s. Extremists in Assyut, Minya, Cairo, and Alexandria pressed for an Islamic revolution, the immediate implementation of Islamic law, separation of the sexes, and the banning of Western music and concerts. The chief militant Islamic challenge to the Mubarak government came from the Gamaa Islamiyya (Jamaat Islamiyya or Islamic Group) and Jamaat al-Jihad who were locked in a deadly battle with security forces and police during the 1990s.

The Gamaa Islamiyya had evolved from student groups active on university campuses and in politics in the Sadat era to an umbrella organization of clandestine groups active in Cairo, Alexandria, Asyut, Minya, and Fayyum. In contrast to the urban-university based Gamaa of the Sadat period, many were now high school age as well as university students, active in small villages and towns as well as urban areas, less educated, living in more desperate conditions of poverty and unemployment, more radical ideologically, and more random in their use of violence. Bent upon destabilizing the Egyptian economy and thus the regime, extremists attacked and murdered Coptic Christians, government officials, and foreign tourists, the most important source of Egypt's foreign revenues providing income for millions of Egyptians. They bombed or burned banks, government buildings, cinemas, theaters, and video and bookstores that popularized western culture.[85] Prominent critics were assassinated (the columnist Farag Foda who had been outspoken in his denunciation of fundamentalism) or physically attacked and injured (Egypt's elderly Nobel laureate, Naguib Mahfouz was stabbed). Others required twenty-four-hour security.

A new round of Muslim-Christian conflict exploded as the battle between the Gamaa and the government intensified. Bombings of churches, homes, and shops, beatings and murders increased not only in large cities but also in small towns (Biba, Sennouris, and Qena) and villages. Coptic Christians, caught in the battle between militants and the government, charged that government officials downplayed the number of incidents and their significance, often attributing such incidents to personal conflicts and vendettas rather than religiously motivated attacks. The Egyptian Organization for Human Rights put the blame squarely on the shoulders of the Islamic Group, condemning the "actions of the organization known as Gamaa Islamiyya [the Islamic Group], which has persisted in its recourse to violence, in its advocacy of the hatred of citizens of the Christian faith, in its incitement to various forms of discrimination against them and in actively taking part in such acts of discrimination."[86] It charged that, despite the government's use of indiscriminate firepower, killings, and arbitrary arrests, militant Islamists were in fact responsible for the bulk of human rights abuses (including the deaths of Christians, police, and a foreign tourist) in Upper Egypt.[87]

Mubarak's "Extreme" War Against Extremism

The Mubarak government mounted a formidable response to the threat of religious extremism and terrorism, utilizing both its military and security forces and special military courts. The spiral of violence and counterviolence contributed not only to law and order but also to a breakdown of law and order. Both extremists and the government became locked in a "holy war" in which the government's police and security forces as well as the militants appeared to have a hit list for murder and assassination rather than arrest and prosecution. An Amnesty International report noted that security forces "appear to have been given a license to kill with impunity."[88] Special military courts, which do not permit defendants a right of appeal, were created to try civilians accused of terrorism. Courts quickly and often quietly dispensed swift, harsh sentences. Lawyers for the defense charged that they were permitted limited access to their clients, many of whom were victims of torture. Lawyers themselves were intimidated and arrested. The number of prisoners executed vastly exceeded those for past politically motivated crimes such as the attempt to kill Nasser or the assassination of Sadat. The U.S. State Department's human rights report on Egypt noted that the government "perpetrated many abuses, including the arbitrary arrest and torture of hundreds of detainees, the use of military courts to try accused terrorists, the failure to punish officials responsible for torture."[89] Systematic torture, long-term detention without charge, taking family members of suspected Islamists or terrorists "hostage" to force their relatives to surrender, and press censorship have led officials of international nongovernmental human rights organizations to declare: "This poor human rights record has yielded resentment, the narrowing of civil society, religious intolerance and erosion of the rule of law in Egypt—and fertile ground for the growth of extremist alternatives."[90]

The war between the government and the Gamaa contributed to a climate in which the state broadened its battle beyond the clandestine Gamaa Islamiyya and other radical groups to curb the growing strength and challenge of the Muslim Brotherhood. The breathing space of the early Mubarak years had enabled Islamic political and social activism to grow more rapidly and to expand its institutions. The Muslim Brotherhood became an effective agent of social and political change, developing alternative socioeconomic institutions and participating in the political process, demonstrating its strength in institution building and popular mobilization. It (and other Islamic organizations) attracted members from the middle and lower middle classes (businessmen, bureaucrats, doctors, engineers, lawyers, journalists) and engaged in a broad range of social and political activities, from the creation of Islamic charitable associations to participation in parliamentary and professional association (physicians, lawyers, engineers) elections. Its network of mosques, hospitals, clinics, day care centers, youth clubs, legal aid societies, banks, and publishing houses multiplied, offering effective civil alternatives to state institutions. Operating within the political system, moderate activists such as the Muslim Brotherhood couched their criticisms and demands within the context of a call for greater political liberalization, democratization, social justice, and respect for human rights.

The Mubarak government's aggressive response to Islamic radicalism in the 1990s increasingly blurred the lines between radical and moderate Islamists, state security and the limits of state authority, prosecution of criminals and human rights. It attempted not only to eradicate violent extremism but also to counter and control the legal institutionalization of Islamic activism politically and socially (social welfare, professional associations, schools, and mosques) in Egyptian society. In its war against "terrorism," a broad government crackdown and massive arrests of suspected terrorists included not only the extremists but also moderate Islamists in an attempt to silence all Islamic opposition. Thousands were held without charge; the Arab Human Rights Organization accused the government of routine torture.[91] By June 1994 the Mubarak government's war was not just against the terrorism of the Gamaa Islamiya but against its strongest legal opposition, the Muslim Brotherhood; it was, in the words of one commentator, an attempt "to curtail not only those movements that have carried out violent attacks, but also one that has come to dominate many municipalities, professional and labor associations and university faculties."[92]

Professional Syndicates

The mainstreaming of Islamic activism had produced a professional class increasingly elected to leadership positions in professional syndicates. Professional syndicates, democratic and voluntary associations of teachers, lawyers, physicians, engineers, and journalists have been a pillar of Egyptian civil society. As Raymond Baker has observed:

Denied access to the political arena, they [the Brotherhood] have made professional syndicates perhaps the most vibrant institutions of Egyptian civil society . . . Islamists have worked to extend medical insurance to syndicate members and their families, establish social and recreational clubs (and not just in large cities), increase the stock of housing available to members at lower prices, and assist the families of those members arrested or otherwise detained by the regime.[93]

The Medical Association became a platform for a national dialogue and debate on major domestic and international issues. In September 1992 the Brotherhood's winning of a majority of the board seats in Bar Association elections, long regarded as a bastion of liberalism, signaled the growing strength and significance of Islamist leadership in the syndicates, disturbing many government officials and secular elites. The government moved decisively in February 1993 to curtail this challenge by the Brotherhood. The government controlled People's Assembly passed legislation (Law 100) that placed stringent quorum requirements on syndicate elections which, if not met, enabled the government to appoint syndicate board members. Attempts to intimidate or silence syndicate opposition continued. On May 10 a protest rally by lawyers over the death in police custody of Abdel Harith Medani, a leading lawyer for the Gamaa Islamiya and a member of the Egyptian Human Rights Organization, led to the arrest of thirty-three lawyers, charged with inciting violence.[94] Abdel Aziz Mohammed the head of the 70,000 member Cairo branch of the Lawyers Syndicate and a lawyer defending a Cairo University professor accused by Islamists of apostasy, charged that the government aimed "to weaken the syndicate as an institution of civil society in the guise of waging a fight against militancy."[95]

Despite these actions by the government, denounced by Islamists and non-Islamists alike, Law 100 proved ineffective. When the Brotherhood continued to win board elections, the state in 1995 and 1996 closed the lawyers and engineers syndicates, placing them under state "guardianship." State appointees were put in charge, financial assets frozen, and most activities curtailed. The doctors syndicate, or Medical Association, where Islamists also continued to win elections to the board, faced a similar threat.

Mosques and Preachers

The government attempted to broaden its control of religious institutions, in particular, private mosques. The vast majority of Egypt's mosques were private (and thus independent in terms of their preachers, content of sermons, and activities) rather than state-controlled. Although both Sadat and later Mubarak (in 1985) announced plans to take control of private mosques, the results were limited given the enormous number of mosques and limited resources. In October 1992 the government again announced its determination to control private mosques and their preachers, which it regarded as a major breeding ground of discontent and radicalism. Mubarak's ministry of religious affairs announced that all sermons at state-controlled mosques would be subject to approval by government appointed officials and that the building of private mosques would be curbed. On November 10, 1992, Mohammed Ali Mahgoub, the minister of religious affairs, announced once again that all private mosques would be brought under the control of the ministry.

In the 1990s Islamic political and social activism in Egypt continued to root itself more deeply and pervasively in Egyptian society, growing among the lower and middle classes, educated and uneducated, professionals, students and laborers, young and old, women and men. Islamists gained cultural legitimacy, becoming a more visible and effective part of mainstream Muslim life and society. State institutions were complemented or challenged by Islamically oriented counterparts. The Muslim Brotherhood and other activists became dominant voices in professional organizations and syndicates of lawyers, doctors, engineers, and journalists. They presented their criticisms and demands within the context of a call for greater democratization, political representation, and respect for human rights.

At the same time, the Egyptian government continued to be "the president's state." In the 1995 presidential elections, Hosni Mubarak won by 94 percent of the vote with no opposition candidate. Both the Independent Commission of Election review and "rulings from the highest courts in the land . . . declared that serious fraud and irregularities had taken place in more than half of the 222 voting districts."[96] The People's Assembly and the bureaucracy continued to be dominated by the Government's National Democratic Party; the government maintained absolute control over the creation and continued existence of political parties. Thus, it continued to refuse legal recognition of the Muslim Brotherhood. In the wake of the 1995 elections, when moderate Islamists from the Brotherhood joined with others (including Christian counterparts) in creating a new political party, Hizb al-Wasat, which advocated the need to democratize the political order and the joint role of Muslims and Christians in Egyptian society, two of its founders and other members were arrested and tried by a military court for "joining an illegal and secret group which aims to overthrow the ruling regime and to circumvent legitimacy by forming Al-Wasat party to act as the voice of the banned Muslim Brothers group." Seven were sentenced to prison.[97]

The reality of Egyptian society, as indeed of many Muslim societies, contributes to a climate in which the influence of Islam and activist organizations on sociopolitical development will increase rather than diminish. Egypt continues to exist in a climate of authoritarian rule, socioeconomic crisis, and cultural alienation in which many citizens experience the failure of the state and of secular ideologies. The government and ruling elites or classes possess tenuous legitimacy in the face of mounting disillusionment and opposition, among whom Islamic activists remain the most vocal, best organized, and effective. The extent to which the government fails to meet socioeconomic needs, restricts political participation, proves insensitive to the need to incorporate effectively Islam and moderate Islamists, or appears exceedingly dependent on the West contributes to the continued appeal of an Islamic political alternative. As one observer has noted, "the future development of the Islamic movement depends on how it is treated (or mistreated) by those in power and not on any inherent conflict between Islam and freedom. . . . Egypt's rulers can expect to see an Islam that faithfully reflects the skill or folly of their own statecraft."[98]

Sudan

On June 30, 1989, a group of military officers seized power in the Sudan, the largest country in Africa and the Middle East, which includes some 597 tribes and more than 400 languages and dialects. For the fourth time since gaining independence in 1956, the Sudan was under military rule. Before long and to the surprise of many, Lt. Gen. Omar Hassam Ahmed Bashir's government was closely aligned with the National Islamic Front (NIF). For many this ideological orientation, or alliance, was strikingly reminiscent of Sudan's previous military ruler, Jafar al-Numayri, whose military dictatorship was toppled on April 5, 1985, by a bloodless military coup d'etat after a sixteen-year rule (1969–85). In the early 1980s, Numayri had struggled to maintain his government and to enhance his legitimacy through his self-proclaimed Islamic revolution in the Sudan. His public commitment to Islamize Africa's largest country resulted in Islamic laws, courts, punishments, and taxes that propelled this Arab socialist state far down the road to becoming a self-proclaimed Islamic state.[99] Understanding these political appeals to Islam in the face of a civil war in which the Sudan People's Liberation Movement (SPLM), established in 1983, has demanded a secular state requires an appreciation of Sudan's Islamic political heritage.

The Sudan has had a rich Islamic past that was central to two major Islamic states: the Funj sultanate (1504–1820) and the Mahdist state (1885–99). The Mahdist movement in particular left a legacy not only of Islamic identification with the state but also of Islam's role as an anticolonialist force and an integral component of Sudanese nationalism and independence owing to its revolt against Ottoman-Egyptian rule (1820–81) and Anglo-Egyptian rule (1899–1955). When the Sudan became independent in 1956, many regarded the Mahdist state as the origin and paradigm of the modern Sudanese nation-state.

Islam continued to be both a pervasive social and cultural presence, a major source of identity, ideology, and values. It served as a source of local and national leadership and inspired Islamic organizations and parties such as the Ansar (followers of the Mahdi), Khatmiyya, and Muslim Brotherhood. Even more secular-oriented nationalists paid homage to Sudan's Islamic past and to its Mahdist tradition as the origin of Sudanese nationalism. The importance of the Sudan's Islamic legacy could be seen in its first government. Although the secular civilian government of Ismail al-Azhari (1956–58) declared Islam the state religion and the *Shariah* a basic source of law, religious organizations (the Ansar and Khatmiyya) demanded an Islamic republic with a parliamentary form of government and the *Shariah* as the main source of law. During 1969–70, when the Free officers, led by Col. Jafar Muhammad al-Numayri, seized power in the May revolution, three important ideological forces were at work in the Sudan: Islam, Gamal Abd al-Nasser's Arab socialism, and communism.

Numayri's Turn to Islam

Like Muammar al-Qaddafi, Jafar al-Numayri was an admirer of Egypt's Gamal Abd al-Nasser and came to power at the head of an Arab socialist revolution. Similarly, within a short period of time, he too turned to Islam to buttress his Arab socialism. Personal as well as political factors influenced Jafar al-Numayri's espousal of an Islamic direction in his life and government. After an abortive coup in 1971 in which he narrowly escaped death, Numayri had become increasingly more religiously observant, abstaining from alcohol, gambling, and carousing. He began to frequent Sufi celebrations and to seek the private counsel of local Sufi shaykhs. At the same time, Numayri's public statements frequently emphasized a holistic understanding of Islam, similar to that espoused by Sudan's traditional Islamic organizations that had opposed his rule, the Ansar (followers of the Mahdi) and the Muslim Brotherhood, both of whom asserted Islam's integral relationship with all aspects of public and private life. In 1976 Numayri issued a directive to government officials to refrain from drinking. He even wrote a book, *Why the Islamic Way?* about his increased emphasis upon Islam, in which he called for the application of Islamic law in the Sudan.[100]

A variety of factors can be identified to explain Numayri's public espousal of Islam. The appeal to Islam offered Numayri a new way out of a deteriorating situation. It was consonant with his opportunistic leadership style, had continuity with the Islamic character of Sudanese political history and social culture, and thus had the potential to consolidate popular support among Sudan's 70 percent Muslim population even if it threatened to alienate the Christian and animist southern third of the Sudanese. Throughout his regime, Numayri had ruled through a variety of alliances, leftist, military, tribal, and religious, which he used only for as long as was necessary, shifting from one partner to another to avoid any becoming too strong in its own right.[101] His strength was in maintaining a balance between building alliances and keeping potential rivals disorganized and relatively weak.

A series of events during the 1970s progressively narrowed Numayri's political options. An abortive Communist coup in 1971 made Numayri resolutely antileftist. His own brand of Arab socialism, unable to garner popular domestic support, had failed as a national ideology. Sudan's economy had deteriorated, and its national debt spiraled out of control. Responding to pressures from the World Bank and the International Monetary Fund, Sudan had lifted government subsidies on staples such as bread and sugar, causing popular anti-government demonstrations and food riots in 1979 (and again in

1982). Insurrection grew in the predominantly non-Muslim South. Numayri continued to be challenged by the National Front, an alliance of national Islamic organizations including the National Islamic Front, led by Sadiq al-Mahdi, the great grandson of the Sudanese Mahdi and a former prime minister.

In the early 1980s, Numayri used the growing political fragmentation to consolidate his power in the North. He then dissolved the regional government in the South and imposed a military regime, completely discarding the Addis Ababa Accords of 1972, which had brought a cease-fire to the seventeen-year civil war between the predominantly Arab Muslim North and the non-Arab, non-Muslim South. Guerilla warfare escalated under the Sudan People's Liberation Movement (SPLM), led by Col. John Garang, an American trained Ph.D., and supported by Libya and Ethiopia. The Muslim government of the North was viewed as dominating the South politically and exploiting its economic resources. Numayri used the rebellion in the South to strengthen his ties with Western allies, particularly the United States. Maintaining that the SPLM were Marxists supported by Libya and Ethiopia, he reinforced the perception of the Sudan as a bulwark against communism in Africa to press for increased military aid from the United States.

While Numayri's turn to Islam troubled many, it had potential popular appeal among Sudan's Muslim majority. In addition Numayri's regime, like many other Muslim governments during the 1970s, looked to Arab oil-rich states and companies for loans and investments. Numayri's approach was similar in this regard to that of Pakistan's Zulfikar Ali Bhutto and his successor, Gen. Zia ul-Haq, who had strengthened their case for aid from Saudi Arabia and other Gulf states by fostering greater Islamization.

The appeal to Islam both resonated with popular Islamic sentiments and co-opted many of the themes of Numayri's major national Islamic opposition, the National Front, with its emphasis on Islamic symbols and rhetoric, criticism of the westernization of society and culture, condemnation of communism, and assertion of the primary importance of Islamic ideology and law.

The National Front represented the major Islamic organizations and banned political parties: the Umma (Ansar) Party of Sadiq al-Mahdi, the Democratic Union Party (DUP, closely associated with Khatmiyya), and the Islamic Charter Front Party (Muslim Brother-

hood) of Hassan al-Turabi. In 1977 Numayri signed a formal agreement of National Reconciliation with Sadiq al-Mahdi, the leader of
the National Front. The major benefactor of National Reconciliation
and its most cooperative participant was, however, the Muslim Brotherhood. Although the other groups remained aloof, the Brotherhood
joined the government. Thus after more than two decades, much of
which time was spent in opposition, the Muslim Brotherhood became
part of the political establishment.

The Muslim Brotherhood had been founded in 1954. Although
inspired by Egypt's Muslim Brotherhood, the Sudanese group is an
autonomous organization. From its creation, the Brotherhood advocated the establishment of an Islamic political and social order
through the adoption of an Islamic constitution based upon the
Quran and the introduction of Islamic law. The Brotherhood offered
an Islamic alternative for traditionally raised Muslims who had then
gone on to receive modern educations. Rejecting the westernization of
society and secularism, it advocated a modern state and society more
firmly rooted in Sudan's Islamic faith and heritage.

The Brotherhood came to prominence during the mid-1960s aided
by Hassan al-Turabi, who had returned from France with a doctorate
in international law, had become dean of the Law School at Khartoum
University, and was then elected secretary general of the Brotherhood
in 1964. When a civilian government, strongly influenced by the Left,
came to power in October 1964, the Brotherhood mobilized popular
support behind its call to eradicate communism and to introduce an
Islamic constitution under the banner of the new Islamic Charter
Front Party. After 1969 the Brotherhood participated in the creation of
the National Front and its efforts to overthrow Numayri's Commu-
nist-supported regime. Under Turabi, a brother-in-law of Sadiq al-
Mahdi, the Brotherhood assisted the Ansar's abortive revolt at Aba
Island in 1970. Sadiq went into exile in Britain, but Turabi and some
of his followers were imprisoned.

The fortunes of Turabi and the Brotherhood were reversed in
1977. Unlike other members of the National Front, the Muslim Brotherhood showed little hesitation in accepting the fruits of National Reconciliation, which included greater involvement in the political process.
The strategy of the Muslim Brotherhood had been to bring about
gradual change from below, from within the system. Their work on
campuses and among educated professionals was aimed at changing

society through the development of a new elite who would enter and influence all sectors of education, the professions, and government. While the long-range goal might be the creation of an Islamic state under a suitable Muslim leader, the Brotherhood was content in the short run to establish itself as a recognized political force or pressure group that any government, whatever its orientation, would have to take seriously. Thus, whether Numayri was sincere or not, Turabi could view Numayri's new initiative as offering an opportunity for the Brotherhood to be in a position to directly influence government policy. Their alliance was motivated on both sides less by a meeting of the minds than by political expediency, as later events illustrate.

From 1978 onward, the Muslim Brotherhood was closely associated with the Numayri regime. Turabi became Sudan's attorney general. Muslim Brothers secured senior appointments in the cabinet and government ministries (law, education, religious affairs), in the judiciary, and in the Sudanese Socialist Union (SSU). In 1980 they also won a substantial number of seats in the elections for a new People's Assembly. Their strength in government was complemented by a continued expansion of their control or influence over nongovernmental institutions: universities, student and professional organizations, mosques and cultural centers, and a burgeoning system of Islamic banks and insurance companies. By 1980 the Islamic Trend Movement, the student wing of the Brotherhood, controlled student unions in every university, except Juba University in the South. In the early 1980s, throughout the Sudan, student government elections were dominated by Islamic issues and invariably Muslim Brotherhood candidates proved most successful. Student politics spilled into the streets as Islamically oriented students led marches, chanting: "Non-Western, Non-Eastern, Islamic 100 percent" in support of the Muslim Brotherhood and Islamization.[102]

Numayri's Islamization Program

Islamization of the Sudan intensified on September 8, 1983, when Jafar al-Numayri declared the Sudan would be an Islamic republic and issued an official decree for the application of the *Shariah* in the Sudan. Numayri proclaimed an "Islamic revolution" that would impact on politics, law, and society.

That the Islamization program in the Sudan was very much "Numayri's Islam" is illustrated both by the process itself and by Numayri's handling of alternative national Islamic leaders and organizations. More than twenty laws and assorted regulations and policies were hastily formulated, with little or no consultation with the attorney general's office or the chief justice. They were issued by presidential decree, not legislative action. Their implementation and application were equally erratic, dependent upon Numayri's presidential decree and special "decisive justice courts," not by the Sudan's duly established judiciary.

Numayri curtailed the powers of Sudan's courts by introducing the decisive justice courts, purportedly to provide swift adjudication and justice in criminal cases. Thousands were arrested and brought before government-appointed judges, whose courts often functioned more like military tribunals, employing "Islamic" punishments such as flogging, done quite liberally, for a variety of crimes. In May 1984, European-style dancing was banned when a nightclub owner was sentenced to twenty-five lashes for permitting heterosexual dancing that was judged contrary to Islam.[103] While the courts were admittedly swift, there were often grave differences of opinion about their independence and the quality of justice that they dispensed.

In the socioeconomic sphere, new guidelines were enacted for taxation and banking. The *Zakat* Tax Act of 1984 replaced much of the state's taxation system with an alms tax that was supposed to become the major source of revenue. The Sudan now joined a number of self-styled Islamic governments, like Pakistan and Iran, in passing legislation that empowered the state to levy, collect, and distribute the *zakat*.

Numayri's stated intention to convert all of the Sudan's banks into interest-free institutions was an especially controversial economic reform. Sudan already had five such banks, including the Faisal Islamic Bank, which had close ties with the Muslim Brotherhood. The move to an Islamic banking system in the Sudan, as in Pakistan and Iran, was to be the first step in basing the entire economy on Islamic principles. These policies greatly disturbed many in the Sudan as well as those foreign interests, particularly U.S.-based multinationals, operating in the Sudan.

Numayri skillfully used Islam to direct, and thus to control, Islamic revivalism within the Sudan and to enhance his political legitimacy by appropriating a religiopolitical status. At the same time, he weakened the power of Hassan al-Turabi, whom he had seen as a competitor, by replacing him with a more subservient attorney general. Turabi was made presidential adviser for foreign affairs, a less influential though important-sounding position. Numayri also took action against Sadiq al-Mahdi who, upon returning from exile in 1982, was first placed in "protective custody" and then imprisoned. Sadiq had always represented a formidable challenge to Numayri. With the greater emphasis upon Islam, Sadiq's direct descent from the Mahdi and his leadership of a national Islamic organization threatened Numayri's own attempt to enhance his legitimacy through an appeal to Islam. Moreover, Sadiq had been critical of Numayri's Islamization program, maintaining that the introduction of the *Shariah* was premature, that society had to be prepared for its introduction.

To enhance his own status as an Islamic political leader, in 1983 Numayri used flamboyant public acts, such as his release of a reported thirteen thousand prisoners to give them a "second chance" under Islamic law, to dramatize the new Islamic order. Similarly, he supervised the destruction of alcohol, worth $11 million, pouring it into the Nile in a public demonstration and media event that gained both national and international attention. In May 1984, he required that senior members of the government, judiciary, military, trade unions, and the SSU pledge their allegiance *(baya)* and loyalty to him, acknowledging him as a Muslim ruler guided by the Quran. This ceremony, combined with his Islamic laws and creation of the decisive justice courts, was a fundamental expression of his appropriation of Islamic leadership and legitimacy to justify authoritarian rule. Indeed Numayri planned to declare himself *Imam,* the religiopolitical leader of the state. On July 11, 1984, however, Numayri was unexpectedly rebuffed by the People's Assembly when it postponed a vote on a series of amendments that would have ratified his Islamic laws and his religiopolitical status.

Initially, Islamization had proved popular in the North. Many felt that the crime rate and corruption were on the decrease. Public floggings and amputations drew large supportive crowds. Nevertheless, Numayri's use of Islam to expand his power and justify an increasingly repressive regime, the erratic rulings of the decisive justice courts, and the indiscriminate use of flogging undermined his image at home and abroad. The Ansar, Republican Brothers, Khatmiyya, secularists, and southern opposition leaders continued to oppose Numayri's Islamization program and, at the same time, to regard the

Muslim Brotherhood as the architect of Numayri's program. Even conservative Muslim states like Saudi Arabia became concerned about a negative image of Islam and Islamic justice as international media coverage of a seemingly endless number of floggings and amputations increased.

Throughout 1984 Sudan's political and economic situation continued to deteriorate. In July a new opposition coalition, the National Salvation Front, was formed by the Ansar, Khatmiyya, Sudanese Communist Party, and others. Their program included civil rights especially for non-Muslims, retention of the *Shariah* as a source of legislation, and the abolition of laws that were regarded as not truly Islamic. Although John Garang of the SPLM participated in the discussions, he refused to join unless complete secularization was accepted. Political instability was exacerbated by the continued deterioration of the economy. The Sudanese pound had been devalued five times in the previous three years. The effects of the famine in Ethiopia (more than 1.2 million refugees) and in the Sudan were inescapable. The United States froze $114 million in economic aid (December 1984), as it sided with the IMF in pressing the Sudan to introduce economic reforms in order to control its spiraling deficit ($9 billion debt).

Numayri responded by a series of reforms that tempered his Islamization program. He discontinued the steady stream of floggings and amputations in the North, backed away from his plan to divide the South, and gave assurances that *Shariah* would not be implemented there. As Numayri moderated his push for Islamization, talk of an imminent introduction of an interest-free Islamic economy also subsided. The *zakat* tax was abolished and the income tax was restored.

In January 1985, amidst growing criticism of Islamization, Numayri selected an easy target, the Republican Brothers, to symbolize his intention of silencing his critics and to rally popular Muslim support. Masking authoritarianism in the guise of being the protector of Islamic orthodoxy, he arrested, tried, and executed the seventy-six-year-old founder and leader of the Republican Brothers, Mahmud Muhammad Taha, for apostasy. Taha had opposed sectarian politics and attempts to implement Islamic law. Many Muslims, including the Ansar, Muslim Brotherhood, and the local Sufi leaders, had long regarded Taha's religious claims and his reinterpretation of Islam as not simply liberal reformism but heresy. Numayri's action seemed the move of a desperate man. It was "seen not only as a violation of Sudan's unwritten law of political tolerance, it was also a violation of Islamic law—as determined by an appeals court ex-post-facto."[104]

In March 1985, Numayri continued his attempt to salvage his tottering regime, answer his critics, and redirect blame for the Sudan's ills away from himself. He followed his long established pattern, co-opting potential rivals into a government coalition and then repudiating them, by moving to eliminate the Muslim Brotherhood as a political force and making it a scapegoat for the failures of his regime. In a statement to reassure his American allies as much as to assuage the Sudanese populace, Numayri claimed to have thwarted a coup by the Muslim Brotherhood, whom he charged were armed by Iran in order to overthrow his pro-American government. Numayri dismissed all members of the Muslim Brotherhood from the government and the SSU and ordered the arrest of two hundred of its leaders, including Hassan al-Turabi.

The removal of Brotherhood leaders from key positions and Numayri's new government "reforms" were a response to the United States, Egypt, and Saudi Arabia as much as to his domestic critics. Indeed they occurred immediately after the visit of then Vice-President Bush and a U.S. delegation. The timing was such that both within the Sudan and in the Arab world, reports maintained that among the four conditions Bush presented for lifting the freeze on American economic aid were discontinuation of Islamic criminal punishments (*hudud*) and dismissal of Islamic fundamentalists from the government and its institutions. The other two alleged points were halting contacts with Libya and accepting the economic reforms demanded by the IMF. The fact that Bush ended his visit by announcing resumption of U.S. aid and that a team from the World Bank left for the Sudan the following day appeared to confirm U.S. responsibility for Numayri's new initiatives. This perception was reinforced in late March, when Sudan's government, yielding to IMF and U.S. pressures, lifted subsidies on staples, an act that proved to be the undoing of the Numayri regime.

The lifting of subsidies on bread and fuel offered Numayri's critics a rallying point that enabled them to transcend their differences and, most importantly, to unite and garner popular support. They formed the "Spring Movement" coalition—composed of trade unions, professional organizations (doctors, lawyers, engineers), and political parties—and demanded Numayri's resignation. Hours after Numayri left the Sudan on March 27, 1985, to meet then President Reagan in Washington, his military and security forces were battling demonstrators in the streets. On April 4, more than twenty thousand demonstrators marched through the streets of Khartoum chanting, "Down with one-man rule" and "Down with the USA." On the morning of April 5, Gen. Abdul Rahman Siwar al-Dhahab, a senior officer, led a military coup that brought sixteen years of the Numayri regime and its Islamic experiment to an abrupt and bloodless end.

The Transition to Democracy

The transitional military government of General Siwar al-Dhahab included a predominantly civilian cabinet and promised elections by April 1986. Once again the major traditional political forces dominated: the Umma Party led by Sadiq al-Mahdi, the Democratic Union Party (DUP), and the National Islamic Front (NIF), an alliance forged by Hassan al-Turabi of the Muslim Brotherhood. Because the Umma and DUP had remained aloof from Numayri, with their leaders often living in exile in Britain or Libya, they were freed from the NIF's political handicap, its past alliance with Numayri. While Turabi and the Muslim Brothers had once thrived as an opposition party, their connection with Numayri now made them, in the eyes of many, the symbol for the excesses of Numayri's Islamization program. In contrast Sadiq al-Mahdi, an outspoken critic of Numayri's *Shariah* experiment, was able to emerge from prison to rally his traditional Ansar supporters and simultaneously to build a coalition of support, projecting the Umma Party as a centrist, pluralistic party.

In April 1986, the Sudan held its first multiparty election in eighteen years. The Umma Party won one hundred seats, the DUP took sixty-three, and the NIF captured a surprising fifty-one seats. Although Turabi lost his bid for a seat in the National Assembly, the NIF swept twenty-two of the twenty-eight seats reserved for university graduates and also demonstrated its ability to win in areas other than their usual urban, professional constituency. The DUP joined with the Umma Party to form a coalition, with Sadiq al-Mahdi returning to power as prime minister of the Sudan. Turabi and the NIF became the major opposition party.

Despite high hopes for the return to parliamentary democracy and for the rebuilding of a strong Sudan, the government of Sadiq al-Mahdi proved incapable of redressing Sudan's major political and economic problems. The Ethiopian-backed SPLM strengthened its hold in the South and continued to demand the abrogation of Islamic law and a secular constitution. The government did not enforce Numayri's September 1983 Islamic laws, but neither would it abrogate them. While Sadiq al-Mahdi had initially been against the imposition of Numayri's laws, given his Mahdist background and stature as an Islamic leader as well as the continued pressure of the Muslim Brotherhood, the government in Khartoum believed that abrogation of the September laws could have been interpreted as being against the implementation of Islam. Sadiq al-Mahdi's position shifted from repeal of Numayri's September laws to talk of their replacement by laws that were based on "true Islamic Values."[105] The situation was exacerbated when a new government coalition, formed in May 1988, in which five members of the National Islamic Front held key cabinet positions (including Hassan al-Turabi, who was appointed minister of justice and attorney general), submitted a draft bill for new Islamic legislation in September 1988. Despite the multilayered political, economic, and social problems that fueled the continuation of the civil war, *Shariah* law had been and continued to be a primary issue cited by the SPLM in their rebellion against what they regarded to be northern religiocultural imperialism as well as political and economic discrimination.

Sadiq al-Mahdi, though an astute politican and gifted intellectual, proved an ineffective prime minister. He failed to resolve the civil war and to make significant headway in reversing the downward spiral of an inherited economy that was in dire straits from the effects of the rebellion in the South, famine, a massive foreign debt, a refugee problem (refugees from the South as well as from Ethiopia), and corruption. Unable to restore political stability, he was forced to rule over a government based upon shifting coalitions. Sadiq neither sought nor enjoyed the same close relationship with the United States but instead pursued a more nonaligned policy that included contacts with Libya and Iran. By 1989 the SPLM had made significant military inroads against government forces, Sudan's foreign debt exceeded $12 billion, and the country was on the brink of bankruptcy. Thus the stage was set for the military coup d'etat of June 30.

In the immediate aftermath of the coup, Lt. Gen. Omar Hassan Ahmed Bashir's military government suspended parliament and all political parties; imprisoned leaders of the major religiopolitical parties, including Sadiq al-Mahdi and Hassan al-Turabi; and pledged itself to the prosecution of corruption, the restoration of political stability freed from sectarian politics, and a freeze on the implementation of Islamic law. The SPLM responded by announcing a cease-fire and its willingness to participate in a national constitutional convention in September 1989. However, the issue of Islamic law again proved an insurmountable obstacle. The SPLM rejected Bashir's decision to resolve the question of implementation of Islamic law through a national referendum rather than a national convention, believing that the northern Muslim majority would thus be put in the position of seeming to vote against Islam.[106] A similar attempt by former President Jimmy Carter in late 1989 to negotiate a settlement between the Bashir government and the SPLM also failed in large part over the issue of Islamic law.

The Bashir regime increasingly showed signs that it was strongly influenced (though not guided), ideologically if not organizationally, by the NIF.[107] NIF members as well as those sympathetic to the NIF held important positions in government, and Bashir became more explicit in his defense of Islamic law despite SPLM insistence on a secular state. Stories of NIF interrogation and even torture of its opponents abounded. The nature of Bashir's personal and political appointments and of purges of the civil and diplomatic services led virtually all of the government's opposition to label it an NIF government, thus contributing to the further polarization of Sudanese society. At the same time, Bashir was quick to crush any and all opposition to the military from professional associations. Also, well-armed local militias had slaughtered and enslaved hundreds of villagers in western Sudan, further contributing to an already unstable political climate.

The realities of Sudan's Islamization of state and society were often at odds with its stated ideals. The NIF-backed government of Bashir promised a new political system, an Islamic state and social order, a federal system with consultative regional and provincial councils. It was to be a nonsectarian, nonmultiparty-based Islamic alternative since Bashir maintained that Sudan's political development had failed because of its sectarian-based politics that resulted in people voting uncritically for members of their own religious sect or group. In fact, the central government remained fully in control on most important policies. Other interest groups were silenced, such as the Khatmiyya and Ansar, as well as secular and non-Muslim citizens who objected to a policy they deemed detrimental to their political and/or religious interests.

Although Hassan Turabi, leader of the National Islamic Front, had long espoused a reformist interpretation of Islam when he was associated with the government, the rhetoric of openness and flexibility gave way to religious authoritarianism. Having long advocated the Islamization of society as a necessary preparation for implementation of the *Shariah*, Turabi when in power supported governments (Numayri and the Bashir) that imposed the *Shariah*, including *hudud* punishments such as amputation for theft.

Sudan's Islamization governments under Numayri and Bashir, although different, raised similar concerns regarding issues of political and religious pluralism, dissent, and tolerance. Government implementation of Islam often seemed more an attempt to legitimate authoritarian rule. Both Numayri and Bashir used religion to justify their continued rule and to stifle political dissent. In the end, the policies of each exacerbated the civil war with southern rebels who demanded a secular state. However, they differed in their relations with the West, particularly the United States. Numayri was for many years an American ally while the Bashir government was regarded as a "radical fundamentalist" government, officially declared a terrorist or rogue state by the United States.

The seriousness of Sudan's crisis is reflected in the observation of a long-time scholar on the Sudan: "The situation in the Sudan is one of multiple crises. The heritage of ineffective rule, both civilian and military, is frightening. The issue may in fact have changed from who will rule Sudan to whether or not Sudan will be able to survive in any meaningful fashion . . . . The military leaders of Sudan will have to be more flexible so that Sudan will not repeat the old cycle again or descend into anarchy."[108]

Shii Politics in Lebanon

Ironically, the two Middle East countries most torn apart by violence and civil strife since the mid-1970s were among those previously regarded as the most stable, modernized, and Western oriented—

Lebanon and Iran. In the aftermath of the Iranian Revolution, Lebanon
became a major theater for Shii political activism, a battlefield where
Shii organizations have struggled against other Lebanese militias, Israeli troops, and Western presence, particularly, American military
and civilian personnel.

Lebanon offers the second most potent example of militant Shii
politics. Since the late 1970s, organizations such as AMAL (acronym
for the Arabic form of the Lebanese Resistance Battalions) and Hizballah (Party of God) have mobilized Shii Muslims into protest and
revolutionary movements. As a result, a religiopolitical community,
long dominated by Maronite Christians and Sunni Muslims within
Lebanon's sectarian system of government, has become a formidable
force in Lebanese politics.

As had happened in Iran, the emergence of Islam in Lebanese
politics was the product of political and socioeconomic factors combined with an effective charismatic religious leadership that skillfully
used key beliefs and symbols to organize and enlist popular support.
In contrast to Iran, however, the Shii of Lebanon had long been a
religious minority community, predominantly rural, poor, disorganized, and lacking an effective clerical organization, or hierarchy.

The Shii of Lebanon existed in a state whose stability was based
upon the delicate balance of confessional political organizations and
parties and their militias. Lebanon's postindependence sectarian system of government, a legacy of the French Mandate, was based upon
an informal agreement, the National Pact of 1943, which institutionalized the relative population strengths of the dominant religious
communities as found in the 1932 census. Key positions in the government, cabinet, parliament, bureaucracy, and military were distributed along confessional lines. Constitutionally, Lebanon was a
parliamentary republic with a strong presidency. Its top leadership
consisted of a Maronite president, Sunni prime minister, and Shii
Speaker of the Chamber of Deputies.

Lebanon's capital, Beirut ("the Paris of the Middle East"), reflected strong foreign influence from its boutiques and banks to its
leading universities—the French Jesuits' Université St. Joseph and the
American University of Beirut (formerly the Syrian Protestant College). Within this context, the Shii were the most politically, economically, and educationally disadvantaged group in the country, a distant
third to the more powerful, better organized, and more prosperous

Maronite Christian and Sunni Muslim communities. Shii disaffection with their lot had resulted in emigration abroad, particularly to West Africa and the Gulf. During the 1970s, Shii grievances increasingly took the form of politicization and involvement in a number of multiconfessional leftist and Communist groups, such as the Syrian Socialist National Party, the Baath Party, and the Communist Party of Lebanon. Within this context, the first Shii-based movement emerged owing in large part to a rather remarkable personality, Imam Musa Sadr.

Musa Sadr and AMAL

As the Ayatollah Khomeini became the living symbol of Iran's revolutionary movement, so too Imam Musa Sadr,[109] an Iranian-born and Qum-educated cleric, became the embodiment of Shii aspirations and militancy in Lebanon. Musa Sadr had gone from Iran to Lebanon in 1959 at the invitation of the Shii community in the southern city of Tyre. By 1969 he emerged as the leading Shii cleric in Lebanon, as confirmed by his election as chairman of the government's newly established Supreme Shii Council. During the early 1970s, Musa Sadr led a series of demonstrations and general strikes to demand reforms to redress socioeconomic injustices and to dramatize Shii concerns in the South regarding the threat of the Israeli military. Increasingly, he called upon the dispossessed of Lebanon to organize and fight against the social injustices that they suffered. In 1974 he founded the Movement for the Dispossessed (Harakat Mahrumin). It was identified as a movement for the emancipation of Lebanon's oppressed and disinherited people from domestic and international domination and exploitation. Although not restricted to Shii, implicit in its language, symbolism, and leadership was an appeal to Shii identity and a sense of community solidarity rooted in its history and religious heritage. As in Iran, Shii Islam was employed to provide an ideology of social protest and struggle against tyranny, disinheritance, and social injustice. Early Shii suffering at the hands of the Caliph Yazid, the Imam Husayn's murderer, was equated to the exploitation and discrimination suffered by Shii under the Lebanese confessional system.

Like the Ayatollah Khomeini, Musa Sadr was a charismatic figure who cultivated his religious persona, often identifying his situation with that of the great *Imams* of early Islam, Ali and his son Husayn, and aligning his role with the spiritual and leadership qualities of the *Imam*. He did not discourage or prevent his followers from calling him *Imam*. Musa Sadr became a cult hero whose portrait and posters could be found everywhere in homes, taxis, village squares, schools, mosques, and at demonstrations and rallies. Similarly, like Khomeini, his role as a symbol, or focus, for Shii political activism was captured in slogans such as "our blood and our souls are yours, *Imam*."[110]

The goals of the movement were true parity: confessional equality that reflected the new demographic realities of Lebanon, increased political power, and a more equitable distribution of wealth and educational opportunities. Thus political and socioeconomic reforms, from government posts and civil service jobs to irrigation projects, schools, and hospitals, were demanded. The movement denounced its domestic domination and condemned Israel as the chief external enemy, a direct threat to the peace and security of southern Lebanon. Attendance at the movement's rallies was a testimony both to popular identification with its agenda and to Musa Sadr's personal charisma. The movement often drew seventy-five to one hundred thousand people, easily eclipsing its leftist competitors. As civil war loomed in 1975, Musa Sadr, following the lead of other Lebanese communities, created a Shii military wing or militia, the Lebanese Resistance Battalions, (Afwaj al-Muqawimah al-Lubnaniyah) whose acronym, AMAL, means "hope."

AMAL remained a relatively small organization, one of a number of outlets for an increasingly politicized Shii youth. Four events between 1975 and 1982 profoundly affected the politics of Lebanon and contributed to growing Shii radicalization. These were the 1975 Lebanese civil war, the disappearance of Imam Musa Sadr in 1978, the Iranian Revolution of 1979, and the Israeli invasions in 1978 and 1982. Despite demographic changes that had resulted in a Muslim majority in Lebanon, Lebanon's Christian-dominated government remained inflexible during the 1970s, refusing to redistribute power more equitably. The Shii in particular had grown from 18 percent of the population in 1968 to 30 percent (approximately 1 million today) of Lebanon's 2.5 to 3 million population to become the largest community in Lebanon. Demographic change and socioeconomic inequities contributed to the marginalization and progressive radicalization of the Shii community. The Lebanese system was seen as perpetuating a status quo that no longer represented proportional distribution of power but Christian minority rule.

The influx of thousands of Palestinians, driven out of Jordan by King Hussein during 1970–71, and their substantial presence in the South exacerbated an already fragile political atmosphere. The PLO's strength was such that it threatened to become a state within a state, dominating the Shii villages of the South. The PLO used southern Lebanon as a base for its operations against Israel. Shii found themselves quite literally caught in PLO-Israeli cross fire, their autonomy and security endangered as their territory became a battleground between entrenched PLO forces and Israeli commandos. In 1975 Muslims, frustrated by government intransigence and the failure to provide a redistribution of power based upon the new proportional population, withdrew their cooperation from the National Pact. The result was a civil war between Christian and Muslim militias and the de facto partitioning of Lebanon into Christian and Muslim regions. Israel's 1978 invasion of southern Lebanon (the Litani operation), with the consequent loss of Shii lives and destruction of their homes and property, realized Shii fears as it brought "an active [Israeli] campaign of air attacks, raids, kidnappings, and house bombings."[111]

While the Lebanese civil war had eclipsed the development of AMAL, the disappearance of Imam Musa Sadr in 1978, during a visit with Muammar al-Qaddafi in Libya, breathed new life into this Shii militia. Although many believed that Musa Sadr died in Libya, his disappearance fit nicely with the traditional Shii doctrines of martyrdom and the occultation of the Hidden Twelfth Imam. In the popular mind, the Imam Musa Sadr became a religious hero and paradigm, a worthy descendant of Imam Husayn and the Hidden Twelfth Imam, who is in seclusion but will return. In the interim, the Shii community would continue to fight on. Thus Musa Sadr's disappearance provided AMAL with a symbol of martyrdom and a messianic hope, an effective rallying point for an embattled Shii community. The Iranian Revolution of 1978–79 reinforced this religiopolitical legacy and interpretation. It was a witness to the power of Shii ideology to produce a religiously based movement for social protest and change.

The discrediting of Qaddafi caused by the disappearance of Musa Sadr, coupled with Iran's example and influence, turned many Shii away from Arab leftist and nationalist ideologies. Students and a rising class of professionals and businessmen offered a fertile ground for recruitment. Financial support came both from within the country and from prosperous members of the Shii diaspora in West Africa and the Gulf.

In 1980 Nabih Berri (born in Sierra Leone in 1938, the son of a southern Lebanese émigré), a lawyer and long-time AMAL member, gained control of the group. Under Berri's leadership, AMAL developed as a Shii nationalist organization, pursuing the redressing of Shii grievances although accepting the framework of a united, Arab multi-confessional Lebanon, a parliamentary republic with a free economic system. It did not speak of Shii dominance or an Islamic state but of full equality and parity for Lebanon's disinherited community. At the same time, AMAL pursued a pragmatic approach in its relations with the Lebanese government and Western powers, particularly the United States.

1982 — A Turning Point

Israel's invasion of Lebanon in June 1982 to eradicate the PLO precipitated further radicalization in the Shii community, as witnessed by the emergence of the Islamic AMAL and Hizballah. At first Shii responses to the Israeli invasion were mixed. In southern Lebanon, Israeli troops were greeted with flowers, welcomed as liberators from the PLO whose military presence and dominance had led to Shii-PLO clashes. As the Israelis settled in, however, they increasingly came to be viewed as an army of occupation. Shii flowers were replaced by growing armed resistance against this new oppression. In Beirut the massacre of Palestinians and Lebanese in the Sabra and Shatila camps by Phalangist (Christian) fighters, with Israeli complicity, shocked and outraged Sunni and Shii alike both within Lebanon and throughout the Muslim world. The tragedy contributed significantly to the radicalization of many hitherto moderate Palestinians as well as Lebanese Shii youth. As a result of the Israeli invasion and the massacres, 1982 became another watershed in the tumultuous politics of war-torn Lebanon, contributing to the rise of more radical Islamic organizations like Hizballah and Islamic Jihad and to a wave of anti-Americanism. The U.S. government was regarded as a partner with Israel, tacitly approving Israel's invasion and continued occupation, and as a major supporter of the regime of President Amin Gemayel (who assumed the presidency after the assassination of his brother), which radical Shii regarded as an unrepresentative, intransigent government. As Shaykh Fadlallah, a noted Shii cleric, observed, "Israel, with the approval of the U.S., invaded Lebanon. The invasion was based on an American decision and American help. Beirut was destroyed and thousands of people were killed by Israeli forces. We consider, the ordinary people consider, [and] if you take a poll you will see that everybody considers the U.S. responsible for what happened. The presence of the Multinational Force was perceived as an umbrella protecting the regime, protecting Israel, not protecting the people."[112]

Nabih Berri's leadership of AMAL was challenged in July 1982 by Hussein al-Musawi (b. 1945), a former schoolteacher and a member of AMAL's command council. When Berri formed an alliance (the Committee of National Salvation) with the Christian Phalangist president elect of Lebanon, Bashir Gemayel (who was assassinated Sept. 14, 1982), and the Druze leader, Walid Jumblatt, Musawi broke with Berri, charging that AMAL had collaborated, in effect, with Israel. Musawi rejected AMAL's secular nationalist objectives as unIslamic and, following Iran's example, advocated an Islamic republic for Lebanon. He withdrew to the Shii center at Baalbek in the Beqaa Valley, where he established Islamic AMAL. Baalbek had become a center for militants. Hizballah was already active there with the support of one thousand newly arrived Revolutionary Guards (Pasdaran) from Iran, ostensibly sent to assist in the resistance to the Israeli invasion.

Islamic AMAL, like a number of groups, functioned as a military arm of Hizballah. Musawi, who repeatedly defended the use of violence as a means to achieve his goals, was linked to the bombings of the U.S. embassy in April 1983 and of the U.S. Marine barracks and French military headquarters in Beirut in October 1983.

Hizballah (Party of God)

Progressively during the 1980s, the influence of AMAL and the dominant role that it had played from 1978 to 1982 were challenged by the more radically oriented Shii movement, Hizballah. Born in Baalbek in the wake of the Iranian Revolution, Hizballah came to prominence as a response to the Israeli invasion of 1982. Pro-Iranian

Lebanese Shii clerics and their mosques provided the critical core leadership and centers. They were assisted by local students and professionals, as well as Iranian Revolutionary Guards. Iran provided both a model and a source of major funding. Posters and pictures of the Ayatollah Khomeini were ubiquitous, and the wearing of the *hijab* (head scarf) became common. Iran provided military training and substantial financial support. By 1987 estimates of Iranian aid were as much as $10 million per month. This aid was used not only to underwrite military activities but also to provide financial support, housing, social services (schools, hospitals, and clinics), and scholarships for victims of the war. Sermons, lectures, films, and media materials from Iran were employed in training programs that indoctrinated and prepared a new generation of holy warriors. The Iranian embassy in Damascus (headed by Ali Akbar Mohtesheimi, who later returned to Teheran to become interior minister) assisted Hizballah and served as a clearinghouse for organizing and planning political violence.

Structurally, Hizballah, like AMAL, lacked the formal arrangement associated with political parties or organizations. It was a loose confederation of smaller groups, or cells, and individuals located in Shii neighborhoods, villages, and towns in the Beqaa Valley; Beirut; and southern Lebanon. In contrast to AMAL, Hizballah was less an organized political party with fixed membership and dues than an ideological movement with associated factions and militias. It has become more structured over the years and is overseen by a Supreme Consultative Council, consisting of religious officials *(ulama)* and militia leaders, as well as regional councils and committees that look after its varied activities (military, educational, and social welfare). Yet one should not conclude that Hizballah is a tight-knit organization with a strong central authority:

> Much ink has been spilt on the issue of who leads Hizballah, but the fact is that—at best—we are dealing with a collegial leadership which subsumes many factions and cliques. Even Iran must cajole rather than direct and order in such an environment. In other words, despite their links to Iran, it would be erroneous to assert that the cliques within Hizballah lack a considerable freedom of action.[113]

While AMAL has been content to focus on Lebanon and to be viewed as a Lebanese Shii political party, Hizballah has assumed a broader Islamic identity; it has represented itself more as an Islamic movement with international concerns (the liberation of Palestine and of oppressed Muslims worldwide) and linkages.

Although Shaykh Fadlallah has denied direct political leadership, he is widely acknowledged as the spiritual inspiration, or guide, of Hizballah. As a Shii resident of the Hizballah-controlled town of Baalbek commented: "He is not a military leader within the group, but when he speaks the faithful listen to him."[114] Born in 1935 of Lebanese parents and educated in the Shii holy city of Najaf in Iraq, he emigrated to Lebanon in 1966, where he quickly established himself as a major Shii religious authority, known for his religious scholarship and exemplary life. He is the most highly regarded scholar and spiritual guide among Lebanese Shii and enjoys significant influence in the Gulf as well. Fadlallah's Friday sermons are among the most attended services at any of Lebanon's mosques. In addition to a multivolume commentary on the Quran, he is the author of a number of other works, including *Islam and the Logic of Force* and *The Islamic Resistance.*

Like the Ayatollah Khomeini and Iraq's Muhammad Baqir al-Sadr, Shaykh Fadlallah and other Shii activist leaders have engaged in a powerful reinterpretation of Shii belief and history, emphasizing political activism and social reform. Muslims were not passively to await the return of the Twelfth Imam but instead to revolt against injustice. The sociopolitical realities of Shii life justify, indeed require, armed struggle *(jihad):* "Muslims are to embark on an 'Islamic revolution' . . . They are to do so under the guidance of religious officials, the *ulama,* whose knowledge and integrity guarantee the ultimate triumph of Islam over the Satanic forces of disbelief."[115] The world is an arena wherein the party of God is locked in combat with the party of Satan, but whereas "the movement's motto, . . . taken from the Quran (58:22) says: 'Party of God will surely be the victors.' The Israelis will be repulsed and the battle eventually extended to Palestine itself; the confessional system in Lebanon will be overturned and eventually an Islamic state established."[116]

Shaykh Fadlallah emerged as the principal ideological spokesman for Hizballah. His political significance grew during the 1980s as a result of both his outspoken sermons and his influence upon Hizballah. Fadlallah maintained that there was little difference between Sunni and Shii; he also advocated interconfessional (Muslim, Chris-

tian, and Druze) tolerance. Although he favored an Islamic state governed by *Shariah* law and accepted the concept of clerical rule *(wilayat
al-faqih)*, Fadlallah maintained that conditions in Lebanon were not
right for an Islamic republic.[117] At the same time, Fadlallah emphasized that an Islamic republic in Lebanon would not be a mere replica
of Iran's but rather would be suited to the Lebanese context.

While rejecting random violence, Fadlallah did, however, accept
the use of force when necessary, regarding it as self-defense. "I call for
the liberation from colonialism. I call to fight colonialism. If colonialism oppresses the people, the people should fight it. But to say that I
lead people to do violent acts—no. The American administration
should understand that it itself is leading people toward violence . . .
Their problem is that they see the tragedy in the reaction to their
action but they do not see the tragedies created by their action . . .
Oppressed people cannot always behave in a reasonable manner. Reason cannot face up to a rocket."[118] For Fadlallah, the cause of Shii
violence was not Islam but Israel: "Violence by the Shiite community
in Lebanon is a reaction to Israeli violence against it . . . The foreign
press call Shiites terrorists, but they never stop to condemn the Israelis who slaughter innocent children and civilians every time their
planes raid Lebanon. Isn't that a crime?"[119]

Thus Hizballah provided a more radical Islamic alternative to
AMAL, viewing violence as the necessary means of self-defense
against U.S. influence and Israeli occupation. The American military
presence was regarded not as a peace-keeping force but as a support
and protection for Lebanon's unrepresentative, illegitimate, oppressive Christian government. By the summer of 1983, Hizballah had
spread to the Shii suburbs of Beirut that surrounded the U.S. Marine
headquarters near Beirut Airport. Thus the location of Marine headquarters in a Shii area symbolized occupation, not peace keeping.
Similarly, given France's strong political and cultural influence as the
protector of Lebanon's Christian community and its former rule during the Mandate period, French U.N. forces were equally disdained.
In April 1983, the U.S. embassy was bombed; and in October 1983,
suicide attacks against the U.S. and French military compounds left
three hundred dead. These acts were attributed to Hizballah and its
related groups, or factions, Islamic AMAL and Islamic Jihad. Hizballah's power and presence were further solidified when it joined forces
with AMAL in the February 1984 Shii takeover of West Beirut.

Shaykh Fadlallah's popularity and influence and the deteriorating situation in Lebanon fed the growth of Hizballah and forced Nabih Berri and AMAL to compete with Hizballah's more militant and Islamic image. Nabih Berri and AMAL's more westernized, nonclerical, and moderate political image contrasted with the militant *mullahs* of Hizballah who presented it as the more authentic Islamic resistance movement. Hizballah's very name, Party of God, and its orientation made it a natural focal point and umbrella for other militant organizations. By 1984–85 many factions (Islamic AMAL; the Hussein Suicide Squad; Jund Allah or the Army of God; and the Islamic Resistance Movement) had become part of Hizballah's fluid organization. Moreover, Hizballah's umbrella encompassed the most radical of all organizations, Islamic Jihad.

Islamic Jihad Organization (Munazzamat al-Jihad al-Islami)

Given the secretive nature of Islamic Jihad, little can be said about this shadowy group. Other than in phone calls taking credit for bombings and kidnappings, no individuals have claimed to be or have been definitively identified as members. Some observers believe that it is a single organization; others maintain that Islamic Jihad is a convenient label for uncoordinated terrorist attacks by commandos associated with Hizballah. The common thread is an undefined commitment to create an Islamic state, an agreement regarding the major obstacles or enemies (United States, Israel, France, pro-Western Muslim governments such as Saudi Arabia and Kuwait, and the Lebanese government), and a common belief that it is a religious duty to eradicate these "enemies of God" through sacrifice and armed struggle.

These common elements, rather than any organizational center or headquarters, may link Lebanon's Islamic Jihad with similar organizations in other parts of the Muslim world. Islamic Jihad has been linked to, or has politically taken credit for, the kidnappings of Americans and others in Lebanon; the bombing and suicide attacks against American and French installations; the hijacking of a Kuwaiti jet and subsequent murder of two American passengers (December 1984); the attempted assassination of Kuwait's ruler (May 1985); and the hijacking of TWA 474 (June 1985), among others. Islamic AMAL has also been accused of many of these same actions. Again because no members of Islamic Jihad have come forward or been captured and thus it is only known through its claim of responsibility for violent acts, the question still remains whether it is a distinct faction or an ascription adopted by Islamic AMAL or some other Hizballah-related militia.

Lebanon's Islamic Jihad, like Hizballah, has been linked to both Iran and Syria. In addition to Hussein al-Musawi (Islamic AMAL) and Shaykh Fadlallah's close contacts with Iran and the presence of Revolutionary Guards in the Beqaa, the Supreme Council of the Islamic Revolution in Teheran provided both financial support and religious and military training for militant Shii at Iranian- and Syrian-run camps in Baalbek. The Iranian connection was further evident in the case of David Dodge, who as acting president of the American University of Beirut, was kidnapped in July 1982 and spent the last months of his captivity in Iran.

Israeli-Shii Struggle in South Lebanon

Although Israel had entered Lebanon to evict the PLO, the equation changed radically. The Israeli-PLO war was transformed into an Israeli-Shiite war in the South. Israeli occupation and policies contributed to further deterioration and radicalization, leading Israeli statesman Abba Eban to observe: "If it turns out that all we have done is traded the hostility of seven thousand Palestinians for the hostility of seven hundred thousand Shiites, then I think we will have made a very poor trade."[120] The very villages that had welcomed Israeli troops as liberators now became the battleground for a full-scale guerilla warfare between Israeli troops and Shiite villagers.

The confrontation reached explosive proportions in April 1985, when more than 750 Lebanese prisoners, mostly Shii, were moved from Ansar prison camp in Lebanon to Atlit, Israel, in apparent violation of the Geneva Conventions. U.S.-Shii relations reached their nadir in March and April 1985, when the United States vetoed U.N. resolutions condemning Israel's "Iron Fist" policy and the transfer of prisoners respectively. These actions, coupled with a car-bomb explosion near Shaykh Fadlallah's home in Beirut, which killed twenty and injured eighty and was attributed to a CIA-influenced Lebanese group, contributed to the TWA hijacking in June 1985 and the taking of American hostages in exchange for those Lebanese held in Israel.

Throughout the negotiations, Nabih Berri, the more moderate and pragmatic leader of AMAL, sought to establish his leadership by gaining control of the hostages from their more militant kidnappers. Yet he did not have the power to gain their release without help from the Syrians, allies of Iran. Berri's moderation and his connections with the United States (he held a green card, and members of his immediate family live in Detroit) undermined his credibility.

With the departure of most of the Israeli forces in the South in 1985, AMAL and Hizballah became locked in an ongoing struggle for dominance that included contrasting relationships with the PLO. AMAL and Hizballah differed in their dealings with Yasser Arafat's PLO. Ironically, although AMAL had received early training from Fatah (the leading faction of the PLO), it was bent on preventing the return of the armed Palestinian force that had existed before 1982 and that the Israeli invasion had sought to extinguish. AMAL became locked in fierce battles, the "War of the Camps," that raged from 1985 to 1988, with the PLO in the Palestinian camps of Beirut and in southern Lebanon. Despite support from Syria, AMAL was not able to subdue the camps and was left greatly weakened in manpower and prestige.[121] In contrast Hizballah tended, albeit somewhat reluctantly, to ally itself with returning PLO forces in the South. Despite the deployment of the majority of Israeli forces to Israel in June 1985, more than one thousand Israeli military advisers, Israeli-supported Maronite Christian militia, and the South Lebanon Army (SLA) of Gen. Antoine Lahad remained. These forces were often locked in combat with the Lebanese National Resistance, a coalition of opposition forces which included the Islamic Resistance Movement led by Hizballah.

Popular Shii resistance to continued Israeli occupation in the South provided the scene for a bitter struggle for followers between AMAL and Hizballah, amidst growing radicalization. AMAL's pragmatic policy of limited restraint toward Israel contrasted with the more combative stance of Hizballah. Hizballah cells grew steadily around local Shii clerics, or *mullahs*, who led the resistance. At the same time, Hizballah threatened to overrun AMAL in West Beirut so much so that Berri had fled to Damascus and ran AMAL from the Syrian capital from 1986 to February 1987. AMAL was saved by Syria, which with forty thousand troops deployed in two-thirds of Lebanon has been the main power broker. Although Syria is an ally of Iran, when Hafez al-Assad saw Hizballah gaining ground in Beirut, he threw Syrian protection and support behind AMAL, sending Syrian troops into West Beirut to limit Iranian/Hizballah influence and thus safeguard Syria's preeminence in Lebanon.

The armed conflict between AMAL and Hizballah came to a head after a Hizballah-related group, the Organization of the Oppressed of the Earth, kidnapped Marine Lt. Col. William R. Higgins of the U.N. peace-keeping force (UNIFIL) in southern Lebanon in February 1988. (Higgins was subsequently executed in retaliation for the Israeli abduction of Shaykh Abdul Karim Obeid, whom they accused of being a Hizballah leader, from his home in South Lebanon.) Although Hizballah had opposed the U.N. presence as another form of foreign (in particular U.S. and Israeli) intervention, Berri had strongly approved its presence as a means to restore stability in the South and regarded AMAL as a guarantor of its security. The abduction of Higgins triggered a ferocious struggle between AMAL and Hizballah for supremacy. As AMAL gained the upper hand in the South, Hizballah seemed poised to take control of Beirut until Syrian troops intervened. The fighting was brought to a temporary end with the signing of the Damascus Agreement in January 1989, a Syrian-Iranian brokered accord between AMAL and Hizballah that acknowledged AMAL's control of the South though permitting a nonmilitary Hizballah presence. It was not long, however, before the hostilities were renewed as Hizballah sought to regain its foothold in the South and reasserted its power in the suburbs of Beirut.

Events in 1988 also signaled a shift in Iran's role and influence in Lebanon. As we have seen, the end of the Iran-Iraq War brought a shift in Iran's priorities. With greater focus on its domestic economic problems and the ascendancy of a more pragmatic leadership, Iran under President Hashemi Rafsanjani cut back its military support for the export of its revolution; sought to work with both AMAL and Hizballah; denounced hostage taking; placed Imad Mughnieh, a reputed architect of hostage taking in Lebanon, under house arrest in Teheran; and offered Iran's assistance in working for the release of foreign hostages held in Lebanon.

At the same time, the death of the Ayatollah Khomeini greatly weakened Iranian influence in Lebanon because neither President Rafsanjani nor Ayatollah Khamenei has enjoyed his prestige, popularity, and power. The battle between AMAL and Hizballah for leadership of Lebanon's thirteen-million Shii community has continued. While most Shii have been caught between the armed struggle of militias, the majority have not been driven by a desire for ideological victory or for the establishment of an Islamic state but a better life for their community.

The Formal Disintegration of the Lebanese Government

Events in Lebanon during 1989–1990 were further complicated by new factors. With the Iran-Iraq truce, Iraq provided support for Christian forces in order to counter the influence of its rivals, Iran and Syria. At the same time, Lebanon's fragile government fell apart. When Amin Gemayel's presidency was about to expire in September 1989, he appointed a six-man interim military government, with Gen. Michel Aoun as interim prime minister, to oversee the government until a president could be elected, a move Muslim leaders rejected. Christian and Muslim political leaders, unable to agree upon a successor, split into two governments, or centers of power. Resolution of the impasse seemed in sight when in October 1989 a majority of the Lebanese Parliament signed a Saudi Arabian-sponsored initiative, the Taif Accords, and in November elected President René Muawwad, who was also accepted by the heads of the major communities (though not Hizballah). However, General Aoun denounced the Taif Accords, refused to recognize Muawwad (or, when he was killed only weeks later, his elected successor, President Elias Hrawi), and refused to vacate the presidential palace at Baabda. Thus the Lebanese war became less a contest between warring Christian and Muslim forces than a battlefield on which AMAL fought Hizballah and where troops (the Lebanese Army's Christian units) loyal to General Aoun, a Maronite Catholic, engaged those (the Lebanese Forces) of his Christian rival, Samir Geagea, as well as Syrian-backed Muslim army units and militiamen.

Lebanon's central government enjoyed a recognition and legitimacy both domestically and internationally that it had not had for some time. Yet, despite this and the diplomatic isolation of General Aoun, the Hrawi government had not been able to displace General Aoun and the ten thousand troops that support him or to end the communal warfare that had ravaged Lebanon for more than fifteen years. Israel's presence and policy in southern Lebanon have remained unchanged. Following attacks on U.S. personnel, and the kidnapping of its citizens, and its abortive attempt (1986) to obtain the release of hostages from Lebanon through arms sales to Iran (Iran-gate), the United States withdrew its diplomatic presence and its direct involvement. Although Syria and Iran continued to be influential actors, Syria remained the most potent force within Lebanon. Its inability to enforce the Hrawi government's economic blockade against Aoun reinforced the belief that it preferred the current climate of relative disunity and instability. The political mix in Lebanon remained combustible and with little hope for an early resolution to civil war. Indeed, partition was a growing reality.

Parliamentary Reforms: The Rebuilding of Lebanon

A turning point occurred in August 1990; the Lebanese parliament broke through the political stalemate that had blocked change and approved constitutional reforms that paved the way for an end to the fifteen-year civil war. The reforms, which were strongly opposed by the Christian right, gave the Muslim majority greater recognition and representation in the government. Although the tradition that calls for a Maronite Christian president, a Sunni Muslim prime minister, and a Shii Speaker of Parliament remained intact, power was shifted from the president to the cabinet as a whole. Moreover, the number of parliamentary deputies was increased from seventy-seven to one hundred and apportioned on an equal basis between Christians and Muslims.

Nevertheless, General Aoun's adamant refusal to recognize the legitimacy of the Syrian-backed government and to vacate the presidential palace continued to block reforms. The situation was finally resolved in October 1990. When neither persuasion, threat of military action, nor economic blockade proved effective, President Hrawi finally asked Syria for help. With the assistance of thousands of Syrian troops, who played a decisive military role, the government's joint Syrian-Lebanese force was able to drive Aoun from his fortress in the presidential palace on October 13. By the end of October, the government, with the agreement of the militias to pull out of the capital, was able to restore its control over a united Beirut; the two main Shii factions, AMAL and Hizballah, reached an agreement brokered by their principal backers, Syria and Iran, for a cease-fire in their three-year battle for control of southern Lebanon. The ability of the Hrawi government to put Lebanon back together again, to implement reforms sponsored by the Arab League and initiated with the Taif Agreement, to reapportion power more equitably to reflect Lebanon's changed demographics, and to attempt to disarm and dismantle the Christian, Druze, and Muslim militias and factions that had carved up Lebanon into warring spheres of influence were bought at a cost: further expansion of the Syrian presence and influence in Lebanon.

The Lebanese civil war produced a confused maze of factions and divided loyalties. Individuals and groups often found themselves in a world of shifting alliances that made yesterday's ally today's enemy. The neat confessional identification of factions and militias and the broader issue of redressing the balance of power between Christians and Muslims often belied to outsiders the deep and conflicting confessional divisions among Christian and Muslim factions. The rivalry among Christian militias, the struggle between Hrawi and Aoun, and the fratricidal battles between AMAL and Hizballah reveal the complex issues of power, personality, economics, ideology, and foreign intervention that tore Lebanon apart. The rebuilding of Lebanon has required a process of reconciliation as much as reconstruction.

Iraq: Islam and the Gulf Crisis

On August 2, 1990, Saddam Hussein did the unexpected; for the first time in modern history an Arab nation invaded, seized, and subsequently annexed another Arab country.[122] A short time later, Saddam Hussein, a secular socialist who had suppressed Islamic fundamentalism at home and abroad, did what some had thought unthinkable. Saddam cloaked himself in the mantle of Islam and called for a *jihad*.

Just as the events of 1979 (the Iranian Revolution) and of 1989 (détente and the triumph of the democratization movement in Eastern Europe) were unforeseen watersheds in world history, so too the Gulf crisis of 1990 altered the map of the Middle East and with it turned upside down and inside out the politics of the region. The Middle East as it has been known and understood is no more.

The Gulf crisis simultaneously presented an apparent united Arab response to a rapacious, expansionist Iraq and, at a deeper level, an Arab and indeed Muslim world divided to an unparalleled extent. Understanding these seeming contradictions requires a perspective that distinguishes between the rhetoric of governments and the Western media and the popular sentiment in the Arab and broader Muslim world. Appreciation of the Islamic dimension of the Gulf crisis and Saddam Hussein's appeal to Islam and call for *jihad,* as well as the Muslim response to his appeals, must be seen against the background of Islamic politics in the 1970s and 1980s in addition to Saddam Hussein's management and manipulation of Islam at home and abroad.

Saddam Hussein, Iraq, and Islam

Saddam Hussein, a follower of Baath secular socialism, came to power in the late 1970s, a Sunni ruler of a Shii majority (60 percent) population, many of whom felt disaffected and dispossessed. He faced Iran's Islamic revolution on his border and an increasingly militant Shii community at home in cities such as Basra and Najaf (where the Ayatollah Khomeini had lived in exile for many years).[123] Domestically, he crushed militant Shii movements. Members of the most prominent organization, *al-Dawa,* the Call Society, were deported, imprisoned, tortured, or executed. In April 1980, the Ayatollah Muhammad Baqir al-Sadr, a leading Shii cleric and the reputed spiritual and ideological guide of *al-Dawa,* was executed.[124] Then Saddam, turning his strategy outward, countered the potential threat of an expansionist revolutionary Islam by invading Iran. With the support of moderate Arab states, the United States, and Europe, and heavily financed by the Gulf states, Saddam Hussein became the defender of Gulf Arabs against an expansionist, fundamentalist Iran. Few denounced this violation of international borders and law; many preferred to see Iraq as an agent of the "civilized world." Thus Iraq received economic and military support from its allies who, at the same time, conveniently overlooked Saddam's use of chemical warfare against the Kurds and the Iranians as well as Iraq's efforts to develop nuclear weapons.

Saddam Hussein's strategy and secret to success has been characterized by a carrot-and-club (not stick) approach. His radical pragmatism included both swift and ruthless punishment accompanied by reward and co-optation. If he crushed his Shii (as indeed all) opposition, he also redressed some of the grievances and inequities of Shii life, pouring large amounts of oil revenue into the development of the infrastucture of Shii areas, the restoration of sacred shrines, and increasing Shii visibility and representation in the government and officer corps of the military.[125] As a result, the Shii of Iraq resisted the Ayatollah Khomeini's call to join with their Shii Iranian brethren in routing Saddam Hussein and, instead, fought in the name of Arab-Iraqi nationalism against the threat posed by the Persian-Iranian state.

The Gulf Crisis of 1990

Two years after the Iraq-Iran truce of 1988, the politics of the Gulf and of the Middle East were reversed. Saddam Hussein did what his Gulf patrons had earlier paid him to prevent. Having turned back the threat to the Gulf from Iranian fundamentalism, he overran Kuwait and confronted his Gulf neighbors in the name of Arab nationalism and of Islam. Ironically, he accomplished this with a military machine paid for in large part by the tens of billions of dollars that Kuwait and the Gulf states poured into Iraq and the weapons and technology provided by the Soviet Union, Germany, and France. Saddam simultaneously sought to appropriate or claim the historic roles of Nebuchadnezzar, Gamal Abd al-Nasser, and Saladin.

While Saddam Hussein failed to win the support of the leadership in the Arab world, he enjoyed a degree of popular support often not fully appreciated in the West, where the tendency was to focus on those governments that supported the United States' initiative and to equate the position of those Arab rulers with that of their people. As a result, little distinction was made between the differing perspectives of Western nations supported by their Arab allies and the views of a significant portion of the populace whose deep-seated grievances and frustrations were given a new voice and champion in Saddam Hussein.

Saddam appealed to many of the same conditions and issues that fed the growth of Islamic revivalism and fueled anti-Western sentiments and acts: the failures of Arab governments and societies (poverty, corruption, and the maldistribution of wealth), the plight of the Palestinians, and foreign intervention leading to Arab dependency.

Following the Iraq-Iran truce, Saddam Hussein stepped into a leadership vacuum, an Arab world with deteriorating economies and grievances. Although not a charismatic leader, he created a popular persona by shrewdly exploiting those conditions and concerns. He appealed to an aggrieved people and made his claim to be the defender of the oppressed. He championed the Palestinian cause and the *intifada* at a time when the Middle East peace process had faltered yet again. In a world in which many Palestinians and non-Palestinian Arabs blamed the United States and the Gulf states for not using their considerable political and economic clout to force Israel to the bargaining table and to resolve the Palestinian issue, he "stood up to Israel," threatening to wipe out half of Israel with his missiles should Israel attack Baghdad.

In Kuwait he combined tough talk with action. Faced with an $80 billion debt and incensed by a bill from Kuwait for its support during the Iran-Iraq War and the refusal of Kuwait and the United Arab Emirates to allow a rise in oil prices that would have yielded much needed revenue for Iraq, Saddam Hussein rationalized his invasion of Kuwait by appealing to populist Iraqi and Arab sentiments. He maintained that Kuwait had historically been and remained a part of Iraq; like many modern Middle Eastern states, its boundaries were artificially drawn by the mandate powers when they carved up the Ottoman Empire after World War I. Iraq had long maintained that Kuwait had been a province of Basra (Iraq). In fact Iraq threatened to annex Kuwait shortly after the British withdrew at independence in 1961. To this charge, Saddam added his denunciation of the ruling al-Sabah family, and he claimed to be responding to popular Kuwaiti sentiment. Stunned by the unexpectedly quick and broadly based international condemnation and response of both the West and the Soviet Union, he increasingly emphasized the Arab and Islamic rationales for his actions to generate popular pressures on Arab rulers from below.

Although the support of Arab and Muslim governments for the U.S.-led alliance against Saddam Hussein has often been emphasized, the divisions tended to be downplayed, thus obscuring the gravity of the situation and its long-range implications for Western and Arab/Muslim relations. Rather than speaking of the successful mobilization of the Arab League, some overlooked the fact that only twelve of its twenty-one members supported the anti-Saddam forces. Those members that demurred included long-time U.S. allies such as Tunisia and Jordan. At the same time, many of the twelve supportive states were slow to render substantive support. Both diplomacy and financial incentives had to be used to increase Arab military presence in the multinational force and support for the anti-Saddam alliance. Some, like Syria, have also had to quell pro-Iraqi popular demonstrations at home. Similarly, although the governments of Pakistan and Bangladesh have sent troops to join the multinational force in the Gulf, these government actions have not reflected popular sentiment. Pro-Saddam and anti-U.S. demonstrations have occurred in many countries, including Tunisia, Yemen, Sudan, and Algeria.

The resignations in September 1990 of both the Arab League's secretary general, Chedli Klibi, and its long-time representative to the United Nations, Clovis Maksoud, reflect the complex realities of the Gulf crisis and its impact upon the Arab and Islamic world. In particular they underscore differences between Western and populist Arab/Islamic perceptions of the crisis. The divisions within the Arab League and the Arab/Muslim world and their toll were vividly reflected in the resignation statement of Clovis Maksoud: "The Arab nation has fallen on itself. . . . the Arab nation has been fragmented to a terrible and unprecedented degree by the events in the Gulf These splits have dealt a grievous blow to the prevailing legitimacy of the Arab order. Our sense of Arab unity has been fragmented and its first casualty is a common national discourse."[126]

Arabs and Muslims (secularists, socialists, and Islamic activists, intellectuals, and the person in the street) were pulled in two directions. It was not so much Saddam Hussein to whom they rallied but the bipolar nature of the confrontation (the West vs. the Arab/Muslim world) and the issues that Saddam proclaimed: Arab unity, dignity, self-sufficiency; freedom from foreign intervention, and social justice (resolution of the Palestinian problem and redistribution of wealth). Thus, for many, not to support Iraq was to choose the Western-led alliance and with it the perpetuation of dependence and expanded foreign presence. Talk of a permanent U.S. presence or new security alliance sounded to many like the rationale for new "protectorates."

An example of this outlook may be found in the following statement of a graduate student from the Arab world who, as an Islamic activist, had been critical in the past of Saddam Hussein:

> The West is playing one group of Arabs off against another to keep us weak and dominate us. It, especially the United States and Israel, cannot tolerate a strong Arab nation. The Arabs are tired of foreign intervention and control. France and Britain came to "protect" the Arabs; their protectorates became a long colonial occupation. We have to take our future in our own hands. The United States defends the status quo not the stability and democratization of the region.

With up to 450,000 U.S. troops in Saudi Arabia and the expansion of air bases in the region, there can be no talk of improving relations with the West. The West is there to destroy the Arab world not to defend its [the Arab world's] interests. If the United States had not sent massive military troops, Saddam would have been isolated. People knew who he was, knew what he had done and was capable of doing. U.S. intervention has forced many Arabs to choose sides between foreign intervention/presence and Arab independence and solidarity. There can only be an Arab solution to an Arab problem.

Jihad in the Gulf Crisis

The divisions within the Islamic world may also be seen in the competing appeals to Islam and calls for *jihad*. As we have seen, in the twentieth century, *jihad* has been used on many occasions: in the struggle for independence from colonial rule as well as loosely by Muslim rulers to mobilize popular support. Anwar al-Sadat cast the 1973 Egyptian-Israeli war as a *jihad*. At the same time, radical groups ranging from the assassins of Sadat in Egypt to extremists in Lebanon and Indonesia have taken the name al-Jihad. The Ayatollah Khomeini declared *jihad* against the shah, Saddam Hussein, and the United States. The call for *jihad* has also been used in Afghanistan against Soviet occupation and, more recently, in Kashmir.

While there are strict limits set on the use of *jihad* in Islamic law, the absence of a central religious authority in Islam enables both its legitimate use and its exploitation. Diversity of interpretation and usage of Islam and of the call to *jihad* were evident in the Gulf crisis.

Saudi Arabia's leading religious leader, Abd al-Aziz Ibn Baz, and Egypt's *mufti*, Shaykh Tantawi, legitimated the presence of foreign troops in Saudi Arabia, the home of Islam's holy sites and cities (Mecca and Medina), which are forbidden to non-Muslims. Despite this endorsement, Saddam Hussein and Iran's Ayatollah Khamenei, Khomeini's successor as *faqih*, declared *jihad* against the U.S./foreign intervention. Similarly, while four hundred religious leaders from across the world, assembled in Mecca by the Saudi-supported World Muslim League, declared that the Kuwaiti leadership had the right to declare *jihad* against Iraq to recover their country, Jordan's *ulama* and the leadership of the Muslim Brotherhood called for a *jihad* against foreign intervention.[127]

Islamic movements, like many people in Arab societies, found themselves pulled in several directions. Ideologically, they rejected secular nationalism or believed that Arab nationalism or Muslim nationalism must be rooted in Islam. Many rejected the legitimacy of most Muslim governments, regarding them as un-Islamic or anti-Islamic. (This ideological rejection has not precluded a willingness to accept financial support, in particular from the oil shaykhdoms.) Finally, all were anti-imperialist. They rejected the legacy of European colonialism, the result of a policy to subdue and divide and thus to assure a weak Arab/Muslim world. Saddam's denunciation of Europe's creation of modern Muslim states with artificial boundaries rang true for Islamic activists and Arab nationalists alike. Anti-American neocolonialism struck a common cord as well. For, as we have discussed, many criticize U.S. policies, ranging from unbalanced support for Israel to the propping up of pro-Western, "puppet" regimes (which the West regards as its moderate allies such as the shah's Iran, Lebanon, Numayri's Sudan, the Gulf states) whose authoritarian governments contradict American ideals of democracy and representative government.

There occurred during the Gulf crisis a shift among many Islamic movements from an initial Islamic ideological rejection of Saddam Hussein, the secular persecutor of Islamic movements, and his invasion of Kuwait to a more populist Arab nationalist, anti-imperialist support for Saddam (or more precisely those issues that he represented or championed) and the condemnation of foreign intervention and occupation. The catalyst was the massive Western (especially U.S.) military buildup in the region, its presence near Islam's sacred cities, as well as the threat of military action against an Arab nation and of a permanent Western presence.

Domestic politics, characterized by pressure to respond in accordance with popular sentiment, as much as religious conviction influenced the receptivity of Islamic movements in Algeria, Jordan, and Egypt to Saddam's appeal to Islam and the call for *jihad*. Although initially thousands of Muslim activists in Algeria demonstrated against Iraq's invasion of Kuwait, on a subsequent visit to Baghdad, Abbas Madani, the leader of Algeria's Islamic Salvation Front, declared: "any aggression against Iraq will be confronted by Muslims everywhere."[128] In Jordan, the Muslim Brotherhood initially condemned the Iraqi invasion; however, after the deployment of American forces, it called for a *jihad* against "the new crusaders in defense of Iraq and the Islamic world." As one American Muslim observer noted: "People forgot about Saddam's record and concentrated on America . . . Saddam Hussein might be wrong, but it is not America who should correct him."[129] In Egypt the Muslim Brotherhood condemned the Iraqi invasion and supported the government's anti-Saddam position; but increasingly, despite Egypt's prominent position in the anti-Saddam alliance, the Brotherhood with other opposition groups criticized the massive presence of foreign (Western) forces in Saudi Arabia. Islamic activist leaders from the Middle East and Asia, including Algeria's Madani, Sudan's Hassan al-Turabi, and Tunisia's Rashid Ghannoushi, traveled to Iraq and Saudi Arabia in an abortive effort to secure peace in the Gulf crisis.[130]

Even in countries that sent forces to support the anti-Saddam "international alliance," popular sentiment often differed from that of the government. In Syria Hafez al-Assad who has a bloody record of suppressing dissent, such as his leveling of much of the city of Hama to crush an uprising by the Muslim Brotherhood, had to contend with pro-Saddam demonstrations. In a poll taken by a Pakistani magazine, *Herald*, 86.86 percent of those polled responded negatively to the question: "Should U.S. troops be defending the Muslim holy places in Saudi Arabia?"[131] In Malaysia and Bangladesh where, like Pakistan, many were critical of Saddam's annexation of Kuwait, popular sentiment reflected an equally strong solidarity with much of the Muslim world's condemnation of America's "double standard." They criticized the United States' excoriation of Saddam for violating international law, demand for Iraq's unconditional withdrawal, and the West's insistence upon a rigorous enforcement of U.N. resolutions because the United States had refused to take the very same stand with regard to the enforcement of U.N. resolutions condemning Israel's occupation of the West Bank and Gaza and even maintained Israel as a close political and military ally, providing it more than $5 billion a year in aid.[132] United States reluctance to link the two issues (or more accurately to acknowledge the existence of a linkage) in resolving the Gulf crisis was seen by many in the Muslim world as an attempt to disengage two already interlocked realities.

The Gulf crisis and Saddam Hussein's appeal to Islam highlight the realities and challenges that confront contemporary Islam in much of the Muslim world today. The mood and temper of many, if not most, is one of frustration and failure. Despite the oil wealth and the opulent life-styles of the few, much of the Muslim world is overpopulated and poor; illiteracy, inflation, unemployment, and even famine are interwoven into the fabric of many peoples' day-to-day existence. Authoritarian regimes have been the norm rather than the exception in countries that range from Libya and the Sudan to Pakistan and Indonesia. Ethnic and regional conflicts (the Gulf, the Palestinians, Pakistan, the Kurds, Kashmir), civil wars (Lebanon, Sudan, Afghanistan), and violence perpetrated by extremist religious groups and governments alike wreak devastating human and socioeconomic consequences. It is no accident that many of the ills addressed by Arab nationalism and socialism in the 1950s and 1960s were subsequently the causes of Islamic revivalism and fundamentalism, and later these same problems were exploited by Saddam Hussein in the name of both Arab nationalism and Islam.

Saddam searched skillfully, if deceptively, for scapegoats as well as symbols of legitimacy to appeal to the Muslim masses and rally popular support. The harsh realities of the Muslim world were juxtaposed with past ideals and glories and reassuring promises of a new socially just order. In this confusing maze of current events and political diatribe, one could locate many of the key issues that remain part of the agenda for contemporary Muslims—social justice, identity, independence, authenticity, legitimacy, and authority.

Like the Ayatollah Khomeini before him, Saddam championed the cause of the oppressed (the poor and the Palestinians), denounced the oil shaykhdoms for their corruption and selfish pursuit of wealth, and condemned the "occupation" of Muslim territory by foreign, "infidel" troops. Given the religious background of the majority of Arabs, their experience of colonialism and tendency to blame the failures of the Middle East upon imperialist forces, the use of *jihad* in the twentieth century in resisting and ultimately overthrowing foreign rule; and the heightened use and sensitivity to Islamic political rhetoric and symbols caused by the impact of the reassertion of Islam in state and society, Saddam's intertwining of religion and politics, however strained in this context, should have come as no surprise.

Democratization in Muslim Politics

Most of the governments in the Middle East and the broader Muslim world have been authoritarian states, led by unelected rulers: monarchs, the military, or ex-military. The facades of parliamentary governments often shield the realities of one man or one party security states. As a result, some have questioned whether this is due to Arab or Islamic culture in contrast to local political conditions.

In the 1990s political liberalization, democratization, and civil society became dominant themes in Muslim discourse and politics. Both the fall of the former Soviet Union and domestic politics from the end of the 1980s propelled democracy to center stage, often more as a political issue than a reality. Both regimes and Islamic movements grappled with the discourse and demand for democratization.[133]

The accepted wisdom in the 1980s reinforced a view that equated "Islamic fundamentalism" or political Islam with the revolutionary Islam of Iran or violent clandestine guerilla groups such as the assassins of Egypt's Anwar al-Sadat. Most governments and analysts believed that Islamic activists and organizations were radical revolutionaries with little support, who would be rejected at the polls. However, because of the authoritarian nature of most governments, there was little opportunity to test this proposition.

In the late 1980s and early 1990s, failed economies, including discredited government development policies, led to political crises, mass demonstrations ("food riots"), and strikes, resulting in limited political liberalization. Governments (Egypt, Algeria, Tunisia, and Jordan) held elections in which Islamic activists ran as candidates (Egypt and Tunisia refused to grant legal recognition as political parties to the Muslim Brotherhood and Ennahda respectively) and in some cases as political parties (Jordan and Algeria). In the post-Gulf war, Kuwait and Yemen held elections, and Saudi Arabia, after hesitant moves to create an appointed consultative council to the king, continued to encounter demands for greater participation and government accountability.

The unexpected occurred and continued to occur throughout the 1990s. Islamists emerged as the leading opposition in such diverse countries as Egypt, Jordan, Tunisia, Algeria, Turkey, Yemen, and Kuwait. Islamists were prominently visible in parliaments and cabinets. More ominously for some, the Islamic Salvation Front in Algeria swept municipal and national elections and seemed poised to form Algeria's first elected Islamic activist-dominated parliament. Turkey, the most secular of Muslim states and long regarded as a paragon of secularism, saw the Refah (Welfare) Party win mayoral elections in 1994 in more than a dozen major cities, including Ankara and Istanbul. In parliamentary elections in December 1995, Refah took 158 seats in the 550 National Assembly to enable Dr. Necmettin Erbakan, its leader, to become Turkey's first Islamist prime minister in its forty-five-year history.[134] However, the Refah Party was declared unconstitutional in 1998, its assets were seized, and it has been banned from political activity.

The specter of Islamists coming to power through ballots rather than bullets heartened some but sent shock waves through the corridors of power in many parts of the world. The record of new Islamic republics in Iran, Sudan, and Afghanistan reinforced old images and fears of the spread of religious authoritarianism. Democratization became a major issue in Muslim politics that led not only to political debate but also to a military takeover and a virtual civil war in Algeria, the suppression of Islamists in Tunisia and Egypt, and a military/secular confrontation with Turkey's first Islamist prime minister. In its most extreme forms, the struggle sometimes appeared to be a battle between "secular fundamentalists" and "Islamic fundamentalists."

North Africa

The conditions which account for the electoral performance of Islamists vary as do the nature of individual countries and Islamic movements. However, some commonalities exist. The examples of Tunisia and Algeria are instructive. After independence, in which Islamically oriented parties and organizations had participated, Tunisia and Algeria for all practical purposes followed more secular paths with continued strong political, economic, and cultural ties with France. Tunisia was a "one man" state ruled by Habib Bourguiba until 1987 when he was overthrown. Algeria became a one-party state governed by the National Liberation Front (Front de Liberation Nationale [FLN]) under a succession of strong men. Both nationalist governments pursued socialist policies of economic development and enjoyed strong ties with France and the West. Islam and Arab culture were subordinated to the interests and culture of a secular Francophone elite. Islamic institutions were controlled by the government. Apolitical or nonpolitical Islamic associations (religiocultural groups) were permitted to exist.

The situation shifted imperceptibly in the aftermath of the 1967 war and quite dramatically by the 1980s. After the Arab defeat in 1967, disillusioned young Arab nationalists like Tunisia's Rashid Ghannoushi and Algeria's Dr. Abbasi Madani turned increasingly to their Arab-Islamic heritage as a counterweight to their European-oriented governments and elites. In time, each became a cofounder of an Islamic movement; Ghannoushi of the Islamic Tendency Movement (MTI) and Madani of the Islamic Salvation Front.

The development of these Islamic movements was shaped by events in the 1970s: the fallout from the 1967 defeat and the discrediting of Arab nationalist ideas; high unemployment and food shortages, which resulted from the failure of the government's planned socialist economic development program; national strikes and food riots; the reemergence of Islam and of Islamic organizations such as the Egyptian Muslim Brotherhood and the Jamaat-i-Islami of Pakistan in Muslim politics; the use of oil revenues by Saudi Arabia and Libya to promote their influence in the Muslim world; and the Iranian revolution.

Although functioning as religiocultural and social movements in the 1970s, by the early 1980s both domestic politics and the impact of Iran's Islamic revolution had served as catalysts for the growth and politicization of Islamic movements. Failed economies in North Africa, as in other parts of the Arab world, triggered popular discontent and street demonstrations. Governments reluctantly adopted limited liberalization policies; Islamic organizations proved increasingly attractive and effective. Mosques became the meeting places for gatherings and provided platforms from which the struggle for Islam could be equated with the needs and grievances of the poor and the oppressed. Students and workers were drawn to organizations that spoke directly to their lives (workers' rights, jobs, wages, poverty, political participation, and Westernization vs. a more authentic national and cultural identity) and presented, as Rashid Ghannoushi observed, a living Islam rather than the "museum Islam," which he had encountered as a student.

The late 1980s brought elections in North Africa. The Islamic Association had been transformed into a political party, the Islamic Tendency Movement (MTI), when the Bourguiba government briefly liberalized Tunisia's one-party political system in April 1981. However, Bourguiba refused to issue a license legalizing the party. MTI's goals and agenda included: the reassertion of Tunisia's Islamic-Arabic way of life and values; the restriction of Tunisia's Westernized (Francophile) profile; and the promotion of democracy, political pluralism, and economic and social justice.

The transformation of the Islamic movement into a sociopolitical organization with its direct involvement in Tunisian political and economic affairs enhanced its attractiveness and popularity but also invited government pressure. Ghannoushi and MTI members were arrested several times between 1981–87. Although the Bourguiba government tried to discredit MTI as "Khomeinists," an Iranian-backed threat to Tunisia, as Dirk Vanderwalle observed, "the Islamic Tendency Movement . . . posed no threat to the country's rulers or its political system. But the movement's criticism of personal power, economic mismanagement, corruption, and moral laxity allowed it to become a symbol—perceived especially by the younger, educated generation as an alternative in a country void of political alternatives."[135]

As the debate raged and a popular uprising seemed likely, Zeine Abedin Ben Ali, Bourguiba's prime minister, seized power in November 1987, promising political liberalization and elections. While Islamist candidates participated in parliamentary elections in 1988, they could do so only as individual candidates. The government maintained firm control over the elections. It refused to recognize MTI as a political party, controlled the media, and restricted political gatherings. Despite these limitations, Islamists won 17 percent of the vote nationally and 40 percent in major urban areas. MTI established itself as the leading political opposition.

MTI continued to press for recognition as a political party. When Ben Ali signaled that the use of *Islamic* was problematic, MTI changed its name to the Renaissance Party (Hizb Ennahda). Despite its offer to work with the new leader and participate in his call for a National Pact in exchange for official recognition as a political party, Ben Ali categorically ruled out in December 1989 any political recognition for the Renaissance Party, stating that his decision "emanates from our firm belief in the need not to mix religion and politics, as experience has shown that anarchy emerges and the rule of law and institutions is undermined when such a mixing takes place."[136]

Two events in particular influenced Ben Ali's "change of heart." The impressive performance of MTI candidates in national elections in 1988 demonstrated the appeal and political potential of MTI and validated its claim as Tunisia's leading opposition group. This was followed by the stunning victory of Algeria's newly recognized Islamic Salvation Front in the 1989 municipal elections. The FIS victory realized the worst fears of many Muslim rulers (and their Western

allies)—the threat or danger of political liberalization or democratization to the stability of their regimes.

Although Nahda avoided confrontational politics in the early
years of Ben Ali's rule, the government's decision to deny Nahda a
visa, i.e., to recognize it as a legal party, and its growing use of force
and repression precipitated a confrontation between the government
and the Renaissance Party. As *The Economist* observed, "his party, the
Constitutional Democratic Rally, rigged the poll in the 1989 general
election and took every seat in parliament. Far from legalizing the
leading opposition group, the Islamic party, Ennahda, the president
has sought to crush it. . . . There is no real democracy and no press
freedom."[137]

In May 1991, the Ben Ali government charged it had uncovered a
plot to overthrow the government and proceeded systematically to
"decapitate" the movement through arrests, repression, and military
trials that were strongly criticized by international human rights organizations. In national elections in 1993, Ben Ali won reelection with
99.91 percent of the vote.

Algeria: The Hijacking of Democracy

If the electoral performance of Islamists in the Arab world rattled
many observers, their electoral victories in Algeria in 1990 and 1991
seemed unthinkable. Algeria proved the ultimate testing ground. An
authoritarian government cautiously opened up the system and allowed Islamic parties (like all other parties) to compete. It lost in both
municipal and national parliamentary elections. The response of the
Algerian military (and of many Muslim and western governments)
and the ensuing civil war raised many issues about the future of
democracy.

The bifurcation of post-independence Algerian society between
the Francophone secular elite and Arabized masses created a powerful, although latent, source of tension and conflict. In the late 1960s
and early 1970s, religiocultural organizations like the al-Qiyam
(Values) Society attracted modern, educated Muslims who reasserted
the central importance of Algeria's Arab-Islamic heritage. By the
1980s, the agenda was broadened beyond culture and ritual to a more
comprehensive Islamically oriented response to political, economic,
and social life. Mosque and university were the scene of debate and

clashes between Arab and French educated. The cultural clash concerned issues of identity, employment, ideology (French-educated individuals were dismissed as leftists and Marxists), and religion (clashes between student and women's organizations over proposed family law reforms).

In Algeria, as in other parts of the Arab world, 1988 proved a turning point. The Algerian government was rocked by street protests that swept the country over high unemployment, severe housing and food shortages, and corruption. The Islamic Salvation Front, a coalition of groups and leaders, emerged as an effective political and social movement, projecting itself as the voice of the oppressed. It created an effective network of "street" mosques and prayer rooms in factories and schools and provided effective social welfare services. Among its paramount leaders was Abbasi Madani, a political activist in the 1950s who joined the National Liberation Front and who was imprisoned by the French for eight years and later by the Benjedid government. In 1963, he had joined the al-Qiyam Society. Disillusioned by the 1967 Arab defeat and increasingly critical of the government's socialist policies, he had returned to school, earned a doctorate in Britain in 1978, become a university professor, and was embroiled in campus and national politics by the 1980s.

On June 12, 1990, in the first multiparty elections since Algeria's independence, the Islamic Salvation Front swept municipal and regional elections despite FLN control of the government, the power of its secular elite and the opposition of Algeria's strong feminist movement. The election results reflected the degree of disaffection with the government as much as it did the electoral strength of the FIS. With a 65 percent voter turnout, the FIS controlled 55 percent (the FLN 32 percent) of the municipal councils and 67 percent (the FLN 29 percent) of the regional assemblies. The FIS won a majority of votes in all the major cities: 64.18 percent in Algiers, 70.5 percent in Oran, 72 percent in Constantine.[138] For many, the unthinkable had happened. An Islamic movement had come to power not in an Iranian style revolution but through a democratic process, not through bullets but with ballots. That it had happened in Algeria seemed unthinkable, a state dominated and controlled by a single party from its inception with a strong secular, French-oriented elite.

The government moved quickly to discredit and contain the FIS victory. Funds to FIS-controlled municipalities were cut off to limit their effectiveness in office, scheduled parliamentary elections were postponed, the FIS leaders Madani and Belhadj were imprisoned, and voting districts were gerrymandered to favor the FLN in future parliamentary elections. With these measures in place and with no access to a FLN-controlled media, the defeat of the FIS in parliamentary elections appeared assured.

On December 26, 1991, Algeria held the first multiparty elections in its thirty-five year history. With 59 percent of eligible voters casting ballots, the FIS scored another victory in the first of two rounds of parliamentary elections. It won 47.54 percent of the vote, 188 of 231 parliamentary seats, 23 votes short of a majority. The FLN finished with 16 seats. In two government-controlled, democratic elections, the FIS had won and now seemed poised to control the parliament with an expected victory in the second round of elections scheduled for January 16, 1992. On January 12, the Algerian military in a de facto coup seized power to prevent the FIS from their democratic victory. Their rationale—the FIS was an antidemocratic "radical" Islamic movement that would use the ballot box to "seize" power. Once in power, it was asserted, they would hijack democracy, taking control of the government.

> Their message, aimed in part at the West, was unmistakable and could be encapsulated as follows: "the governments in power are worth preserving. For no matter what their shortcomings, ranging from political exclusion to severe human rights violations, they form the only barrier against fanatics who want to confront the West." According to this interpretation, local forms of authoritarianism are regrettable, but they are the only road toward western-style political pluralism.[139]

The military takeover was followed by a move to suppress the FIS, precipitating a virtual civil war in which more than 100,000 Algerians have lost their lives. The military and security forces moved quickly, arresting FIS leaders and imprisoning more than 15,000 members in detention camps, closing down their institutions, and seizing their properties and funds. After initially eschewing violence, as government repression and violence mounted, Islamists responded both defensively and offensively. The military's crackdown saw many in the FIS move from a nonviolent legal opposition to a combative, and for some, revolutionary movement. Reminiscent of the results of Nasser's suppression of the Muslim Brotherhood in the 1960s, the FIS split into a moderate and more militant wing, the Islamic Salvation Army.

The spiral of government and Islamist violence and counter-violence swept across Algeria's cities and countryside. As the battle raged between government security forces and those in the FIS who also turned to violence, both the security forces and the Islamists developed radical militias, the military's eradicateurs (eradicators) and the Armed Islamic Group (GIA). The GIA, an extremist guerrilla group, rejected any attempt at a political solution or compromise, demanded an Islamic state, and waged a war *(jihad)* of terrorism against all opponents (progovernment, Islamist, or noncommitted). Like other radical movements in the Muslim world, their world was divided into "true believers" (those who fully accepted their views and agenda) and unbelievers *(kafirs)*, Muslim and non-Muslim alike. They condemned the FIS for its moderation and killed military and civilians (leading secularists, journalists, and school children), combatants and noncombatants alike.

The spiral of violence deepened the culture war in society between militant secularists and Islamists and contributed to a growing polarization in society. In 1994 the government refused to attend (or to recognize) a summit sponsored by the San Egidio Catholic community in Rome or to discuss the agreement arrived at by representatives of all opposition parties (including the FLN). While the government continued to pursue the eradication of its "radical Islamic threat" and maintained that the FIS was out to "hijack democracy," its critics noted:

> That the government, army, and FLN were unwilling to allow the process to evolve speaks volumes to the strong residue of authoritarianism which continues to permeate Algerian political culture, attitudes, and behavior. . . . It is only by abandoning its traditionalist commitment to an authoritarian and autocratic state that Algeria may proceed with its democratic experiment.[140]

On June 5, 1997, Algeria held parliamentary elections, in which the FIS was excluded from participation, and the country elected its first multiparty assembly since gaining independence in 1962. Amid criticism from United Nations observers and charges of "massive fraud" by losing parties, an Islamic movement, Mahfoud Nahnah's Movement of Society for Peace (MSP), formerly HAMAS, earned the second highest number of votes. Ennahda, another Islamic party, won 34 seats. Positioning itself as a modern, moderate, nonviolent Islamic alternative, the MSP appealed both to those who were tired of the violence and economic hardship (unemployment stood at 28 percent of the working population) and to those who wanted an alternative to the military-backed regime of President (formerly General) Liamine Zeroual. The MSP won 69 seats (as compared to the 156 of President Zeroual's National Democratic Rally) of the 380 legislative seats and were given 4 (of 30) cabinet and 3 secretary of state posts in the new government.

The experiences of Algeria and Tunisia, however diverse, underscore commonalities that extend to other parts of the Middle East and are critical to understanding the nature and dynamic of Muslim politics. In many ways, Islamic revivalism and political activism are both a response to the failures of modern states/regimes and yet a further stage in the development of nationalism. Islamic movements like Ennahda, FIS, and the Muslim Brotherhood, however much they acknowledge to a broader Islamic community *(ummah)*, have taken up the nationalist struggle but grounded it in the more popular discourse and symbolism of Islam. Thus, they accept an Islamically legitimated nation while rejecting past experiments in secularism and socialism. They appeal to issues and slogans that resonate more broadly in their societies though not among their western-oriented secular elites: religious identity and values, anticolonialism (European and American), dependence on the West, the economic and social failures of the state, maldistribution of wealth, and corruption.

Finally, Tunisia and Algeria are a testimony to the debate and battle over democratization and civil society in the 1990s. Both governments and Islamic movements have appealed to democracy in legitimating their actions and policies. Islamic activists and movements are a testimony at the same time to the existence of civil society, but of a civil society that exists independent of the state. Many Islamic movements win members and/or votes because of the effectiveness of their social welfare services and institutions. Islamic movements in North Africa, like those in the broader Muslim world, remind us that, while economic factors are important, they are not the only factors. The membership of Islamic organizations in North Africa as elsewhere is drawn not only from the poor but also from a professional technocratic class (teachers, professors, doctors, lawyers, engineers, and scientists); it is not only lower class but also middle class; well educated as well as uneducated. Finally, the examples of Tunisia and Algeria reflect the broader policy issues. Do Islamic movements or parties have the same rights (as well as duties) as other religious and political organizations? Do electoral results indicate that they are indeed representative of a legitimate constituency and alternative vision for society? How representative are governments and ruling elites? Are Islamists out to hijack democracy or are governments using fear of an "Islamic threat" to justify a reneging on promises of political liberalization? Is the use of violence and repression by state security forces a necessary and effective antidote or does it polarize societies, contributing to a spiral of violence that results in radicalization and extremism among the militant factions of security forces and Islamists?

Conclusion

For more than two decades religion has been a major factor in Muslim politics. If the early decades of independence had seen many emerging nation states pursue a more secular path of political development and modernization, by the 1990s there were new Islamic republics in Iran, Sudan, and Afghanistan, and Islamic political actors, organizations, and parties seemed ubiquitous. Islamic ideology, symbols, religious leaders, organizations, and institutions took on a level of importance that moved Islam from the periphery to the center of political discourse and action.

Governments, ranging from conservative monarchies to revolutionary or populist states, have appealed to Islam to enhance their political legitimacy and mobilize popular support. Opposition movements and political parties have mobilized under the banner of Islam calling for reform or for revolution. While many have participated within the political system, others have chosen a more radical violent alternative. Islam has been appealed to as an alternative political or social order as well as a yardstick by which existing governments have been judged autocratic, corrupt, economically unjust, or religiously and morally bankrupt.

The Islamic tide/wave swept across much of the Muslim world; at first, for example, most spectacularly visible in Iran, Lebanon, Pakistan, Libya, and Egypt and later in Algeria, Tunisia, Jordan, and Turkey. At times it seemed to crest and recede (Lebanon and Libya), only to rise again in new areas (Algeria, Tunisia, and Turkey) or to return to old sites (Egypt, Sudan, Afghanistan, and Saudi Arabia). If the 1980s were focused on Iran and its export of revolution, Muslim politics in the 1990s revealed a more diverse and multifaceted profile. While revolutionary regimes continued to exist and extremist groups wreaked their havoc through acts of terrorism, Islamists also emerged as major players in politics and society. They operated within the system, at the center, not the periphery, of society. Their educational, economic, and social welfare institutions and services, presence in the professions and state institutions, and their performance and successes in electoral politics were clear signs of the quiet Islamization of society from below. Many governments and secular elites felt threatened not only by violent revolutionary groups but also by those who offer a critique of the status quo and an alternative vision of state and society. At the turn of the century, after several decades of political turmoil and change, the significant reemergence of Islam in politics raises many questions and issues about the future direction of Muslim societies and their relations with the West.

... 6 ...

Issues and Prospects

Within several decades, the modern Middle East has undergone major political and socioeconomic changes. From Morocco to Pakistan, European colonialism was terminated and newly independent Muslim states pursued the process of nation building. Most Muslim nations took modern Western states as their models for political and socioeconomic development. In addition Israel was created and with it have come decades of warfare in Palestine creating both an international political problem as well as an Islamic issue.

For many Muslims, the 1970s signaled an important turning point in modern Muslim history. The centuries-long decline of Islamic fortunes seemed reversed by the Egyptian "victory" over Israel in the 1973 war and by the Arab oil embargo. The attention of the West was drawn to an Arab/Islamic world whose new-found oil wealth transformed its geopolitical and strategic significance. The Iranian Revolution provided a political victory that seemed a watershed for Shii and Sunni alike. For its supporters, Iran provided living proof that a return to Islam could work miracles as the government of an invincible shah was brought to its knees by an "Islamic" revolution. The restoration of success, pride, and self-confidence was accompanied by a significant revival in Islamic practice and politics. The reassertion of religiocultural identity in public as well as personal life became a major factor in contemporary Muslim life and politics at the national and international levels.

During the 1980s, the force of a politicized Islam continued to assert itself in public life. Egypt's Jamaat al-Jihad assassinated Anwar al-Sadat in 1981. President Hafez Assad's army ruthlessly leveled much of Hama (1982), Syria's third largest city, to suppress the Muslim Brotherhood. Radical Islamic groups calling themselves Islamic Jihad and al-Jihad took credit for the terrorist attack against American troops in Lebanon (October 1983) and similar car-bomb attacks in Kuwait (December 1983). In 1983 Saudi Arabia, Kuwait, and other Gulf states established a commission to study and develop a unified code of *Shariah* law. Fear of an expansionist, revolutionary Iran led to the formation of the Gulf Cooperation Council (GCC) to coordinate national efforts militarily and economically. In North Africa, Algeria, Morocco, and Tunisia cracked down on Islamic activists, banning their existence or activities as well as imprisoning their members. In Turkey, Turgut Ozal, who had been a candidate for the "Islamic" National Salvation Party (NSP) in the prejunta elections, became prime minister and then subsequently president. From the Sudan to Malaysia, Islamic leaders held cabinet level positions; international Islamic universities were established; Islamic banks, finance houses, and insurance companies were created; and Islamic laws were implemented.

By the early 1990s, the winds of democracy that had blown across Eastern Europe were also experienced in the Muslim world. Calls for greater liberalization and democratization resulted in demands for greater autonomy in Soviet Central Asia, Kosovo, Yugoslavia, Kashmir, and the West Bank and Gaza. Islamic candidates and parties scored impressive victories in elections in Egypt, Algeria, Tunisia, and Jordan, where they emerged as the strongest political opposition. Islamic revivalism in the 1990s had become normalized and institutionalized, part of the mainstream, rather than the periphery, of Muslim society. The force of the Islamic resurgence or of "Islamic fundamentalism" is not to be reduced to the activities of marginalized, violent revolutionaries. For many in the Muslim world today, Islam has become a more self-conscious component of their lives, informing personal piety, dress, and behavior as well as public life, generating new or transforming old educational, economic, and social institutions.

Islam and Development

The resurgence of Islam has challenged many of the presuppositions and expectations of development theory. Modernization for the Muslim world did not necessarily follow the general wisdom of Western political theories by resulting in the progressive secularization of state and society.[1] While a minority elite class accepted and implemented a Western secular world view along with its ideologies and values, the majority of the Muslim population has not truly accepted and internalized a secular outlook.[2] Daniel Crecelius' observation regarding Egypt, which was second only to Turkey in its pursuit of westernization, is true for much of the Islamic world:

> Most studies on the process of modernization or secularism recognize the necessity for all systems by which man lives, the psychological and intellectual no less than the political and economic, to undergo transformation. We do not find this change in Egypt, whether at the level of state or society, except among a small minority of westernized individuals. Traditional beliefs, practices, and values reign supreme among Egypt's teaming village population and among the majority of its urban masses. It should be emphasized that adherence to tradition is not confined to any single class or group of occupations but is characteristic of a broad spectrum of all Egyptian social classes.[3]

Ironically, the technological tools of modernization have often served to reinforce traditional belief and practice as religious leaders who initially opposed modernization now use radio, television, audio—and videotapes to preach and disseminate, to educate and to proselytize. The message of Islam is not simply available from a preacher at the local mosque. Sermons and religious education from leading preachers and writers can be transmitted to cities and villages, domestically and internationally. As any visitor to the Muslim world is quick to observe, the message of Islam has become an integral part of daily media programming and an available commodity in inexpensive pamphlets, books, and cassette tapes sold on the streets in kiosks and book stalls as well as in hotels and mosques. The writings and taped sermons of these "Muslim media evangelists" now enjoy mass distribution from Khartoum to Jakarta. Thus technology and the mass media have become an effective means to spread the message of Islam and to reinforce an international or transnational Islamic consciousness among Muslims.

Modernization has not led to the triumph of secular political and economic ideologies. Liberal nationalism, Arab nationalism and socialism, capitalism and Marxism have, in fact, come to be viewed as

the sources of Muslim political and economic failures. Disillusionment with political rulers and deteriorating socioeconomic conditions
have translated into a repudiation of foreign systems that, like any
inappropriate transplant, have been rejected. Islamic activists have instead advocated a more authentic, Islamic framework for Muslim society. Though often described in monolithic terms as "the Islamic
alternative" or "the system of Islam," a diverse and prolific assortment
of Islamic ideologies, actors, political parties, and organizations have
reemerged in Muslim politics, grouped under the umbrella of Islam
during the past decade: conservative religious states (Saudi Arabia
and Pakistan); radical Islamic experiments (Libya and Iran); military
officers; kings; ayatollahs; state-supported religious organizations;
and militant, secret Islamic opposition movements—all have advocated an Islamically oriented future and employed Islamic symbols
and rhetoric. Islam has proven a meaningful and effective mobilizing
force among modern as well as traditional Muslims. For some Islamic
activists, the means to achieve their Islamic goals are persuasion and
gradual change; for others it is violent confrontation, armed revolution through holy war.

The adaptability of Islam to modern political conditions continues
to be a hotly debated question. Despite the euphoria of the 1970s and
early 1980s, the realities of contemporary Islamic politics have often
led to disappointment over unfulfilled dreams and expectations. Muslim critics of contemporary attempts to Islamize society denounce the
arbitrary, self-serving use of Islam by autocratic governments in
Libya, the Sudan, Iran, and Pakistan. Muslims have seemed incapable
of turning great wealth into effective power nationally and transna-
tionally. A greater divisiveness rather than a pan-Islamic unity of purpose and cooperation has plagued the "brotherhood of believers"
since the 1980s: Iraq's seizure of Kuwait; the Iran-Iraq War; the assassination of the "Believer-President" of Egypt by an Islamic organization; Sunni-Shii conflicts in Pakistan; AMAL and Hizballah's bitter
internecine battles in Lebanon; Qaddafi's confrontations with Egypt,
Chad, and the Sudan as well as with his own *ulama;* and Iran's radical
religious propaganda and encouragement to Shii in Iraq, Saudi Arabia, Kuwait, and other Gulf states to overthrow their Sunni governments. International Islamic organizations such as the Organization of
the Islamic Conference as well as Islamic governments proved ineffec-
tual in resolving the crises in Afghanistan, Lebanon, and between Iran

and Iraq. In addition economic polarization occurred within and among many Muslim countries between those who profited handsomely from an oil-based economy and modernization and their less fortunate Muslim brethren. The defenders of the "have nots" continue to denounce economic oppression in the name of Islamic egalitarianism and social justice.

For many Western and Muslim observers, the failures of a resurgent political Islam demonstrate the inherent inability of Islam to play a constructive role in modern political development. The juxtaposition of the certitude and commitment of Islamic activists with such skepticism once again raises for students of Islamic politics the questions that modern Islamic reformers, like Jamal al-Din al-Afghani, Muhammad Abduh, Ahmad Khan, and Muhammad Iqbal, have addressed since the late nineteenth century: "Are Islam and modernization compatible?" "Can Islamic history and tradition (culture) support modern sociopolitical change?" If so, "What might this Islamic future look like?" "What are the issues that accompany contemporary calls for the Islamization of state and society?"

Islam and Modernization

The study of modernization in Islam is too often fraught with unwarranted dichotomies: tradition versus change, fundamentalism versus modernism, stagnation versus progress and development. For many Western analysts and Muslim secularists, Islam is a major impediment to meaningful political and social change in the Muslim world. For Islamic activists and other believers, Islam remains eternally relevant and valid. A key factor in the discussion of political modernization is the status and hold of tradition, the authority of the past, in Islam.

Despite the important place of Arab customary practice and non-Arab influences on Muslim life, during the early Islamic centuries the very meaning of tradition was redefined and standardized. This process obscured the complex, dynamic historical development of Islamic tradition with its inclusion of non-Islamic sources. Originally, tribal tradition, *sunnah*—"beaten or trodden path," meant the accumulated wisdom or practice of Arab tribal society, passed down from generation to generation in oral law. During the early Islamic centuries, this tribal tradition was replaced by the notion of "Islamic" tradition. All beliefs and practices were "Islamized" by maintaining that the Islamic community's way of life was rooted not simply in the handed down wisdom and experience of the community but in revelation: the word of God (Quran) and the example or model behavior of the Prophet *(Sunnah).* In particular the established practice of the tribe was subsumed under and replaced by the practice of the Prophet. Tribal practice or customary law *(sunnah)* gave way to Prophetic practice *(Sunnah).*

With the development of Islamic law, the traditional Islamic way of life was no longer simply viewed as the product of human wisdom but rather as the divinely revealed blueprint for society, the straight path *(Shariah)* of Islamic law, based upon the Quran and Prophetic tradition. By the tenth century, this Islamic framework for state and society was essentially seen as determined and fixed—preserved in Islamic law, guarded and interpreted by the *ulama.* It was law that provided the statement and synthesis representing the unity and guidance of Islam amid the diversity of Muslim life and historical experience. Within Sunni Islam, the notion of the closing of the door to personal interpretation *(ijtihad),* reflected and reinforced the general belief that the guidelines for Muslim individual and communal life had been fully determined and set forth. Henceforth, society was simply to emulate, follow *(taqlid)* the revealed guidelines of a sacred tradition. The net result was a system that effectively standardized and sanctified tradition by grounding it more directly in revelation and religious sanctions. It preserved Islamic identity and the power of the *ulama.* The preservation of a normative ideal was obtained, however, at the expense of Muslim remembrance and awareness of Islam's dynamic historical development and adaptability.

As we have seen, the Islamization of state and society during the early Islamic centuries had included a process of borrowing and assimilation, through adoption and adaptation of non-Muslim beliefs and institutions. Islamic law itself was the product of reasoning and decision making by early caliphs, legal scholars, and judges. In the attempt to establish its unity and authority, the classical formula for the sources of law, which later jurists accepted as expressing the development of Islam's code for state and society, emphasized its revealed character and origins at the expense of its human input. Islamic law was described as a set of laws derived directly from revealed sources (Quran and *Sunnah* of the Prophet), and regulations deduced through analogical reasoning based on revelation and accepted by the consensus of the community, which was deemed infallible. The significant role of personal judgment and local customary laws was "officially" overlooked or forgotten. At most this human endowment was acknowledged as contributing to subsidiary principles of law. No wonder that Islamic tradition became fixed and sacrosanct for many; future generations were simply to follow the ideal pattern as comprehensively and authoritatively set forth in Islamic law. Departure from the revealed law or practice of the community—that is, any substantive addition or change—was viewed as heresy.

The sacrosanct nature of tradition in Islam, based upon a romanticized understanding of Islamic history, is of primary significance in contemporary Islamic political development; for it serves as an inspirational reality for traditionalists and, at times, as a major obstacle for modern reformers. There are two general approaches to Islamic renewal and reform: the traditionalist desire to restore the past, to replicate an early Islamic ideal; and the reformist call for renovation or reconstruction through Islamic (as distinct from Western) reform. Both approaches emphasize reliance on Islamic sources and distance themselves in varying degrees from the uncritical westernization of secular elites as well as from the heritage of an earlier Islamic modernism like that of Muhammad Abduh and others, which is viewed as being heavily influenced by the West. A key difference between Islamic traditionalists and reformers is their understanding and use of Islamic history and tradition in addition to the degree of change that they advocate. The compatibility of Islam and modernity itself is not the issue. Most Muslims, of varying persuasions, would acknowledge the traditional place and acceptability of Islamic renewal and reform. Traditionalist and reformer alike can assent to Mawlana Mawdudi's observation that "Islam needed in every age and still needs . . . groups of men and institutions which could change the course of the times and bring the world round to bow before the authority of the One, Almighty."[4] However, they disagree about the direction, method, and the extent of the changes required.

Muslim Attitudes Toward Change

Four positions or attitudes toward modernization and Islamic sociopolitical change may be identified among Muslims today: secularist, conservative, neotraditionalist, and Islamic reformist. These views are not mutually exclusive but often overlap.

Secularists advocate the separation of religion from the state. They view appeals to Islam in politics as retrogressive or inappropriate to modern political and social realities. Thus they would limit Islam to the private sphere of life. It is only the other three positions that are concerned with the implementation of Islam in public life and for whom the relationship of Islam to the sociopolitical aspects of life is an important task. The conservative position is represented by the majority of the *ulama* for whom the Islamic blueprint for society continues to be that classical synthesis developed during the early Islamic centuries and preserved in manuals and commentaries on Islamic law. For conservatives Islam is a closed cultural system fully articulated in the past, preserved in medieval Islamic texts, and valid for all ages. Religious conservatives, who constitute the majority of religious leaders, accepted as an interim measure the imposition of Western secular law because it left their "ideal blueprint" intact for implementation in a later, more Islamic period. Because Islamic law is the divinely revealed pattern for life, they believe it is not Islamic law that must change or modernize but society that must "return to Islam," conform to God's will. Nevertheless, when the opportunity to create an Islamic society has occurred—in Iran and Pakistan and to a lesser degree in the Sudan, Egypt, and Malaysia—conservatives equate an Islamic order with the restoration or following of traditional formulations of Islamic law.

Neotraditionalists, however, maintain the need, and their right, to go back to the Quran and *Sunnah* of the Prophet in order to bring about the renewal of Muslim society. Although they value the classical Islamic synthesis, they are not wedded to it as are the conservatives. Movements like the Muslim Brotherhood and the Jamaat-i-Islami reflect a neotraditionalist approach. While they accept much of classical law, they believe that law historically incorporated many un-Islamic practices. Therefore, Muslims must return to their revealed sources to revitalize the Islamic community. (In this sense, they may be called fundamentalists.) Claiming continuity with eighteenth—and nineteenth-century Islamic revivalists like Muhammad ibn Abd al-Wahhab and Shah Wali Allah, neotraditionalists maintain that the only authority to be followed is that of the Quran and *Sunnah;* they claim the right to interpret *(ijtihad)* the Quran and *Sunnah* to respond to the needs of modernity. Neotraditionalists, like conservatives, reject both Muslim secularism and early twentieth-century Islamic modernism. Islamic modernism, in its attempt to harmonize Islam and the West, is judged guilty of westernizing Islam, sacrificing its authentic vision and voice. Neotraditionalists emphasize the complete self-sufficiency of Islam—the comprehensiveness and totality of the Islamic world view. Muslims need only look to Islam's sources to find the answers for Islamic society today. They believe that what is required is a rearticulation of Islam's eternally valid message. As we have seen, for neotraditionalists like Sayyid Qutb and Mawlana Mawdudi, Islam is the divinely mandated alternative to the materialism and secularism of Western capitalism and communism. While westernization is rejected, selective modernization is not. Western science and technology are to be appropriated cautiously and "Islamized"; however, Western values and mores are rejected, for Islam has its own answers for humankind.

In contrast to religious conservatives and neotraditionalists, there are contemporary Islamic reformers. They too look to the early period of Islam as embodying the normative ideal. Reformers distinguish more sharply between the principles and values of Islam's immutable revelation and the historically and socially conditioned Islamic institutions and practices that can and should be changed to meet contemporary conditions. Many reformers, like Ali Shariati, are Western educated but Islamically oriented. They are committed to an "Islamic modernization," that is, a future in which political and social development are more self-consciously and firmly rooted in Islamic history and values. They learn from the West but do not wish to westernize Muslim society.

Unlike the Islamic modernism of Muhammad Abduh and Ahmad Khan, contemporary reformers do not see themselves as responding apologetically or polemically to the West but rather as seeking in a more independent, indigenous, and authentic manner to meet the needs of Muslim societies. They view Islamization as a process by which Islamic principles and values are reapplied to meet the circumstances and needs of a changing sociopolitical milieu. The greater implementation of Islamic law, the establishment of Islamic banks and insurance companies, the creation of Islamic universities and curriculum reform are viewed as part of this process. As in the formative period of Islam, Islamization can include adoption and adaptation of other cultures' political and economic systems. Whether in politics, education, economics, or law, Islamically acceptable development eschews the uncritical transplanting of foreign models. Programs and policies must be appropriate to the specific needs of Muslim societies and must either embody Islamic principles and values or, at the very least, not be contrary to Islam. Unlike Islamic modernists of the early twentieth century, today's Muslim reformers believe that they live at a time and in political and social circumstances when specific programs may be developed and implemented, not simply advocated and written about by pioneering voices.

Islamic Pioneers

Jamal al-Din al-Afghani, Hasan al-Banna, Sayyid Qutb, Mawlana Abul Ala Mawdudi, and Muhammad Iqbal paved the way for contemporary Islamic activism by alerting the Islamic community to the dangers of Western domination and arguing for a modernity grounded in Islam. They reasserted Islam's role in politics and society in a milieu dominated by secular elites and Western models of development. Despite the differences between neotraditionalists and early Islamic modernists, both were trailblazers of contemporary Islamic revivalism. They rekindled an awareness of the totality of Islam, the integral relationship of religion to all areas of life—politics, law, and society. They restored pride in Islamic history and civilization and, by extension, acceptance of reason, philosophy, modern science, and technology. The contribution of these Islamic actors occurred in two particular areas: organization and interpretation. Islamic organizations like the Muslim Brotherhood and the Jamaat-i-Islami provided the vanguard for what has developed into a more broad-based Islamic movement. They have served as the organizational models for a proliferation of Islamic societies that bring together small groups, or cells, of committed Muslims to live, train, and work for the transformation of society. Throughout much of the Islamic world, Muslim Brotherhoods have been established along with a host of Islamic political and social reform societies. Islamic student societies exist at most major schools and universities, often capturing student elections. For a minority of Islamic organizations, the struggle for Islamic renewal has taken a violent, revolutionary path.

Islamic pioneers, through their preaching and writings, provide an ideological interpretation of Islam that sets forth the principles and guidelines for a more authentic, Islamic alternative for state and society. Given the growing polarization in many Muslim states, the reassertion of Islam in politics, the proliferation of Islamic societies with their improved resources, a new phase of implementation and experimentation has occurred. Islamic organizations such as Pakistan's Jamaat-i-Islami; Turkey's Refah (Welfare) Party; the Muslim Brotherhoods of the Sudan, Egypt, and Jordan; Tunisia's Ennahda (Renaissance); and Algeria's National Salvation Front participate in elections. Moreover, since the late 1970s, Islamic activist leaders have obtained cabinet-level positions not only in Iran and Pakistan but also in the Sudan, Jordan, Turkey, Kuwait, Yemen, and Malaysia. Theory has given way to practice.

Throughout the Muslim world innumerable conferences and experiments in Islamic politics, law, economics, and education have occurred. Governments have introduced Islamic laws and levied Islamic taxes. Islamic banks and insurance companies exist in much of the Muslim world and in non-Muslim countries. The burgeoning literature on Islamic economics reflects a growing sophistication in conceptualization and analysis. Education is a priority. New Islamic universities have been created, and required courses in Islam have been introduced at every level of education. More significantly, in addition to Islamic student associations at schools and universities, broader-based Islamic youth and professional organizations have been created such as the Saudi-based World Assembly of Muslim Youth, the Islamic Society of North America, the Muslim Youth Movement in Malaysia, and the Association of Muslim Social Scientists. These organizations, whose members are modern educated, bring together students and younger professionals (university professors, government bureaucrats, business people) who are committed to the implementation of more Islamic states and societies. They develop programs and materials to foster modern, Islamically oriented youth; run social centers; and, where political conditions permit, engage in politics.

The Nature of Islamic Government

The widespread sentiment, discussion, and attempt to reestablish Islamic states and societies have again focused attention on the ques-

tion of the nature and necessity of Islamic government. As we have
seen, there was and is no single, agreed upon model of an Islamic
state. The Islamic past was, in fact, quite diverse. Although the revealed material sources (Quran and *Sunnah* of the Prophet) of Islam
and the early caliphate period are viewed by Sunni Muslims as exemplifying the Islamic ideal in which religion and power were fused in
an Islamic government and delineated in Islamic law, the reality of
Umayyad and Abbasid caliphal rule was often quite different from
the normative vision or ideal. Indeed many devout Sunni Muslims
believe that the Islamic imperative was realized solely under Muhammad and the first four Rightly Guided Caliphs. For Shii, only the rule
of Ali, and not the other caliphs, is acknowledged as legitimate. The
Shii imamate remained an eschatological hope to be realized when
the Twelfth Imam returns as the Mahdi. The reality of Islamic history,
with de facto fragmentation of the Islamic Empire after A.D. 850 as
well as the un-Islamic character or concerns of many Muslim rulers,
belie the existence of an ideal Islamic state.

The conclusion that the Islamic state/empire became a secular
state is equally unwarranted and misleading. To begin with, secularization is a modern term describing the separation of religion and
state. This concept did not reflect the political reality in the Muslim
world. Throughout Islamic history, the legitimacy of the ruler and the
ideal makeup of the state, whether caliphate, imamate, or sultanate,
continued to be official adherence to Islamic law as the basis for state
and society. The caliph-sultan remained a symbol of Islamic unity;
Islam continued to be operative in political notions of society and
citizenship, law and judiciary, education and taxation, war and peace.
State institutions concerned with law, the judiciary, education, and
social welfare services were administered in large part by the *ulama*.
The state was often a major patron of Islam for Muslim institutions,
scholars, disciplines, and sources. Although Islam may not have been
the guiding force in the life of its rulers, both in theory and, albeit in a
more limited manner, in practice, religion remained organically related to state and society. Until the colonial period, most Muslims—
despite differences owing to time and place—could well believe and
maintain that, however imperfect, they lived in an Islamic state and
society officially guided by the *Shariah*. Moreover, Islam has remained
a primary principle of social cohesion and identity in spite of its loss

of power and autonomy occasioned by colonialism and the Western secular path followed by most Muslim governments. Its continued presence among the vast majority of Muslims explains the continued appeal to and acceptance by many Muslims of "Islamic" politics.

Lack of a single, concrete, historical model has led to confusion as well as to a lack of consensus regarding what an Islamic state is. Summarizing what we have noted, this confusion is caused by several factors: (1) The Medinan ideal (the state under Muhammad and the Rightly Guided Caliphs) does not offer much in the way of a detailed model. (2) The later caliphal practice of the Umayyads and Abbasids provides only a skeletal system of political institutions, taxes, and so forth; and it also was not accepted by Shii. (3) Failure to fully establish an Islamic state led to the formulation of ideal formulae: Islamic law and political theory that, at best, constitute a theoretical, idealized version of a utopian society. (4) The relationship of religion to the state, like most beliefs and practices and indeed revelation itself, has throughout the ages been subject to a variety of interpretations.

The process of interpretation and application of religious truths to society is conditioned not only by the authority of past practice but also by the very sociohistorical realities to which it speaks. Neither individual religious scholars and leaders nor religious organizations and institutions can escape this hermeneutical fact. Both the Umayyad caliphs and their critics appealed to Islam; Sunni and Shii, who possess the same Book and Prophet, deduced different political theories of the caliphate and imamate. Islamic law developed the doctrine of diversity *(ikhtilaf)* to account for differences in law, conditioned by personal interpretation and preference and by differing social and historical conditions among the various law schools. Diversity of interpretation and lack of consensus are reflected in contemporary Islamic politics, in the variety of Islamically oriented states: Saudi Arabia's monarchy, Pakistan's martial law regime under Zia ul-Haq, Iran's clergy-run Islamic republic, Libya's "state of the masses," and the Sudan under Numayri. Competing Islamic visions and claims, often pit Islamically oriented leaders and opposition movements against Muslim governments as has occurred in Iran, Pakistan, Egypt, Syria, Iraq, and Saudi Arabia. Nevertheless, there has been little consensus or specificity to Islamic militants' agendas, as seen in the case of those who seized Mecca's Grand Mosque in 1979 or the Muslim militants in

Egypt and Syria, beyond their denouncing "un-Islamic" regimes and their general references about the need to restore the Medinan ideal and *Shariah* law.

The history of two countries in particular, Pakistan and Iran, exemplify the problems of agreement and definition among Islamic activists during the twentieth century. As discussed in chapter 4, the *Munir Report* on the anti-Ahmadiyya riots in Pakistan in the early 1950s noted that extensive questioning and testimony of religious leaders revealed a one-sided consensus on who was not a Muslim. However, the *ulama* were incapable of agreeing on such fundamental questions as: "Who is a Muslim?" or "What is an Islamic State?" The critical nature of this problem and its implications were summarized in the *Munir Report:* "Keeping in view the several definitions of a Muslim given by the *Ulama,* need we make any comment except that no two learned divines are agreed on this fundamental . . . if we adopt the definition given by any one of the *Ulama* we remain Muslims according to the view of that *alim* [religious scholar] and *kafirs* [unbelievers] according to the definition of everyone else."[5] Similarly, as indicated in chapter 5, in Pakistan religious forces that were able to unite under the banner of Islam in an opposition movement proved unable to achieve any consensus regarding the nature of Pakistan's Islamic republic. Iran's Constitutional Revolution of 1905–11 and Islamic Revolution of 1979 provide striking examples of a reversal of Islam's unifying role once an opposition movement moved beyond the common object of concern, beyond Islamic rhetoric to the formulation and implementation of government institutions and policy.

During the Constitutional Revolution, conservative religious leaders insisted upon full implementation of the *Shariah* and rejected liberal constitutionalist adoption of a Belgian-based constitution with religious clauses and a "supreme committee" of interpreters (*mujtahids*) who would assure that no law was contrary to the *Shariah*. So, too, in postrevolutionary Iran, conservatives and liberal constitutionalists again divided when clerics rejected the liberal constitutionalist option and instead implemented a clergy-dominated state.

Contemporary Islamic revivalism with its movement beyond talk of Islamization to actual implementation has highlighted a variety of issues regarding the relationship of Islam to modern politics. Islamic activists call for the introduction of a more Islamically oriented way of life in Muslim states—an Islamic order; in general this means

"Muslim" states whose inspiration and general orientation are derived from Islam. More particularly, the ideal is to establish "Islamic" states in which religion and politics are integrally related: economically, legally, and socially. The ideological foundation of an Islamic state is to be the doctrine of God's absolute unity *(tawhid)*, sovereignty, and totality of God's will for humankind.

The organic relationship of religion to all areas of life is viewed as distinguishing the Islamic community from Christianity as well as from Western secularism and communism. Islam is to provide the ideological basis for both individual and communal life, for state and society. This Islamic alternative is referred to as an Islamic order or the system of Muhammad. Given the lack of a specific, agreed upon authoritative model for an Islamic state, Islamic activists, organizations, and governments have had to address a number of issues that include the nature of Islamic government, political institutions, and international relations.

Early twentieth-century Islamic activists, such as Afghani, al-Banna, Qutb, Mawdudi, and Iqbal, were pioneers, ideological visionaries rather than practitioners. Their writings concerning Islamic government and institutions tend to be sketchy, dealing more with general principles and ideals rather than specific details. There is some general agreement regarding certain required features: (1) The state is the means by which an Islamic order or way of life is fostered and regulated. (2) The Islamic state is primarily a community of believers bound by a common faith and commitment to their divinely mandated mission to obey God and spread God's just rule and governance throughout the world. (3) The consensus of the community is the source of authority regarding the particular form of Islamic government as well as the selection and removal of the head of state. (4) Based upon Quranic prescription (Quran 42:38 and 3:159) and early Islamic practice, the ruler must be selected or elected. This may occur through direct elections or indirectly by representatives of the people, a consultative assembly. These may be a group of community leaders or an elected parliament. (5) The ruler is to govern according to and assure implementation of the *Shariah* to which ruler and ruled alike are bound. (6) The ruler is required to consult with representatives of the people. However, the ruler is not bound to follow their advice. (7) The checks on the ruler's power are the limits of the *Shariah*, an independent judiciary, and the right of the people to remove an unjust ruler.

In light of these general principles as well as recent Muslim writings and state practice, a preliminary assessment can be made regarding the ideology and political institutions of an Islamically oriented state and the issues raised by shaping such a process.

Islamic State(s)

There is some specific agreement regarding what is not an Islamic government and less regarding what is. Most Muslims agree that hereditary succession, monarchy, dictatorship, and military rule are not Islamic although historical circumstances may require such interim forms of government. Thus, in recent times, the monarchies of Saudi Arabia and of Iran, the military government of Pakistan, and the increasingly dictatorial policies of Anwar al-Sadat became easy targets for Islamic critics.

Historically, Islam has had a strong executive exemplified by Muhammad and the early caliphs as well as medieval sultans and shahs. Sunni notions of the caliphate and Shii doctrines of the imamate also envision a strong central authority. Within the limits of the *Shariah*, the caliph or *Imam* retains final political, administrative, military, and judicial authority. Contemporary Islamic political activists, though still retaining a strong executive, tend to provide some checks on the ruler's authority, such as elections (direct or indirect) of the head of state, the formation of a parliament as a modern version of the caliph's advisory councils, and the subordination of the ruler to the *Shariah*. Yet, for Islamic leaders like Mawlana Mawdudi and the Ayatollah Khomeini, the head of government remained quite powerful because, for all practical purposes, he controls the government. He must consult with the parliament but is not necessarily bound by its decisions. He oversees the appointment of the judiciary and military leadership. Furthermore, there is a sharp difference between Sunni models of Islamic government and the Shii model of the Ayatollah Khomeini. Sunni Muslims do not advocate a theocracy, governed by the *ulama*. They emphasize *Shariah* (what some call a nomocracy) governance with the *ulama* serving as advisers. For Khomeini, as noted previously, the *faqih*, or legal expert, is the ultimate guide of a government dominated by clerics. It should be noted that this is not the Shii model but a model of government because many Shii, including the Ayatollah Shariatmadari and Mehdi Bazargan, have regarded clerical rule as an innovation. They restrict clerical input to an advisory rather than governing role.

The ideological orientation of an Islamic state is reflected in Islamic activists' expectation and demand that governments be led by the most virtuous, observant Muslims. In societies in which the governments are often viewed as corrupt and autocratic regimes, such moral idealism has proven attractive. Not only neotraditionalists like Egypt's Muslim Brotherhood and Pakistan's Jamaat-i-Islami but Islamic reformers would subscribe to the position that "the prevailing criteria of political merit for the purposes of candidature for any political office revolves on moral integrity as well as other relevant considerations. All this would, no doubt, influence the form and spirit of accession to positions of power."[6]

This moral idealism is extended to the process of candidate selection, especially of the ruler. Candidates should not actively seek office or undertake a modern political campaign; rather, an independent nominating committee would select these best of men.

Democracy

Although Islamic leaders have been critical of "Western" democracy, in recent years, many leaders and organizations have espoused some form of democratically elected national assembly with legislative powers. Most conservative *ulama* and neotraditionalists have tended to believe that the national assembly or parliament should be a consultative body. The tendency toward a strong executive, coupled with restrictions that flow from the Islamic ideology and commitment of the state, has led critics to speak of Islam's totalitarian or autocratic nature.[7] Islamic advocates themselves, though arguing that the principles of consultation and consensus indicate Islam's democratic spirit, do distinguish between Western and Islamic democracy because the political ideology of an Islamic state is centered around God, not man. This orientation does include guidelines or limits. Sovereignty belongs to God alone; the *Shariah* is law. All additional or supplementary laws and state policies must be formulated within the limits of the *Shariah;* that is, they may not contradict it. Therefore, legislation is not based solely on the popular will. Actions proscribed by the Quran and *Sunnah* can never be introduced, no matter how popular. To those who view such a political system as autocratic or totalitarian, Muhammad Natsir, a former Indonesian prime minister and leader of the Islamically oriented Masjumi Party, responds: "Islam is not one hundred percent democracy, neither is it one hundred percent autocracy. Islam is . . . Islam."[8]

Calls for the liberalization and democratization of society from secular and Islamic activists alike have increasingly been influenced by the democracy movement in Eastern Europe. At the same time, Islamic candidates and parties have participated in elections and in many countries (Algeria, Tunisia, Egypt, Jordan, Lebanon, Turkey, Yemen, Kuwait, Pakistan, and Malaysia) have emerged as leading opposition forces. These events have challenged the preconceptions of many development specialists who had seen Islam as an obstacle to change and incompatible with democracy. The Judeo-Christian tradition has proved historically to be flexible and open to multiple interpretations and has adapted itself to modern notions of democracy and political pluralism through a process of reinterpretation and reform. So too, the Islamic tradition has been used to support a spectrum of governments from dictatorship to democracy, as witnessed most recently in such countries as Iran, Pakistan, the Sudan, Saudi Arabia, Egypt. Although some Islamic movements continue to speak out against democracy, their reactions are often caused more by a general rejection of dependency on the West. Most Muslims today accept the notion of democracy; similarly, Islamic activists' critique of many Muslim governments has included a denunciation of autocratic rulers as unIslamic and a demand for democratic elections, political parties, and human rights. Yet their endorsement of democracy would be qualified by its subordination to God's law. In practice this process varies from implementation of Islamic law to constitutional provisions that no law be contrary to the Quran or to Islam.

The Islamization of democracy or the attempt to generate Islamic forms of democracy has been based upon a process of reinterpretation of traditional concepts and institutions. Consultation or political deliberation *(shura)* and community consensus *(ijma)* have been reinterpreted to support religiopolitical reform: parliamentary democracy, representative elections, political parties. Thus, for example, the consultative group or assembly *(majlis al-shura)* who selected or elected the caliph has been transformed and equated with a parliament or national assembly.

Yet the record thus far is inconclusive. Many of those who advo-

cate democracy, such as Tunisia's Rashid Ghannoushi, have not come
to power. Algeria's Abbas-Madani, the leader of the Islamic Salvation
Front, affirmed his acceptance of democracy to counter accusations
that he had opposed it in the past; yet some younger more militant
voices rejected democracy. Moreover, the examples of Iran, the Sudan,
Afghanistan, and Zia ul-Haq's Pakistan raise many serious problems.
In addition many Muslim rulers appear reluctant if not opposed to
democratization. Only time will tell whether the espousal of democracy by contemporary Islamic movements and their participation in
the electoral process are simply a means to power or a truly embraced
end, or goal. One can anticipate that democracy in the Middle East,
whether under the current rulers or Islamic activists, will remain a
source of contention until time and experience have enabled the development of new political traditions.

While many debated the meaning of democracy and its compatibility with Islam, political liberalization and democratization became
widespread themes in Muslim political discourse in the 1990s. If
many entrenched regimes democratized reluctantly or seemed to reverse earlier trends towards liberalization, Islamists displayed a range
of positions from rejection to advocacy of democracy. The demand by
Islamic organizations for recognition as political parties and their
right to participate in electoral politics have been countered by governments and elites who charge that they are out to "hijack democracy," to use the ballot box to seize power. Many warned of the
dangers of the spread of religious extremism, of Islamists seizing
power through the ballot box, imposing their will, threatening the
security and stability of governments in the region and the West, and
jeopardizing the Middle East Peace Process, human rights, the status
of women, and minorities. For rulers, such fears provided a rationale
for intervention, suppression, or severe constraints on Islamic movements.

The concern that Islamists will hijack democracy is balanced by
the policies of many regimes which demonstrate that they only believe in "risk free democracy" or, as one western diplomat put it,
"democracy without dissent." Thus, many continue to outlaw Islamic
political parties or to suppress them. The massive violation of human
rights by autocratic states is often justified by the charge that Islamists
are an inevitable threat to the stability and security of regimes and to
the West (most notably its access to oil supplies).[9]

The attempt by governments like Algeria to eradicate the FIS underscored a further danger, the creation of self-fulfilling prophecies. As with Gamal Abd al-Nasser's repression of the Muslim Brotherhood in the 1960s, the Algerian government's repression of the FIS fostered greater radicalization, an emergence of avowedly violent extremist organizations like the Armed Islamic group, and a prolonged and devastating civil war.

In the 1990s governments and experts have been divided in their assessment of political Islam and of appropriate policy options.[10] Some of these experts insist that there are no Islamic moderates and that all Islamic activists and organizations should be excluded from participation in the political process. Others distinguish between violent extremists and moderates who, if given the opportunity, participate within the system. The latter group, they argue, should be permitted, indeed should have the right, to function as social and political organizations and parties. Those who advocate greater political liberalization and a policy of inclusion rather than exclusion of Islamic parties maintain that a more open system provides more competition and more options for voters and weakens the strength of Islamists who often attract not only their followers but also those who wish to cast a protest vote against failed or discredited governments. They believe that, faced with political reality, Islamists will prove more accommodating both to survive politically and because it is in the national interest. Inclusion also tests the capacity of Islamic activists to move beyond slogans and to prove or disprove their capacity for real political vision and leadership.

Both the nature of some Islamic regimes (Sudan, Iran, and Afghanistan) as well as the actions of more secular governments (Tunisia, Algeria, Turkey, and Egypt) reflect the authoritarianism, violence, and repression of Muslim politics and the need to strengthen the values and institutions of civil society.

Islam and Pluralism

A critical issue in Muslim politics is that of pluralism. Historically, the monotheistic visions of both Islam and Christianity and the belief of each—that it possessed the final and complete revelation of God and was charged to call all to salvation—resulted in competing claims and missions and produced theological and political conflict. In the nineteenth and twentieth centuries, much of mainstream Christianity grappled and came to grips with the realities of pluralism in the modern world. The outcome was the result of a process of reform in which doctrines were reexamined and reinterpreted. For example, Roman Catholicism in the late nineteenth and first half of the twentieth century resisted and condemned much of what was termed "modernism" (from popular sovereignty and elections to pluralism). However, at Vatican II, the church for the first time officially recognized and accepted pluralism.

For Muslims the issue of pluralism is directly related to the status of Muslims as *dhimmi* or protected minorities in Islamic law, as well as to that of Muslim minority communities living under non-Muslim rule. While historically Islam often proved more flexible in tolerating non-Muslims (Peoples of the Book) as minorities whose protected *(dhimmi)* status enabled them to live and practice their faith under Muslim rule, that status amounts to second-class citizenship in the modern world. The persecution and suppression of non-Muslims by some Muslim governments and by some Islamic movements underscore the need for reinterpretation and reform if the rights of all citizens are to be guaranteed.

Due to an unprecedented number of Muslim immigrants and refugees, there are in 1998 more Muslim minority communities in existence around the globe than at any previous time in history. While some wish some day to return, most face living in new non-Muslim homelands. This reality raises many questions from loyalty and political participation to living in societies whose laws are not based upon (or reputed to be based upon) Islamic law. Thus, for Muslims and for Muslim reformers, pluralism is a critical concern both for Muslim majority countries and for Muslim minority communities. From Egypt to Indonesia, scholars debate and engage in a reinterpretation of Islamic doctrines and laws. As with other faiths, the lines of the debate are often drawn between traditionalists who wish to simply follow the authority of the past, that is, to retain the classical law and modernists or reformers who argue the need and acceptability of a fresh interpretation of Islamic sources, a reformulation of Islam.

Islamic Law

Because *Shariah* rule is the sine qua non of an Islamic state, law reform is a fundamental issue in the Muslim world today. During the colonial period, Western-inspired legal codes replaced much of Islamic law in most Muslim countries. The major exception was Muslim family law. Family law, which includes laws governing marriage, divorce, and inheritance, had always enjoyed pride of place within the *Shariah,* reflecting the centrality of the family in Muslim society. Throughout Islamic history, although caliphs and sultans might circumvent other areas, family law was the one area of the *Shariah* that remained enforced. Similarly, despite modernization of law during the eighteenth and nineteenth centuries, it was not until the post–World War I period that change in this sensitive area of Muslim life first occurred in Egypt and after World War II in.many other Muslim countries. Even then, unlike previous legal reform that introduced modern legal codes, reform in Muslim family law was accomplished through selective changes in traditional Islamic law.

The process of legal change did not reflect widespread societal change so much as the desires of modern elites. Governments imposed reforms from above through legislation. Though attempts were made to provide an Islamic justification or rationale, as we saw in our discussion of the debate surrounding Pakistan's Muslim Family Laws Ordinance of 1961, the religious establishment objected to this tampering with the law. It was an incursion into an area of Muslim life that religious scholars, not politicians or bureaucrats, had developed and controlled. They denounced reforms as a further erosion of the *Shariah* through an introduction of Western, and thus un-Islamic, regulations and values by parliamentary bodies composed of nonexperts. Regardless of the lack of religious and popular support, modernizing elites, who constituted a small percentage of the population, enacted family law legislation from Morocco and Tunisia to Indonesia. While some reform-minded religious leaders supported change, the more conservative majority did not. Most were content to bide their time until a more favorable period when Islamic law might again be implemented.

Modern Islamic legal reform has been directly challenged by the contemporary resurgence of Islam. Khomeini's Islamic republic repudiated Iran's Family Protection Act and conservative *ulama* in Pakistan called for the repeal of The Muslim Family Laws Ordinance. Demands for a return to the *Shariah* are common in many parts of the Muslim world. Countries as different culturally as in degree of modernization and westernization as Egypt, the Sudan, Libya, Iran, Pakistan, and Mauritania have declared the *Shariah* as the source of law. As we saw in the previous chapter, many have enacted Islamic legislation enforcing traditional Islamic penalties for theft, alcohol consumption, fornication, and adultery. Even more have curbed gambling, night-clubs and cinemas. Muslim governments like the Sudan and Malaysia, which have significant non-Muslim populations, have introduced Islamic legislation.

The place of the *ulama* in a modern Islamic state and society has become a thorny problem. Because the national assembly or parliament is permitted to pass legislation in areas not covered by Islamic law, most religious leaders have advocated a committee of religious experts to advise parliament in the drafting of legislation. The classical view of legal development is that Islamic law is the product and province of the *ulama*. Thus they believe that they alone have the requisite learning to function as interpreters of the law and thus to advise the elected assembly (most of whose members tend to be lay, not religious leaders of the community) as well as to assist in resolving jurisprudential problems in draft legislation.

Many Islamic modernists, in order to justify lay contributions to legislating as well as to limiting the powers of the *ulama*, whom they regard as out of touch with modern realities, have challenged the status, power, and scope of *ulama* authority. These modernists recall that in Islam all Muslims are equal and have a direct relationship with God. There are neither sacraments nor clerical intermediaries. Strictly speaking there should be no clergy or clerical class in Islam. They argue that the title *ulama* (plural of *alim*, "learned") simply means one who has knowledge or is an expert. Modernists argue that this title belongs properly not to a specific clerical group or class but to any Muslim who is qualified. The issue is raised subtly by Hassan al-Turabi, a long-time leader of Sudan's Muslim Brotherhood:

> The *ulama* should have a role in this procedure [parliamentary deliberations or legislation] . . . not as the ultimate authority determining what the law is, but as advisors in the *shura* [assembly] to enlighten the Muslims as to the options which are open to them. What do I mean by *ulama*? The word historically has come to mean those versed in the legacy of religious (revealed) knowledge *(ilm)*. However, *ilm* does not mean that alone. It means anyone who knows anything well enough to relate it to God. Because all knowledge is

divine and religious, a chemist, an engineer, an economist, or a jurist are all *ulama*. So the *ulama* in the broad sense, whether they are social or natural scientists, public opinion leaders, or philosophers, should enlighten society.[11]

The real issue in law, as in sociopolitical change in general, is the question of change. How much change is required and how much departure from tradition is legitimate? Conservatives see little need for substantive change; neotraditionalists who accept *ijtihad* in principle, reinterpret sparingly in practice. Islamic modernism created a climate for the acceptance and Islamic legitimacy of reform but failed to provide an agreed upon method to render such change. As a result the resurgence of Islam in politics and society has tended to be a process of revivalism, restoration of past practice, rather than reconstruction through reinterpretation and reform. This orientation is especially evident in issues regarding women's status and the rights of non-Muslims in an Islamic state.

Women's Rights

All sane, male, adult Muslims are entitled to citizenship, to vote, and to hold office in most Muslim states. In recent decades, Muslim women in modernizing Muslim states have been given the right to vote and to serve in government. However, contemporary Islamic revivalism has often threatened to reverse these gains. The return of Islam has included a return to the veil, with increased emphasis on the separation of sexes and the restriction of women's role in public. Although the veiling of women in Islam is not based upon revelation but rather is borrowed from non-Islamic sources, the practice has, like many others, become so embedded in tradition that it came to be viewed by many as integral to Islam. Thus Mawlana Mawdudi reflects the outlook of many religious leaders:

> People have tried their very best to prove that the present form of Purdah was a custom in pre-Islamic communities, and that the Muslims adopted this custom of ignorance long after the time of the Holy Prophet. The question is: Where was the necessity of carrying out this historical research in the presence of a clear verse of the Quran, the established practice of the time of the Holy Prophet, and the explanations given by the Companions and their pupils? Obvi-

ously this trouble was taken in order to justify the objective of life prevalent in the West. For without this, it was not possible to advocate the Western concepts of "progress" and "civilization" that have got deeply fixed in the minds.[12]

After the Iranian Revolution, women who had donned the veil as a symbol of opposition to the shah and because of the anonymity it afforded in public antigovernment demonstrations were soon demonstrating in March 1979 against the compulsory wearing of the veil. Though the regulation was rescinded, veiling was still made compulsory in government and public offices in the summer of 1980. In addition coeducation was banned; women judges lost their positions; women were barred from the judiciary and legal professions. Similarly, as noted in the previous chapter, Islamization in Pakistan included implementation or advocacy of traditional Islamic measures regarding dress, the separation of the sexes, and legal rights. In many countries in Africa and Southeast Asia, such as the Sudan and Malaysia, women were never segregated publicly and many have been part of the work force. In recent years, however, Islamic revivalism has unleashed the voices of those who advocate more restrictive dress codes for women and who would also restrict their activities in public life. At the same time, some Islamic activists and intellectuals have in recent years engaged in a reassessment of women's status and role in society, emphasizing not only greater gender equality in worship and piety but also in education and employment. They represent a range of positions. Some Islamic movements like the Muslim Brotherhoods of Egypt and Jordan and Tunisia's Ennahda have emphasized increased access to education and employment. Women are becoming more visible in the councils of Islamic organizations. Islamist women are more and more visible in the professions (physicians, journalists, lawyers, engineers, social workers, and university professors) and as administrators and staff in schools, clinics, and social welfare agencies and services.

Today women are increasingly writing and speaking out for themselves on women's issues. Muslim women empower themselves not just as defenders of women's rights but as interpreters of the tradition. Many argue that patriarchy as much as religion, indeed patriarchy linked to religion, accounts for many customs affecting gender relations which became long-standing traditions. The primary interpreters of Islam (of the Quran, traditions of the Prophet, and law) were males functioning in, and reflecting the values of, patriarchal societies. Religion was linked to patriarchy through its interpreter-scholars and their appeal to Islam to legitimate their interpretations of doctrine and law.

Women scholars and activists draw on the writings and thought not only of male scholars but also—and most importantly—on the work of a growing number of Muslim women scholars and activists who utilize an Islamic discourse to address issues ranging from dress to education, employment, and political participation. In areas as diverse as the Arab world, Iran, and South and Southeast Asia, women have begun their own magazines and contribute to newspapers in which they set forth new interpretations and visions of gender relations. Organizations like Women Living Under Muslim Laws (Geneva) and Sisters in Islam (Malaysia) have become visible and vocal representatives within their own countries as well as internationally, writing, publishing, speaking out, and participating in international conferences such as the Cairo conference on population and Beijing's conference on women. Although small in number, they may well, as has occurred in other religions, prove to be a vanguard in a long-term process of reassessment, reform, and transformation.

Non-Muslim Minority Rights

The revivalist mood and orientation of resurgent Islam has also raised concerns about the status and rights of non-Muslims. Tensions and clashes between Muslim and non-Muslim communities have increased: the Copts in Egypt, Bahai in Iran, Chinese in Malaysia, Christians in the Sudan and Pakistan. Often non-Muslim minorities such as Christians in Egypt, the Sudan, and Pakistan or the Ahmadiyya of Pakistan are regarded as having cooperated in the past and benefitted from European colonial rule. Similarly, the Chinese in Malaysia, Bahai in Iran, and Ahmadiyya in Pakistan, who tend to be more advanced educationally and economically, have encountered resentment and discrimination. Reactionary religious leaders have found it easy to mobilize or incite their followers against minorities, viewed as disproportionately successful, who have become the targets for pent-up socioeconomic frustrations.

Although Muslim-Copt relations in Egypt had been relatively

calm, during the 1970s the situation slowly altered with a series of communal disturbances. As Egyptians were returning to their Arab-Muslim heritage, the Coptic community underwent a similar revival, returning to their Coptic monastic heritage under the strong leadership of their patriarch and bishops. The spirit of the renewal was summarized in the declaration: "All authentic service begins and ends with the Church."[13] Tensions mounted between two increasingly militant communities. The conflict escalated and took on a national dimension in 1977, when a bill was introduced in parliament to reinstate the death penalty, the traditional Islamic punishment, for apostasy from Islam. The draft legislation was directed at Copts who, unable to divorce their wives according to their own religious tradition, converted to Islam and then, after the divorce, returned to Christianity. Public protests against the proposed legislation were led by Pope Shenouda III, the Coptic leader, and stopped only after Sadat's government declared its opposition to the bill.

Tensions between Muslims and Copts continued with incidents involving church bombings, stonings, disruption of Christian celebrations, and harassment of Coptic students at universities in Cairo, Alexandria, and Asyut. In April 1980, Pope Shenouda called off public Easter celebrations in protest. In June 1981, a major Muslim-Christian confrontation in Cairo took eighteen lives and required riot police. Throughout the 1980s and 1990s militants in Asyut, Fayyum, and Cairo, when venting their criticisms of the state, have often attacked Christian churches, stores, and neighborhoods. Consequently for many Copts, Islamic revivalism, with its push for more *Shariah* law and greater popular religious enthusiasm, is a threat to their legal rights, religious freedom, and personal safety.

Muslim-Bahai confrontations in Iran, like Muslim-Ahmadiyya conflicts in Pakistan, have a long history. As discussed in chapter 4, during the late 1950s the *ulama* had mounted a campaign against the Bahai, whom they considered apostates from Islam. The dome of Teheran's Bahai center had been destroyed, and the religious authorities tried unsuccessfully to persuade the government to pass legislation that would have suppressed the Bahai and dismissed its members from public office. After the Revolution of 1979, the Bahai again came under heavy attack: their religion was declared illegal, their property seized, and many were imprisoned and executed. Although government officials insist that Bahai have been punished for political crimes and not religious reasons, the rights of non-Muslim minorities in an Islamic state remains an unresolved issue.

According to Islamic law, non-Muslims belong to a second class of citizens, the *dhimmi* ("protected"), who constitute their own community. In exchange for their allegiance to the state and payment of a poll tax, they are free to practice their faith and are governed by their religious leaders and laws in matters of worship, private life, education, and family laws. Most Muslim states have granted equality of citizenship to all regardless of religious faith. Nevertheless, the contemporary resurgence has resurrected pressures to reassert legally the often widespread, traditional attitude toward non-Muslims that, though changed by modern legislation, has remained operative in the minds and outlooks of many Muslims. This attitude has been further reflected in the extension of new Islamic public laws, such as the banning of alcohol to non-Muslim citizens in the Sudan, Iran, and Pakistan.

Non-Muslim minorities face another potential limitation in Islamic states. Given the state's Islamic ideology, many Muslims now ask: "Should non-Muslims be permitted to hold key government positions?" In most contemporary Muslim states, with the exception of the head of state or prime minister, citizens regardless of faith may hold office. This modern, liberal, secular pluralistic approach is contested in many quarters today by those who argue that the state's Islamic ideology requires a commitment to Islam. This rule would preclude non-Muslims from holding key posts in the government, legislature, judiciary, and military, which formulate and implement the ideology of the state. Despite modern constitutional reforms, Islamic organizations like the Muslim Brotherhood and the Jamaat-i-Islami and many religious leaders have continued to teach and preach a restricted role for non-Muslims. In Pakistan the 1953 anti-Ahmadiyya riots in the Punjab had been caused by Muslim demands that the Ahmadiyya be declared non-Muslims and that Zafrullah Khan and other Ahmadi government officials be dismissed from office. Similar demands and confrontations continued to occur for decades. In Iran Islamic opponents criticized the shah for permitting Bahai to occupy important government and military positions. In both Pakistan and Iran, the Islamic opposition eventually succeeded: Pakistan declared the Ahmadiyya a non-Muslim minority, and the Islamic Republic of Iran suppressed the Bahai faith.

In practice, in many Muslim countries, non-Muslims have been absent from top posts in government. This is caused not only by their limited numbers but also by government recognition and acceptance of widely held traditional attitudes toward the place of non-Muslims in an Islamically oriented state. Finally, radical Islamic organizations today reject non-Muslim involvement in government both as contrary to Islam and, in the case of Christians, as recognition of their past ties with Christian, European colonial powers and their continued association with the Christian West.

Pluralism

Yet, since the 1980s, from Egypt to Indonesia, a diverse group of Muslim intellectuals and activists (Rashid Ghannoushi, Muhammad Selim al-Awa, Yusuf Qaradawi, Mahmoud Ayoub, Kamal Aboul Magd, Fahmy Howeidy, Abdurahman Wahid, Nurcholish Madjid, Abdulaziz Sachedina, Fathi Osman) has produced a growing body of literature that reexamines Islamic traditions and addresses issues of pluralism both at the theoretical and the practical levels. Recognizing the need to open up the one party or authoritarian political systems that prevail as well as the need to face the multireligious and multicultural demographic realities of their societies, they have both reinterpreted Islamic principles to reconcile Islam with democratization and multiparty political systems and recast and expanded traditional doctrine regarding the status (*dhimmi*) of non-Muslim minorities. In addition to employing traditional concepts like "consultation" (*shura*) and "consensus" (*ijma*) to limit the authority of rulers, words like "party" (*hizb*) have been reinterpreted, acknowledging a positive connotation rather than one of difference and division which would undermine rather than promote the good of society.[14]

Islamists and other Muslim intellectuals have marshalled scripture and history to argue that Islam supports the equality and pluralism of the human community. Quranic passages which affirm that God chose to create the world with different nations and tribes (Sura 5:48, 30:22, 48:13) are emphasized. They argue that the pluralism of the Quran was in fact practiced by Muhammad and the early community in its recognition and extension of freedom of religion, worship, and protection (*dhimmi*) to non-Muslims. Some, like Professor Mahmoud Ayoub, assert that rather than implying a second-class citizenship, the word *dhimma* (which is not in the Quran but found in the *hadith*) was intended to designate a special covenant of protection between Muslims, on the one hand and Christians and Jews on the other.[15] Others note that the term *dhimma* refers to the form of a covenant, not its content, and that content can be redefined in light of new realities.

Increasingly, both the writings of Muslim intellectuals and the experience of Islam in Southeast Asia become more relevant to the broader Muslim world. The multireligious and multiethnic societies of Malaysia and Indonesia provide a substantial example of pluralism— the issues, problems and possibilities for change, accommodation, and coexistence.[16] Although Malaysia experienced Malay-Chinese riots in 1969, Malaysians continue to construct a Muslim majority society in which non-Muslims enjoy a degree of political and religious equality (as well as democracy) unknown in many parts of the Muslim world. Indonesia's depoliticization of Islam has ironically engendered both a deeper Islamization of Indonesian society and a diverse group of voices (Muslim and Christian) committed to a pluralist society.[17]

Just as Muslim politics reveal the profound debate and conflict over issues of political liberalization, democratization, and pluralism, so too a generation of Muslim intellectuals and leaders is attempting to reexamine and reinterpret their faith in light of modern realities, debating critical questions of pluralism, democracy, and minority and women's rights. Whether this new current will prevail in the face of authoritarian regimes, conservative religious authorities, and secular forces remains to be seen.

Nationalism and Pan-Islam

The current reassertion of Islam in politics, with its emphasis on Islamic identity and ideology, has implications for international relations as well as domestic internal politics.[18] The agendas and actions of radical Islamic groups, combined with statements by many traditionist leaders, directly challenge existing political structures, in particular the nation-state. Many condemn not only specific political regimes but also nationalism as un-Islamic. They reaffirm the pan-Islamic ideal of the unity and solidarity of a supranational community. The tendency of Islamic revivalism to look to the Medinan ideal and the traditional belief in a pan-Islamic caliphate would seem to reinforce this expectation. Both neotraditionalists like Mawdudi and Islamic modernists like Iqbal repudiated nationalism as a tool used by colonialism, as Iqbal said, "to shatter the religious unity of Islam in pieces."[19] Political realities and the passing of time have, however, tempered the normative ideal for many Muslims. Modern states, even with their once artificially drawn boundaries, have become an accepted fact of life for most. Islamic movements shape their agendas and goals to national realities and participate in national politics as they continue to acknowledge the transnational community of believers and shared international concerns, such as the liberation of Palestine.

The trend in both self-styled Islamic states and in Muslim states is to supplement acceptance of the nation state with support for pan-Islamic cooperation, more than for political unity. Saudi Arabia (as well as other Muslim countries such as Iran, Libya, and Kuwait) seeks and exercises influence over other Muslim states and organizations while guarding its boundaries and national identity jealously. Although Libya has had a number of abortive unions with other Arab countries, these were to foster Qaddafi's brand of Arab nationalism. Qaddafi's engagement in international Islamic politics, whether in Lebanon, the Sudan, or the Philippines, has been aimed primarily at enhancing his stature and promoting his revolutionary beliefs, not in uniting the community. Khomeini, despite his pan-Islamic statements and support for revolutions in other states, was first and foremost an Iranian Shiite national leader. The Iran-Iraq War, regardless of Khomeini's Islamic rhetoric, was fueled as much by Arab-Persian historic rivalry and animosity as by Islamic sentiments. Though some Sunni Muslim activists admired and wished to emulate Khomeini in toppling Western-oriented and supported regimes, few wished to unite under the leadership of a Shiite ayatollah. The traces of Sunni-Shiite historical differences run deep. Pakistan, like many other Muslim states, willingly courted development assistance from Arab oil countries, but not political union.

Finally, major international Islamic organizations, like the Organization of the Islamic Conference, retain their nation-state orientations while pursuing greater Islamic cooperation. Indeed one could argue that, as has long been the case, there continues to be a great gap between normative vision (ideal) and political reality. Whatever agreement Muslims muster in closing ranks when faced by threats from non-Islamic countries is in the nature of an opposition movement whose unity soon passes and is displaced by a return to national self-interest. Neither the Palestinian problem nor recent Islamic political issues such as those in Afghanistan, the Philippines, and Kashmir have produced an effective transnational Islamic front. The Pakistan-Bangladesh civil war, Lebanon, the Iran-Iraq War, Libyan-Saudi rivalry, and Iraq's conquest of Kuwait counter images of a united Muslim world.

The passing of time has brought about a gradual transformation in which the sharp dichotomy between a pan-Islamic supranational ideal and modern nationalism has been softened and transformed.[20] Though the modern Western concept of nationalism and the nation-state adopted by Muslim political elites initially seemed Islamically unacceptable, the seeds for an Islamic adaptation or Islamization of nationalism were present. Objections to modern nationalism were primarily a reaction to the continuation of Western imperialism through the displacement of Islamic institutions by Western secular models. For some, nationalism represented the further division and weakening of an already debilitated Islam before a militant, colonial Christian West. It undermined the Islamic solidarity and unity of the community, replaced God's sovereignty with ultimate allegiance to the nation, and its implicit secularism reduced Islam to the private sphere of life. Yet a case for a more Islamically acceptable nationalism can be made. Islamic modernists like Afghani, Rida, and Iqbal had realized the necessity for some acceptance of nationalism while continuing to speak of pan-Islamism as the source of a Muslim's most basic identity, solidarity, and strength. For most, actual transnational political union remained at best a future goal: "In order to create a really effective political unity of Islam, all Moslem countries must first become independent, and then in their totality they should range themselves under the caliph. Is such a thing possible at the present moment? If not today, one must wait." Muhammad Iqbal reflected a more pragmatic revolution that many Muslims today have come to espouse: "God is slowly bringing home to us the truth that Islam is neither Nationalism nor Imperialism but a League of Nations which recognize artificial boundaries and racial distinctions of reference and not for restricting the social horizon of its members."[21]

Mawlana Mawdudi of the Jamaat-i-Islami and Sayyid Qutb of the Muslim Brotherhood, major influences on Muslim political thought, dismissed nationalism as a product of Western imperialism. They believed that the implicit values of nationalism sustained a narrow, self-centered, secular, materialist world view that emphasized national, racial, or class interests and conflicted with the God-centered, moral, egalitarian, universal message of Islam, which invisioned a world-state governed by the *Shariah*.[22] Yet, in practice, while always affirming the universal ideal of Islam, Mawdudi reluctantly accepted the Muslim nationalism of Pakistan as the Brotherhood had accommodated Arab nationalism. Moreover, as we have seen, both the Jamaat and the Brotherhood have become major political actors and participants in their respective nation-states. Similarly, most Islamic activists and organizations espouse a dual citizenship. While affirming and participating in a transnational community (*ummah*), they have as their proximate focus and goal the transformation of their nation-states.

Different language, tribal, and ethnic groups have always existed under the umbrella of Islam. In the Quran, God declares: "We . . . made you into tribes and nations" (49:13). Muslims have long recognized the political force and sociological reality of local or national identity as well as a more basic, universal supranational pan-Islamism. As Fazlur Rahman notes: "This 'nationalism,' therefore, is not averse to a wider loyalty and, in face of a non-Muslim aggressor (as we have often witnessed during this and the preceding century), the two sentiments make an extraordinarily powerful liaison." Still, for many Muslims, such local or national group sentiment must be subservient to a broader Islamic identification and commitment. It must also eschew a secularism that would reduce Islam solely to the private sphere of life. The problem occurs when: "this primitive 'nationalism' comes to be formulated as a political ideology and is transformed into a nation-state claiming sovereignty and demanding paramount loyalty."[23]

Modern liberal nationalism is objectionable more for its Western secular origin and orientation than for its organization of Muslims in modern states. The general climate today is one that seeks to reformulate or reconstruct the nation-state rather than to reject it, to make it compatible with Islam. The process is one of Islamization.

Islamization

Appeals to Islamization again underscore the revivalist versus reformist differences among Islamic activists. The term is used by both
traditionalists and reformers to describe the method by which more
Islamically oriented states are to be implemented. However, their use
of the term differs. For traditionalists, Islamization is primarily the
reintroduction of past institutions and practices with little adaptation
or change, for example, veiling of women, public separation of men
and women, traditional Islamic laws and punishments. Reformers'
understanding of Islamization is more faithful to history, recognizing
the creative process by which Islam developed. They see themselves
as continuing a dynamic process that is as old as Islam itself. Muslims
borrowed freely from the cultures that they conquered, adopting and
adapting political, legal, social, and economic practices as long as they
were not contrary to Islam. Therefore, Islamic systems of government
and the *Shariah* were not simply based upon Quranic and Prophetic
guidelines but upon those ideas, practices, and institutions from Arabia, Byzantium, and the Sasanid empires that did not contradict Islam
and were adopted or modified. While traditionalists take great pains
to emphasize the total self sufficiency of Islam, reformers insist that,
though some past laws and institutions may be valuable, new
circumstances and problems require new solutions formulated in light
of Quranic principles and through selective borrowing. This process
brings about Islamic modernization not simply wholesale westernization.

Sadiq al-Mahdi, Oxford-educated grandson of the Sudanese Mahdi and recent prime minister of the Sudan, is representative of a
reformist approach. He describes Islamization as separating Islam
from the traditionalist formulation of Islam, which is based upon a
historically conditioned understanding of the Quran and *Sunnah*. The
purpose of Islamization is to separate modernization from westernization. The goal is to establish a synthesis that is both Islamic and
modern.[24] Given this view of the historical conditioning of past Islamic practice, al-Mahdi can declare that there is no single Islamic
political or economic system but historical applications of Islamic political and economic injunctions.[25] Similarly, in law, "even the most
specific injunctions, injunctions which have been explicitly specified
by holy texts, are contingent upon conditions which permit a high

degree of flexibility. Thus the canonical punishments known as *hudud* (e.g., amputation for theft) . . . are associated with elaborate conditions which allow circumstantial considerations to qualify their application."[26]

Another reformist understanding and approach to Islamization or Islamic sociopolitical change is taken by Hassan al-Turabi:

> Any form or procedures for the organization of public life that can ultimately be related to God and put to his service in the furtherance of the aims of Islamic government can be adopted unless expressly excluded by the *Shariah*. Once so received, it is an integral part of Islam whatever its source may be. Through the process of Islamization, the Muslims were always very open to expansion and change. Thus, Muslims can incorporate any experience whatever if not contrary to their ideals. Muslims took most of their bureaucratic forms from Roman and Persian models. Now much can be borrowed from contemporary sources, critically appreciated in the light of the *Shariah* values and norms, and integrated into the Islamic framework of government.[27]

However, as noted in chapter 5, when Turabi and the National Islamic Front were associated with government, government policies and practices often contradicted his reformist thought.

The Islamic reformist task has required think tanks of Muslims to develop models appropriate to differing conditions of Muslim societies as well as experimentation. Given the orientation of the majority of religious leaders and the Muslim masses, the tendency of Islamic experiments has been traditionalist, exemplifying the distinctly different visions and orientations of traditionists and modernists.

Education

The key to resolving the problem of tradition and change is education. Traditionally, education and religious scholarship were the province of the *ulama*. In the past, religious schools trained the leaders of society; however, as we have seen in the nineteenth and twentieth centuries, many Muslim countries introduced secular education alongside the *ulama's* traditional religious education. This existence of two parallel systems has actually caused a bifurcation of Muslim society. Despite some curriculum reform, the traditional system remains relatively isolated from the mainstream. Government-funding priority has been given to secular schools because they provide the training and academic degrees for prestige positions in a modern society (science, engineering, medicine, law, journalism). Graduates of religious schools, with predominantly traditional educations, continue to serve as religious leaders or teachers. But they are often ill prepared to understand and respond to the demands of modernity. Most are unable to provide creative reinterpretation of traditional values, which is the kind of religious leadership required in modern society. On the other hand, modern elites trained in Western-oriented secular schools are well versed in modern disciplines but are often lacking in the true awareness of their tradition necessary to make changes that are sensitive to the history and values of their cultural milieu. As a result, Western models and presuppositions have been uncritically adopted by modern elites. Opportunities to render change reflecting some continuity with the past have gone unrecognized as well as unrealized. Thus both traditional and modern elites have failed to provide a new synthesis that clearly offers some continuity between tradition and modernity.

Too often the Muslim world has seen, on the one hand, a Western-oriented elite minority convinced that they must forge ahead regardless of the obscurantist opposition of religious leaders and, on the other, a religious leadership suspicious of and resistant to an alien process—modernization—characterized as Western and secular, materialist and godless. To date, the religious leadership is seen as an obstacle to change while Western secular Muslims and their governments are conveniently blamed for the social and spiritual ills of society.

The bifurcation of education and the consequent training of two separate mind-sets or outlooks (traditional and modern) are clearly illustrated in the contemporary Islamic revival. The demand for more Islamically oriented states requires a reexamination of political, social, legal, and economic institutions as well as of the principles and values that inform them. If secularists have denied the necessity, let alone feasibility, of undertaking such a task, the religious leadership has generally proven incapable of it. More conservative religious leaders tend to be fixated on the past. They view tradition not so much as a source of direction and inspiration but rather as the very map to be followed in all its details. Conservatives fail to distinguish between revealed, immutable principles and historically conditioned laws and institutions that were the product of the early jurists' human reason.

The hold of tradition is to be found in a more hidden form among those who advocate reinterpretation *(ijtihad)* and change in principle but who, when pressed on specific changes, often reflect a *"taqlid mentality,"* a tendency to follow past practice reflexively. Thus, when religious forces gain power (Iran) or influence (Pakistan) or become more vocal in calling for the Islamization of society (Egypt), the Islam that many advocate or introduce is that of the past, not simply in its revealed principles but often in its derivative prescriptions and forms. Even those Islamic leaders who are more reform-minded often temper their statements and policies in order to avoid the criticism of conservative religious leaders and to maintain their credibility among a more tradition-oriented populace.

Yet we must avoid the oversimplified distinction between intransigent traditionalists and reform-minded modernists. The tendency of the more tradition bound to view their understanding of Islam as definitive has not precluded actual change. The very process of preserving and passing on a religious tradition requires interpretation and application, thus contributing to Islamic change. The study, preaching, and interpreting of Islam by individual religious scholars and teachers as well as its implementation occur within changing social contexts. Diversity results from the very fact that normative Islamic ideologies espoused in a particular time and place are themselves the product of both the carriers and the contexts.[28]

Thus, although all Muslims are bound by Islamic law, its overall unity incorporates a diversity in practice that reflects differences in juristic reasoning as well as in the customs of the various geographic areas in which the laws developed. So, too, traditional beliefs, practices, and institutions take on new meanings in the teachings of even the most orthodox. The Ayatollah Khomeini's interpretation of government under the *faqih* and Zia ul-Haq's implementation of Islamic measures, though ostensibly justified as a "restoration" of past practice, are viewed by others, both traditionists and modernists, as innovative interpretations. The application of Islamic history and values to modern concerns and deeds have produced fresh interpretations or extensions of Islamic concepts. Shii beliefs and rituals have been transformed from quietistic, messianic expectation of the Hidden Imam to an ideology of political and social activism and revolution to hasten his return. Consultation and consensus are used to Islamically legitimate modern parliamentary forms of "Islamic" government. In the name of Islam, constitutionalism, democracy, and parliamentary forms of government have been adopted and rendered Islamic. Muslims, drawing on a rich and diverse tradition, reconstruct an ideologized Islam: a systematic, integrated ideology encompassing politics, law, economics, and education. As a result, most conservatives, neo-traditionalists, and Islamic reformers accept "Islamized" versions of modern government and administrative institutions.

Differences in Islamic visions are accompanied by profound disagreements regarding the implementation of Islamic rule. For the vast majority of Muslims, the resurgence of Islam is a reassertion of cultural identity, formal religious observance, Sufi practice, family values, and morality. The establishment of an Islamic society is seen as requiring a personal and social transformation that is a prerequisite for true Islamic government. Effective change is to come from below through a gradual process brought about through the implementation of Islamic law. For the majority of Muslims, the process is one of transformation through educational and social reform.

The more significant outcome of contemporary Islamic revivalism has been the occurrence of a quiet revolution, a process of Islamically oriented social and political change in many Muslim countries. The impact of Islamic revivalism is reflected in the life and institutions of mainstream Muslim society. Most governments have found it necessary to become more Islamically sensitive, building more mosques, funding Islamic schools, projects, and conferences, and generally increasing public observance of religious norms. Even a secularist leader like Saddam Hussein deemed it useful to call for *jihad* in his confrontation with the United States over Kuwait. At the same time, Islamically inspired schools, day-care centers, clinics, hospitals, legal aid societies, and youth groups have proliferated. Many are run by pious individuals and professionals, and others by specific Islamic organizations. Some are political; others are nonpolitical. Women have initiated their own Quran study groups in which they seek to better understand scripture and tradition in order to protect their status and rights, to address issues of identity, dress, and social life more authentically and autonomously.

Despite media images of gun-toting *mullahs*, the majority of contemporary Islamic leaders and movements have been lay rather than clerical. The leadership in Muslim societies is no longer easily divided into Western-oriented and traditional-Islamic. Increasingly, one finds a third group, a new generation of modern educated but self-consciously Islamically inspired and grounded professionals in every strata of society: in government, the bureaucracy, the military, education, the media, the corporate sector as well as in nongovernment organizations and agencies. Continued emphasis on education and on youth groups and centers reinforces the building of this cadre in society. In fact this new group of professionals has begun to establish their own schools as well as to create a presence in the administration and faculty of state schools and universities.

Yet a minority continue to view the societies and governments in Muslim countries as so hopelessly corrupted that violent revolution is perceived as the only effective method for systemic change. They regard their existing societies as pagan (i.e., un-Islamic) societies and their leaders as no better than infidels who must be eradicated. Islamic revolutionaries reject not only the political, economic, and social status quo but also the official religious establishment. In most countries, the official *ulama* and Sufi leaders are regarded as having been co-opted by their governments. Therefore, militants believe that both established political and established religious elites, in whose hands power is concentrated, must be overthrown. Power must be seized by a new Islamically committed leadership, the *Shariah* imposed, a deviant society restored to its divinely revealed path and thus governed Islamically. Radical revolutionary groups have remained relatively small in membership. Though effective in political agitation, disruption, and assassination, they have generally not been successful in mobilizing the masses.

Islamic Threat or Clash of Civilizations?

In recent years, there are those who speak of a clash of civilizations, a clash between Islam and "our" modern secular (or Judeo-Christian), democratic culture or between Islamic civilization and the West.[29]

The underestimation of religion in modernization or development theory as a source of identity and a potential force in politics has led to its overestimation. New recognition of religion's significance in international affairs has reinforced an exaggerated belief among some in the impending clash of civilizations. The clearest, most provocative, and influential articulation of this position is Samuel P. Huntington's "Clash of Civilizations" in which Huntington declared that in the post–cold war period: "The clash of civilizations will dominate global politics. The fault lines between civilizations will be the battle lines of the future. . . . The next world war, if there is one, will be a war between civilizations."[30]

Religious and cultural differences are emphasized in this position over similarities; political, economic, and cultural differences are necessarily equated with confrontation. Areas of cooperation and the fact that most countries are primarily, although not solely, driven by national and regional interests are overlooked or deemphasized.

The creation of an "imagined" monolithic Islam has led to a religious reductionism that views political conflicts in the Sudan, Lebanon, Bosnia, and Azerbaijan in primarily religious terms—as "Islamic-Christian conflicts." Although the communities in these areas may be broadly identified in religious or confessional terms as Christian and Muslim communities, as is the case of Northern Ireland's Catholic and Protestant communities or Sri Lanka's Tamil (Hindu) and Buddhist communities, local disputes and civil wars have more to do with political (e.g., ethnic nationalism, autonomy, and independence) and socioeconomic issues/grievances than with religion.

The challenge in an increasingly global, interdependent world is to recognize both competing and common interests. America's policy towards Japan or Saudi Arabia is not based upon a sense of shared culture, religion, or civilization but upon national or group interests. Cooperation can result from common religious and ethnic backgrounds; however, more often than not it comes from the recognition of common national and strategic interests. While a clash of civilizations can become the clarion call that justifies aggression and warfare, future global threats and wars will be due less to a clash of "civilizations" than to a clash of interests, economic and otherwise.

Implicit in the analysis of many critics of political Islam is a "secular fundamentalism," a modern secular perspective which views the mixing of religion and politics as necessarily abnormal (departing from the secular norm), irrational, dangerous, and extremist. Those who do so are often dubbed "fundamentalists" (Christian, Jewish, or

Muslim) or religious fanatics. Thus, when secular-minded peoples in the West (government officials, political analysts, journalists, and the bulk of the general public) encounter Muslim individuals and groups who speak of Islam as a comprehensive way of life, they immediately dub them fundamentalist and simply equate them with retrogressive forces, obstacles to change, or zealotry that is a threat.

The assumption that the mixing of religion and politics necessarily and inevitably leads to fanaticism and extremism has been a major factor in concluding that all Islamic movements are extremist and that Islam and democracy are incompatible. Failure to differentiate between Islamic movements, that is, between those that are moderate (willing to participate within the system and seek change from below) and those that are radical (violent) and extremist, is misleading and counterproductive. Few equate the actions of Jewish or Christian extremist leaders or groups with Judaism and Christianity as a whole. Similarly, the American government does not condemn the mixing of religion and politics in Israel, Poland, Eastern Europe, or Latin America. A comparable level of discrimination is absent when dealing with Islam. Therefore, questions remain. Can the ills of societies be reduced to a single cause or blamed on "fundamentalist fanatics"? Are the activities of a radical minority a convenient excuse for the failures of many governments to build strong and equitable modern states? Does this perceived threat support authoritarian, military/security governments, whose nonelected rulers' primary wish is to perpetuate their own power?

The use of violence is a particularly contentious and problematic issue. Distinguishing between moderates and extremists can be difficult. The line between movements of national liberation and terrorist organizations is often blurred or dependent upon one's political vantage point. America's revolutionary heroes were rebels and traitors to the British crown. Menachem Begin and Yitzak Shamir, the Irgun and Stern Gangs, Nelson Mandela and the African National Congress, and until recently, Yasser Arafat and the PLO were regarded by their opposition as terrorists leading terrorist movements. Similar questions or issues exist elsewhere. Is Christian liberation theology and its derivative movements in Latin and Central America simply a crypto-Marxist revolutionary force or an authentic populist movement? Yesterday's terrorists may be just that—terrorists, or they may become today's statesmen.

The challenge is to move beyond an imagined monolithic political Islam. The diversity reflected in differences between state Islam as seen in Saudi Arabia, Morocco, Malaysia, Iran, Sudan, Pakistan, Libya, or Afghanistan can also be seen in differences among Islamic movements, from moderate/pragmatist (those that participate within the system) to radical extremist (those that simply seek to overthrow regimes and impose their own brand of Islam). The Muslim Brotherhoods of Egypt and Jordan, Pakistan's Jamaat-i-Islami, Turkey's Refah Party, Tunisia's Ennahda, and Algeria's Islamic Salvation Front, to name a few, eschewed violence and participated in electoral politics. At the same time, Egypt's Gamaa Islamiyya, Algeria's Armed Islamic Group, and *jihad* organizations in many countries have engaged in violence and terrorism.

The challenge for students of Muslim politics is to avoid an easier, monolithic approach and instead to evaluate each country and each Islamic movement separately and within its specific context. Just as democratic, Western Christian, European, or Chinese nations, despite commonalities, possess distinctive differences and national interests, so too a rich diversity of peoples, governments, and interests are found in the Muslim world and within political Islam.

Conclusion

In many parts of the Islamic world, Muslims stand at a crossroads. Although independent states for several decades, the political legitimacy of many Muslim governments is far from established. To the extent that incumbent governments fail to satisfy the political and economic needs of their societies and to pursue a path of modernization that is sensitive to their Islamic heritage, these governments will remain in precarious positions in which stability is based more often than not on authoritarian rule and force. If Muslim governments strive to achieve a new synthesis providing some continuity between the demands of modernity and their Islamic tradition, then a broad range of possibilities stretches out before them—from a conservative, fundamentalist to a more reformist state and society. Although the outcome will vary from country to country depending upon political, social, and economic variables, the process itself is inevitable because it involves national identity as well as religious understanding and commitment.

Notes
Selected Bibliography
Index

Notes

1. Religion, Politics, and Society

1. Bernard Lewis, *The Arabs in History* (New York: Harper and Row, Torchbooks, 1966), 62.

2. Marshall S. G. Hodgson, *The Venture of Islam,* 3 vols. (Chicago: Univ. of Chicago Press, 1974), 1: 209.

3. Fred R. Donner, *The Early Islamic Conquests* (Princeton: Princeton Univ. Press, 1981), 269.

4. Lewis, *Arabs,* 67–68.

5. Reuben Levy, *The Social Structure of Islam* (1957; reprint, Cambridge: Cambridge Univ. Press, 1971), 299.

6. N. J. Coulson, *A History of Islamic Law* (Edinburgh: Edinburgh Univ. Press 1964), 28; Levy, *Social Structure,* 334.

7. See John L. Esposito "Law in Islam," in *The Islamic Impact,* ed. Yvonne Y. Haddad (Syracuse, N.Y.: Syracuse Univ. Press, 1984), chap. 4; Coulson, *History,* chap. 3.

8. Hodgson, *Venture,* 1: 252.

9. Laura Veccia Vaglieri, "The Patriarchal and Ummayad Caliphates," in *The Cambridge History of Islam,* ed. P. M. Holt, Ann K. S. Lambton, and Bernard Lewis (Cambridge: Cambridge Univ. Press, 1978), 1A: 103.

10. Fazlur Rahman, *Islam,* 2d ed. (Chicago: Univ. of Chicago Press, 1979), 79.

11. See Yvonne Y. Haddad, ed., *The Islamic Impact* (Syracuse, N.Y.: Syracuse Univ. Press, 1984).

12. Hodgson, *Venture,* 1: 237.

13. Norman Itzkowitz, *Ottoman Empire and Islamic Tradition* (Chicago: Univ. of Chicago Press, 1971), 3.

14. Erwin I. J. Rosenthal, *Political Thought in Medieval Islam* (Cambridge: Cambridge Univ. Press, 1958), 27.

15. Hamilton A. Gibb, *Studies on the Civilization of Islam* (Princeton: Princeton Univ. Press, 1982), 45.

2. Revival and Reform

1. See John O. Voll, "Renewal and Reform in Islamic *Tajdid* and *Islah*," in *Voices of Resurgent Islam*, ed. John L. Esposito (New York: Oxford Univ. Press, 1983), chap. 2.

2. Barbara Daly Metcalf, *Islamic Revival in British India, 1860–1900* (Princeton: Princeton Univ. Press, 1982), 56 ff.

3. Ibid.

4. See Aziz Ahmad, *Studies in Islamic Culture in the Indian Environment* (Oxford: Oxford Univ. Press, 1964), 209–17.

5. As quoted in John O. Voll, "The Sudanese Mahdi: Frontier Fundamentalist," *International Journal of Middle East Studies* 10 (1979): 159.

6. P. M. Holt and M. W. Daly, *The History of the Sudan: From the Coming of Islam to the Present*, 3d ed. (Boulder, Colo.: Westview Press, 1979), 95.

7. Hodgson, *Venture*, 3: 136.

8. Ibid., 3: 152.

9. See Metcalf, *Islamic Revival*, 46 ff. for a discussion of differing interpretations of this *fatwa*.

10. The Hijrat movement in India had inspired more than thirty thousand Muslims to migrate to Afghanistan, clogging the Khyber Pass. See Gail Minault, "Islam and Mass Politics: The India Ulama and the Khilafat Movement," in *Religion and Political Modernization*, ed. Donald E. Smith (New Haven: Yale Univ. Press, 1974), 178–79.

11. Albert Hourani, *Arabic Thought in the Liberal Age, 1798–1939* (Oxford: Oxford Univ. Press, 1970), 41.

12. As quoted in Ibid., 48.

13. Ibid., 194; and Sylvia G. Haim, ed., *Arab Nationalism* (Berkeley: Univ. of California Press, 1976), 21 ff.

14. Daniel Crecelius, "The Course of Secularization in Modern Egypt," in *Islam and Development: Religion and Sociopolitical Change*, ed. John L. Esposito (Syracuse, N.Y.: Syracuse Univ. Press, 1980), 60.

15. For a fuller analysis of Afghani see Hourani, *Arabic Thought*, chap. 5; and Nikki R. Keddie, *Sayyid Jamal al-Din "al-Afghani": A Political Biography* (Berkeley: Univ. of California Press, 1972).

16. Aziz Ahmad, *Islamic Modernism in India and Pakistan, 1857–1964* (London: Oxford Univ. Press, 1967), 126.

17. Hourani, *Arabic Thought*, 109.

18. See Wilfred Cantwell Smith, *Islam in Modern History* (Princeton: Princeton Univ. Press, 1957), 47–51; and Hourani, *Arabic Thought*, chap. 5.

19. Also referred to as the Manar movement, after its journal, *Al-Manar*.

20. *Taammulat* (Cairo: Dar al Maarif, n.d.), 68–69, translation in John J. Donohue and John L. Esposito, eds., *Islam in Transition: Muslim Perspectives* (New York: Oxford Univ. Press, 1982), 70.

21. Ibid., 71.

22. *Ara wa ahadith fi al-wataniyya wa al-qawmiyya* (Views and Speeches on Nationalism and Patriotism) (Cairo: Mahbaat al-risala, 1944), 20.

23. Rahman, *Islam*, 227.

24. Ahmad, *Islamic Modernism*, 34.

25. As quoted in Rahman, *Islam*, 267.

26. Ahmad Khan, "Lecture on Islam," in *Islam*, ed. Donohue and Esposito, 42.

27. Ibid.

28. Chiragh Ali, *The Proposed Political, Legal and Social Reforms in the Ottoman Empire and Other Mohammedan States* (Bombay, 1883), 118.

3. Nationalism

1. Hourani, *Arabic Thought*, 227.

2. *Al-Manar wal Azhar*, 179, in ibid., 226.

3. Malcolm H. Kerr, *Islamic Reform: The Political and Legal Theories of Muhammad Abduh and Rashid Rida* (Berkeley: Univ. of California Press, 1966), 190.

4. *Al-Manar*, 3 (Cairo, 1900): 172, 290–92.

5. Ibid., 33 (Cairo, 1933). Translated in Donohue and Esposito, *Islam*, 57–58.

6. Nadav Safran, *Egypt in Search of Political Community* (Cambridge: Harvard Univ. Press, 1961), 83

7. Rashid Rida, *al-Wahabiyyun wal Hijaz* (Cairo, 1926), 47.

8. Kerr, *Islamic Reform*, 187.

9. *Taamulat*, as translated in *Islam*, ed. Donohue and Esposito, 70–71.

10. Ibid., 71.

11. Ibid., 72.

12. *The Future of Culture in Egypt*, excerpted in *Islam*, ed. Donohue and Esposito, 74. Subsequent citations to this volume will be carried in parentheses in the text.

13. *Al-Islam wa usul al-hukm* (Cairo, 1925); translated into French by L. Bercher, *L'Islam et les bases du pouvoir*, in *Revue des etudes islamiques* 7 (1933): 353–91; 8 (1934): 122–63; selections translated into English as "Islam and the Bases of Authority," in *Islam*, ed. Donohue and Esposito, 29–37.

14. For summaries of Abd al-Raziq's position and the controversy see Hourani, *Arabic Thought*, 183–92; and Leonard Binder, "Ali Abd al-Raziq and Islamic Liberalism," *Asian and African Studies* 16, no. 1 (Mar. 1982): 31–58.

15. Muhammad Rashid Rida, *al-Khilafa* (Cairo: Manar Press, 1923). French translation: *Le Califat dans la doctrine de Rashid Rida*, trans. H. Laoust (Beirut, 1938).

16. Ali Abd al-Raziq, "Islam and the Bases of Authority," in Donohue and Esposito, *Islam*, 30. Subsequent citations will be carried in parentheses in the text.

17. *Our Decline and Its Causes* excerpted in *Islam*, ed. Donohue and Esposito, 61. Subsequent citations will be carried in parentheses in the text.

18. "Muslim Unity and Arab Unity," in *Islam*, ed. Donohue and Esposito, 69. Subsequent citations will be carried in parentheses in the text.

19. Abd al-Rahman al-Bazzaz, "Islam and Arab Nationalism," in *Islam*, ed. Donohue and Esposito, 84. Subsequent citations will be carried in parentheses in the text.

20. David Ottoway and Marina Ottoway, *Algeria: The Politics of a Socialist Revolution* (Berkeley: Univ. of California Press, 1970), 30.

21. David C. Gordon, *The Passage of French Algeria* (New York: Oxford Univ. Press, 1966), 30 n. 58.

22. See L. Carl Brown, "The Islamic Reform Movement in North Africa," *Journal of Modern African Studies* 2 (1964): 55–63.

23. See Jamil Abun Nasr, "The Salafiyya Movement in The Religious Bases of the Moroccan Nationalist Movement," in *St. Antony's Papers, No. 16, Middle Eastern Affairs No. 3,* ed. Albert Hourani (London: Chatto and Windus, 1963), 90–105.

24. John Waterbury, *Commander of the Faithful: The Moroccan Political Elite* (New York: Columbia Univ. Press, 1970), 48.

25. As cited in Gordon, *French Algeria,* 24.

26. Ibid., 50.

27. Bernard Lewis, *The Middle East and the West* (New York: Harper and Row, 1964); and Joseph Desparment, "Les Guides de l'opinion indigene en Algerie," *L'Afrique Française* (1933): 11–16.

28. Mangol Bayat, *Mysticism and Dissent: Socioreligious Thought in Qajar Iran* (Syracuse, N.Y.: Syracuse Univ. Press, 1982), 15–20.

29. Ann K. Lambton, "Quis custodiet custodes?" *Studia Islamica* 6 (1956): 133.

30. See E. G. Browne, *Persian Revolution of 1905–1909* (Cambridge: Cambridge Univ. Press, 1916); and Hamid Algar, *Religion and State in Iran 1785–1906* (Berkeley: Univ. of California Press, 1969).

31. Nikki R. Keddie, Iran: *Religion, Politics, and Society* (London: Frank Cass, 1980), 41.

32. See Ann K. S. Lambton, "Persia: The Breakdown of a Society," in *Cambridge History,* ed. Holt, Lambton, and Lewis, 465. See also Lambton's "Persian Political Societies, 1906–1911," in *St. Antony Papers, No. 16,* ed. Hourani, 41–89.

33. Hamid Algar, "The Oppositional Role of the Ulama in Twentieth Century Iran," in *Scholars, Saints, and Sufis,* ed. Nikki R. Keddie (Berkeley: Univ. of California Press, 1972), 234.

34. Algar, *Religion,* 252.

35. Shaykh Fazl Allah Nuri, "Refutation of the Idea of Constitutionalism," trans. Abdul Hadi Hairi, *Middle Eastern Studies* 13, no. 3 (Oct. 1977): 329; excerpt in *Islam,* ed. Donohue and Esposito, 292–96.

36. Donohue and Esposito, *Islam,* 289, 288.

37. Gail Minault, "Islam and Mass Politics: The Indian Ulama and the Khilafat Movement," in *Religion and Political Modernization,* ed. Smith, 170–71.

38. Al-Hillul 1, no. 4, as quoted in M. U. Haq, *Muslim Politics in Modern India* (Lahore: Book Traders, n.d.), 83.

39. S. Abul Hasan Ali Nadwi, *Islam and the World* (Lahore: Muhammad Ashraf, reprint. 1967), 139.

40. Abul Ala Mawdudi, *Nationalism and Islam* (Lahore: Islamic Publications, 1947), 10.

41. Ahmad, *Islamic Modernism,* 186.

42. *Struggle for Independence: 1857–1947* (Karachi, 1958), app. 4, 14.

43. Ibid., 18.

44. Jamil-ud-din Ahmad, ed., *Speeches and writings of Mr. Jinnah* (Lahore: Muhammad Ashraf, 1952), 1:177.

4. The Modern State

1. Stanford J. Shaw and Ezel Kural Shaw, *History of the Ottoman Empire and Modern Turkey,* vol. 2 (Cambridge: Cambridge Univ. Press, 1977), 375.

2. Don Peretz, *The Middle East Today*, 2d ed. (New York: Holt, Rinehart, and Winston, 1971), 160.

3. Howard A. Reed, "Attaturk's Secularizing Legacy and the Continuing Vitality of Islam in Republican Turkey," in *Islam in the Contemporary World*, ed. Cyriac K. Pullapilly (Notre Dame, Ind.: Cross Roads Books, 1980), 331.

4. Kemal H. Karpat, "Modern Turkey," in *Cambridge History*, ed. Holt, Lambton, and Lewis, 562–63.

5. G. L. Lewis, "Turkey," in "Islam and Politics," *The Muslim World 56*, no. 4 (Oct. 1966).

6. Serif Mardin, "Turkey," in *Islam in the Political Process*, ed. James P. Piscatori (Cambridge. Cambridge Univ. Press, 1983), 134.

7. Ibid., 144.

8. For background information on the early history of Saudi Arabia, see John L. Burckhardt, *Notes on the Bedouins and Wahabys* (London: Colburn and Bentley, 1831); H. St. John Philby, *Saudi Arabia* (Beirut: Librairie du Liban, 1968); and George S. Rentz, "Muhammad ibn Abd al-Wahhab (1703–1792) and the beginnings of the Unitarian Empire in Arabia" (Ph.D. diss., Univ. of California at Berkeley, 1948).

9. James P. Piscatori, "The Formation of Saudi Arabia: A Case Study in the Utility of Transnationalism," in *Ethnic Identities in a Transnational World*, ed. John Stack (Westport, Conn.: Greenwood Press, 1981). See also "The Iraq-Najd Frontier," *Journal of the Central Asian Society* 17 (Jan. 1930): 85–90; and George Rentz, "Wahhabism and Saudi Arabia," in *The Arabian Peninsula: Society and Politics*, ed. Derek Hopewood (London: Allen and Unwin, 1972), 64–65.

10. Ronald R. MacIntyre, "Saudi Arabia," in *The Politics of Islamic Reassertion*, ed. Mohammed Ayoob (New York: St. Martin's Press, 1981), 13.

11. James P. Piscatori, "The Roles of Islam in Saudi Arabia's Political Development," in *Islam and Development*, ed. Esposito, 134.

12. As quoted in Yvonne Y. Haddad, "The Arab-Israeli Wars, Nasserism and Islamic Identity," in *Islam and Development*, ed. Esposito, 239, n. 23.

13. *The Islamic Pact: An Obvious Trick* (Cairo: Supreme Council of Islamic Affairs, n.d.), 50.

14. David Holden and Richard Johns, *The House of Saud* (New York: Holt, Rinehart, and Winston, 1981), 512.

15. The following analysis is based upon my "Pakistan: Quest for Islamic Identity," in *Islam and Development*, ed. Esposito, chap. 8.

16. Leonard Binder, *Religion and Politics in Pakistan* (Berkeley: Univ. of California Press, 1961); E. I. J. Rosenthal, *Islam in the Modern National State* (Cambridge: Cambridge Univ. Press, 1965), 181–281; Fazlur Rahman, "Islam and the Constitutional Problems of Pakistan," *Studia Islamica* 32, no. 4 (Dec. 1970): 275–87.

17. *Constitution of the Islamic Republic of Pakistan* (Karachi: Government of Pakistan, 1956), Pt. 1, Art. 1. Subsequent citations from this document are in parentheses in the text.

18. *Report of the Court of Inquiry Constituted under Punjab Act II of 1954 to Inquire into the Disturbances of 1953* (Lahore, 1954), 231 ff.

19. As quoted in M. Ahmed, "Islamic Aspects of the New Constitution of Pakistan," *Islamic Studies* 2 (June 1963): 262.

20. Ibid., app. C, 283.

21. *Report of the Commission on Marriage and Family Laws* as excerpted in *Islam*, ed. Donohue and Esposito, 201–2. Subsequent citations given in text.

22. For a detailed analysis see John L. Esposito, *Women in Muslim Family Law* (Syracuse, N.Y.: Syracuse Univ. Press, 1982), 83–101.

23. Sharough Akhavi, *Religion and Politics in Contemporary Iran* (Albany: SUNY Press, 1980), 42 ff.

24. Ibid., 38.

25. Ervand Abrahamian, *Iran Between Two Revolutions* (Princeton: Princeton Univ. Press, 1982), 259.

26. Sharough Akhavi, "Shii Social Thought and Praxis in Recent Iranian History," in *Islam*, ed. Pullapilly, 183.

27. Hamid Algar, "The Oppositional Role of the Ulama in Twentieth-Century Iran," in *Scholars*, ed. Keddie, 247.

28. Ibid., 247.

29. In Fayez Sayegh, "The Theoretical Structure of Nasser's Arab Socialism," in *St. Antony Papers, No. 17, Middle Eastern Affairs No. 4* (London: Oxford Univ. Press, 1965), 13.

30. Gamal Abd al-Nasser, *Egypt's Liberation: The Philosophy of the Revolution* (Washington, D.C.: Public Affairs Press, 1955), 86–87.

31. Morroe Berger, *Islam in Egypt: Social and Political Aspects of Popular Religion* (Cambridge: Cambridge Univ. Press, 1970), 47.

32. Shaykh Mahmud Shaltut, "Al-Ishtirakiyya wal-Islam" (Socialism and Islam), in *Islam*, ed. Donohue and Esposito, 99.

33. Ibid., 101.

34. Ibid., 102.

35. See, for example, a *fatwa* on land reform in ibid., 197–99.

36. Crecelius, "Course of Secularization," in *Islam and Development*, ed. Esposito, 234, n. 30.

37. As quoted in Guenter Lewy, "Nasserism and Islam," in *Religion*, ed. Smith, 270–71.

38. As quoted in Christina Phelps Harris, *Nationalism and Revolution in Egypt* (The Hague: Mouton, 1964), 144.

39. Ibid., 145.

40. Richard P. Mitchell, *The Society of the Muslim Brothers* (London: Oxford Univ. Press, 1969), 9, 14.

41. For my interpretation of Sayyid Qutb, I am especially indebted to Yvonne Y. Haddad, in particular for her "Sayyid Qutb: Ideologue of the Islamic Revival," in *Voices*, ed. Esposito, chap. 6, and her "Quranic Justification for an Islamic Revolution: The view of Sayyid Qutb," *Middle East Journal* 37, no. 1 (Winter 1983): 14–79.

42. Muhammad al-Ghazzali, *Our Beginning in Wisdom* (Min Huna Nalam), trans. Ismail R. al-Faruqi (Washington, D.C.: American Council of Learned Societies, 1953), 54.

43. Sayyid Qutb, as quoted in Haddad, "Sayyid Qutb," in *Voices*, ed. Esposito, 73.

44. Ibid., 74.

45. Ibid., 70.

46. Hasan al-Banna, "Min al-qadim: Ittijah al-nahda al-jadida fi al-ulam al-lslami," translated excerpts in *Islam,* ed. Donohue and Esposito, 78.

47. Safran, *Egypt,* 209.

48. Sayyid Qutb, *Khasais,* in Haddad, "Sayyid Qutb," in *Voices,* ed. Esposito, 74.

49. Ibid., 76.

50. Ibid.

51. Ibid., 71.

52. Hasan Ismail Hudaybi, *al-Musawwar,* as quoted in Mitchell, *Muslim Brothers,* 258.

53. For an introduction to Mawdudi's development and thought see Charles J. Adams, "Mawdudi and the Islamic State," in *Voices,* ed. Esposito, chap. 5; and Adams, "The Ideology of Mawlana Mawdudi," in *South Asian Politics and Religion,* ed. Donald E. Smith (Princeton: Princeton Univ. Press, 1966), chap. 7.

54. Abul Ala Mawdudi, *Tarjuman al-Quran* (Nov.–Dec. 1938): 48.

55. Abul Ala Mawdudi, "Political Theory of Islam," in *The Islamic Law and Constitution,* ed. Khurshid Ahmad 6th ed. (Lahore: Islamic Publications, 1977), 130.

56. Mawdudi, "The Islamic Law," in *Islamic Law,* ed. K. Ahmad, 5.

57. Adams, "Mawdudi," in *Voices,* ed. Esposito, 116.

58. Mawdudi, "First Principles of the Islamic State," in *The Islamic Law,* ed. K. Ahmad, 23.

59. Ibid.

60. Mawdudi, "Political Theory of Islam," 159. Subsequent citations noted in text.

61. Mawdudi, "First Principles of the Islamic State," 214.

62. Mawdudi, "The Islamic Law," 66.

5. Contemporary Politics

1. Ali E. Hillal Dessouki, ed. *Islamic Resurgence in the Arab World* (New York: Praeger 1982); Ayoob, *Politics;* Edward Mortimer, *Faith and Power* (New York: Random House, 1982); and John O. Voll, *Islam: Continuity and Change in the Modern World* (Boulder, Colo.: Westview Press, 1982). For case studies, see Esposito, *Islam and Development;* and Esposito, *Voices.*

2. See John J. Donohue, "Islam and the Search for Arab Identity," chap. 3 in *Voices,* ed. Esposito; and Ali Merad, "The Ideologisation of Islam in the Contemporary Muslim World," chap. 3 in *Islam and Power,* ed. Ali E. Hillal Dessouki and A. S. Cudsi (Baltimore: Johns Hopkins Univ. Press, 1981).

3. Donohue, "Islam and the Search," in *Voices,* ed. Esposito.

4. For Qaddafi's use of Islam, see Lisa Anderson, "Qaddafi's Islam," chap. 6 in *Voices,* ed. Esposito; and Lisa Anderson, "Religion and Politics in Libya," *Journal of Arab Affairs* 1, no. 1 (Autumn 1981); Ann Mayer, "Islamic Resurgence or a New Prophethood: The Role of Islam in Qadhdhafi's Ideology," in *Islamic Resurgence,* ed. Dessouki.

5. Anderson, "Qaddafi's Islam," in *Voices,* ed. Esposito, 136.

6. Mahmoud Mustafa Ayoub, *Islam and the Third Universal Theory: The Religious Thought of Muammar al-Qadhdhafi* (London: KPI Ltd., 1987), 94.

7. "The Libyan Revolution in the Words of Its Leaders," *Middle East Journal* 24 (1970): 208.

8. Lela Garner Noble, "The Philippines: Autonomy for Muslims," in *Islam in Asia: Religion, Politics and Society*, ed. Esposito (New York: Oxford Univ. Press, 1987), 101.

9. Cesar Adib Majul, "The Iranian Revolution and the Muslims of the Philippines," in *The Iranian Revolution: Its Global Impact*, ed. John L. Esposito (Miami: Florida International Univ. Press, 1990), 261–62.

10. Sulayman S. Nyang, "The Islamic Factor in Libya's Foreign Policy," *Africa and the World*, 1, no. 2 (Jan. 1988): 17–18.

11. Muammar al-Qadhdhafi, *The Green Book*, excerpted as "The Third Way" in *Islam*, ed. Donohue and Esposito, 103.

12. Ibid.

13. Ibid., 105.

14. Ibid., 104.

15. For a useful summary of Qaddafi's socialist program, see Raymond H. Habiby, "Muammar Qaddafi's New Islamic Scientific Socialist Society," chap. 18 in *Religion and Politics in the Middle East*, ed. Michael Curtis (Boulder, Colo.: Westview Press, 1980), 247.

16. Anderson, "Qaddafi's Islam," in *Voices*, ed. Esposito, 143.

17. George Joffe, "Islamic Opposition in Libya," *Third World Quarterly* 10, no. 2 (Apr. 1988): 624.

18. Ibid., 629.

19. Jennifer Parmelee, "At Home, Gadhafi May Face Religious Turmoil," *International Herald Tribune*, Jan. 11, 1989.

20. Adel Darwish, "Gaddafi's Garbled Message," *Middle East* (Dec. 1989): 14.

21. William L. Richter, "The Political Dynamics of Islamic Resurgence in Pakistan," *Asian Survey* 19, no. 6 (June 1979): 547–57.

22. See, for example, Waheed-uz-Zaman, ed., *The Quest for Identity* (Islamabad: Islamabad Univ. Press, 1973).

23. Philip E. Jones, "Islam and Politics under Ayub and Bhutto: A Comparative Analysis." (Typescript, Seventh Conference on South Asia, Madison, Wis., Nov. 1978.)

24. *Dawn* (Pakistani newspaper), Sept. 30, 1977.

25. *Pakistan Affairs*, 35, no. 1 (Jan. 1982): 1.

26. *Dawn Overseas* (Pakistani newpaper), Sept. 17–23. 1982.

27. "News from the Country," al-Mushir (Rawalpindi) 23, no. 3 (1981): 115.

28. *Zakat and Ushr Ordinances, 1980* (Islamabad: Government of Pakistan, 1980), 33.

29. *Introduction of Islamic Laws: Address to the Nation by President General Zia-ul-Haq* (Islamabad: Government Printing Office, 1979), 16.

30. *Islamic University Ordinance* (Islamabad: Government Printing Office, 1980), 6.

31. *Dawn Overseas Weekly* (Pakistani newpaper), Apr. 12, 1989.

32. Anthony Hyman, "The Shine Wears Off," *Middle East* (Dec. 1989): 20.

33. See, for example, the comments of Mawlana Ahmad Noorani, president of the Jamiyyat i-Ulama-i-Pakistan (JUP), in *Dawn*, Oct. 2, 1979, 3.

34. The author wishes to acknowledge a debt to Mumtaz Ahmad for this information.

35. "The Muslim Community," *News From the Country, 1980–84* (Rawalpindi, Pakistan: Christian Study Center, 1985), 146–47.

36. For a discussion of Pakistan's Shii movement, see Maleeha Lodhi "Pakistan's Shia Movement: An Interview with Arif Hussaini," *Third World Quarterly* (Apr. 1988): 806–17.

37. *Dawn Overseas*, Feb. 3, 1983.

38. Ervand Abrahamian, *Iran: Between Two Revolutions* (Princeton: Princeton Univ. Press, 1982), 447.

39. Ibid., 448.

40. Jalal Al-e-Ahmad, *Gharbzadegi* ["Weststruckness"], trans. John Green and Ahmad Alizadeh, (Lexington, Ky.: Mazda Press, 1982), 11.

41. Ibid., 59.

42. Ali Shariati, *On the Sociology of Islam*, trans. Hamid Algar (Berkeley: Mizan Press, 1979), 17. For Shariati's life and thought, see Abdul Aziz Sachedina, "Ali Shariati: Ideologue of the Iranian Revolution," chap 9 in *Voices*, ed. Esposito.

43. Ervand Abrahamian, "Ali Shariati: Ideologue of the Iranian Revolution," MERIP Reports 102 (Jan. 1982): 25.

44. Ali Shariati, *Man and Islam*, trans. Fathollah Marjani (Houston, Tex.: Free Islamic Literature, 1980), xi.

45. As quoted in Shariati, *Sociology of Islam*, 23.

46. Ali Shariati, *Intizar Madhab-i-itiraz*, trans. Mangol Bayat, in *Islam*, ed. Donohue and Esposito, 297.

47. As quoted in Abrahamian, "Ali Shariati," *MERIP Reports:* 26.

48. Donohue and Esposito, *Islam*, 302.

49. Khomeini, "Message to the Pilgrims," in *Islam and Revolution: Writings and Declarations of Imam Khomeini*, trans. Hamid Algar (Berkeley: Mizan Press, 1981), 195.

50. Ibid.

51. Khomeini, "Islamic Government," *Islam*, 127.

52. Abrahamian, *Iran*, 505.

53. Ibid.

54. Ibid.

55. Khomeini, "Islamic Government," *Islam*, 43.

56. For this discussion of clerical control of Iran's government, I am especially indebted to Shahrough Akhavi's "Iran: Implementation of an Islamic State," in *Islam in Asia*, ed. Esposito.

57. Said Amir Arjomand, *The Turban for the Crown: The Islamic Revolution in Iran* (New York: Oxford Univ. Press, 1988), 164.

58. Ibid.

59. "Constitution of the Islamic Republic of Iran," *Middle East Journal* 34 (1980): 185.

60. For divergent but overlaping analyses, see Ali Banuazizi, "Faltering Legitimacy: The Ruling Clerics and Civil Society in Contemporary Iran," *International Journal of Politics, Culture and Society* 8, no. 4 (1995): 563–78, and Mohsen M. Milani, "Political Participation in Revolutionary Iran," in *Political Islam: Revolution, Radicalism, or Reform?*, ed. John L. Esposito (Boulder, Colo.: Lynne Rienner, 1997), 77–94.

61. Jean-François Legrain, "The Palestinian Islamicisms: Patriotism as a preparation for their Expansion," in *Accounting for Fundamentalisms: The Dynamic Character of Movements*, ed. Martin E. Marty and R. Scott Appleby (Chicago: American Academy of Sciences, 1994), 425.

62. Article 11 in Raphael Israeli, *Fundamentalist Islam and Israel* (New York: Univ. Press of America, 1933), 138–39.

63. Articles 12 and 15, ibid., 139, 142.

64. Sarah M. Roy, "Gaza: New Dynamics of Civic Disintegration," *Journal of Palestine Studies* 22, no. 4 (Summer 1993): 29.

65. Jean-François Legrain, "Hamas: Legitimate Heir of Palestinian Nationalism?" in *Political Islam: Revolution, Radicalism, or Reform?* ed. John L. Esposito (Boulder, Colo.: Lynne Rienner, 1997), 166.

66. Ibid., 172.

67. Hasan Hanafi, "The Relevance of the Islamic Alternative in Egypt," *Arab Studies Quarterly* 4, nos. 1, 2 (Spring 1982): 63.

68. As cited in Fadwa El Guindi, "Religious Revival and Islamic Survival in Egypt," *Middle East Insight* 2, no. 1 (Nov.–Dec. 1981).

69. Saad Eddin Ibrahim, "Islamic Militancy as a Social Movement: The Case of Two Groups in Egypt," in *Islamic Resurgence*, ed. Dessouki, 118.

70. Saad Eddin Ibrahim, "Egypt's Islamic Militants," *MERIP Reports* 103 (Feb. 1982): 11.

71. Fadwa El Guindi, "The Killing of Sadat and After: A Current Assessment of Egypt's Islamic Movement," *Middle East Insight* 2, no. 5 (Jan.–Feb. 1982): 21.

72. *Middle East International* 95 (Mar. 16, 1979): 2.

73. Louis J. Cantori, "Religion and Politics in Egypt," in *Religion*, ed. Curtis, 86.

74. El Guindi, "Killing of Sadat," 23.

75. Gilles Kepel, *Muslim Extremism in Egypt: The Prophet and the Pharoah* (Berkeley: Univ. of California Press, 1986), 192.

76. Hamied N. Ansan, "The Islamic Militants in Egyptian Politics," *International Journal of Middle East Studies* 16, no. 1 (Mar. 1984): 123–44.

77. Ibid., 134.

78. *New York Times*, Oct. 1, 1984.

79. Robert Bianchi, "Egypt: Drift at Home, Passivity Abroad," *Current History* (Feb. 1986): 73.

80. John Kifner, "Egyptian Opposition Lionizes Guard Who Killed Seven Israelites," *New York Times*, Dec. 27, 1985.

81. Paul Magnelia, "Islam on the Rise," *Africa News* (Feb. 1988): 8.

82. Saad Eddin Ibrahim, "Egypt's Islamic Activism in the 1980's," *Third World Quarterly* (Apr. 1988): 643.

83. Jane Freedman, "Democratic Winds Blow in Cairo," *Christian Science Monitor*, Jan. 17, 1990.

84. *New York Times*, Sept. 3, 1989.

85. Amira El-Azhary Sonbol, "Egypt," in *The Politics of Islamic Revivalism*, ed. Shireen Hunter (Bloomington: Indiana Univ. Press, 1988), 25.

86. Egyptian Organization of Human Rights, "A Statement of Recent [Incidents] of Communal/Religious Violence," Apr. 3, 1990, 1.

87. "Assiut Bears the Brunt of Islamists' Human Rights Abuse," *Middle East Times*, May 16–22, 1994, 2.

88. Christopher Hedges, "Seven Executed in Egypt in Move to Suppress Islamic Rebel Group," *New York Times*, July 9, 1993.

89. Ibid.

90. Virginia N. Sherry, "Egypt's Trampling of Rights Fosters Extremism," *New York Times*, Apr. 15, 1993. For an analysis of the Egyptian Organization for Human Rights report for 1996, see "The Year in Review," *Civil Society* (July 1997), 11–12.

91. Jane Freedman, "Democratic Winds Blow in Cairo," *Christian Science Monitor*, Jan. 17, 1990.

92. Chris Hedges, "Egypt Begins Crackdown on Strongest Opposition Group," *New York Times*, June 12, 1994, 3.

93. Raymond William Baker, "Invidious Comparisons: Realism, Postmodernism, and Centrist Islamic Movements in Egypt," in *Political Islam: Revolution, Radicalism or Reform?*, ed. John L. Esposito (Boulder, Colo: Lynne Rienner, 1997), 124.

94. "Militants Rally to Lawyer's Death," *Middle East Times*, May 16–22, 1994, 1.

95. "Fugitive Lawyer Remains Defiant," *Middle East Times*, June 27–July 3 1994, 16.

96. Saad Eddin Ibrahim, "A Spring of Democracy," *Civil Society*, July 1997, 4.

97. "The Year in Review," 11.

98. Robert Bianchi, "Islam and Democracy in Egypt," *Current History* vol. 88 (Feb. 1989), 104.

99. I have drawn on materials from my "Sudan's Islamic Experiment," *Muslim World* 76 (July/Oct. 1986): 181–201. I am especially indebted to my colleague John O. Voll for information contained in his *Political Impact of Islam in the Sudan* (Washington D.C.: U.S. Department of State, 1984) and for his comments.

100. Jafar al-Numayri, *Al-Nahj al-Islami li madha* (Cairo: al-Maktab al Misri al-Hadith, 1980).

101. Bona Malwal, *The Sudan: A Second Challenge to Nationhood* (New York: Thornton Books, 1985).

102. *Sudanow* 7, no. 12 (Dec. 1982): 5.

103. *Arab News*, May 31, 1984.

104. Peter Bechtold, "The Sudan Since the Fall of Numayri," in *The Middle East from the Iran-Contra Affair to the Intifada*, ed. Robert O. Freedman (Syracuse, N.Y.: Syracuse University Press, 1991), 371.

105. Ibid., 24.

106. John O. Voll, "Political Crisis in the Sudan," *Current History* 89, no. 546 (Apr. 1990): 179.

107. Ann Lesch, "Khartoum Diary," *Middle East Report*, no. 161 (Nov–Dec. 1989): 37.

108. Voll, "Political Crisis," 179–80.

109. See Richard Augustus Norton, *Amal and the Shia: Struggle for the Soul of Lebanon* (Austin: Univ. of Texas Press, 1987); and Fouad Ajami, *The Vanished Imam: Musa al-Sadr and the Shia of Lebanon* (Ithaca, N.Y.: Cornell Univ. Press, 1986).

110. Salim Nasr, "Roots of the Shii Movement" *MERIP Reports* (June 1985): 14.

111. Augustus Norton, "Harakat AMAL—The Emergence of a New Lebanon Fantasy or Reality," in Islamic Fundamentalism and Islamic Radicalism (Washington, D.C.: House Committee on Foreign Affairs, 1985). 347.

112. George Nader, "Interview with Sheikh Mohammad Hussein Fadl Allah," *Middle East Insight* (June/July 1985): 19.

113. Augustus Richard Norton, "Lebanon: The Internal Conflict and the Iranian Connection," in *Iranian Revolution*, ed. Esposito, 128.

114. Edward Alan Yeranian, "Iran Clamps Down on Hizbullah," *Christian Science Monitor*, Oct. 10, 1989, 3.

115. James P. Piscatori, "The Shia of Lebanon and Hizbullah, the Party of God," in *Politics of the Future: The Role of Social Movements*, ed. Christine Jennett and Randal G. Stewart (Melbourne: Macmillan, 1989), 310. I am indebted to the author for this summary of Hizballah's ideology.

116. Ibid.

117. Nader, "Interview with Sheikh Fadl Allah," *Middle East Insight*, 19.

118. Ibid.

119. Yeranian, "Iran Clamps Down," 3.

120. Thomas L. Friedman, "Israel's Dilemma: Living with a Dirty War," *New York Times Magazine*, Jan. 20, 1985, 42.

121. Norton, "Lebanon: The Internal Conflict," 19.

122. This analysis of the Gulf crisis is based in large part on my article, "Jihad in a World of Shattered Dreams: Islam, Arab Politics, and the Gulf Crisis," in *The World and I* (Feb. 1991): 515–27.

123. Chibli Mallat, "Iraq," in *Politics of Islamic Revivalism*, ed. Shireen T. Hunter (Bloomington: Univ. of Indiana Press), 76ff; and Philip Robbins, "Iraq: Revolutionary Threats and Regime Responses," in *Iranian Revolution*, ed. Esposito, 86ff.

124. Chibli Mallat, "Religious Militancy in Contemporary Iraq: Muhammad Baqer as-Sadr and the Sunni-Shii Paradigm," *Third World Quarterly* (Apr. 1988): 75ff.

125. Robbins, "Iraq," in *Iranian Revolution*, ed. Esposito, 90–95.

126. *New York Times*, Sept. 12, 1990.

127. *Washington Post*, Sept. 14, 1990; and the *Los Angeles Times*, Sept. 22, 1990.

128. "Islam Divided," *Economist* (Sept. 22, 1990): 47.

129. Abdurrahman Alamoudi, *Washington Report on Middle East Affairs* (Oct. 1990): 69.

130. *New York Times*, Oct. 4, 1990.

131. *Herald* (Pakistani newspaper), Sept. 1990, 30.

132. "The Gulf Crisis," *Aliran* 10, no. 8 (1990): 32.

133. For an analysis of this issue, see John L. Esposito and John O. Voll, *Islam and Democracy* (New York: Oxford Univ. Press, 1997); John L. Esposito and James P. Piscatori, "Democratization and Islam," *The Middle East Journal* 45 (Summer 1991), 427–40; John L. Esposito, "Islam, Democracy, and U.S. Foreign Policy," in *Riding the Tiger: The Middle East Challenge After the Gulf War*, ed. Phebe Marr and William Lewis (Boulder, Colo.: Westview, 1993), 187–210; and Timothy Sisk, *Islam and Democracy: Religion, Politics, and Power in the Middle East* (Washington, D.C.: United States Institute of Peace, 1993).

134. For Refah's impact on Turkish politics see Ben Lombardi, "Turkey—Return of the Generals," *Political Science Quarterly* 122, no. 2: 191–215; and Sabri Sayari, "Turkey's Islamist Challenge," in *Middle East Quarterly* (Sept. 1996): 35–43.

135. Dirk Vanderwalle, "From New State to the New Era: Toward a Second Republic in Tunisia," *Middle East Journal* (Autumn 1988): 603.

136. "Ben Ali Discusses Opposition Parties, Democracy," *FBIS-NES*, 29 (Dec. 1989).

137. "The Autocrat Computes," *The Economist* (May 18, 1991), 47–48.

138. François Burgat, *The Islamic Movement in North Africa* (Austin: Univ. of Texas Press, 1993), 279.

139. Dirk Vanderwalle, "Ben Ali's New Tunisia," *Field Staff Reports: Africa/Middle East*, 1989–90, no. 8, 3.

140. John P. Entelis and Lisa J. Arone, "Algeria in Turmoil: Islam, Democracy and the State," *Middle East Policy* 1, no. 2, (1992): 33–35.

6. Issues and Prospects

1. For examples of the conventional wisdom, see Manfred Halpern, *The Politics of Social Change in the Middle East and North Africa* (Princeton, N.J.: Princeton Univ. Press, 1963); Daniel Lerner, *The Passing of Traditional Society* (New York: Free Press, 1958); Gabriel Almond and G. Bingham Powell, *Comparative Politics: A Comparative Approach* (Boston: Little, Brown, 1966); and Donald E. Smith, *Religion and Political Development* (Boston: Little, Brown, 1970).

2. Michael C. Hudson, "Islam and Political Development," in *Islam and Development*, ed. Esposito, esp. 7 ff.

3. Crecelius, "The Path of Secularization in Egypt," in *Islam and Development*, ed. Esposito, 68–70.

4. Abul Ala Mawdudi, *A Short History of the Revivalist Movement in Islam* (Lahore: Islamic Publications, 1973), 33.

5. *Report of the Court of Inquiry Constituted under Punjab Act 11 of 1954, to Inquire into Punjab Disturbances of 1953*, 218. See also Muhammad Munir, *From Jinnah to Zia* (Lahore: Vanguard Books, n.d.), esp. 38–73.

6. Hassan al-Turabi, "The Islamic State," in *Voices*, ed. Esposito, 248.

7. As Mangol Bayat concludes in "Islam in Pahlavi and Post-Pahlavi Iran: A Cultural Revolution?" in *Islam and Development*, ed. Esposito, 106.

8. Deliar Noer, *The Modernist Muslim Movement in Indonesia* (London: Oxford Univ. Press, 1973), 287–88.

9. For a presentation of contending positions, see John L. Esposito and John O. Voll, *Islam and Democracy* (New York: Oxford Univ. Press, 1996); Bernard Lewis, "Islam and Democracy," *The Atlantic* 271 (Feb. 1993): 87–98; Martin Kramer, "Islam vs. Democracy," *Commentary* 195 (Jan. 1993): 35–42; John O. Voll and John L. Esposito "Islam's Democratic Essence," *Middle East Quarterly* 1 (Sept. 1994): 3–11 with ripostes, 12–19, and Voll and Esposito reply, *Middle East Quarterly* 1 (Dec. 1994): 71–72; Robin Wright, "Islam, Democracy and the West," *Foreign Affairs* 71 (Summer 1992): 131–45. See also John L. Esposito and James P. Piscatori, "Democratization and Islam," *Middle East Journal* 45 (Summer 1991): 427–40.

10. See, for example, Robert H. Pelletreau, Daniel Pipes, and John L. Esposito, "Resurgent Islam in the Middle East," *Middle East Policy* 3 no. 2 (1994): 1–21.

11. Ibid., 245.

12. Abul Ala Mawdudi, *Purdah and the Status of Woman in Islam*, trans. and ed. al-Ashari (Lahore: Islamic Publications, 1972), 200–201.

13. Matta al-Maskin, as quoted in "The Coptic-Muslim Conflict in Egypt. Modernization of Society and Religious Renovation," *CEMAM Reports* (Beirut: Center for the Study of the Modern Arab World, 1976), 34.

14. For a summary discussion of Arab Islamists and pluralism, see Yvonne Y. Haddad, "Islamists and the Challenge of Pluralism," occasional paper (Washington, D.C.: Center for Contemporary Arab Studies and the Center for Muslim-Christian Understanding, 1995).

15. Mahmoud Ayoub, "Islam and Christianity: Between Tolerance and Acceptance," in *Religions of the Book: The Annual Publication of the College Theology Society*, vol. 38, ed. Gerard Sloyan (Lanham, Md.: College Theology Society, 1992), 28.

16. See, for example, Robert Heffner, "Modernity and the Challenge of Pluralism: Some Indonesian Lessons," *Studia Islamika* 2, no. 4 (1995), 25.

17. Nurcholish Madjid, "In Search of Islamic Roots for Modern Pluralism: The Indonesian Experience," in *Toward a New Paradigm: Recent Developments in Indonesian Thought*, ed. Mark R. Woodward (Tempe: Arizona State Univ. 1996), 90; and Olaf Schumann, "Christian-Muslim Encounter in Indonesia," in *Christian-Muslim Encounters*, ed. Yvonne Y. Haddad and Wadi Z. Haddad (Gainesville: Univ. of Florida Press, 1995), 285–99.

18. James P. Piscatori, "Islam in the International Order," in *The Expansion of International Societies*, ed. Hedley Bull (Oxford: Oxford Univ. Press, 1984).

19. Muhammad Iqbal, in *Speeches and Statements of Iqbal*, ed. Shamloo (Lahore: Muhammad Ashraf, 1948), 224.

20. James P. Piscatori, *Islam in a World of Nation-States* (Cambridge: Cambridge Univ. Press, 1986), chaps. 3–7.

21. Muhammad Iqbal, *The Reconstruction of Religious Thought in Islam* (Lahore: Muhammad Ashraf, 1968), 159.

22. See, for example, Abul Ala Mawdudi's, *Nationalism and India* (Pathenkot: Maktaba-e-Jamaat-e-Islami, new ed. 1947); and *Unity of the Muslim World*, ed. Khurshid Ahmad (Lahore: Islamic Publications, 1967).

23. Rahman, *Islam*, 227.

24. Sadiq al-Mahdi, "Islam—Society and Change," in *Voices*, ed. Esposito, 239.

25. Ibid., 236–37.

26. Ibid., 238.

27. Al-Turabi, "The Islamic State," in *Voices*, ed. Esposito, 249–250.

28. Dale F. Eickelman, "The Study of Islam in Local Contexts" *Asian Studies* 27 (1982): 12.

29. Bernard Lewis, "The Roots of Muslim Rage," *Atlantic Monthly* 226, no. 3 (Sept. 1990); Samuel P. Huntington, "The Clash of Civilizations," *Foreign Affairs* (Summer 1993), 222–49; John L. Esposito, *The Islamic Threat: Myth or Reality?* 2d ed. (New York: Oxford Univ. Press, 1995), chap. 6.

30. Huntington, "The Clash of Civilizations," 22, 39.

Selected Bibliography

Abd-Allah, Umar F. *The Islamic Struggle in Syria*. Berkeley: Mizan Press, 1983.

Abdillah, Masykuri. *Responses of Indonesian Muslim Intellectuals to the Concept of Democracy (1966–1993)*. Hamburg: Avera Verlag Meyer, 1997.

Abrahamian, Ervand. *Iran Between Two Revolutions*. Princeton: Princeton Univ. Press, 1982.

Abu-Amr, Ziad. *Islamic Fundamentalism in the West Bank and Gaza: Muslim Brotherhood and Islamic Jihad*. Bloomington, Ind.: Indiana Univ. Press, 1994.

Ahmad, Aziz. *Islamic Modernism in India and Pakistan, 1857–1964*. Oxford: Oxford Univ. Press, 1967.

———. *Studies in Islamic Culture in the Indian Environment*. Oxford: Oxford Univ. Press, 1964.

Ahmad, Kurshid, ed. *The Islamic Law and Constitution*. 6th ed. Lahore: Islamic Publications, 1977.

Ahmed, Akbar A. *Discovering Islam*. London: Routledge, 1988.

———. *Resistance and Control in Pakistan*. London: Routledge, 1991.

Ajami, Fouad. *The Arab Predicament*. New York: Cambridge Univ. Press, 1982.

———. *The Vanished Imam: Musa al-Sadr and the Shia of Lebanon*. Ithaca, N.Y.: Cornell Univ. Press, 1986.

Akhavi, Shahrough. *Religion and Politics in Contemporary Iran*. Albany: SUNY Press, 1980.

Al-e-Ahmad, Jalal. *Gharbzadegi*. Trans. by John Green and Ahmad Alizadeh. Lexington, Ky.: Mazda, 1982.

———. *Iranian Society*. Comp. and ed. Michael C. Hillman. Lexington, Ky.: Mazda, 1982.

Algar, Hamid, trans. "Message to the Pilgrims." In *Islam and Revolution: Writings and Declarations of Imam Khomeini*. Berkeley: Mizan Press, 1981.

———. *Religion and State in Iran 1785–1906*. Berkeley: Univ. of California Press, 1969.

Anderson, James Norman. *Islamic Law in the Modern World.* Westport, Conn.: Greenwood Press, 1976.

Antoun, Richard T., and Mary Elaine Hegland, eds. *Religious Resurgence: Contemporary Cases in Islam, Christianity and Judaism.* Syracuse, N.Y.: Syracuse Univ. Press, 1987.

Arjomand, Said Amir. *The Shadow of God and the Hidden Imam: Religion, Political Order, and Societal Change in Shi'ite Iran from the Beginning to 1890.* Chicago and London: Univ. of Chicago Press, 1984.

———. *The Turban and the Crown: The Islamic Revolution in Iran.* New York: Oxford Univ. Press, 1988.

Arjomand, Said Amir, ed. *From Nationalism to Revolutionary Islam.* Albany: SUNY Press, 1984.

Ayoob, Mohammed, ed. *The Politics of Islamic Reassertion.* New York: St. Martin's, 1981.

Ayoub, Mahmoud M. *Islam and the Third Universal Theory: The Religious Thought of Muammar al-Qadhdhafi.* London: KPI, 1987.

Ayubi, Nazib. *Political Islam.* London: Routledge, 1991.

Bakhash, Shaul. *The Reign of the Ayatollahs: Iran and the Islamic Revolution.* New York: Basic Books, 1984.

Bani-Sadr, Abolhassan. *Islamic Government.* Trans. M. R. Ghanoonparva. Lexington, Ky.: Mazda, 1981.

Bannerman, Patrick. *Islam in Perspective.* London: Routledge, 1988.

Banuazizi, Ali, and Myron Weiner, eds. *The State, Religion, and Ethnic Politics: Afghanistan, Iran, and Pakistan.* Syracuse, N.Y.: Syracuse Univ. Press, 1986.

Batatu, Hanna. *The Old Social Classes and the Revolutionary Movements of Iraq.* Princeton: Princeton Univ. Press, 1978.

Bayat, Mangol. *Mysticism and Dissent: Socioreligious Thought in Qajar Iran.* Syracuse, N.Y.: Syracuse Univ. Press, 1982.

Berger, Morroe. *Islam in Egypt: Social and Political Aspects of Popular Religion.* Cambridge: Cambridge Univ. Press, 1970.

Bill, James A. *The Eagle and the Lion.* New Haven: Yale Univ. Press, 1988.

Binder, Leonard. *Religion and Politics in Pakistan.* Berkeley: Univ. of California Press, 1961.

Bonine, Michael E., and Nikki R. Keddie, eds. *Modern Iran: The Dialectics of Continuity and Change.* Albany: SUNY Press, 1981.

Burgat, François. *The Islamic Movement in North Africa.* 2d ed. Trans. William Dowell. Austin: Univ. of Texas, 1997.

Burke, Edmund, and Ira M. Lapidus. *Islam, Politics, and Social Movements.* Berkeley: Univ. of California Press, 1988.

Chelkowski, Peter J., ed. *Taziyeh: Ritual and Drama in Iran.* New York: New York Univ. Press, 1979.

Cole, Juan R. I., and Nikki R. Keddie, eds. *Shiism and Social Protest.* New Haven: Yale Univ. Press, 1986.

Coulson, N. J. *Conflicts and Tensions in Islamic Jurisprudence.* Chicago: Univ. of Chicago Press, 1969.

————. *A History of Islamic Law.* Edinburgh: Edinburgh Univ. Press, 1964.

Curtis, Michael, ed. *Religion and Politics in the Middle East.* Boulder, Colo.: Westview Press, 1982.

Dekmejian, R. Hrair. *Islam in Revolution: Fundamentalism in the Arab World.* Syracuse, N.Y.: Syracuse University Press, 1985.

Dessouki, Ali E. Hillal, and Alexander S. Cudsi. *Islam and Power.* Baltimore: Johns Hopkins Univ. Press, 1981.

Dessouki, Ali E. Hillal, ed. *Islamic Resurgence in the Arab World.* New York: Praeger, 1982.

Donner, Fred R. *The Early Islamic Conquests.* Princeton: Princeton Univ. Press, 1981.

Donohue, John J., and John L. Esposito, eds. *Islam in Transition: Muslim Perspectives.* New York: Oxford Univ. Press, 1982.

Eickelman, Dale F. *The Middle East.* 2d ed. Englewood Cliffs, N.J.: Prentice Hall, 1989.

Enayat, Hamid. *Modern Islamic Political Thought.* Austin: Univ. of Texas Press, 1982.

Esposito, John L. *Islam: The Straight Path.* 3d ed. New York: Oxford Univ. Press, 1997.

Esposito, John L. *The Islamic Threat: Myth or Reality?* 2nd ed. New York: Oxford Univ. Press, 1995.

————. *Women in Muslim Family Law.* Syracuse, N.Y.: Syracuse Univ. Press, 1982.

Esposito, John L., and John Obert Voll. *Islam and Democracy.* New York: Oxford Univ. Press, 1996.

Esposito, John L., ed. *The Iranian Revolution: Its Global Impact.* Miami: International Univ. Press, 1990.

————. *Islam and Development: Religion and Sociopolitical Change.* Syracuse, N.Y.: Syracuse Univ. Press, 1980.

————. *Islam in Asia: Religion, Politics and Society.* New York: Oxford Univ. Press, 1987.

————. *Oxford Encyclopedia of the Modern Islamic World.* 4 vols. New York: Oxford Univ. Press, 1995.

————. *Political Islam.* Boulder, Colo.: Lynne Rienner, 1997.

————. *Voices of Resurgent Islam.* New York: Oxford Univ. Press, 1983.

Evans-Pritchard, E. E. *The Sanusi of Cyrenaica.* New York: Oxford Univ. Press, 1949.

Fernea, Elizabeth Warnock. *Women and the Family in the Middle East.* Austin: Univ. of Texas Press, 1985.

Fernea, Elizabeth, and Basima Bezirgan, eds. *Middle Eastern Muslim Women Speak.* Austin: Univ. of Texas Press, 1977.

Fischer, Michael M. J. *Iran: From Religious Discourse to Revolution.* Cambridge: Harvard Univ. Press, 1980.

Gaffney, Patrick D. *The Prophet's Pulpit: Islamic Preaching in Contemporary Egypt.* Berkeley: Univ. of California Press, 1994.

Gellner, Ernest. *Muslim Society.* New York: Cambridge Univ. Press, 1981.

Gibb, Hamilton A. R. *Mohammedanism: An Historical Survey.* 2d ed. New York: Oxford Univ. Press, 1953.

————. *Studies on the Civilization of Islam.* Princeton: Princeton Univ. Press 1982.

Gibb, Hamilton A., and Harold Bowen. *Islamic Society and the West.* Oxford: Oxford Univ. Press, 1960.

Gilsenan, Michael. *Recognizing Islam: Religion and Society in the Modern Arab World.* New York: Random House, Pantheon, 1983.

Goldschmidt, Arthur, Jr. *A Concise History of the Middle East.* 2d ed. Boulder, Colo.: Westview Press, 1983.

Gordon, David C. *The Passage of French Algeria.* New York: Oxford Univ. Press, 1966.

Green, Jerrold D. *Revolution in Iran: The Politics of Countermobilization.* New York: Praeger, 1982.

Haddad, Yvonne Y. *Contemporary Islam and the Challenge of History.* Albany: SUNY Press, 1982.

Haddad, Yvonne Y., and John L. Esposito, et al. *The Islamic Revival Since 1988: A Critical Survey and Bibliography.* Westport, Conn.: Greenwood Press, 1997.

Haddad, Yvonne Y., John Obert Voll, et al. *The Contemporary Islamic Revival: A Critical Survey and Bibliography.* New York: Greenwood Press, 1991.

Haddad, Yvonne Y., ed. *The Islamic Impact.* Syracuse, N.Y.: Syracuse Univ. Press, 1984.

Haddad, Yvonne Y., and John L. Esposito, eds. *Islam, Gender and Social Change.* New York: Oxford Univ. Press, 1997.

Haim, Sylvia G., ed. *Arab Nationalism.* Berkeley: Univ. of California Press, 1976.

Hiro, Dilip. *Iran under the Ayatollahs.* London: Routledge, 1985.

————. *The Longest War: The Iran-Iraq Military Conflict.* New York: Routledge, 1991.

Hodgson, Marshall S. G. *The Venture of Islam.* 3 vols. Chicago: Univ. of Chicago Press, 1974.

Holt, P. M., and M. W. Daly. *The History of the Sudan: From the Coming of Islam to the Present.* 3d ed. Boulder, Colo.: Westview Press, 1979.

Holt, P. M., Ann K. S. Lambton, and Bernard Lewis, eds. *The Cambridge History of Islam.* New York: Cambridge Univ. Press 1978.

Hourani, Albert. *Arabic Thought in the Liberal Age 1798–1939.* Oxford: Oxford Univ. Press, 1970.

———. *A History of the Arab Peoples.* Cambridge: Harvard Univ. Press, 1991.

Hourani, Albert, ed. *St. Anthony's Papers, No. 16, Middle Eastern Affairs, No. 3.* London: Chatto and Windus, 1963.

———. *St. Anthony's Papers, No. 17, Middle Eastern Affairs, No. 4.* London: Oxford Univ. Press, 1965.

Hudson, Michael C. *Arab Politics: The Search for Legitimacy.* New Haven: Yale Univ. Press, 1977.

Hunter, Shireen T., ed. *The Politics of Islamic Revivalism: Diversity and Unity.* Bloomington: Indiana Univ. Press, 1988.

Iqbal, Muhammad. *The Reconstruction of Religious Thought in Islam.* Lahore: Muhammad Ashraf, 1968.

Itzkowitz, Norman. *Ottoman Empire and Islamic Tradition.* Chicago: Univ. of Chicago Press, 1971.

Jafri, J. H. M. *The Origins and Early Development of Shii Islam.* London: Longman, 1979.

Johnson, Nels. *Islam and the Politics of Meaning in Palestinian Nationalism.* London: Routledge, 1983.

Keddie, Nikki R. *Iran: Religion, Politics, and Society.* London: Frank Cass, 1980.

———. *Roots of Revolution: An Interpretive History of Modern Iran.* New Haven: Yale Univ. Press, 1981.

———. *Sayyid Jamal al-Din "al-Afghani": A Political Biography.* Berkeley: Univ. of California Press, 1972.

Keddie, Nikki R., ed. *Religion and Politics in Iran: Shiism from Quietism to Revolution.* New Haven and London: Yale Univ. Press, 1983.

———. *Scholars, Saints, and Sufis.* Berkeley: Univ. of California Press, 1972.

Keddie, Nikki R., and Lois Beck, eds. *Women in the Muslim World.* Cambridge: Harvard Univ. Press, 1978.

Keddie, Nikki R., and Eric Hooglund, eds. *The Iranian Revolution and the Islamic Republic.* New ed. Syracuse, N.Y.: Syracuse Univ. Press, 1986. (This contains some papers not included in the earlier version of this book published by the Middle East Institute in 1982.)

———. *The Iranian Revolution and the Islamic Republic.* Conference Proceedings of the Woodrow Wilson International Center for Scholars. Washington, D.C.: Middle East Institute and Woodrow Wilson Center, May 21–22, 1982.

Kepel, Gilles. *Muslim Extremism in Egypt: The Prophet and Pharaoh.* Trans. by Jon Rothschild. Berkeley and Los Angeles: Univ. of California Press, 1986. (This translation includes an afterword covering the years 1981 through 1985.)

Kerr, Malcolm H. *Islamic Reform: The Political and Legal Theories of Muhammad Abduh and Rashid Rida.* Berkeley: Univ. of California Press, 1966.

Khomeini, Ayatollah Ruhollah. *Islam and Revolution: Writings and Declarations of Imam Khomeini.* Trans. and annot. Hamid Algar. Berkeley: Mizan Press, 1981.

Kramer, Martin. *Political Islam.* Beverly Hills: Sage Publications, 1980.

———. *Shiism, Resistance, and Revolution.* Boulder, Colo.: Westview Press, 1987.

Lambton, Ann K. S. *State and Government in Medieval Islam.* Oxford: Oxford Univ. Press, 1981.

Lapidus, Ira M. *Muslim Cities in the Later Middle Ages.* Cambridge: Harvard Univ. Press, 1967.

Lassner, Jacob. *The Shaping of Abbasid Rule.* Princeton: Princeton Univ. Press, 1980.

Lee, Robert D. *Overcoming Tradition and Modernity: The Search for Islamic Authenticity.* Boulder, Colo.: Westview Press, 1997.

Levy, Reuben. *The Social Structure of Islam.* 1957. Reprint. Cambridge: Cambridge Univ. Press, 1971.

Lewis, Bernard. *The Arabs in History.* New York: Harper and Row, Torchbooks, 1966.

———. *The Emergence of Modern Turkey.* 2d ed. New York: Oxford Univ. Press, 1968.

———. *The Middle East and the West.* New York: Harper and Row, 1964.

———. *The Muslim Discovery of Europe.* New York: W. W. Norton, 1982.

Lisbesny, Herbert. *The Law of the Near and Middle East.* Albany: SUNY Press, 1975.

Malik, Hafeez. *Sir Sayyid Ahmad Khan and Muslim Modernism in India and Pakistan.* New York: Columbia Univ. Press, 1980.

Mardin, Serif. *Religion and Social Change in Turkey.* Albany: SUNY Press, 1989.

Marr, Phebe. *The History of Modern Iraq.* Boulder, Colo.: Westview Press, 1985.

Martin, B. G. *Muslim Brotherhoods in Nineteenth-Century Africa.* New York: Cambridge Univ. Press, 1977.

Mawdudi, S. Abul Ala. *A Short History of the Revivalist Movement in Islam.* Lahore: Islamic Publications, 1973.

Metcalf, Barbara Daly. *Islamic Revival in British India, 1860–1900.* Princeton: Princeton Univ. Press, 1982.

Milton-Edwards, Beverley. *Islamic Politics in Palestine.* London: Tauris Academic Studies, 1996.

Minai, Naila. *Women in Islam.* New York: Putnam, 1981.

Minault, Gail. *The Khilafat Movement.* New York: Columbia Univ. Press, 1982.

Mitchell, Richard P. *The Society of the Muslim Brothers.* New York: Oxford Univ. Press, 1969.

Mortimer, Edward. *Faith and Power.* New York: Random House, 1982.

Mottahedeh, Roy P. *Loyalty and Leadership in an Early Islamic Society.* Princeton: Princeton Univ. Press, 1980.

———. *The Mantel of the Prophet.* New York: Random House, Pantheon, 1986.

Munson, Henry, Jr. *Islam and Revolution in the Middle East: Religion and Politics in Iran.* New Haven: Yale Univ. Press, 1987.

Nagata, J. *The Reflowering of Malaysian Islam.* Vancouver: Univ. of British Columbia Press, 1984.

Nashat, Guity, ed. *Women and Revolution in Iran.* Boulder, Colo.: Westview Press, 1983.

Nasr, Seyyed Vali Reza. *Mawdudi and the Making of Islamic Revivalism.* New York: Oxford Univ. Press, 1996.

Norton, Augustus Richard. *Amal and the Shia: Struggle for the Soul of Lebanon.* Austin: Univ. of Texas Press, 1987.

Peters, Francis E. *Allah's Commonwealth.* New York: Simon and Schuster, 1974.

Peters, Rudolph. *Islam and Colonialism: The Doctrine of Jihad in Modern History.* The Hague: Mouton, 1979.

Piscatori, James P., and Dale Eickelman. *Muslim Politics.* Princeton: Princeton Univ. Press, 1996.

Piscatori, James P., and the Royal Institute of International Affairs Staff. *Islam in a World of Nation-States.* Cambridge: Cambridge Univ. Press, 1986.

Piscatori, James P., ed. *Islam in the Political Process.* Cambridge: Cambridge Univ. Press, 1983.

Polk, William R., and Richard L. Chamber, eds. *Beginnings of Modernization in the Middle East: The Nineteenth Century.* Chicago: Univ. of Chicago Press, 1968.

Pullapilly, Cyriac K., ed. *Islam in the Contemporary World.* Notre Dame, Ind.: Cross Roads Books, 1980.

Rahman, Fazlur. *Islam.* 2d ed. Chicago: Univ. of Chicago Press, 1979.

———. *Islam and Modernity.* Chicago: Univ. of Chicago Press, 1982.

Rajaee, Farhang. *Islamic Values and World View: Khomayni on Man, the State, and International Politics.* Lanham, Md.: Univ. Press of America, 1983.

Ramazani, Rouhollah K. *Revolutionary Iran: Challenge and Response in the Middle East.* Baltimore: Johns Hopkins Univ. Press, 1986.

Rodinson, Maxime. *Muhammad.* Trans. Anne Carter. New York: Random House, Pantheon, 1980.

Roff, William R., ed. *Islam and the Political Economy of Meaning.* London: Croom Helm, 1987.

Rosenthal, Erwin I. J. *Political Thought in Medieval Islam.* Cambridge: Cambridge Univ. Press, 1958.

Roy, Olivier. *The Failure of Political Islam.* Cambridge, Mass.: Harvard Univ. Press, 1994.

Rubin, Barry. *Paved with Good Intentions: The American Experience in Iran.* New York: Penguin Books, 1981.

Ruedy, John, ed. *Islamism and Secularism in North Africa.* New York: St. Martin's Press, 1994.

Safran, Nadav. *Egypt in Search of Political Community.* Cambridge: Harvard Univ. Press, 1961.

Sahliyeh, Emile, ed. *Religious Resurgence and Politics in the Contemporary World*. Albany: SUNY Press, 1990.

Saunder, J. J. *The History of the Mongol Conquests*. Boston: Routledge, 1971.

Savory, Roger M. *Iran under the Safavids*. New York: Cambridge Univ. Press, 1980.

Schacht, Joseph. *An Introduction to Islamic Law*. New York: Oxford Univ. Press, 1964.

Shariati, Ali. *Marxism and Other Western Fallacies*. Trans. R. Campbell. Berkeley: Mizan Press, 1980.

———. *On the Sociology of Islam*. Trans. Hamid Algar. Berkeley: Mizan Press, 1979.

Shaw, Stanford J., and Ezel Kural Shaw. *History of the Ottoman Empire and Modern Turkey*. Vol. 2. Cambridge: Cambridge Univ. Press, 1977.

Siddiqui, Kalim, ed. *Issues in the Islamic Movement*. London: Open Press, 1983.

Sivan, Emmanuel. *Radical Islam: Medieval Theology and Modern Politics*. New Haven: Yale Univ. Press, 1985.

Smith, Donald E. *South Asian Politics and Religion*. Princeton: Princeton Univ. Press, 1966.

Smith, Donald E., ed. *Religion and Political Modernization*. New Haven: Yale Univ. Press, 1974.

Smith, Jane, ed. *Women in Contemporary Muslim Societies*. Lewisburg, Penn.: Bucknell Univ. Press, 1980.

Smith, Wilfred Cantwell. *Islam in Modern History*. Princeton: Princeton Univ. Press, 1957.

Sonn, Tamara. *Between Quran and Crown*. Boulder, Colo.: Westview Press, 1990.

Stowasser, Barbara, ed. *The Islamic Impulse*. London: Croom Helm, 1987.

Tabatabai, Muhammad H. *Shiite Islam*. 2d ed. Albany: SUNY Press, 1979.

Taheri, Amir. *The Spirit of Allah: Khomeini and the Islamic Revolution*. Bethesda, Md.: Adler and Adler, 1986.

Taleqani, Mahmood. *Islam and Ownership*. Trans. from Persian by Ahmad Jabbari and Farhang Rajaee. Lexington, Ky.: Mazda, 1983.

Trimingham, J. Spencer. *The Sufi Orders in Islam*. New York: Oxford Univ. Press, 1973.

Vaglieri, Laura Veccia. "The Patriarchal and Ummayad Caliphates." In *The Cambridge History of Islam*, ed. P. M. Holt, Ann K. S. Lambton, and Bernard Lewis. Cambridge: Cambridge Univ. Press, 1978.

Voll, John O. *Islam: Continuity and Change in the Modern World*. 2d ed. Syracuse: Syracuse Univ. Press, 1994.

Von Grunebaum, Gustave E. *Classical Islam*. Winchester, Mass.: Allen and Unwin, 1970.

Waterbury, John. *Commander of the Faithful: The Moroccan Political Elite*. New York: Columbia Univ. Press, 1970.

Watt, W. Montgomery. *The Formative Period of Islamic Thought.* New York: Columbia Univ. Press, 1973.

———. *Islamic Political Thought.* New York: Columbia Univ. Press, 1980.

———. *Muhammad: Prophet and Statesman.* New York: Oxford Univ. Press, 1974.

Weiss, Anita M., ed. *Islamic Reassertion in Pakistan: Islamic Laws in a Modern State.* Syracuse, N.Y.: Syracuse Univ. Press, 1986.

Wright, Robin. *In the Name of God: The Khomeini Decade.* New York: Simon and Schuster, 1989.

———. *Sacred Rage: The Crusade of Modern Islam.* New York: Simon and Schuster, Linden Press, 1985.

Zabih, Sepehr. *Iran since the Revolution.* Baltimore: Johns Hopkins Univ. Press, 1982.

Index

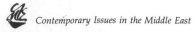